D1276662

HOUGHTON MEMORIAL LIBRARY
HUNTINGDON COLLEGE
1500 E FAIRVIEW AVENUE
MONTGOMERY, ALABAMA 36194-6201

Dane Morrison, Editor

AMERICAN INDIAN STUDIES

An Interdisciplinary Approach to Contemporary Issues

Foreword by Ron Welburn

HOUGHTON MEMORIAL LIBRARY
HUNTINGDON COLLEGE
1500 E FAIRVIEW AVENUE
MONTGOMERY, ALABAMA 36194-6201

PETER LANG
New York • Washington, D.C./Baltimore
Bern • Frankfurt am Main • Berlin • Vienna • Paris

305.897073
A512M8
1997

Library of Congress Cataloging-in-Publication Data

American Indian studies: an interdisciplinary approach to contemporary issues/
Dane Morrison, editor.

p. cm.

Includes bibliographical references and index.

1. Indians of North America—Study and teaching. 2. Indians of North
America—History. 3. Indians of North America—Social life and customs.
I. Morrison, Dane Anthony.

E76.6.A44   305.897'073—dc21   96-50438

ISBN 0-8204-3101-X (Hardcover)
ISBN 0-8204-3916-9 (Paperback)

Die Deutsche Bibliothek-CIP-Einheitsaufnahme

American Indian studies: an interdisciplinary approach to contemporary issues/
Dane Morrison, editor. - New York, Washington, D.C./ Baltimore; Bern;
Frankfurt am Main; Berlin; Vienna; Paris: Lang.

ISBN 0-8204-3101-X

NE: GT

The paper in this book meets the guidelines for permanence and durability
of the Committee on Production Guidelines for Book Longevity
of the Council of Library Resources.

© 1997 Peter Lang Publishing, Inc., New York

All rights reserved.
Reprint or reproduction, even partially, in all forms such as microfilm,
xerography, microfiche, microcard, and offset strictly prohibited.

Printed in the United States of America.

Contents

Illustrations

Foreword

This collection of essays, addressing contemporary Native American issues and concerns, arrives at a crucial moment. More and more students and faculty now exhibit a surge of genuine interest in the classroom instruction of Native American topics. Yet, offering Native American—or American Indian, if you wish—subject courses and Native Studies programs ultimately involves questions about the agendas and budgets of colleges and universities. Such programs and courses, whether they already grant certificates or degrees or are in the process of evolving from idea to proposal, are forced to pursue building their own foundations and expansion at a time when many institutions, including their hosts, want to downsize curricular needs and reallocate intellectual and teaching energies to other academic or administrative areas.

Under these conditions, students throughout the United States and Canada clamor to enroll in the scattered, few, and momentary Native subject courses that are available, often learning of them at the last minute, as such offerings seem to be hidden in course listings or are brand new additions. Student enthusiasm is strongest when driven by their own predisposition to learn something valuable and accurate about Native peoples. They respond with open minds to issues affecting Native communities, for sooner or later they realize that so much historical "American law," for instance, deals with Indian treaties and land and resource rights issues that may involve their own towns and their parents' properties.

Academic departments find the large enrollments encouraging, and where there are no courses in Native literatures, histories, and expressive traditions, requests for their installment persist. Of course, critics at such institutions may target a particular course to allege its lack of scholarly foundation and purpose. They may disparage it for having no clear pedagogy except to allow venting for and about the downtrodden while catering to a pot-boiler mentality fomenting "political correctness." Although the integrity of academic benefits and the scholarly worth of Native Studies curricula may be under debate, Native students are the principal group desiring to learn about their collective presence on their own continent. Furthermore, they want others to appreciate how they respond to the political construct of "America." They face administrative obstacles less in outright resistance than primarily in the ineffectual efforts of institutions of higher learning to make a commitment to their academic and counseling needs. The inert campus bureaucracy of fact-finding meetings, proposals and revisions, more meetings, agenda delays, and senate approvals before the implementation of a certificate or degree-awarding curricular structure can occur seems the norm for program developers.

Developing new courses and reformatting old ones (particularly those in departments of Anthropology) continue to stimulate and provoke everyone involved, even if some of the most sincere workers fail to grasp the issues' historical and present-day ramifications. The growing population of sympathetic non-Native students and faculty wrestle with their own values and ethics regarding Native peoples. More than any previous generation, they realize how their own perceptions and expectations of Indians derive from stereotypes, and they find just as painful their inability to articulate their distress. As Americans and Canadians in the social mainstream, they inherit a vast ignorance of conflicting images about Indians: the contemporary perception of the non-existence of Native Americans in favor of a romanticized portrayal as icons from long ago; that all Indians are assimilated and therefore no longer are "real" Indians; that Indians and their culture today are "so spiritual!" with their ceremonies, pottery, and prophecies about ecological disaster and how possibly to avert it; that Indians are lazy, thieving drunkards; and that Indians live in the past because they want whites to honor two hundred-year old treaties affecting land acquisitions.

Even where budgetary fortunes permit and aggressive students and faculty succeed—as in a course series of guest lecturers from various Indian reservations, urban centers, and nations recognized or not recognized by state or federal governments, offered at the University of Massachusetts in Amherst during the spring of 1996—the offerings may distress the naive by their differing points of view, speakers' priorities about economic development and sovereign nation status, and whether or not lecturers are entitled to express their anger. Contemporary issues in Indian Country stimulate students to think about important questions and definitions, such as what and who is an Indian, a tribe, community, band, nation; what is meant by sovereign nations and domestic dependent nations; in Native expressive traditions, what is "art" and what is artifact; what determines the sacred and the ceremonial; why are Native stories not myths but embodiments of the spirituality and history of the people who live by them; why is there such emotion about graves, remains, collections of sacred objects believed to be housed in the students' universities and museums; what does it mean in modern stories for the characters to come home; and what is a "Hollywood Indian" and what impact do films make on the collective expectations about Native Americans? Such questions may puzzle students at the beginning of a course, and thinking about them enables those students to articulate better what they do not know about Indians and Native cultures and histories. Students also will be forced to think about their own communities, some of whose place names identify them as derived from an indigenous language and meaning and which are accompanied here and there by advertising symbols and images they now realize are offensive to many Native Americans.

Teachers of Native Studies find themselves accountable to the Native communities they study with little room for the orthodoxies of cultural debate. In unwitting association, the romantic feature film, *Dances with Wolves*, and legislation such as the Native American Graves Protection and Repatriation Act (NAGPRA) produced some encouraging results. Native Americans in the 1990s renewed a modest faith in the kinds of cultural integrity they realize the society is (sometimes reluctantly) able to protect; and non-Natives began reconsidering their attitudes about what Indians believe is appropriate and important.

Written in response to this new era for introducing Native Studies to academia, these essays prepare students to meet some of the intellectual questions and ethical foundations in this holistic discipline. As introductory discourses on education, spirituality, literary expression, language, movies, and legal history, just to name a few, they offer a sophisticated approach to a sorely needed fundamental appreciation of this subject area. I believe the broad range of subjects these essays cover contributes to ending the search for an elusive but substantive text geared to introductory courses about contemporary American Indian concerns, for it will encourage students to explore the various bibliographies that buttress scholarly inquiry and encourage them to listen carefully to the remarks spoken and in print from Native peoples.

Implicit in these essays are efforts to answer such questions as, why we need Native Studies at all, and, is Native Studies geared solely for Native students or for the general population? They show that, certainly, a college or university that seeks to increase Native enrollments can try to provide an environment and services that not only encourage Native students to apply, but even more so to maintain ties to home. Scholarships and intellectual benefits aside, the idea of going away to school is daunting. The experience reinforces in Native students the pains and distress they learn about from elders whose school experiences away from their communities often involved kidnapping, abuse and violence, and being told that as "savages" they would never amount to anything. Furthermore, both non-Native students and administration and counseling staff need to learn about what that legacy in Indian education means and how it will demand their reformulating notions about the American dream. In this context, *American Indian Studies: An Interdisciplinary Approach to Contemporary Issues* affirms the idea that North American education stands only to gain from Native American Studies because it will help us to demystify romanticism and begin to comprehend why our relationships to the world around us differ as strongly as they do.

Native Studies allows us to renew ourselves in the kinds of knowledge and information we already have or could have learned from our people; it assists our becoming useful contributors to the survival of our communities, to "return the gift" so that all the Creation will be honored, supported, protected, and sustained; it encourages all its students (faculty included) to pursue holistic learning and interdisciplinary methods, instilling an appreciation for how deeply and inextricably Native ways of knowing accept a connection between all things; and it exposes students to the multicultural realities of the original inhabitants of this hemisphere. Respect for the people and their traditions, as well as a willingness to listen, stand paramount in or outside any Native Studies classroom or topic. From there, the reader can use this text as a guide to thresholds of knowledge to bring about broader humanistic tolerance and change.

Ron Welburn
University of Massachusetts, Amherst

Preface

The essays in Native American Studies collected here offer college students and the general public a text that, while decidedly scholarly, remains accessible and provocative. The book's contributors, who work at a sampling of community colleges, state colleges, liberal arts colleges, research universities, and museums, raise stimulating, important, and even controversial issues offered in fresh, clear, and accessible prose. The contributors worked to develop essays that are:

* broadly applicable rather than specialized;
* scholarly, but accessible, and
* problem-oriented.

This collection tells no story; nor does it present a singular point of view. You will find, instead, a variety of interpretations. This diversity is intentional. We hope to invite discussion, debate, even controversy. It is, after all, a part of our academic traditions to continually confront our assumptions, to question our perceptions, and to revise how we see the world.

Those interested in Native American Studies face two challenges. The first, a difficulty posed by any new area of knowledge, is the need to master the content of the subject. Given the historical context of hundreds of tribes and a myriad of languages, one cannot hope to become expert in the many cultures that have made up the Native American world, at least in one college career. Students may feel burdened by the two or five or seven books assigned in a course. Yet, the professor often feels the weight of responsibility to teach the material, and wonders, "How can I get across all the important and interesting things there are to know about this area with only two (or five or seven) books?" The problem of content is compounded by the false assumptions many non-Native Americans bring to their study. Native Americans are not the mythical, one-dimensional figures of conventional films and stories. The realities of American Indian life defy simple typecasting, ranging as they do from the oppressive poverty found on many reservations to the successful strategic planning of Indian casinos to the exciting creativity of Native American literature.

The second challenge Native American Studies presents to students is its interdisciplinary nature. Native Studies draws upon the expertise and knowledge of many distinct disciplines, such as economics, education, history, literature, museum studies, popular culture, and religion. Each of these disciplines champions its particular set of questions and concerns, approaches and strategies, tools and techniques, goals and objectives. The difficulty of learning a variety of approaches to knowing the world can be daunting for the student, especially if past academic encounters emphasized "the facts" over the process of how historians or economists or literary scholars go about their work.

The essays in *American Indian Studies: An Interdisciplinary Approach to Contemporary Issues*, then, introduce you to both the domain of Native American Studies and to some of the disciplines through which you can approach this important and fascinating topic. Most of the essays ask you to consider both the content—i.e., "the facts" of some aspect of Native American experience—and the process—i.e., the way in which scholars of a particular discipline study that experience. However, a scholar trained in one discipline is not necessarily limited to a particular area of study. Indeed, you will find in this collection a historian who examines economic problems, religious studies people who discuss historical developments, a sociologist who describes religious conflicts, a psychologist who interprets film, a literary scholar who analyzes an aspect of the history of education, and more.

Despite the challenges of content and process, the effort to come to terms with the many aspects of the Native American experience is rewarding. The contributors to this volume hope that, after you have immersed yourself in their essays, you come away enriched. We believe this collection will endow you with greater insight into both academic endeavor and the lives of the First Americans. Their experience is that of a people who shaped—and who continue to influence—the development of American society; their lives demonstrate, as well, the indefatigable power human beings summon to surmount great obstacles, both natural and man-made.

Dane Morrison
Barrington, New Hampshire

Publisher's Note

Books, research papers, and essays that draw on secondary sources usually include a list that places the texts the author has cited in a consistent order. Most academic disciplines have a preferred handbook or style manual that they follow. However, because *American Indian Studies: An Interdisciplinary Approach to Contemporary Issues* is truly interdisciplinary, the contributors to the volume were asked to document their sources according to the manual commonly used in their respective fields.

This book encompasses disciplines in the humanities and social sciences. Hence, the three manuals most commonly used in these areas of study were employed: *The Chicago Manual of Style*, 14th edition, published by the University of Chicago Press in 1993; the *Publication Manual of the American Psychological Association*, 4th edition, published by the American Psychological Association in 1994; and the *MLA Handbook for Writers of Research Papers*, 4th edition, by Joseph Gibaldi, and published by the Modern Language Association in 1995.

The Chicago Manual of Style comprises two general methods of documentation: a notes/bibliography system and an author-date system. The notes/ bibliography method includes information about the sources, as well as explanatory notes, in a section entitled "Notes." The "Bibliography" places the sources in alphabetical order. However, a bibliography is not mandatory in the case of relatively short essays. Therefore, and because the essays in this book are self-contained, it was not considered necessary to have corresponding bibliographies for the "Notes" in each essay prepared according to the guidelines of *The Chicago Manual of Style*. The authors who employed this method of documentation are religion scholars Ross Enochs and Eric Mazur, museum director Dan L. Monroe, and historians Pauleena MacDougall and Dane Morrison.

The second method of documentation for *The Chicago Manual of Style* is the so-called "author-date" system. Sally Midgette, the author of the linguistics essay, used those guidelines. According to the author-date system, parenthetical documentation (usually the name of the author who is cited and the year of publication) is given in the text, and the complete information about the sources mentioned in the text is given in the "References." However, there also may be explanatory "Notes" preceding the references, as is the case for Sally Midgette's essay. In addition, the author-date system of *The Chicago Manual of Style* allows variations within that system.

The *APA Manual* also uses an author-date system. As with *The Chicago Manual of Style*, explanatory notes may or may not precede the "References." In fact, these two author-date systems share other similarities. Even so, the student needs to remember that these two methods of documentation are similar, but certainly not identical. Wayne J. Stein, Jon Reyhner, and William Asikinack, authors of three of the education essays, employed the *APA Manual* to document their sources. Karen Coody Cooper, who discusses museum-related issues, used this method of documentation, as well. Two of the economics essays, authored by Miriam R. Jorgensen and Wayne J. Stein, also were prepared according to the *APA Manual*. Gabrielle A. Tayac, who is a sociologist, employed this form of documentation for her essay, as well; her topic combines issues dealing with sociology and religion.

The *MLA Handbook* typically is used in research papers dealing with English literature and film studies. It recommends in-text documentation, i.e., sufficient information is given in the text to identify the source in the "Works Cited" section. In contrast to the references of the *APA Manual* and the author-date system of *The Chicago Manual of Style*, the parenthetical documentation usually includes the name of the author of the source cited and the pertinent page number(s), no matter whether the author quotes directly or whether the information is paraphrased. If a source's author is not identified, a brief title is given and again the page number(s), when appropriate. As with the author-date systems of the *APA Manual* and *The Chicago Manual of Style*, a section with explanatory "Notes" may or may not precede the "Works Cited" section.

The authors who used this form of documentation are Robert M. Nelson, Irene Moser, Tom Matchie, and Laura Browder, for the essays on literature. For the essays on films and icons, they are Ellen L. Arnold, Mary Alice Money, and Jane Frazier. Debra K. S. Barker, a literary scholar, followed the guidelines of the *MLA Handbook*; her contribution combines issues concerning education, history, and identity.

Readers might wonder why a single style of documentation was not used for this book. The reason is that we wanted to expose the reader, and especially the student reader, to the different styles of documentation most frequently used in the humanities and social sciences, and, even more importantly, to reemphasize the interdisciplinary nature of American Indian Studies and the fact that almost all academic disciplines encompass issues pertaining to Native American and First Nations cultures.

Heidi Burns
Senior Acquisitions Editor
Peter Lang Publishing
Baltimore, Maryland

Acknowledgments

Grateful acknowledgment for permission to reprint is made to:

Abbe Museum, Bar Harbor, Maine: "Greetings from Bar Harbor." Postcard. From the collection of the Abbe Museum. Reprinted by permission of the Abbe Museum, Bar Harbor, Maine.

American Indian Higher Education Consortium: Map and List of Tribally Controlled Community Colleges. Reprinted by permission of the American Indian Higher Education Consortium.

Joseph Bruchac, III: From "The Geyser," *Entering Onondaga* (Austin, TX: Cold Mountain, 1977); rpt. *The Remembered Earth: An Anthology of Contemporary American Indian Literature*, ed. Geary Hobson (Albuquerque: U of New Mexico P, 1980). Reprinted by permission of Joseph Bruchac, III.

Joy Harjo: From "the last song," *The Last Song* (Las Cruces, NM: Puerto del Sol, 1975); rpt. *The Remembered Earth: An Anthology of Contemporary American Indian Literature*, ed. Geary Hobson (Albuquerque: U of New Mexico P, 1980). Reprinted by permission of Joy Harjo.

Hudson Museum, University of Maine, Orono: Plates: Gauges. Crooked knife and block. Reprinted by permission of the Hudson Museum, University of Maine, Orono.

Maine Folklife Center, University of Maine, Orono: Map of Wabanaki Communities, drawn by Stephen Bicknell. Plates: Pack basket and pack basket block; oblong basket, made by Edward Newell. Edward Newell using a gauge to make even strips of ash. Wastebasket and picnic basket (from the Bicknell collection). Fancy baskets and acorn basket (from the author's collection). Basket makers from Indian Island, Maine, ca. 1850 (from the Fogler Library, University of Maine, Orono). Ash logs and strips in Edward Newell's workshop. Reprinted by permission of the Maine Folklife Center, University of Maine, Orono.

Simon J. Ortiz: From "To Insure Survival," *The Remembered Earth: An Anthology of Contemporary American Indian Literature*, ed. Geary Hobson (Albuquerque: U of New Mexico P, 1980); rpt. *Woven Stone*, Sun Tracks, vol. 21 (Tucson: U of Arizona P, 1992). Reprinted by permission of Simon J. Ortiz.

Scholars Press: From Joel W. Martin's "Before and beyond the Sioux Ghost Dance: Native American Prophetic Movements in the Study of Religion," *Journal of the American Academy of Religion* 49, no. 4 (winter 1991). Reprinted by permission of Scholars Press.

IN THE WORLD

I

History, Language, Identity

The three essays in this section explore aspects of how Native American history has been told, the language through which a Native identity is created and maintained, and the means through which that identity is passed on to younger generations of Native Americans. As Debra K. S. Barker reminds us in recounting a Lakota proverb, "A people without a history is like wind across the buffalo grass." A people's ability to pass on these traditions from one generation to the next is vital for the continuity of their culture. When the passage has been interrupted or distorted, as it often has been in the history of contact between Native Americans and Euro-Americans, the result is often dysfunctional communities and broken lives.

In the first selection, "In Whose Hands Is the Telling of the Tale?" historian Dane Morrison explores the ways in which historians have written about Native peoples. Morrison's focus is historiography—the study of the works of historians, of how these texts came to be written the way they were, and of the common themes that emerge in these works. He points out that the way Native American history is told is contingent on who does the telling. In the hands of mainstream white men, for example, Native contributions have been ignored or Native peoples denigrated. In this essay, Morrison is concerned that, until the 1960s, "our histories have painted a picture of the first Americans that reflects a distorted impression of our own culture . . . with partial, distorted images of Indians tossed in." Misrepresentations of Native peoples have formed a prominent feature of historical writing because, in part, "historians generally have incorporated the values of their own times" into their writing. Indeed, the distortions of Native Americans that emerge in our chronicles are often so great that we should call them myth rather than history. Morrison's essay describes the schools of interpretation that have characterized the telling of the American story; it concludes by suggesting that "Writing from the differing perspectives of multiple participants helps us to see history develop as those witnesses may have seen it." He calls for a "style which [incorporates] the many voices of the past to present . . . a more balanced" history.

In "The Native Languages of North America: Structure and Survival," Sally Midgette of the University of New Mexico explores dimensions of

Native American language and culture. We find two levels of analysis in Midgette's essay: the words and grammar a Native people use and the rhetoric of academic discourse. Her focus here is on the Navajo language. Following an overview of how linguists have studied Native American languages and an examination of the categories of Navajo grammar, she asks us to consider a question of ongoing controversy among linguists: To what degree is language shaped by culture, the reflection of a people's ways of thinking. From the observation that the languages of North America differ from those of Europe "in ways that are often startling as well as illuminating," Midgette notes that these differences not only "help us to understand the full diversity and range of human thinking," but also have been used as a basis for comparing different cultures. For instance, earlier linguists argued that Native American cultures are "primitive" because the languages their people speak are "simple." Finally, Midgette reminds us of the importance of Native language. Language is not simply an artifact, she contends, but an integral element in the continuity of Native culture. Thus, she decries the political efforts to create an English-only society.

For English Professor Debra K. S. Barker of the University of Wisconsin at Eau Claire, the voices that call for a hearing are not those of historians or linguists, but rather Native voices that tell us how her people perceived and experienced their history. In the testimony of those who were forced to attend boarding schools organized and run by whites, we can see why many Native Americans continue to see the American experience as a history of oppression and why many remain bitter. Her essay, "Kill the Indian, Save the Child: Cultural Genocide and the Boarding School," draws upon primary evidence, such as testimony from oral interviews, biographies, and agent reports, and secondary evidence, such as historical studies. Barker describes a government program "that has emotionally and spiritually devastated generations of American Indian people, setting in motion a concatenation of repercussions, including cultural genocide and generations of family pain." She concludes that "the boarding school robbed generations of Indian children of the stories of their families and tribes, stories that would have otherwise empowered them with knowledge, wisdom, survival skills, and a spiritual foundation."

1

"In Whose Hands Is the Telling of the Tale?"

Dane Morrison

> For most people, serious learning about Native American culture and history is different from acquiring knowledge in other fields, for it requires an initial, abrupt, and wrenching demythologizing.
>
> —Michael Dorris,
> "Indians on the Shelf"[1]

The Historian's Methods

For many college students, even those who have read about American Indians in high school, Michael Dorris's assertion may appear curious. Why should studying Indians—or anything else, for that matter—require "a . . . wrenching demythologizing?" After all, do we not just list the values and practices of a tribe to describe its culture? And, is history not just what happened in the past? Do we not still study history as we did in high school—as a subject, with the emphasis on content, on what happened and when, and, especially, endlessly, on memorizing dates?

These questions are of particular concern to me because, as a college professor who researches and teaches Native American history, I hear them frequently. It is true that this is often how history gets taught in our public schools. More often than not, history textbooks are written as if everything that happened in the past was inevitable. This approach to writing history puts the student at a disadvantage. It suggests the false idea that people in the past did not struggle to find answers, did not search to identify solutions to their problems, did not endeavor to create order in their world. Worse still, perhaps, it makes history seem predictable, even boring. High school history may have seemed to you, as it often seemed to me when I was on the other side of the desk, just "a confused heap of facts," as Lord Chesterfield described.[2]

At the college or university level, history is studied quite differently, and, as many first-year students discover, "wrenchingly." Your professors treat the study of history not as a subject, but as a discipline: that is, as a formally structured way of thinking about some aspect of past human experience. For professional historians, including your professors, the "discipline" or "structure" within this way of thinking begins from a set of assumptions.

The assumptions which underlie this structured way of thinking have their own heritage. Developed by historians in Europe and the United States as a better way of going about the difficult tasks of discovering and reconstructing the past, this structure became part of the formalized training of American historians when the early graduate schools were established in the United States during the 1870s. The first academic historians (or, those who worked out of universities and colleges) decided they would treat history as the study of the past; they would focus their research and teaching on explaining the causes and effects of events; they would base their conclusions on analysis of documents (the "evidence"), and they would organize this evidence into patterns or "themes" that seem to characterize particular eras or "periods" of time.

Thus, the scholar who researches and writes history does not do so in the way a textbook describes the past. Indeed, our research usually proceeds in just the opposite fashion. The historian begins with a question ("Why did an event such as the Civil War, the Western Movement, or World War II develop when it did or in the way that it did?"), collects documents ("What evidence is available?"), examines written documents and alternative materials to find clues or evidence that tell him what happened and perhaps why ("What does this document or source from a particular period tell us about that time?"), and, finally, analyzes a collection of documents to see if a common pattern emerges ("What trends developed during this period?"). If you think about history in this way (and this is how your professors hope to train you to think about it), you will discover that the historian operates in a fashion that is similar to a detective who looks for clues to solve a mystery, a scientist who seeks to uncover the sources of a disease, or an artist who sees the various parts of the world in fresh, creative ways.

Working through this "methodology," historians of Native American history have made a discovery that is both exciting, as academic discoveries can be, and quite disturbing. By re-examining the documents left behind more closely, by comparing one with another, by looking more critically at the motivations for writing these documents, we have discovered that the standard story of American Indians compiled by earlier historians has been a myth. The nature of the myth becomes clearer if we outline the elements of a good Indian history.

In a 1990 publication, Helen Roundtree, a very good historian of Native Americans of the Colonial Period, offered her definition. The elements of a sound Native American history would include an interdisciplinary perspective, reconstruction of the American Indian experience, and a more complete description of how Native societies adapted to changing conditions.[3] We historians have not always written such enlightened histories.

Consistent with our country's treatment of Native American peoples, our histories have painted a picture of the first Americans that reflects a distorted impression of our own culture, tracing our own ambivalences and anxieties about carving "civilization" out of the wilderness. Our chronicles were dictated by missionaries, influenced by government agencies, couched by politicians, shaped by publishers' marketers, and happily unchallenged by audiences of farmers and ranchers, laborers and corporations. These histories were not influenced by input from Native Americans and, so, they have not been true histories of Native Americans. They have been the myths of mainstream America, with partial, distorted images of Indians tossed in.

Whose History Is This?

To whom does Native American history belong? The question is not as obvious as it appears on the surface. When I ask this question in my college classrooms, white students tend to answer that it is a part of American history. Native American students, conversely, often respond by saying that it is "our" history; that is, the history of their peoples. This statement represents a meaning different from the one put forth by white students. Our history, it says, is our identity.

The issues raised by these dual answers to the question mirror a controversy that disturbs academic studies today, including my field of history. It is: How should academic scholars write and teach American Indian history? As Native American poet Ron Welburn asks, "in whose hands is the telling of the tale?"[4] What makes the effort to research and write American Indian history, and other histories, as well, so difficult today is the realization that those responsible for "the telling of the tale" render up different versions of the story. From the pens of earlier historians, many of whom were well-to-do white males, the conventional history of this land and its peoples became a mythology of "great men" of Western heritage overcoming "wild lands and wild men" to plant the seeds of "civilization." Through the integration of deeper research and our own experiences during the past three decades, however, later historians have learned that the myth does not explain what really happened. The standard assumptions underlying the myth have not worked well in guiding historians to research and write a more authentic American history—one that more accurately depicts the role of Native Americans in the story.

Furthermore, some voices say whites cannot, and therefore should not, write Native American history at all. Some critics believe that only Native Americans can appreciate the nuances of culture and experience that make up their history.[5] This is a challenge white male historians hear in women's and African American history classes, as well. In response, one could counter, "Is it legitimate to claim that it is inappropriate for an American historian to examine and interpret French or German, Chinese or Japanese history because he or she does not 'understand our experience' or cannot appreciate the sensibilities of that culture?" Yet, the point is an important one, and it should not be lost. In the debate, the undergraduate student may legitimately ask, "Do the sophisticated problems that confront a few scholars doing advanced research affect how I study history? Do the myths of American history continue to influence my textbooks even in the wake of the 'political correctness' wave of the 1990s?" Unfortunately, yes. Despite the efforts of historical researchers to present a balanced picture of American history that includes the experiences of Native Americans, African Americans, and women—the approach derided by political commentators as "political correctness"—the myths still find their way into too many American history college textbooks. As James Axtell, Daniel Richter, and R. David Edmunds have shown, although American History college textbooks are presenting a more complete picture of the past—recognizing not so much a single American *experience*, as rather, a collection of American *experiences*—too many texts continue to be filled with errors about American Indians because they neglect recent research. Hence, they perpetuate myths and, as Richter complains, channel our thinking away from the real people and into stereotypes—sometimes silly, often harmful. As long-time ethnohistorian James Axtell writes: "Authors who still use words and phrases like 'red man,' 'superstitious,' 'war-whooping,' 'primitive,' . . . need a crash course in cultural relativism and ethnic sensitivity."[6] The historian who continues to describe the human experience in such terms, we might add, could benefit from a remedial course in historical methodology, as well.

The problem of how to do Native American history involves another fundamental domain of the historian's method—collecting and organizing the evidence she needs to support the interpretation she puts forth. Building on poet Ron Welburn's question, we might express the question as: On what sources do we base the telling of the tale? As I suggested earlier, one of the tasks of the historian is to prove that the events she claims to have happened really did occur, and that they occurred as she describes. Furthermore, she must show that these events form a pattern in which we can see how her interpretation develops. To accomplish these tasks, she must bring forward evidence. Evidence may take the form of laws, battlefield casualty figures, census data, diary entries, probate records (wills), or depositions, to name just a few examples. What this means, in the practice of researching and writing academic history, is a focus on documents. Historian Arthur Schlesinger, Jr., expressed it well when he observed, "History springs in great part from documents, and the historian's assumption is that documents mean something and that history written on the basis of documents means something too."[7]

Academic historians do not have a monopoly on an interest in the past, of course. Like other peoples, a rich part of Native American community life has been a recalling and celebration of their collective experience. Even so, there is a difference in methods. Generally, when American Indian communities have reconstructed the past, they have done so primarily in terms of oral traditions handed down through generations or through the use of mnemonic (remembering) devices such as wampum belts. However, these sources are not seen as reliable evidence in the traditional definition of history, and the events they describe are therefore held in question. Many historians still balk at using such "oral history" because oral tales are organic; they change over time and with the teller. Historians mistrust this approach. With Schlesinger, they hold that "Documentation is not the end of history, but . . . it is the beginning."[8] Professional historians have good reason to take this "critical" approach. For example, popular writers make the claim that the U.S. Constitution was based on the political system of the Iroquois Confederacy. Their assertion rests on the "fact" that Benjamin Franklin and other colonial leaders held treaty negotiations with the Iroquois during the 1750s, and these same leaders helped to draw up the Constitution. Yet, historians require a more detailed analysis of both the oral and written evidence. Although Native American cultures did indeed help to shape mainstream culture, this is one example of how a story can be oversimplified when the writer neglects to study the evidence of the past.[9]

In insisting upon the primacy of documents, however, academic historians may have gone too far in limiting the exact forms of evidence we may use. Only recently, and still too rarely, have historians begun to draw upon the oral traditions of Native American peoples to provide explanations of why events developed as they did. Importantly, the way one selects evidence shapes the story that one tells. Let me offer an example. Historian William Simmons collected folk tales and origin myths for his book, *Spirit of the New England Tribes*.[10] The stories examine the origins and development of the original people of New England, as well as their perceptions of European colonists. Yet, we might ask, how many history textbooks have incorporated such stories to describe and explain Native responses to European colonization? In fact, some Native American scholars have challenged the conventional historian's methods as simply a reflection of the biases of Western ethnocentrism. "Only Indians can truly understand Indian experience," these critics claim, "and native orally transmitted histories must take precedence over Euro-American documentation."[11]

This realization challenges us to think about Welburn's question in still another way: How will the tale be told? Historians are story-tellers. They have traditionally described their versions of the past through narrative. Considering the myriad of events viewed from a great many perspectives, you might expect to see an outpouring of a great many "tales to tell." Yet, it is an interesting fact that in all the histories we read, there have been few truly different stories. This has been so especially in the telling of the histories of Native Americans and their interactions with their white neighbors.

As historian Richard White, in his excellent study of Native American history about the Great Lakes, *The Middle Ground,* has observed, "The history of Indian-white relations has not usually produced complex stories."[12] Indeed, we can identify two plots that have dominated the writing of Native American history since the beginnings of white occupation. The original plot described American history in terms of the spread of "civilization" over the "heathen" and the wilderness. By the latter part of the nineteenth century, the tragedy of the "vanishing American" preoccupied some writers, with Helen Hunt Jackson's *A Century of Dishonor* as a prime example.[13]

The Rise and Fall of the "Grand Narrative"

In trying to find a place for the dispossessed and the powerless of our society in their versions of this country's history, historians generally have incorporated the values of their own times. Each generation grows up within the context of particular social, political, economic, and other forces—forces which not only characterize the generation, but also which shape it.[14] As historian Earl Lewis notes in writing about African-American historiography, "most historians found themselves in lock-step with their time. . . ."[15] We should not be too critical, however. The effort to stand outside mainstream values invokes, perhaps, the highest levels of intellectual endeavor—the attempt to reflect upon *how we think* about the past, to understand the forces that act on us as we try to make sense of the evidence we collect and analyze, and to consider the influence of our own biases upon the works we write. If we survey the several ways in which historians have included Native Americans in their "telling of the tale," we can see more clearly how groups that have been forced to live on the margins of our society have not fared well "in the hands" of historians.

These different ways of telling the story of American history—what we call interpretations—have shared common assumptions about Native American peoples and their cultures. We can group these interpretations in different categories of thought according to the traits they hold in common, what we call schools of historical interpretation. Although historians of the several schools have differed in their broad interpretations of American history, they have shared one thing in common—a view of the various Native American peoples as, simply, "the Indian." In this convention, the image of "the Indian" is that of someone who is inferior to Europeans and to Americans of European heritage.

Nationalist Period History
During the early nineteenth century, historians created a "grand narrative" of American history. On the foundations of their writings, they developed

the myth that has continued to dominate our understanding of the American experience. Even those historians whose interpretations depart from this version—known as revisionists because their conclusions *revise* the conventional story—must respond to the "grand narrative" in order to explain to their readers why their stories differ. In her essay on the development of this "nationalist school," Dorothy Ross describes the tale they told as "the story of Western progress, a liberal story of growing commercial development, representative political institutions based on democratic consent, and the advance and diffusion of knowledge—processes that were projected to remake the entire world."[16]

The mythic tale of the progress of American civilization began with a group of historians who wrote in the early and mid-nineteenth century. In the hands of George Bancroft, Francis Parkman, William Hickling Prescott, and J. L. Motley, it became "the liberal/republican story of American exceptionalism, which seated world progress in the American nation."[17] The plot grew as much out of the popular values of the time as from principles of scholarship and was linked to the emerging ideology of Manifest Destiny—the belief that the Christian deity had ordained a mission in which white Americans would spread liberal Western ideals and institutions across the continent. In describing the American Revolution, for instance, Bancroft wrote of "the change which Divine Wisdom ordained, and which no human policy or force could hold back, [proceeding] as majestically as the laws of being."[18] He saw in the rise of the American people the political regeneration of the world; "in America," he asserted, liberty "was the breath of life of the people."[19]

The work of Francis Parkman demonstrates another characteristic feature of this school. A careful writer, he penned volumes that described the struggle between England and France for the mastery of the North American continent in a style that has been described as "a lurid and fascinating . . . grand adventure."[20] Virtually obsessed with the collection of primary source materials, Parkman was typical of the Nationalist School in his capacity for reconstructing historic scenes, perfected by careful analysis of documents and his own travels to observe the sites where events had occurred. As in the works of Bancroft, Motley, and Prescott, "great men" representing the "forces of history" walked the pages of Parkman's books, shaping events to conform to the divine design for the progress of humanity.[21] By 1889, when Congress chartered the American Historical Association "in the interest of American history, and of history in America," and history was becoming a profession and a career, the tale told by the Nationalist School had established the framework for a myth that would shape their readers' understanding of the American experience.[22]

Why do I describe this way of telling the story of American history as a myth? For most students, the version put forth by Bancroft and Parkman probably sounds reasonable. It is, perhaps, essentially the story they have heard most of their lives, in classrooms, on TV, in film, and in public history exhibits (museums or re-enactments of famous events). Perhaps college professors like myself too often assume that our students share an interest in our life's work of examining and re-examining the stories other historians tell. We ought to explain more clearly both the outlines of the old view and the evidence we uncover that shows how this view presents a story of American history that is faulty in many places. To uncover the outlines of the myth, ask yourself this: In the interpretations of Bancroft and his colleagues, who were "the people?" Have we included all Americans in the progress achieved by this nation? Have the laws and customs of our society and the values of our culture left anyone out? In fact, in the time in which Bancroft first wrote, four million African Americans were enslaved, women in some states could be divorced simply on the word of husbands, receive no property, and be separated from their children, and Native Americans were repeatedly betrayed by treaties that American government officials signed, but often had no intention of honoring. Why, then, was the myth of an inclusive, progress-bound democracy so influential?

In praising the work of Bancroft, William Sloane identified characteristics that help us to understand why the Nationalist School of interpretation was so successful, and how it left Native Americans on the margins. In analyzing the historian's interpretation of the frontier, Sloane wrote, "By this compulsion of origins, the environment, though eliminating all that cannot be assimilated, retains all useful elements, incorporating them into an intricate but orderly whole."[23] When I pull a dusty volume of Bancroft's *History of the United States* off my shelf and examine the index, I cannot find an entry for Native Americans (a term concocted in the mid-twentieth century, of course), nor American Indians, nor even Indians; what I do find is "Red Men."[24] They are embedded within the story of white Americans, predominately male; their role in a kind of morality play depicts them as weak obstacles, "primitive" in comparison to the technologies and social organization of "civilized" Europeans, almost casually pushed aside.

These historians wrote for a society which showed little interest in more than a sketch of the indigenous cultures and the role they played in contributing to the American experience. Although Parkman and his colleagues were fervent collectors of primary documents, the sources they sought rarely included accurate depictions of Native American cultures.[25] What emerged in their studies, then, was a caricature of the peoples they wrote of, and, consequently, a faulty picture of their influence on the development of the country or of how the development of the country affected their lives and cultures. In the plot line of the grand narrative, "the American forest and the American Indian . . . received their final doom" as Europeans conquered the "wild land and wild men" of this "new world" and Americans expanded the contours of "civilization" westward.[26] By "eliminating all that [could] not be assimilated" in their works, then, the

Nationalist School retained only what they saw as "the useful elements, incorporating them into an intricate but orderly whole."

The "New History" of the Progressive Era

Changes in American society and within the historical profession at the turn of the century pushed the writing of history in a new direction. Social transformation in the form of industrialization, urbanization, and immigration, so rapid and widespread as to warrant the title "the tyranny of change," combined with a more rigorous approach to the analysis of documents to provoke historians to reconsider the Nationalist School's version of events. Even so, the place these historians accorded Native Americans in their revised version of the tale continued unaltered, and the historical Indian remained marginalized and unimportant.

From the 1890s through the 1920s and beyond, some historians began to question the happy, harmonious Nationalist interpretation that dominated public perceptions of the country's history. The complicated affairs of modern life convinced these historians that life in the past could not have been so simple. In particular, they "searched for what they considered the 'real' forces shaping society [and] focused their attention on the economic aspect of life."[27] In the classic study of this "new history," *An Economic Interpretation of the Constitution of the United States* (1913), Charles Beard developed a fresh interpretation in which the merchants, plantation owners, and land speculators who came to Philadelphia in 1787 framed the structure of the Constitution to benefit their own economic interests.[28] Despite their rather jaded views, these historians were part of their era; they considered themselves "progressives" and maintained that "new political leadership and rapidly expanding technology would restore social order and economic prosperity . . . education, skillful management, and a renewed interest in the public's welfare would ensure political, economic, and social reform."[29] Although Beard and others critiqued the class interests of the country's founders, they found no place for the ethnic, racial, or gender interests of the dominant majority. Instead, an equally significant part of the tale—the ongoing dispossession and exploitation of Native Americans and others —had no obvious place in the Progressive School's economic orientation.

R. David Edmunds notes that historians produced few essays on Native Americans during these years, and those pieces that were written described the first peoples as little more than a "supporting cast" in a European drama. "Indians," he observes, "were rarely portrayed as initiating any important activity; they participated in or responded to European initiatives but seemed to be incapable of formulating agendas of their own."[30] In an important study more relevant to Native American history, in 1893 the University of Wisconsin historian Frederick Jackson Turner described his "frontier thesis" at the annual meeting of the new American Historical Association in Chicago. One might expect that in an interpretation that highlighted the frontier, Native Americans would play a prominent role. In Turner's hands, however, "the Indian trade pioneered the way for civilization," yet the "Indian frontier" was nothing more than a "consolidating agent . . . a common danger demanding united action."[31] As in the Nationalist interpretation, "the Indian" stood only as a foil; like the conquest over the wilderness itself, Native peoples served as an obstacle to be dominated. Turner and his Progressive colleagues praised the struggle as one in which white Americans developed "character."

The Consensus School Arises
during the Mid-Twentieth Century
The struggle of Western democracies against fascism during the 1930s and 1940s and then Soviet socialism during the 1950s and 1960s shaped American historians' writing yet again. The effort to make sense of the disturbing events of their own times found expression in another round of revisionism, this time a reaction against the economic cynicism of the Progressive historians. The postwar generation came to appreciate the ideals championed by the Western democracies. Furthermore, this new wave of historians believed they had been part of a united front of all Americans against common enemies, and interpreted this coming together as more typical of the American experience than not. The "consensus history" they wrote focused on the commonalities of their nation's history and decried those historians who emphasized class conflict and economic rift. The Consensus School of professional historians, generally working in colleges and universities, saw no place in their interpretation for events that undermined an image of a harmonious past. Indeed, they could not accept interpretations that included Native Americans, African Americans, women, or other minorities in active, contributing roles as serious history. Instead, they relegated such treatments to the domain of less scholarly popular history. As Edmunds shows, the major scholarly journal of this period, the *American Historical Review*, published only two relevant essays in the 1930s (one on early American Indian policy, the other on Braddock's Defeat), one in 1949 (an effort to show the Welsh origins of prairie tribes), and one in 1958 (on Indian removal under Jackson).[32] Yet, ironically, the seeds of change emerged during these years as an undercurrent; with the dramatic social explosions of the 1960s, it would become an intellectual tidal wave.

The "New Social History"
The civil rights movements of the late 1950s and 1960s and the dramatic social upheavals they triggered broke the lethargy of postwar conformity. Red Power, Women's Liberation, Hispanic Rights, and others, all largely inspired by the successful Black Civil Rights movement, prompted another generation of historians, sometimes challenged by their students, to re-examine the tale of America's past in yet new ways.[33] The War in Vietnam

(really, the American phase of a war for Indochina) and the threat of nuclear war intensified the awareness of events "too immediate and crushing in their impact, too challenging in their demand that we as individuals take the responsibility for encounter and resolution." As the radical Students for a Democratic Society observed in their 1964 charter, dubbed the Port Huron Statement,

> We are the people of this generation . . . looking uncomfortably to the world we inherit . . . maturing in complacency. As we grew, however, our comfort was penetrated by events too troubling to dismiss . . . we began to see complicated and disturbing paradoxes in our surrounding America.[34]

Most disturbing, this generation found, was "the permeating and victimizing fact of human degradation, symbolized by the Southern struggle against racial bigotry. . . ."[35] The hypocrisy of a wealthy society that espoused democratic rhetoric while millions remained mired in poverty and deprived of fundamental rights fostered demands for redress. Most significantly, perhaps, it seemed as if wherever one looked, common people in countless little ways—rather than "great men" through heroic events leading the nation toward progress, as the grand narrative would have it—were changing the course of history. This social revolution and the accompanying countercultural revolt against mainstream values did not fit the interpretations of any of the major schools of historical thought. The chroniclers of this generation—budding students of history in the graduate schools, in particular—realized they must find ways to reconcile their versions of the past with the realities of the American experience appearing before their eyes.

Thus was born a new approach to historical inquiry—the "new social history." The historians who developed and refined the strategy—sometimes styled "history from the bottom up"—sought the common people and everyday experiences as subjects of their studies. They reached beyond the conventional approaches of historical research to incorporate the insights of other disciplines and to examine fresh types of sources. In the context of the stale interpretations to which we felt subjected—yet more on the framing of the Constitution, the place of slavery in causing the Civil War, Truman's decision to drop an atomic bomb on Hiroshima—the studies that came out of this approach opened our eyes to what we believed were innovative ways of envisioning historical development, especially the examination of life as we believed it was really lived. For the budding graduate student, as I was in the late 1970s and early 1980s, this was exciting business. It was easy to feel a part of a revolution of ideas that would help us to make sense of our world and to create a more authentic picture of the past—and, so, of who we are today—by incorporating the experiences of peoples who had been largely excluded from the telling of the tale. Women's history, African-American history, the history of poverty, legal history, demographic history, film history, and other paths promised to open areas of research that would explain the human condition in more detail than earlier historians had ever conceived. One new direction that many of us found particularly exciting was the effort to create a Native American history, or "new Indian history," as it is known today.

We were fortunate to have some inspiring mentors. William Fenton was one who recognized that historians needed to do more to incorporate the role of Native Americans in their interpretations. At a conference on Early American Indian and White Relations, held at the Institute of Early American History and Culture in 1953, Fenton spoke of the need to find "common ground" that linked the peoples of early America.[36] Following the publication of his 1957 work, *American Indian and White Relations to 1830, Needs and Opportunities for Study*, historical literature began to seek new ways to include Native American history in the telling of American history.[37]

It is interesting to note that Fenton was an anthropologist. His participation in the debate signaled a dramatic change in the methods of historical research. Increasingly, historians recognized that many of the questions that were being raised about Native American history—many for the first time—could be answered through the work of anthropologists, as well as their colleagues in archaeology, sociology, religion, art, and other academic fields. The emerging recognition that a more authentic Native American history would have to be an interdisciplinary effort contributed to the development of a new subfield—ethnohistory.[38] Defined by James Axtell, a leading practitioner, as "the use of historical and ethnological methods and materials to gain knowledge of the nature and causes of change in a culture defined by ethnological concepts and categories," ethnohistory became the model for approaching research and writing in Native American history, although it was not always as rigorously applied as its authors promised.[39] A few examples—some pathbreaking, some more recent—will give us an idea of the kinds of work historians have done in this area of research.

One approach, which I have called the "cultural domination" school, exemplified the promises and pitfalls of the new approach to Native American history. In *Dispossessing the American Indian* (1972), Wilbur Jacobs, to cite one example, sought to "restore highlights of a historical canvas that [was] not often seen clearly in our histories . . . the tenacious struggle of the woodland tribes . . . to preserve their landed heritage."[40] In the hands of such historians, we read interpretations that reframed the tale in the rhetoric of Cold War revisionism and the antiwar movement. The theme that underlay these studies was one of "white cultural imperialism" and "cultural domination." For Jacobs, "the whole process of conquering the Indian . . . exhibited the development of racist attitudes. . . ."[41] Francis Jennings's 1976 work, *The Invasion of America: Indians, Colonialism, and the Cant of Conquest* further developed the interpretation.[42] Jennings challenged the new generation of scholars to go beyond Parkman's "history of the American forest" and consider the continent not as the empty "virgin land" that earlier historians had described, but rather a world "widowed" by the epidemic holocaust that wiped out millions of Native people and undermined Native cultures. At the same time, he developed a plot in which Euro-American culture came to dominate the indigenous peoples of North America through elaborately contrived conspiracies. Popular histories such as Dee Brown's *Bury My Heart at Wounded Knee*, which reached a broader audience, framed Native American history along similar lines.[43]

While inspiring their colleagues to examine the history of Indian-white relations in new ways, the story that these historians told, ironically, retained some of the elements that previous schools had used to marginalize Native Americans. I saw that works such as *The Invasion of America*

> have continued to depict the first Americans as passive victims in a tragic history . . . [and] continue the conventional historiographical focus on proactive European beliefs, initiatives, and behaviors. To the neglect of a comparable examination of the underlying thought and overt behavior of Native American participants, historians who follow this school of thought invoke a model of "cultural domination." The overall interpretation . . . is a polemic which asserts that Anglo-American culture . . . converged and even "conspired" toward a single, all-inclusive, and unswerving goal—the complete delegitimization and marginalization of [Native peoples].[44]

Although these studies offered fresh insights, they followed the single confining theme that Native Americans were passive victims or pawns before a white "invasion," an interpretation Helen Hunt Jackson had developed one hundred years earlier in *A Century of Dishonor*.[45] The emphasis on "great men," the few pivotal leaders who shaped events, frequently remained, as well. In addition, many of these texts interpreted the past through the lens of the present, evaluating the behavior and thought of earlier periods in twentieth-century terms—the approach we label anachronism. For example, in the post-Watergate atmosphere, such studies describe seventeenth-century events in terms of "backcountry Euroamerican thugs" engaged in "stonewalling," "missionary rackets," and "deed games." Significantly, this interpretation of Indian-as-victim too often continued to focus attention on white motivations, white strategies, and white behaviors. One came to wonder if, in the effort to heed Dorris's call for "an initial, abrupt, and wrenching demythologizing," the new generation of historians were not substituting one mythology for another.

Another approach, which we might label the "ethnic interaction" school, was more deeply grounded in ethnohistorical methods while developing less inflammatory interpretations. About the time Jacobs and Jennings produced *Dispossessing the American Indian* and *The Invasion of America*, Gary Nash developed a textbook for Colonial American history which describes the early American experience as the interaction of the different peoples who came to the New World. *Red, White, and Black: The Peoples of Early America* (1974) redefined the American experience by "attempting to understand not only how . . . Europeans 'discovered' North America and proceeded to transplant their culture there, but also how societies that had been in North America and Africa for thousands of years were actively and intimately involved in this process."[46] So, he examined the cultures of the major ethnic groups before contact and over decades of interaction. The history Nash described was the creation of a new culture, a blend of the contributions of each group, shaped by the many acts of conflict and cooperation between them.[47] Nash's narrative went beyond what had been previously written in positing each set of peoples as active agents, an important distinction from histories which made Native Americans, African Americans, and women the passive victims of progress. James Axtell, likewise, wrote a host of studies in this area. In essays such as "The Unkindest Cut, or Who Invented Scalping?" Axtell not only challenged historians to think more deeply about the nature of the interaction between Native Americans and Anglo-American settlers, but also to define fundamental terms such as *culture*.[48]

For the undergraduate student, this can be heady stuff—especially if you are new to the level of scholarship expected in college. If, as I suggested at the beginning of this essay, you have come away from your high school experience thinking that history is just what happened in the past and that the focus of the discipline is on content, on what happened and when, and on memorizing dates, it may be difficult to make sense of ideas such as schools of historical interpretation. Whether you accept the conclusions of the "cultural domination" or "ethnic interaction" school, it may be clear by now that historians have made some strides in undoing the mythologies of the grand narrative. Yet, historians continue to struggle with the concerns raised by poet Ron Welburn. How to write the Native American experience—"in whose hands is the telling of the tale?"—continues to challenge us.

Why Does the Problem of "Whose History" Remain?

If there have been such strides in bringing a Native American perspective to the discipline of history, why, then, does stinging criticism continue? Both Native American representatives and academic scholars worry that the myths historians have written about Native Americans have not died. To understand why, let us look at two areas in which the myth seems to operate.

Texts

Surveying the field of history in 1989, James Merrell could celebrate. "The study of Indians in colonial British America clearly has arrived," he noted, "and—if the number of younger scholars busily scratching away at their own plots of that common ground is any indication—it is just as clearly here to stay."[49] Even so, Merrell found cause for concern. Beyond the writing of specialized studies of specific events, called monographs, Merrell cautioned: "But with the good news comes the bad: the products of these labors . . . are for the most part ignored by the larger community of scholars studying early America."[50] In his 1993 piece, "Whose Indian History?" Daniel Richter also was concerned about the "scant impact" of ethnohistory or the New Indian History "on larger areas of scholarship, on high school and college textbooks, and on the popular mind."[51] Richter recounts how, to his disbelief, during the 1992 celebration of the five hundredth anniversary of Columbus' landing in the New World, a fast-food chain distributed a map recalling many of the old myths.[52] Although Edmunds's 1995 review suggests optimism is warranted by the "more recent scholarship [that] has altered this pattern" even in textbooks, you should examine your own texts to determine how much of Native American history is woven into the tales they tell. Some would lament that, in the hands of white scholars, the tale now told will differ little from tales told by earlier historians.[53]

Voice

This phenomenon—whites continuing to control the telling of the tale—leaves at least some Native Americans and even some academic scholars suspicious. As Richter has found, Native Studies specialists and tribal leaders

> argue that Euro-American documents are so inevitably tainted by biases and falsehoods and . . . Western concepts of history are so invariably foreign to Indian culture, that almost nothing written by white academics—no matter how attuned they may be to cultural differences—can be trusted.[54]

Starting from the tenet that the concept of the "Indian" is a fabrication of ethnocentric Euro-American thinking, these critics "have questioned the content, methodology, and even the purpose of Native American history."[55] Indeed, in one of the more extreme positions of this view, ethnohistorian Calvin Martin has demanded that "we historians need to get out of history, as we know it, if we wish to write authentic histories of American Indians."[56]

Such critics maintain that only Native Americans have the authority to tell the tale because, in the hands of others, it has become so twisted. "Indians have repeatedly claimed that much of 'academic' Indian history does not reflect a Native American perspective; it reflects only what non-Indian academics think is important in the lives of Indian people," Edmunds has observed.[57] This is a serious charge; it is also one that this essay has demonstrated to be an accurate one. The critics' call for an "Indian voice"—one that would "address those historical questions considered important by Indian communities but should also present a Native

American perspective . . ."—is worthy of incorporation into the tale.[58] At a deeper level, however, we must consider the question of "whose voice tells the tale" even further. Is there a singular voice that speaks for all Native Americans? As Edmunds asks,

> Do historians who are members of the tribal communities possess particular insight into these historical issues? Are their insights into recent events more valid than those in the distant past? Can historians (non-Indian) who are not members of the tribal communities speak with an "Indian voice?"[59]

Who speaks for the Massachusett, for instance? Given the documentary evidence that suggests that the tribe died out during the nineteenth century, who speaks for them? In the same vein, we might ask, can Native men accurately present the experience of Native women? Certainly, the practice has been challenged in the New Social History field of women's history; given the insistence upon authentic voice that some critics raise, is it any less relevant in this case? "The danger," as Edmunds cautions, "is the potential atomization of scholarship and the failure of different groups even to communicate."[60]

Resolution?

Is there some way to resolve these problems of writing the Native American experience into mainstream American history? I would maintain that the methodological dilemma—the challenge posed by Native American history to the conventional approaches to doing history—contains the seeds of its own solution. At its best, and most recently in some examples of the New Social History, historical writing has attempted to both recognize the limits imposed by the perceptions and perspectives of the writer and to remind the reader that any conclusions drawn are based on the writer's analysis of the evidence at hand. I have always found this a more honest approach to my discipline, both for the people we are describing and for the people we are teaching. It offers a way of presenting history not as a set of dates or collection of events, but as a process of research in which both familiar and novel sources are explored through innovative methods and in which fresh discoveries are made. This organic research-in-process approach sets a tone that is document-based, as Schlesinger and others would expect, but which, to a greater degree than in earlier histories, reminds the reader that its conclusions are not the "truth" of a grand narrative, but the findings of one researcher and contingent upon the documents selected and the perspective employed.

Regarding the selection of evidence to be collected and analyzed, here, again, the historian's methods suggest a strategy. We are trained to treat all documents with careful, critical analysis. Is this not always done in researching and writing history, you might ask? It has not been carried out rigorously in re-counting Native American history, as I suggested earlier, due to the biases that earlier historians brought to the task. Richter has demonstrated a more balanced approach in tracing the history of the Iroquois covenant chain in a study which combines an analysis of colonial written documents with Iroquois oral testimony.[61] As he has argued,

> Of course, texts do not objectively mirror "reality"; of course, documents tell us more about their authors than about their subjects; of course, the meaning a text constructs for its author is not transmitted intact to modern readers. . . . But such cautions simply drive home in new, and sometimes more effective, ways lessons that any good historian already knows: read skeptically; question sources; verify assertions; understand the assumptions of the past and those of your own generation and class; and, even then, remember that all historical writing is interpretative rather than objective. . . .[62]

Regarding the inclusion of different peoples in American history textbooks, I am always rather surprised, when reading the complaints of Native American, African-American, and women's historians, how few seem to be reading each other's concerns. For a white male historian trying to write balanced histories—and, I imagine for the undergraduate student trying to make sense of all of this, it must seem like a Tower of Babel—there are some clear parallels that underlie these subfields. Take, for instance, Joan Scott's wonderful study, *Gender and the Politics of History*.[63] The "extraordinary tensions" Scott describes—between academic scholarship and political/cultural interests, between the assigned methods required in the separate disciplines and the usefulness of interdisciplinary approaches, and between theory and the historian's preference for the primacy of evidence—are common to the many subfields of the New Social History. In addition, scholars in each subfield struggle with the effort to find documents that help us to understand the issue of agency; that is, the proactive decisions and actions of peoples who have been dominated or disadvantaged by the dominant society.

What would this approach look like? The history of American experiences can be depicted as contemporary historians believe it was—the history of how different groups perceived events and how these perceptions led to the responses that reshaped the direction of their societies. Some scholars, such as Gary Nash in *Red, White, and Black* and James Axtell in *The European and the Indian*, have demonstrated ways to integrate the methods and insights of other disciplines in order to write histories that incorporate the peoples they study into narratives of American history that are tales of American experiences (in the plural).[64] Richter describes the approach in anthropological terms, as the differences between the "etic" and the "emic."[65] In the traditional "etic" style, historians tried to convey the impression of objectivity, as if they were standing above events and were describing how these occurrences actually unfolded. In the "emic" writing style, the historian offers a more subjective approach and describes events and historical processes as they were understood by participants. For example, the "etic" style might write of Metacomet's War in 1675–76,

> The Indians launched an assault upon Puritan settlements . . . ;

in the "emic" style,

> Driven by their perceptions of overpopulation, the farmers of the colony extended their holdings deeper into the frontier. Yet, increasingly, as the repeated protests of Metacomet to Plymouth authorities demonstrate, members of Wampanoag and Nipmuk bands came to see that the expansion of colonial farms threatened their lands and that their only hope lay in a preemptive assault upon encroaching settlements. In response, during the summer of 1675 Wampanoag and Nipmuk warriors attacked Puritan outposts. . . .

Writing from the differing perspectives of multiple participants helps us to see history develop as those participants may have seen it; it challenges us, also, to interpret the symbols through which they understood events and to reconstruct the historical meanings they attributed to events. By integrating "etic" and "emic" perspectives, then, the historian also writes in a voice that not only describes the realities of research-in-process, but which also addresses the differing viewpoints of the participants of past events. As Edmunds counsels, "Designed to place the tribal communities within the broader American perspective, this history also illustrates how Native American people were motivated by their unique cultural patterns and how those patterns adapted to change." Edmunds has described the calls for "an 'Indian-centered' perspective: an account of Indian-white relations that analyzes this interaction from the Native American point-of-view."[66] Such a view certainly offers us a different side of the story. Yet, it still leaves us with only one side. A true "etic-emic" style incorporates the many voices of the past to represent the many American experiences this essay calls for. This approach squares not only with concerns for a more authentic Native American history, but also with the objectives of more mainstream historians such as Charles Beard, who observed:

> It is by looking calmly at ourselves as well as others, . . . by recognizing frankly and with good humor that we stand somewhere—it is by doing this that we can approach, but never reach, that ideal of objectivity which [earlier historians] claimed to have attained.[67]

The ensuing result might not be an objective history, perhaps, but, hopefully, it would be a more balanced one. It could be—in the hands of the person reading this essay, perhaps—a tale of American experiences. By including Native as well as white voices, and, indeed, by working across a fuller range of perspectives, this more balanced history might help future generations avoid another necessary and "wrenching demythologizing."

Notes

1. Michael Dorris, "Indians on the Shelf," in *The American Indian and the Problem of History*, ed. Calvin Martin (New York: Oxford University Press, 1987), 103.

2. To be fair to both Chesterfield and the study of history, the Lord is frequently quoted out of context. His famous advice to his son was, "Lay down a method also for your reading. . . . Never read history without having maps and a chronological book, or tables, lying by you, and constantly recurred to; without which history is only a confused heap of facts." Phillip Dormer Stanhope, Earl of Chesterfield, *Letters to his Son by the Earl of Chesterfield, on the Fine Art of Becoming a Man of the World and a Gentleman*, ed. Oliver H. Leigh (New York: Tudor, 1937), 291.

3. Helen C. Roundtree, review of *The Indian's New World: Catawbas and Their Neighbors from European Contact Through the Era of Removal*, by James H. Merrell, *American Historical Review* 95, no. 5 (December 1990): 1619–20.

4. Ron Welburn, "Apess after Words," *Quarter after Eight* 2 (1995): 11–14.

5. Daniel K. Richter, "Whose Indian History?" *William and Mary Quarterly*, 3d ser., 50 (April 1993): 383. A curious example of the lengths to which political correctness can be taken is seen in the unfortunate case of the Roman Catholic scholar who has been criticized for holding the position of Director of the Jewish Studies Program at Queens College. Mona Charen, "Do You Have to Be Jewish to Teach Jewish Studies?" *Boston Globe*, 21 July 1996, p. C7.

6. James Axtell, "Europeans, Indians, and the Age of Discovery in American History Textbooks," *American Historical Review* 92 (June 1987): 627; R. David Edmunds, "Native Americans, New Voices: American Indian History, 1895–1995," *American Historical Review* 100 (June 1995): 726–27; Richter, "Indian History," 381.

7. Arthur Schlesinger, Jr., "History: Text and Context," Massachusetts Historical Society *Proceedings* 103 (1991) (Boston: Massachusetts Historical Society, 1992), 5.

8. Schlesinger, 2.

9. Richter, "Indian History," 383. For a good example of how a professional historian would reconstruct such a connection, see Donald A. Grinde, Jr., *The Iroquois and the Founding of the American Nation* (San Francisco: Indian Historian Press, 1977).

10. William Simmons, *Spirit of the New England Tribes: Indian History and Folklore, 1620–1984* (Hanover, NH: University Press of New England, 1986).

11. Richter, "Indian History," 383.

12. Richard White, *The Middle Ground: Indians, Empires, and the Republics in the Great Lakes Region, 1650–1815* (New York: Cambridge University Press, 1995), ix.

13. Helen Hunt Jackson, *A Century of Dishonor: A Sketch of the United States Government's Dealings with Some of the Indian Tribes* (Boston: Roberts Brothers, 1891).

14. Cynthia Larson, conversation with author, Barrington, NH, 20 May 1996.

15. Earl Lewis, "To Turn as on a Pivot: Writing African Americans into a History of Overlapping Diasporas," *American Historical Review* 100 (June 1995): 767.

16. Dorothy Ross, "Grand Narrative in American Historical Writing: From Romance to Uncertainty," *American Historical Review* 100 (June 1995): 652.

17. Ross, 652.

18. Ernst Breisach, *Historiography: Ancient, Medieval, and Modern* (Chicago: University of Chicago Press, 1994), 257.

19. Breisach, 257.

20. Breisach, 258.

21. Bert James Loewenberg, *American History in American Thought: Christopher Columbus to Henry Adams* (New York: Touchstone, 1972), 288.

22. Sandria Freitag, "How Will We Do History in the 21st Century?" *Perspectives: Newsletter of the American Historical Association* 34 (January 1996): 3.

23. Cited in Ross, 654.

24. George Bancroft, *History of the United States of America, from the Discovery of the Continent*, 6 vols. (New York: D. Appleton, 1885), 6: 551–52.

25. Loewenberg, 299.

26. Breisach, 258; William Bradford, *Of Plimouth Plantation*, ed. Harvey Wish (New York: Capricorn, 1962), 60.

27. Breisach, 300.

28. Charles Beard, *An Economic Interpretation of the Constitution of the United States* (New York: Macmillan, 1913).

29. Edmunds, 717.

30. Edmunds, 718.

31. Cited in Edmunds, 717.

32. Edmunds, 721–22.

33. Edmunds, 723–24; Alice Kessler-Harris, *Social History* (Washington, DC: American Historical Association, 1990), 3.

34. Students for a Democratic Society, "The Port Huron Statement," in *America Since 1945*, 4th ed., eds. Robert D. Marcus and David Burner (New York: St. Martin's Press, 1985), 203–4.

35. "The Port Huron Statement," 203.

36. James H. Merrell, "Some Thoughts on Colonial Historians and American Indians," *William and Mary Quarterly*, 3d ser., 46 (January 1989): 94.

37. William Fenton, *American Indian and White Relations to 1830, Needs and Opportunities for Study: An Essay* (Chapel Hill: University of North Carolina Press, 1957).

38. Edmunds, 725; Merrell, 94.

39. Cited in Edmunds, 725.

40. Wilbur Jacobs, *Dispossessing the American Indian: Indians and Whites on the Colonial Frontier* (New York: Scribner, 1972), xi.

41. Jacobs, xi-xii.

42. Francis Jennings, *The Invasion of America: Indians, Colonialism, and the Cant of Conquest* (Chapel Hill: University of North Carolina Press, 1976).

43. Dee Brown, *Bury My Heart at Wounded Knee* (New York: Holt, Rinehart & Winston, 1971).

44. Dane Morrison, *A Praying People: Massachusett Acculturation and the Failure of the Puritan Mission, 1600-1690* (New York: Peter Lang, 1995), xv-xvi.

45. Jackson.

46. Gary Nash, *Red, White, and Black: The Peoples of Early America* (Englewood Cliffs, NJ: Prentice-Hall, 1974), 3.

47. Nash, 3.

48. James Axtell, "The Unkindest Cut, or Who Invented Scalping? A Case Study," in *The European and the Indian: Essays in the Ethnohistory of Colonial North America* (New York: Oxford University Press, 1981), 16–35.

49. Merrell, 95.

50. Merrell, 95.

51. Richter, "Indian History," 380.

52. Richter, "Indian History," 380.

53. Edmunds, 726, 739.

54. Richter, "Indian History," 383.

55. Edmunds, 737.

56. Cited in Richter, "Indian History," 383.

57. Edmunds, 737.

58. Edmunds, 738.

59. Edmunds, 738.

60. Edmunds, 738.

61. Daniel K. Richter, *The Ordeal of the Longhouse: The Peoples of the Iroquois League in the Era of European Colonization* (Chapel Hill: University of North Carolina Press, 1992).

62. Richter, "Indian History," 386.

63. Joan Wallach Scott, *Gender and the Politics of History* (New York: Columbia University Press, 1988).

64. Scott, 16–17, 20.

65. Richter, "Indian History," 387–88.

66. Edmunds, 725.

67. Cited in Schlesinger, 3.

2

The Native Languages of North America: Structure and Survival

Sally Midgette

The languages of Native America are an enormous resource for anyone who is interested in understanding something about the tremendous diversity of human languages and the cultures in which they are rooted. Native American languages are, as well, an important starting point for scholars interested in the cultures and histories of America's original people. Linguists—the scholars who study the origins, evolution, and varying structures of the world's languages—estimate that there were approximately 300 distinct languages on the North American continent before the coming of the Europeans.[1] What has always intrigued those who study these languages and cultures is how completely they differ, in myriad ways, from those of Western Europe. It is not just that the sounds are strange to the ears of non-Native peoples, but also that both the grammatical categories and the systems of classifying things verbally tend to differ greatly from those of Europe, in ways that are often startling to us as well as illuminating. These multiple differences help us to understand the full diversity and range of human thinking and categorizing. One might imagine that there is little controversy in the linguistic study of Native American peoples. After all, what can there be to argue about? But when we consider that scholars have long maintained that language is a mirror of culture—that language reflects the conditions of "civilization" and "advancement" of a people—the potential for using language to label a people as inferior is clear. My own work as a linguist has led me to conclude that these languages are far from "primitive" or "backward," and that the peoples who speak these languages have much to teach scholars about culture.

Another important point of debate has to do with the relationship between a people's language and their ways of perceiving the world—what anthropologists call mindset or world view. I had studied the Navajo language for several years before becoming aware that, although there is some connection between a people's perceptions and how these perceptions are expressed, the relationship is not always very direct, and is often difficult to analyze (see Midgette 1995 for one attempt to do just that).

The Historical Background of the
Study of Native American Languages

Europeans who arrived on the North American continent for the first time and encountered these new languages and cultures were suffering from an initial geographical misapprehension and lumped them all together under the name "Indian." Gradually, among the waves of people who subsequently arrived, one or two explorers appeared who began to create lists of the words they were hearing from the different peoples they encountered in order to understand these languages which were new to them.[2] In several cases, tragically, these lists are all that remains of the culture in question, as tribes became decimated by European diseases or were forcibly removed from their home territories and became extinct.

It was not until several hundred years after the first contact (by then a large number of word lists had been gathered) that a major attempt was made to consolidate the heretofore rather scattered knowledge of Native North American languages. The effort was initiated by John Wesley Powell, who is known primarily for his explorations of what is now the American West (he and his party were the first Europeans to traverse the Grand Canyon by boat). Powell was also passionately interested in the cultures and languages of the country he was exploring. In 1891 he published a definitive listing of the language families of the North American continent (excluding Mexico); the list, which included fifty-eight separate language families, not only demonstrated the wealth of different cultures represented in the area; but it also provided the basis for all further scholarship involving these languages (Powell [1891] 1966). Today some of the language families he listed have been given different names, some errors have been found, and there have been many attempts to sort out the relationships between them and to group them in different ways, but Powell's list still remains the bedrock for all subsequent studies.

Language Groups

Linguists have discovered significant similarities between certain of the world's languages, which enable them to organize these languages into groups called language families. Those that share a number of words that have similar sounds and meanings are said to belong to the same language family. Thus, we can see that English is closely related to German because there are hundreds of word pairs like Mann/man, Weib/wife; Milch/milk, and Wasser/water. From this resemblance we can conjecture that originally (perhaps several thousand years ago), the two were a single language and can then be said to belong to the same language family. Scholars in the last century expanded on this idea by tracing relationships even further back in time. By discovering more distant sound-meaning correspondences between English and languages like Russian, and, finally, even like Sanskrit and other languages of India, they evolved the notion of a "super-family" or **phylum** (from the Greek word for "class" or category), which they called **Indo-European**. To give an example, it has been deduced that the Indo-European word for 'old' was something like *sen- (Watkins 1992). Although this word stem does not correspond to the English word for this concept, it appears in words relating to old age, such as **sen**ile ('mentally incapacitated because of age') and **sen**escence ('growing old'). Many other languages of Europe and India use something akin to this syllable to express notions related to age, enough so that it and hundreds of other examples provide a reason to deduce that at one point a common Indo-European culture and language existed across Europe and parts of Asia, perhaps as long as 4000 years ago.

Relatively recently, linguists have used these same methods to analyze words in the various language families on Powell's list, in order further to organize the families he described. They assemble them into larger, related groups, or **phyla** (plural of **phylum**), on the basis of correspondences between sound and meaning. The task is more difficult here because scholars must rely on only a few fragmentary word lists instead of being able to draw on written documents dating back several thousand years. The families themselves are easily established; for instance, it is not hard to deduce from the examples below that words from the language of the Slave people of northeastern Canada belong to the same language family as those of the Sekani of Alaska and the Navajo of the southwestern U.S.:

	'knife'	'water'
Slave	**beh**	**tu**
Sekani	**bes**	**tu**
Navajo	**béésh**	**tó**

Again the fact that there are hundreds of other similar word pairs demonstrates that there is a close relationship between all the languages of this family (called Athabaskan, after the lake in Alaska from which the tribes are supposed to have originally migrated). Some scholars have gone back even further in history, reconstructing an original "Proto-Athabaskan" language from which Slave, Sekani, and Navajo are all derived; the derivations are deduced in the same way, from correspondences of sound and meaning (see Krauss 1964, 1965, 1969, 1992; and Leer 1979, 1996).

Powell's list, then, consists of distinct language families, including Athabaskan, (which might have comprised about forty languages at the time he wrote). Roughly ten of the fifty-eight he lists were either extinct or near extinction in 1891. Powell made no attempt to group the languages further. Indeed, linguists today recognize that the list was in itself a major accomplishment, demonstrating the amazing variety of languages and cultures existing at the time. William Bright (1994) points out an interesting fact about their distribution: thirty-eight of the language families were spoken by tribes living west of the Rocky Mountains, and fully twenty of these were in California (although the California figure was later challenged). Thus, well over half of these language families (around 65%) are spoken in the western third of the United States and Canada. This suggests something about patterns of migrations across the Bering Straits from Asia to North America: that in successive waves of migration, those peoples who arrived earlier continued to move in an easterly direction and their languages tended to blend with each other, while those who arrived later remained distinct from each other and maintained their separate languages.

It was not long before scholars began to try to determine which of the language families could be grouped into phyla, a significant strategy because it might reveal some of the history and prehistory of the peoples who spoke them (as in the example above). Franz Boas' (e.g., Boas [1891]1966) studies of the northwest coast Native Americans laid much of the groundwork. Later, Roland Dixon and Alfred Kroeber (1913a, 1913b), doing further research on language families of California, amended Powell's list by consolidating the twenty down to only twelve. Later, the great American linguist Edward Sapir determined that all the language families mentioned could be sorted into just six major phyla (or superordinate groups):

1. Eskimo-Aleut
2. Algonkian-Wakashan
3. Na-dene
4. Penutian
5. Hokan-Siouan
6. Azteco-Tanoan   (Sapir [1929] 1990)

These were intended to be tentative categories, but given Sapir's status as a linguist, they were for many years taken to be definitive. Many of the recent groupings are based on Sapir's phyla. As an example, I have adapted part of William Bright's (1994) listing of the categories:

Phylum: Eskimo-Aleut (two families)[3]
Family: *Aleut* (Aleutian Islands)
Family: *"Eskimo"*: Yupik (spoken in Siberia, Alaska) and Inuit (spoken in Alaska, Canada, Greenland)

Phylum: Na-Dené (two families)
Family: *Athabaskan*: Northern Athabaskan: Slave, Koyukon, etc. (spoken in Alaska and across Canada); Pacific Coast Athabaskan: Tolowa, Hupa, etc. (spoken in Oregon, California); and Apachean: Navajo and the Apache languages (spoken in Arizona, New Mexico)
One isolate (see note 3)

Phylum: Macro-Algonkian (two branches[4]; nine families)

I. Algic Branch (three families)

Family: *Algonkian* (Algonquian): Cree, Ojibwa, Algonkin, Shawnee, Cheyenne, Arapaho, etc. (spoken in central and eastern Canada, Great Lakes, New England, Central Atlantic Coast, south central U.S., Western Great Plains)

Two isolates

II. Gulf Branch (six families)

Family: *Muskogean*: Choctaw, Chickasaw, Alabama, Seminole, etc. (spoken in Georgia, Alabama, Mississippi, Oklahoma, Florida, Texas)

Five isolates, all extinct

Phylum: Macro-Siouan (four families)

Family: *Siouan*: Crow, Dakota, Omaha, Kansa, Winnebago, etc. (spoken on the Northern & Central Plains, Wisconsin, Gulf Coast, southeastern U.S.)

Family: *Iroquoian*: Seneca, Cayuga, Mohawk, Huron, Cherokee, etc. (spoken in the northeastern and southeastern U.S.)

Family: *Caddoan*: Caddoan, Pawnee, Wichita, etc. (spoken on the Central Plains)

One isolate

Phylum: Hokan (13 families)

Six families which consist of some surviving languages and many extinct ones: Shastan, Pomoan, Chumashan, etc. (spoken in California, Arizona, Texas, Mexico)

Five isolates

Two families which are entirely extinct

Phylum: Penutian (16 families)

(spoken in California, Oregon, Idaho, California, British Columbia)

Nine families with many extinct members

Chinookan, Miwokan, Costonoan, etc.

Six isolates, including Tsimshian and Zuni

One extinct family

Phylum: Aztec-Tanoan (two families)

Family: *Kiowa-Tanoan*: Kiowa (spoken in Oklahoma); Tanoan (spoken in the New Mexico and Arizona pueblos)

Family: *Uto-Aztecan*: Paiute, Shoshoni, Comanche, Ute, Hopi, etc. (spoken in the Great Basin and California)

(There is also a large number of "unclassified" families and isolates; no one knows which other languages they are related to.)

Bright's formulation is based on that of Sapir, except that Bright (in agree-ment with most other scholars now) separates out a "Macro-Siouan" phylum as distinct from Hokan. Many scholars have adopted this type of categoriza-tion. Indeed, Bright represents a middle ground between two groups of scholars who specialize in Native American languages. One side in this debate is represented by those who follow Powell's original theory. They argue that Powell's language families are not truly related, since there is not enough evidence to proclaim a common ancestor or "proto-language" for so many of them (Campbell and Mithun 1979, for example). On the other hand, scholars like Joseph Greenberg (1987) state that all these languages can be included under only three phyla: Eskimo, Na-Dené (which includes Athabaskan), and all the rest (which he calls "Amerind").

The disagreement has generated much discussion. It is clear, for instance, that the relationships between the Algonkian, Siouan, and Hokan groups are a great deal closer than those between the Eskimo and Atha-baskan groups, which remain distinct and clearly defined. However, this similarity does not necessarily mean that they all had a common ancestor. The confusion may stem from the fact that closer intercultural relationships existed between certain tribes, either in the form of friendly "areal contact" (in trade relationships, for instance), or unfriendly contacts such as territo-rial disputes and conquests (such as the Norman Conquest, which had such a profound effect on modern English). Some peoples more easily develop the habit of borrowing words from other languages than others do. Consider the Navajo, for instance; they have borrowed remarkably few words, either from Spanish or English contact, or even from the more inti-mate contact they had with the Pueblos of New Mexico, after taking many of them in after the famous Pueblo revolt against the Spanish in 1694. Like the Germans, the Navajo have preferred to create new, compound words when the need arises. For example, "shovel" when it was adapted as a tool, was represented by the word **łeezh bee hahalgeedí**, "that with which dirt is scooped up" rather than by an approximation of the English word. Simi-larly, "telephone" (English borrowed the term from the Greek words mean-ing 'far' and 'sound') is **béésh bee hane'é** in Navajo: literally, 'metal by means of which one speaks.' Thus, there are relatively very few borrowings within this language family; as a result, it remains distinct from the others, even those of neighboring tribes.

However, many of the other tribes living nearby borrowed both words and linguistic traits from each other, as well as from the English, French, and Spanish speakers around them. Sherzer (1976) cites many examples of linguistic "areal traits" which have spread among tribes living adjacent to each other. The tendency toward wholesale borrowing, both of words and of linguistic traits such as sounds and grammatical structures, tends to obscure the regular processes of sound change through which we can trace the ways in which "genetically" related languages within language families gradually become differentiated from each other. Thus, it is much harder to determine exactly how closely Central Pomo (a Hokan language of the Pomoan family and Sierra Miwok (Penutian phylum, Miwokan family) are related (because they have borrowed from each other) than it is with the non-borrowing and distinctive Eskimo and Athabaskan language families. In the latter, interestingly, the similarities in languages hold across thousands of miles, from Alaska to Greenland in the first case, and from the Arctic Circle to the American Southwest in the second.

Differing Categorizations

One of the most interesting aspects of studying Native American languages is the continual discovery by speakers of European languages—including English—of new ways of putting things into the categories which structure the language. In Native American languages, for instance, these language structures differ profoundly from the Indo-European model, and they show us that there are many more types than we had previously imagined. Each language, then, represents not only an entire culture with a shared set of values, but also ways of categorizing, which directly or indirectly reflect these values.

1. Differences in basic structure

One important difference is in the grammar of these languages at a basic level. Linguists have been able to categorize the world's languages according to the way in which sentences are structured. If sentences in a given language are created by accumulating a number of relatively short and simple words, as in English, linguists call it an **analytic** language. At the opposite extreme are the languages in which sentences often consist of single, very complex words, with roots, prefixes and suffixes occurring in a fixed order. Linguists call these **polysynthetic languages.** Navajo is such a language; scholars class it at the opposite end of the spectrum from English. For example, contrast two sentences, in Navajo and Eskimo, with their English translations:

Navajo: Naa'ahéłgo'
           'I pushed them and made them fall over one after another.'
                          (Young and Morgan 1992, 217)
Eskimo: Tł'imsh-ya-'is-'ita- 'itł- ma
           boil -ed eat-ers go-for   he-does
           'he invites people to a feast'
                          (Whorf 1956, 243)

We have found another interesting characteristic of polysynthetic languages—in a single-word sentence, the word is always a verb; thus, the verb word has more importance than it does in English. In these languages, nouns are often incorporated into the verb word itself, so that expressions such as "we're going **berry-picking** (verb)" rather than "we are going to **pick berries** (verb plus noun)" are created. Native American languages abound in formations like the first one:

Comanche: **puku**makwI?eti̵ uri̵i̵
           horse-chasing they
           They're chasing horses ("horse-chasing")
           (Charney 1993, 123)

Koyukon: nee**haał**nee'onh
           to a point **trap**.handle compact obj
           S/he set a trap ("did trap-setting")
                              (Axelrod 1990, 191)

What this tells us, then, is that nouns in some Native American languages tend to be subordinate to verbs and to play a subservient role in the grammar, which is not the case in English.

It is tempting to draw conclusions from these facts about Native American language structures, and to make generalizations about differences in mindsets and in world view between the cultures which mirror these linguistic traits. (Astrov 1950 and Witherspoon 1977, for instance, provide detailed discussions of the Navajo world view that might be said to reflect their "verb-oriented" language.) Linguists (in particular Benjamin Whorf 1956 and Edward Sapir 1921) have debated the issue of the ways in which "thought" (or mindset) is influenced by the categories of language. (See also Midgette 1995 for a more recent in-depth analysis of this problem.) In general, however, it is very hard to demonstrate that grammatical factors such as the importance of the verb play a major role in shaping ways of thinking, since so many other factors come into play. It is much easier to demonstrate the connection in the case of different categories of *meaning* within a given language; I will discuss this below.

2. Differences in semantic categories: time, plurality, shapes

Other differences that linguists have discovered to exist between languages have to do with meaning—what we call **semantic** categories. Some of these form what we call "regular language systems," such as **number** (singular and plural words) and **tense** (past, present, future). I will discuss these below, as well as a category that is foreign to Indo-European speakers, the system of classifying objects linguistically according to their shape and consistency.

One category that operates differently in many Native American languages is that of **number**: specifying how many persons or entities are involved in a given situation. In English, the sentence, 's/he's lying under the pine tree' contrasts in number with its plural form 'they're lying under the pine tree.' In the Navajo equivalent, one says:

ńdíshchíí-yaa- gi sitį   (-tį = 'single person lies')
pine tree- under-at singular-person-is-lying
's/he is lying under a pine tree'

In its plural form this becomes:

ńdíshchíí-yaa- gi ndaaztį   (da- + -tį = 'plural individuals lie separately')
pine tree- under-at plural-people-are-lying (singly, not in a group)
'they (three or more individuals) are lying, each under a separate pine tree'

In English, only a single distinction is expressed, that between one subject lying and many of them. However, the Navajo system offers a number of other choices, depending on the exact arrangement of the people lying:

ńdíshchíí-yaa-gi shi**téézh**   (-**téézh** = 'two people, a pair, are lying')
'they (two individuals) are lying under a single pine tree'
ńdíshchíí-yaa-gi ndaazh**téézh**   (da- + -**téézh** = 'plural pairs lie separately')
'they (at least three pairs) are lying under separate trees'

ńdíshchíí-yaa-gi shi**jéé'**   (-**jéé'** = 'three or more are lying')
'they (three or more individuals) are lying (in a group) under a single tree'

ńdíshchíí-yaa-gi ndaazh**jéé'**   (da- + -**jéé'** = 'plural groups of 3+ lie separately')
'they (at least three groups, each consisting of at least three members), are lying under
    the trees (with each group lying under a separate tree)'
               (Young and Morgan 1987, grammar section 63)

In this area, the Navajo language, then, has a complex and sophisticated system. It requires its speakers to mark plurality with extreme care and in detail. These verb stems have either singular meaning, as in the stem -**tį**, dual or two subject meaning, as in the stem -**téézh**, or plural meaning, as with -**jéé'**. There is also a special pluralizing prefix (-**da-**), to define the configuration (whether the subjects are lying individually or in a group).

Another characteristic of Navajo and other members of the Athabaskan language family is their tendency to categorize the subjects (or direct objects) of verbs as to the shape or consistency of the object being referred to. This phenomenon occurs mainly with verbs describing the handling or propelling of an object. We see it also in verbs that describe an object as it moves independently or stays in one position. A set of twelve different verb stems offers a choice between categories; for example:

ńdii'**á**   'I picked it up' (a solid roundish object like a hat, ball)
si'**á**   'it's (sitting) there' (a solid roundish object)

ńdii**łtsooz**   'I picked it up' (a flat flexible object like a blanket, piece of
              paper)

siłtsooz	'it's (sitting) there' (a flat flexible object)
ńdiitłéé'	'I picked it up' (something mushy, like a handful of mud)
sitłéé'	'it's (sitting) there' (something mushy)

(Nine other verb stems are used to refer to picking up or otherwise moving other types of objects: slender stiff objects (-tą̄ — ńdiitą̄ 'I picked it up [a pole]); plural objects (-nil — ńdiinil "I picked them up [plural things]'); something in an open container (-ką̄ — ńdiiką̄ 'I picked it up [something in a container]'), etc.

These distinctions are an important part of the Navajo verb system. They allow Navajo speakers to have greater precision in defining concrete objects. They create, as well, many opportunties for metaphor and humor.

Still another important difference between Native American and Indo-European languages has to do with time distinctions and time categories. I had studied the Navajo language for several years before becoming aware of the reason for an uneasy feeling, in a given conversational exchange, that I was not quite sure exactly *when* in the past the events being described had actually occurred. Analyzing this feeling, I discovered that it arose from the fact that the distinction between a past, present, or future action or state is not considered very important within the Navajo language system. A given verb representing an action, such as **yitł'ó**, meaning 's/he *is weaving*,' is usually taken to refer to the present but can equally well be used in a past or future context: **yitł'óogo i'íí'ą̄**, meaning 's/he *wove* all day' or **yitł'ó dooleeł**, meaning 's/he *will weave*.' These types of uses would be impossible in English or other Western European languages, where the tense of every verb must be marked.

Conversely, Navajo and the languages related to it are very specific about such notions as whether a given activity takes a long or a short time to accomplish. One group of verbs with certain distinctive characteristics expresses instantaneous actions like 'punch,' 'kick,' and 'peck.' Similarly, verbs of motion have predictable markings which show whether they can occur with durative expressions such as 'for a while.' So, one can say in Navajo:

Hooghangóó **yishwołgo** hodíina'
house-toward I was running for a while
'I ran along toward the house for a while'

but not:

*Hooghangóó **nílwodgo** hodíina'
house-toward I ran for a while

The sentence with an asterisk is not acceptable because the second verb **nílwod** is marked with a prefix indicating arrival. Arriving, though, is a short-term action and therefore cannot be used with the durative expression 'for a while.'

Another type of marking in Navajo indicates whether certain types of activity (such as "kicking" or "hitting") have occurred a single time or are repeated: **sétał** means 'I kicked him/her once,' as opposed to a different form of the verb, **nanétááł**, meaning 'I kicked him/her repeatedly.' This distinction does not exist in English, where the one word 'kicked' covers both the case of the single and of the repeated action.[5]

This brings us to a central debate in ethnic studies—a controversy that linguistic research has been able to clarify: What does the presence or absence of certain distinctions in the language have to do with actual conceptualizations and ideas of the people who speak it? Is it possible to say that among the Navajo the motivating force for the well-known concept of "Indian time," which involves, among other things, an unwillingness to regulate one's behavior to a clock, derives from the linguistic indeterminacy of the Navajo verb system in terms of past and present? Are Navajo speakers therefore to be thought of as deficient in this way, unable to perceive the difference between past and present because this distinction is not important to them? It is perhaps tempting to think of it this way; however, linguists have done a great deal of research on this very question, and the answer is a resounding "no."

Most of the research in this area has been done on the relationship between the number of color terms in a given language and the ease with which its speakers can discriminate between, for example, blue, green, and various shades of bluegreen. Language experts found that there was no real difference in the ability to discriminate colors between speakers of a language which had terms for both green and blue, and those whose language uses a single term for both colors. In laboratory experiments in which the subjects were timed to determine how quickly they could recognize a given color as being "blue" or "green" (using examples of bluish-green or greenish-blue, where it was not easy to decide) the experimenters observed little difference between the rapidity of responses on the part of speakers of languages which had separate words for these two colors and those which had only a single word for both colors. However, when the task was changed to require a verbal response (the subject was told to reply with the word "blue" or "green," rather than simply pressing a button), those whose language had only a single word were not quite as quick to respond as those whose language distinguished each color by a distinct word. It seems that a particular language system *does* reflect the thinking and the categories of its users, but probably mostly in tasks which relate more to the use of the words themselves, rather than ones having to do with perceptions of the world. Thus, the conclusion was that it is not actually the *perception* of the colors which differs according to the language system, but only the ability to *name* a given color more quickly. (See Kay and McDaniel 1978 for a summary of this type of research.)

Linguists have also shed light on a related issue in examining how different languages treat abstract notions. English deals with these easily because of the large number of abstract nouns in the language: words such as "color," "time," "space," "knowledge," "grief," and "happiness." In Navajo, such ideas are expressed by verbs, which situate the notion in time, as verbs are supposed to do. Thus, one can describe individual entities with precision in terms of their color by words like **dootł'izh** ('it is blue'), or **łitsxo** ('it is orange'). Yet, in Navajo, it is difficult to speak about the abstract concept of "color perception," since there is no general word for "color." Again, English has the abstract notion of "time." The closest Navajo equivalent to this word is a verb, **hoolzhiizh**, which means '(a period of) time passed.' Here the concept refers to a dimension of human existence which, by definition, passes, rather than to some sort of entity (as in English). From the perspective of another academic discipline, a physicist might argue that the Navajo representation is closer to physical reality as a person understands it; the idea of "time" cannot truly be abstracted from the fact that it is something which "passes" in a particular context.

At various times in the history of the studies of Native American languages and cultures (linguistics and anthropology), the analysis of these types of differences have been used to compare one culture to another. Often, such comparisons have been used to demonstrate the "superiority" of one culture as against the "inferiority" of another. Thus, it used to be said that Native American languages—as well as those of other non-Western peoples—are "primitive" because they lack this ability to name (and thus manipulate) abstract concepts. It later became clear that this idea is ethnocentric because it ignores the many ways in which these languages are more precise and perhaps reflect reality more accurately than the structures of Indo-European languages. Is "time" best represented as an entity or as a "thing" which "does" something ("passes")? What else does it do but pass? I would suggest that these languages are far from "primitive" or backward and that we have at least as much to learn from them as they do from us.

The Survival of Native North American Languages

It is a sad fact—and in cultural terms a tragic one—that many of the Native American languages of North America are rapidly dying out. Because of required schooling which is exclusively in English, and because in some cases children are forbidden to speak their native tongue in school, and also because of television and other instruments of Anglo culture, more and more children are not taught to speak the Native language in their homes. The current situation is not unlike the plight of the German, Italian, Irish, and other immigrants who came to the United States during the late nineteenth and early twentieth centuries. They and their children learned to speak English and found themselves unable to communicate with their own grandparents. The difference is that most immigrants have the option of returning to a homeland where their language is flourishing. For Native Americans, the gradual loss of child speakers means that their language and, with it, eventually, their culture will become extinct. It is difficult for members of the dominant culture to imagine what this loss means to the individuals involved. For all of us, our native language is part of our "deep-rooted identity" (Fishman 1991). I have heard several Native Americans speak feelingly about their sense of rootlessness and despair, and how they recovered when their grandmothers taught them to speak Tolowa, or Navajo, and they regained a sense of themselves and their heritage. As things are going, however, this means of language preservation may not be possible in another fifty years, as the elders die out and the children fail to learn. The loss to our society will be immense if these languages die out—although some politicians still urge everyone to "assimilate" in the "melting pot" of American culture, it is not a pleasant thought to imagine a homogenized culture where everyone thinks alike, nor is that really our aim as a society.

A major cause of this cultural crisis seems to be the attitude which prevails at least in the U.S., and to a lesser extent perhaps in Canada, that it is really only possible for a society to function well through a single language. As a result, many educational policymakers at the local, state, and national levels insist that children learn English and *only* English, so that they can function in the dominant culture. This attitude ignores the fact that in most countries of Western Europe, children are routinely educated to speak at least one other language besides their native one; in small countries like Holland, it is usually two or three, by necessity. The case of one Navajo school tends to disprove this prevailing insistence on monolingualism: at Rock Point, on the Navajo Reservation, elementary school children are now taught all subjects in both English and Navajo, and it is this Reservation school which sends by far the highest percentage of its students to college. This tendency toward monolingualism that guides our educational system is not only false but could have the long-term effect of even further undermining Native American cultures on our continent. It is vitally important, then, to encourage bilingualism among these groups, with the goal of achieving complete fluency in both languages, rather than insisting that the children learn *only* English.

What can be done to reverse the decline of Native American languages in North America? Several writers (Watahomigie and Yamamoto 1992; Craig 1992; Jeanne 1992; England 1992) in their assessments, as well as the articles by Wayne Holm (1996) and Martha Austin et al. (1996), describe some successful programs and put forward various suggestions. As they show, government legislation can help, as can the efforts of trained linguists to teach literacy, transcribe materials and documents, and so forth. Jeanne (1992) proposes a Native American Institute in order to train Native linguists and to provide them with career opportunities in this area. But, as Joshua Fishman (1991) points out, only determined efforts by the communities whose languages are threatened can reverse the "language shift" to the exclusive use of the dominant language. He points out that "the destruction of languages is an abstraction which is concretely mirrored in the concomitant destruction of intimacy, family and community, via national and international involvements and intrusions, the destruction of local life by mass market hype and fad, of the weak by the strong, of the unique and traditional by the uniformizing" (Fishman 1991, 4). Since one's native language is associated with one's identity, efforts to maintain or re-establish a threatened language must begin at the local level, with family and communities. Furthermore, such efforts must be dissociated from the more public area where the dominant language holds sway, and where power relationships are important. It is a question of reversing attitudes as well: attitudes of the dominant culture which remains unaware of the problem, the sense of shame expressed by Native Americans for speaking a language which is not valued in the wider society, and which is perceived as "irrelevant" in terms of earning a living, and, finally, the attitude that everyone can learn *only* one language, which must then inevitably be the dominant one.

Conclusion

It is interesting and instructive to realize that not all peoples use a linguistic system which functions just as ours does. Not everyone marks verbs according to whether the activity expressed precedes or coincides with the present time of the speaker. Nor does everyone employ several words rather than a single complex one to express a complete proposition or sentence. Analyzing how the different systems work is a wonderful intellectual challenge. Equally fascinating are the many "untranslatables" of each language, in which several important ideas can be fused into a single core concept. A fascinating example I have come across in my research is the Navajo word **hózhǫ́**, which lies at the heart of their world view (Hozhǫ́ǫ́jí, the "Blessingway" Ceremony being one of the most important of the chants). This word can only be translated by three separate English words: "peace," "harmony," and "beauty." Similarly, the word **nahaghá** in Navajo is used to express the equivalent of our word "religion"; but it literally means "living" or "walking around." One's religion is thereby equated with the ongoing motion of daily living, a wonderful concept.

To undertake to understand the intellectual and cultural differences between other languages and our own is not only a challenge in itself, but it helps us to understand more fully what these cultures have to offer us, and to comprehend the full range of human expression. It leads us, also, to a new appreciation of the uniqueness of our own cultures and invites us to discover how different peoples can live together, respecting their differences and discovering their commonalities.[6] The study of languages—especially the Native American ones—is a vitally important tool to help us gain this understanding.

Notes

1. This estimate, set forth by William Bright (1994), is phrased in a tentative manner ("The Native North American languages may have originally numbered as many as 300" [427]). Because these languages were not recorded, the evidence is so scarce that it is difficult to estimate the actual number of languages and cultures that existed before the Europeans came. Many basic texts on the subject, such as Spencer, Jennings et al. (1965), and Driver (1961), tend to hazard only tentative guesses as well: "In Alaska, Canada and the United States mainland, about 200 separate languages can be verified for the period immediately preceding contact" (Spencer, Jennings et al., 101).

2. English settlers such as William Wood in *New England's Prospect* ([1634] 1865) and Roger Williams in *Key into the Language of America* ([1643] 1936), created some of the first lexicons for Native American languages north of the Rio Grande.

3. Some families consist of many languages; others, called isolates, consist of only a single language which seems to be unrelated to any others.

4. A *branch* is just another level of grouping, consisting of language families which seem to be loosely related.

5. Here I have dealt exclusively with Navajo; see also Axelrod (1993) for a complete description of these kinds of differences in a related language, Koyukon.

6. Adrian J. Martinez, conversation with the author, Roswell, NM, 20 July 1995. See also Hale (1992) on the importance of linguistic diversity.

References

Astrov, Margot. 1950. "The Concept of Motion as the Psychological Leitmotif of Navaho Life and Literature." *Journal of American Folklore* 63: 45–56.

Austin, Martha, Bernice Casaus, Daniel McLaughlin, and Clay Slate. 1996. "Diné Bizaad Yissohígíí: The Past, Present and Future of Navajo Literacy." In *Athabaskan Language Studies: Essays in Honor of Robert W. Young*, edited by Eloise Jelinek et al. Albuquerque: University of New Mexico Press.

Axelrod, Melissa. 1990. "Incorporation in Koyukon Athapaskan." *International Journal of American Linguistics* 56, no. 2 (April): 179–95.

———. 1993. *The Semantics of Time: Aspectual Categorization in Koyukon Athabaskan*. Lincoln: University of Nebraska Press.

Boas, Franz. [1891] 1966. *Introduction to Handbook of American Indian Languages*. Reprint, *American Indian Languages*, edited by Preston Holder. Lincoln: University of Nebraska Press.

Bright, William. 1994. *American Indian Linguistics and Literature*. Berlin: Mouton.

———. 1994. "Native American Languages." In *The Native North American Almanac*, edited by Duane Champagne. Detroit: Gale Research Inc.

Campbell, Lyle, and Marianne Mithun, eds. 1979. *The Languages of Native America: Historical and Comparative Assessment*. Austin: University of Texas Press.

Charney, Jean O. 1993. *A Grammar of Comanche*. Lincoln: University of Nebraska Press.

Craig, Colette. 1992. "Endangered Languages: A Constitutional Response to Language Endangerment: The Case of Nicaragua." *Language* 68, no. 1 (March): 17–24.

Dixon, Roland B., and Alfred L. Kroeber. 1913a. "New Linguistic Families in California." *American Anthropologist* 15: 647–55.

———. 1913b. "Relationship of the Indian Languages of California." *Science*, n.s. 37: 225.

Driver, Harold E. 1961. *Indians of North America*. Chicago: University of Chicago Press.

England, Nora C. 1992. "Doing Mayan Linguistics in Guatemala." *Language* 68, no. 1 (March): 29–35.

Fishman, Joshua. 1991. *Reversing Language Shift: Theoretical and Empirical Foundations of Assistance to Threatened Languages*. Philadelphia: Multilingual Matters Inc.

Greenberg, Joseph H. 1987. *Language in the Americas*. Palo Alto: Stanford University Press.

Hale, Ken. 1992. "Language Endangerment and the Human Value of Linguistic Diversity." *Language* 68, no. 1 (March): 35–42.

Holm, Wayne. 1996. "On the Role of 'YounganMorgan' in the Development of Navajo Literacy." In *Athabaskan Language Studies: Essays in Honor of Robert W. Young*, edited by Eloise Jelinek et al. Albuquerque: University of New Mexico Press.

Jeanne, LaVerne Masayesva. 1992. "An Institutional Response to Language Endangerment: A Proposal for a Native American Language Center." *Language* 68, no. 1 (March): 24–28.

Jelinek, Eloise, Sally Midgette, Keren Rice and Leslie Saxon, eds. 1996. *Athabaskan Language Studies: Essays in Honor of Robert W. Young*. Albuquerque: University of New Mexico Press.

Kay, Paul, and Chad McDaniel. 1978. "On the Linguistic Significance of the Meanings of Basic Color Terms." *Language* 54, no. 3 (September): 610–46.

Krauss, Michael E. 1964. "Proto-Athabaskan-Eyak and the Problem of Na-Dene I. The Phonology." *International Journal of American Linguistics* 30: 118–31.

——. 1965. "Proto-Athabaskan-Eyak and the Problem of Na-Dene II. The Morphology." *International Journal of American Linguistics* 31: 18–28.

——. 1969. "On the Classifers in the Athapaskan, Eyak and Tlingit Verb." *International Journal of American Linguistics* Memoirs nos. 23 and 24.

——. 1992. "Endangered Languages: The World's Languages in Crisis." *Language* 68, no. 1 (March): 4–10.

Leer, Jeff. 1979. *Proto-Athabaskan Verb Stem Variation, Part I: Phonology*. Fairbanks: Alaska Native Language Center.

——. 1996. "The Historical Evolution of the Stem Syllable in Gwich'in (Kutchin/Loucheux) Athabaskan." In *Athabaskan Language Studies:*

Essays in Honor of Robert W. Young, edited by Eloise Jelinek et al. Albuquerque: University of New Mexico Press.

Midgette, Sally. 1995. *The Navajo Progressive in Discourse: A Study in Temporal Semantics.* New York: Peter Lang.

Powell, John Wesley. [1891] 1966. *Indian Linguistic Familes of America North of Mexico.* Reprint, *American Indian Languages,* edited by Preston Holder. Lincoln: University of Nebraska Press.

Sapir, Edward. 1921. *Language.* New York: Harcourt, Brace and World.

———. [1929] 1990. "Central and North American Indian Languages." Reprint, in *The Collected Works of Edward Sapir, Vol. V: American Indian Languages, Part 1,* edited by William Bright. Berlin: Mouton de Gruyter.

Sherzer, Joel. 1976. *An Areal-Typological Study of American Indian Languages North of Mexico.* Amsterdam: North-Holland.

Spencer, Robert F., Jesse D. Jennings, et al. 1965. *The Native Americans.* New York: Harper and Row.

Watahomigie, Lucille J., and Akira Y. Yamamoto. 1992. "Endangered Languages: Local Reactions to Perceived Language Decline." *Language* 68, no. 1 (March): 10–17.

Watkins, Calvert. 1992. "Indo-European and the Indo-Europeans." *American Heritage Dictionary,* 3d ed., s.V. Appendix 2081–91. New York: Houghton Mifflin.

Whorf, Benjamin Lee. 1956. *Language, Thought and Reality: Selected Writings of Benjamin Lee Whorf,* edited by John B. Carroll. Cambridge, MA: The MIT Press.

Witherspoon, Gary. 1977. *Language and Art in the Navajo Universe.* Ann Arbor: University of Michigan Press.

Young, Robert W., and William Morgan Sr. 1987. *The Navajo Language: A Grammar and Colloquial Dictionary.* Albuquerque: University of New Mexico Press.

———, with the assistance of Sally Midgette. 1992. *Analytical Lexicon of Navajo.* Albuquerque: University of New Mexico Press.

3

Kill the Indian, Save the Child: Cultural Genocide and the Boarding School

Debra K. S. Barker

You, who are wise must know that different Nations have different Conceptions of things and you will therefore not take it amiss, if our Ideas of this kind of Education happen not to be the same as yours.

—Canassatego,
Leader of the Six Nations,
Lancaster, Pennsylvania, 1744

If you are familiar with the centrality of the oral tradition within American Indian cultures, you will understand how carefully we listen to the stories of our parents and relatives. As they tell us stories about their lives, they bequeath to us a living text of memory to help us structure our understanding of who we are and how we fit into the larger, more encompassing story of our tribe and culture. You will understand, also, that an integral part of the oral tradition is the voices of those offering testimony from their wisdom and experience.

The voices and testimony that follow speak to the family stories a good number of us have heard from our parents, grandparents, and elders; especially, they recall the story of their unwilling participation in the federal government's effort to re-educate on a massive scale thousands of American Indian children. Of course, education is valuable and empowering. Of course, education—in its most positive aspect—can afford all of us the skills and knowledge to help us realize whatever type of success we can imagine, whether we are talking about a conventional Western education or an education grounded in traditional, tribal ways. The key is that the education be undertaken with respect for the dignity of the students and be designed to empower them, not to diminish them. The process of education that I will be discussing here is one that has emotionally and spiritually devastated generations of American Indian people, setting in motion a concatenation of repercussions, including cultural genocide and generations of family pain.

In recent years documentaries and studies on Indian history only briefly touch on the boarding school system, contextualizing it with a host of other oppressive measures taken by the federal government to destroy the cultures of the people who stood in the way of progress. With one exception, however, studies have relied less on the testimony of Indian witnesses than on the published research of white historians. Indian voices, for the most part, have gone unheard. Given the fact that in the last century Indian education became a national political issue, involving Congress, the War Department, and the Department of the Interior, I wanted to counterpoint Native voices with those of the politicians and policymakers whose philosophical positions and decisions so profoundly affected the lives of our ancestors.

Like so many other experiments and policies implemented by the federal government during the past few hundred years in its attempt to deal with "the Indian problem," the boarding school system ultimately did more harm than good. Understating the point, Fuchs and Havighurst assert that this federal policy, "rooted in forced assimilation, paradoxically grounded in white humanitarianism . . . left a legacy of unpleasant memories that affect attitudes and policies today" (225). This legacy bequeathed more than simply "unpleasant memories" for generations to come, however. Although it appeared to be the solution the federal government had sought to the Indian problem, it became an instrument that emotionally scarred generations of innocent children, leaving them and their children, as well, victims of institutionalized cultural genocide.

If one were to ask those people who endured, fled, or simply survived boarding school about their memories of their teachers and their education, one might hear some surprising answers. John Lame Deer, a Lakota medicine man, relates in his 1972 autobiography that the Catholic mission boarding school he attended on the Rosebud reservation in South Dakota was run like a prison. My own Aunt Margaret, who attended the same school, loved the bread the students made in the bakery and enjoyed the Saturday night movies, especially *King Kong*. Feeling persecuted by the nuns, however, dreading their unceasing unkindness, she made a successful escape to Aunt Mary Cordier's house in St. Francis, never returning to earn her diploma. My mother, an alumna of 1952, also felt quite bitter about her experiences. She recalled constant hunger, incidents of physical abuse, and traumatic public humiliations for even minor infractions of rules. A particularly vivid memory she shared with me was that of one of the youngest girls at school being punished for wetting her bed. Determined to teach her a lesson, one of the nuns wrapped the child up in her wet sheets and threw her down the outdoor fire escape tunnel. Years later, my mother would still recall the child's terrified screams.

In her 1990 autobiography, *Lakota Woman*, Mary Crow Dog compares children who survived Indian boarding schools to "victims of Nazi concen-

Plate 1. Graduation photograph of the women, St. Francis Mission School, Rosebud, 1952. Teresa Lillian Prue, the author's mother, is in the front row, second from the left.

tration camps trying to tell average, middle-class Americans what their experience had been like" (28). As a child, I listened to my mother's stories of her own bleak, joyless childhood. Feeling helpless to comfort her, I could not even comprehend what it must have been like to be without one's family and utterly powerless in the hands of a group of people committed to not only controlling one completely, but also to erasing one's personal and tribal identity. Mary Crow Dog is indeed correct in her analogy.

Extermination by Civilization: Some American History

Indian education in America had been undertaken initially during the colonial period. One of the more successful efforts was that of the Society for Propagation of the Gospel in New England, a London organization which funded the establishment of an Indian college at Harvard during the 1650s. This group also underwrote the expense of books and of Bibles translated into Algonquian, as well as ministers and teachers to convert and educate the "heathen." Yet, as historian Christine Bolt points out, the Native peoples "were able to educate the whites in the ways of the wilderness without making comparable demands on them and preferred the newcomers' material goods to their culture" (210). Later, in 1701, another English missionary organization, the Society for the Propagation of the Gospel in Foreign Parts, established 170 missions in the colonies (210), inciting a tide of missionization and education that gained momentum as the numbers of Euramericans grew and encroached relentlessly upon Indian land. Even as early as 1744, however, tribal leaders recognized that the curricula and objectives of a Euramerican education were irrelevant to the Indian graduates returning home. Furthermore, colonial educational practices compromised graduates' chances of even surviving in their native environment. Respectfully declining the Euramericans' request to inculcate any more of their young people, the sachems of the Iroquois Confederacy explained:

> Several of our young people were formerly brought up at the colleges of the Northern Provinces; they were instructed in all your science; but when they came back to us, they were bad runners; ignorant of every means of living in the woods; unable to bear either cold or hunger; knew neither how to build a cabin, take a deer, or kill an enemy; spoke our language imperfectly; were therefore neither fit for hunters, warriors, or counselors; they were totally good for nothing. We are, however, not the less obliged by your kind offer, though we decline accepting it; and to show our grateful sense of it, if the gentlemen of Virginia will send us a dozen of their sons, we will take great care of their education, instruct them in all we know, and make men of them. (Qtd. in Franklin 98)

Bolt supports the chiefs' objections and suggests yet another reason why a Euramerican education afforded Indians little benefit in the white world: "Patronized and coerced, required to undertake irksome and sometimes unintelligible tasks and finally offered no secure place in the white world if they wanted, the lot of the small number of educated Indians was an unenviable one" (211).

The federal government and the American public as a whole registered ambivalence when it came to solutions to the Indian problem. In 1792, Benjamin Lincoln, politician and former Revolutionary War general, expressed his hope that Indians would be treated fairly and humanely. Nevertheless, he called for a plan to defoliate the land, thus starving out the "beasts of the forest upon which the uncivilized principally depend for support" (qtd. in Pearce 68). The Trail of Tears, which followed as a result of President Andrew Jackson's deliberate enforcement of the unconstitutional Indian Removal Act of 1830, evoked sympathy among many of those who learned of the death march that claimed thousands of Indian lives as they walked the thousand miles between their homes in the Southeast and Oklahoma. Ironically, the tribes immediately involved, the Five Civilized Tribes, were friendly and "civilized" by Euramerican standards. The Cherokee, for instance, had established their own schools for their children and were printing books and a newspaper in their own language. According to Fuchs and Havighurst, the Choctaw, another of the "Civilized" tribes, had established "a comprehensive school system of their own with twelve schoolhouses and non-Indian teachers, supported by tribal, missionary, and federal funds" (223).

Yet another factor that inflamed public sentiment regarding "the Indian problem" was the phenomenal popularity of the captivity narrative. This was a genre of popular literature which disseminated to the general public the melodramatic image of the Indian as "the consummate villain, the beast who hatcheted fathers, smashed the skulls of infants, and carried off mothers to make them into squaws" (Pearce 58). In accepting this representation, people easily viewed Native people as sub-human and, therefore, undeserving of the same sympathy they might extend to people of their own race. Politicians and philanthropic organizations devoted to the cause of saving this inevitably "vanishing" people would finally conclude that Indians must either conform entirely to the values, religious beliefs, and vocations of white Americans or they would become extinct. As David Adams points out, "The option to maintain a separate cultural identity simply did not exist" (36). Henry Price, the Commissioner of Indian Affairs in 1881, established the position of the federal government in no uncertain terms:

> There is no one who has been a close observer of Indian history and the effect of contact of Indians with civilization, who is not well satisfied that one of two things must eventually take place, to wit, either civilization or extermination of the Indian. Savage and civilized life cannot live and prosper on the same ground. (Qtd. in David Adams 1–2)

In the wake of post-Civil War westward expansion, the growth of the railroad, and Manifest Destiny—the credo buoying up pioneers and entrepreneurs westward in quest of gold and land—the Indian problem became a national issue. Clearly, philanthropists working in behalf of Indian interests would not tolerate all-out extermination; as historian Robert M. Utley points out, "public sentiment overwhelmingly favored destruction by civilization rather than by killing" (35).

A federally controlled policy of civilization through education and aggressive missionization appeared to be the most promising avenue of endeavor. After all, according to one Indian agent's report to Congress, the Brule Sioux, my ancestors, had shown potential to be civilized. Pointing out that, although in the past they had been "splendid animals, having but few human hopes, and much more of the animal than intellectual in their composition," they had begun to live in log cabins (qtd. in David Adams 40). What modern people might not realize, however, was that the Brule Sioux—like other tribes—were given no other choice. The federal government had ordered them to surrender themselves so they could be assigned to reservations.

Indian agents noted in their reports to Congress, however, the apparent futility of civilizing Native children who continued to live within families that persisted in practicing their traditional religion and language. Thomas Morgan, Commissioner of Indian Affairs from 1889 to 1893, warned that if Native children were allowed to grow up within their parents' homes, they would become corrupted by "fathers who are degraded and mothers who are debased." Rather than embrace white Christian values, Indian children would inevitably come to "love the unlovely and to rejoice in the unclean." In Morgan's view, the only way children could "escape the awful doom" of savagery was "for the strong arm of the Nation to reach out, take them in their infancy and place them in its fostering schools . . ." (qtd. in Prucha, *Americanizing the American Indian* 243).

The education of thousands of Indian children became not only a monumental undertaking, but an expensive one, as well. A solution to the problem was offered by Captain Richard Pratt, a former overseer of the Ft. Marion Indian prisoner-of-war camp in Florida and self-styled expert on rehabilitating Indians. His solution was to convert abandoned military forts into boarding schools and then implement an educational program based on a military model. Like others who felt they had special insight into Indian cultures, he thought that Indian people valued neither punctuality nor respect for government authority, clearly hallmarks of "civilized" behavior. The structure and discipline of military training seemed to be the answer to the problem, provided that schools could work with pupils young enough to be successfully indoctrinated.

His first project, the Carlisle Indian School, was established in 1878 in Carlisle, Pennsylvania, and would provide the model upon which federal and mission boarding schools, as well as reservation day schools, based their programs. By 1902, there were ninety reservation boarding schools in existence (David Adams 65), all essentially operating with the ideology espoused by Richard Pratt in an 1881 letter to Senator Henry Dawes. Acknowledging the price the Indian child would have to pay in order to gain the privilege of assimilating into mainstream American life, the Indian would be forced to

> lose his identity as such, to give up his tribal relations and to be made to feel that he is an American citizen. If I am correct in this supposition, then the sooner all tribal relations are broken up; the sooner the Indian loses all his Indian ways, even his language, the better it will be for him and for the government. . . . (Pratt 266)

In an address to a Baptist convention in 1883, Pratt elaborated upon the philosophy of education that guided his work with Indian children: "In Indian civilization I am a Baptist, because I believe in immersing the Indians in our civilization and when we get them under holding them there until they are thoroughly soaked" (Pratt 335).

Even as the ideological groundwork was laid for the detribalization of indigenous nations, no one thought to consult Indian people about the prospect of their cultures being eradicated. In fact, policymakers could not understand why Indians were not eager to embrace "civilization." Bolt suggests the paternalistic ethnocentrism that prompted white policymakers to view their culture as clearly superior to any other, observing that whites quite naturally viewed their "home environment" to be more wholesome than those of African Americans and Indians. Because their "home environment" was "held by whites to be the cause of the 'inferiority' of the two races, educators assumed that they would gratefully abandon their values and institutions when prompted to do so by their 'superiors'" (217). Unfortunately, the time soon came when many parents were given no choices regarding their children's education or even their religious training.

Having no ready pupils for his experiment, Pratt embarked on a recruiting mission that took him to my family's reservation in South Dakota, where he persuaded reluctant parents to hand their children over into his care. Pratt, whom historian Robert M. Utley deems wrongheaded but well-meaning, at least gave Indian parents the choice of rejecting his offer. From 1879 to 1918, the Carlisle Industrial School represented a successful model of Indian education that other schools in the United States and Canada would emulate. According to Utley, "During his twenty-four-year tenure the school educated, in all, 4,903 Indian boys and girls from seventy-seven tribes" (xiii).

What made possible the realization of the Carlisle school, as well as that of other federal boarding schools, reservation day schools, and mission schools, was the intrinsic nature of the reservation system itself. Advocates such as Francis Walker, Commissioner of Indian Affairs in 1872, argued that policymakers needed to be hardheaded when it came to "the treatment of savages by a civilized power." As Walker observed, reservations were necessary to bring "the wild beasts [the Indians] to the condition of supplicants for charity" (qtd. in Thomas 60–61). Assigned to reservations, designated wards of the government, and forced into complete economic dependency, Indians were at the mercy of government attempts to control and coerce them into compliancy. Having conquered them militarily, the federal government could then undertake a well-planned campaign to exterminate Indian cultures, resulting in "devastating cultural implications" for the human beings involved (Utley xvii).

In the years to come, Indian agents, serving on reservations as representatives of the federal government, condoned any means necessary to fill boarding schools, lending new significance to the term, "compulsory education." In fact, Congress enacted legislation in 1892 formally empowering government officials to use force when Native parents balked at the prospect of their children being taken from them, herded onto trains, and transported hundreds of miles away to boarding schools. David Adams notes that not until 1904 were officials required to obtain parental consent to remove their children to non-reservation boarding schools (89).

To enforce compliance with the new compulsory attendance law, Indian agents used whatever means necessary. For example, at the Yankton Agency in South Dakota, the home reservation of my great-grandfather, John Cordier, agents withheld rations to reluctant parents (David Adams 202).

Consequently, children at the Pine Ridge agency knew that if they played truant, their parents might starve. J. B. Harrison, of the Indian Rights Association, reported: "When a child was absent from school without a good reason, the rations of the whole family were cut off til he returned" (qtd. in David Adams 203).

During the autumn, agents often supervised what were essentially kidnapping raids. Agency police were ordered to hunt down and seize bodily children who were hiding or had been hidden by their parents. Fletcher J. Cowart, agent of the Mescolero Agency in New Mexico, described in his annual report for 1886 the cries and "lamentations" of Indian mothers and the stark terror of small, uncomprehending children about to be taken away by impatient strangers, perhaps never seeing their parents again (199). After witnessing such a particularly wrenching scene, one agent understated a dimension of Indian culture that he had observed, noting in his annual report to the Commissioner of Indian Affairs, "I have been impressed with the great fondness Indians have for their children. This may be one cause why they do not like to part from them" (qtd. in David Adams 205). A remarkably empathetic agent, W. D. C. Gibson, reported in 1887,

> It is really a pitiful sight to witness their distress and sorrow at times when they come to talk about the children and ask how many 'moons' before they come home, while their appearance indicates that they had passed a restless night, or perhaps not slept any. (163)

In comparison with the tone and tenor of other agents' reports, this agent appears to be one of the few who viewed Indians as human beings, rather than as obstinate and godless savages.

One of the most dramatic accounts of parents' resisting the kidnapping of their children comes from an annual report filed by an agent at the Yakima agency. In his 1885 report, Agent R. H. Milroy explained that he was forced to arrest and lock up Cotiahan, a Yakima tribal leader who refused to reveal where he had hidden his child. Making an example of him to the other band members, Milroy chained the father's leg and "put him to sawing wood, and told him if he refused to work, he would be tied to a tree and whipped" (200).

Had the children and parents been able to foresee the humiliation, anguish, and deprivation that constituted their children's "education" in these boarding schools, they might have resisted the agents' overtures even more aggressively than they did. As he was being led onto the train bound for Carlisle, Luther Standing Bear recalls thinking at the time that he was being taken away to be killed. "I could think of no reason why white people wanted Indian boys and girls except to kill them, and not having the remotest idea of what a school was, I thought we were going East to die," he writes (*Land of the Spotted Eagle* 230–31).

Barbed Wire and the Bible

In one sense those children would "die," passing from one life to another: stripped naked of the clothes their mothers had made for them, renamed with the names of American Civil War heroes and famous Indian fighters, and re-educated to adopt the "civilized" values of the race that had conquered them. In a quite literal sense, however, hundreds of children died. Neglect, hunger, disease, homesickness—even suicide—left the testimony of acres of little tombstones at boarding schools all over the United States. Luther Standing Bear tells us that "In the graveyard at Carlisle most of the graves are those of little ones" (*Land of the Spotted Eagle* 234). Chief Standing Bear goes on to say that by the third year Carlisle Indian School was in operation, almost one-half of the Plains children had died. Sadly, anxious parents back home might never be notified that their children were ill, much less dead and buried. Too often, rather than deal with the questions and tears of bereft parents, Indian agents would leave telegrams and letters to gather dust on their desks (*My People, the Sioux* 162–63). Ojibwa scholar Basil Johnston recalls a particularly virulent epidemic at his boarding school that claimed "between thirty to fifty boys at a time: chicken pox, measles and mumps . . ." (82). Not surprisingly, John Cook, Indian agent at the Rosebud reservation, warned that given "the large percentage of deaths among the scholars" at Carlisle, parents would not allow their children to be taken away (*Annual Report* 1881, 52).

When military and prison systems induct a new member into their respective institutions, their first step is to dismantle the individual's identity. Boarding school inductions followed similar lines. When Basil Johnston first met his new classmates at Peter Claver's Residential School, he was struck by the fact that they all had been shaven bald. In a 1900 article she published in *The Atlantic Monthly*, Dakota writer Zitkala-Ša (Gertrude Bonnin) describes being dragged screaming into a chair, where she was tied and her hair cut. (A shocked student once asked me, "Did they do the same thing to white girls who went away to school?") Zitkala-Ša explained to her readers that in Dakota culture, to have one's hair cut meant two things, both momentous. Either one had been publicly exposed as a coward or one was in the throes of grief at the loss of a dear one. Along with the haircut, the children were then subjected to a further humiliation—delousing—a practice that persisted until the 1960s, according to Mary Crow Dog. An alumna of my mother's school, who attended in the late 1960s, Crow Dog reports in the chapter of her autobiography entitled "Civilize Them with a Stick" that the nuns would "dump the children into tubs of alcohol, a sort of rubbing alcohol, 'to get the germs off'" (35).

Stripped of their clothes, which were usually burned, children were issued uniforms that distinguished them as inmates, so to speak. In the last century, girls were given dresses which were close-fitting and to Zitkala-Ša's

Plate 2. Corinne M. Cordier, the author's maternal grandmother, photographed in her school uniform, ca. 1914.

thinking, immodest. Boys were issued little military uniforms, which they later learned to sew for themselves and their classmates. Betty Eadie writes in her 1992 memoir that after the haircut and delousing, girls were issued "two dresses each, one color for one week, the other for the following week. These uniforms would help identify runaways" (7).

Just as children were stripped of all outward marks of identity, they were threatened, bullied, and beaten to conform to their teachers' expectations of what constituted civilized behavior. When Congress considered enacting legislation banning corporal punishment in boarding schools, Captain

Richard Pratt was incensed, insisting that such a ban "would mean the end of Indian schools" (qtd. in Hyde, *A Sioux Chronicle* 57). Children received a spectrum of punishments for speaking their own language, for instance. Marcella La Beau remembers that children caught speaking Lakota would have their mouths washed out with soap before they were punished (qtd. in Josephy 436). A Klamath man recalls that older boys were forced to walk around a tree stump for an hour, carrying a fence rail on their backs (David Adams 125). One of the most dramatic incidents of punishment is recounted by a Blackfoot student, Lone Wolf, who witnessed the event. Angered at hearing a boy speaking his Native language, a white supervisor threw the boy across a room, breaking his collarbone (qtd. in Josephy 435).

Because the constitutional right of freedom of religion was denied to Indians, Indian children were forced to practice the religion of whatever Christian denomination prevailed at their school. Children were also punished for not worshipping with the zeal the teachers demanded of them. Mary Crow Dog's grandmother told her a story that happened when she was very young and caught by the nuns playing jacks instead of praying. As a punishment, she was locked in a tiny cell in an attic, in the dark, and fed only bread and water for a week (Crow Dog 32). Betty Eadie recalls, "My sister Thelma was often beaten by [the nuns] with a little hose and was then forced to thank the Sister who had done it or be beaten again" (9).

Unable to bear the regimentation, spoiled food, bleak living conditions, and utter lack of emotional support, many children ran away. Consequently, one agent at Cheyenne and Arapaho Agency felt compelled to place bars on the dormitory windows and padlock the doors to prevent children from escaping (David Adams 127). Even in this century, according to Betty Eadie, children were locked in their rooms at night (8). Punishment for running away was usually severe. As Mary Crow Dog explains, her grandmother and her fellow inmates were made examples to other children after they were found and returned to school: "The nuns stripped them naked and whipped them. They used a horse buggy whip on my grandmother. Then she was put back into the attic—for two weeks" (32). One particularly incensed school principal hunted down a group of escaped Ute students, drove them back at gunpoint "like wolves," then threatened to hang them (David Adams 219). Luckily, my Aunt Margaret was never caught. Just last summer, while we were at Rosebud, she pointed out to me the route she took to escape what had become an intensely miserable period of her life.

As I look at old photographs of my mother and Aunt Margaret's school grounds, as well as those of other schools, I am struck by two images that recur with frequency: the barbed wire fences and the rows of little children behind those fences, identically dressed, staring warily into the camera. From all the accounts I have read and heard, from the 1880s to the 1960s, the typical boarding school operated on a daily basis like a military prison for children. Basil Johnston and his classmates objected to the absolute lack of privacy, of having every hour of day scheduled: "The boys resented the never ending surveillance that began in the morning and ended only late at night, after they had all fallen asleep; a surveillance that went on day after day, week after week, month after month, year after year" (137). My mother recalls having only two hours of free time a week outdoors—on Sunday afternoon. She said that boys and girls could mingle and talk on the grounds, but everyone had to remain standing for that time; no one was allowed to sit on the ground, unless the person had a telephone book to sit on. (My mother would later laugh about the irrationality of this stipulation: "Where on earth were we going to get telephone books?") Apparently, the nuns were concerned that students might engage in sexual activity on the school grounds in full sight of everyone. "They treated us like we were savages," my mother said.

Children awoke each morning to reveille and fell asleep to taps. Medicine man John Lame Deer remembers falling in for roll call four times each day. He recalls, "We had to stand at attention, or march in step" (25). His grandson Archie Lame Deer, who is my mother's age and perhaps a classmate of hers at St. Francis, tells us that a priest would order the boys to march around the playground holding sticks as if they were rifles. "If we'd had blond hair and blue eyes," he jokes, "you might have taken us for Hitler youth in Nazi Germany" (49).

Even girls were not exempt from the military regimentation. In her book *Oglala Women*, Marla N. Powers presents testimony from a woman who attended Rapid City Indian School, recounting the bugles and bells that dictated when they awakened, ate, worked, had inspections, and slept. The girls marched, too: "We fell into formations. We had officers for each company . . . a captain and a major. . . . We knew every drill there was to be known, right flank, left flank, forward march, and double time" (111). Thomson Highway adds that he knew of girls getting their heads shaved for "minor infractions" of rules (*War against the Indians*).

The education and training most children received was equally regimented, culturally irrelevant, and ultimately a waste of time, according to a number of disillusioned graduates. Understanding nothing about Indian people, teachers assumed that the children were unfeeling and impervious to humiliation. Charles Eastman, who earned his M.D. at Boston College, writes in his autobiography *From the Deep Woods to Civilization* of the humiliation of class recitation at Dr. Alfred Riggs Santee Training School: "For a whole week we youthful warriors were held up and harassed with words of three letters . . . rat, cat, and so forth . . . until not a semblance of our native dignity and self-respect was left" (46). To make the learning process even more fraught with anxiety, students reciting their lessons were asked to do so "taking the position of a soldier at attention" (Pratt 244).

Christine Bolt notes that in both white and Indian cultures children learned by memorization. However, the rote learning by which Indian children were inculcated with the religion and values of the dominant culture must have been not only tortuous, but bewildering as well. Bolt explains,

> The Indian mission children were asked to memorize hymns and passages from Scripture which they frequently did not understand and which contradicted all their own learned traditions. Incomprehension was compounded by the fact that pupils of every degree of attainment were at first taught together. . . . (213)

The ninth-grade students at Pierre Indian School in South Dakota must certainly have puzzled over the usefulness and relevance of *Julius Caesar* and *Lady of the Lake* to the lives they would lead as they adapted to their dramatically changing world. Indeed, how could Shakespeare help a Cheyenne person negotiate the cultural transition from tribal values to those of the American West? No doubt Paiute children in Nevada prior to 1931 were equally mystified by the following lines they were forced to memorize and recite:

> What do we plant
> When we plant the tree?
> We plant the ship
> That sails the sea. . . . (Qtd. in Szasz 33)

My aunt Margaret never did have an occasion to use the Latin she was taught after she learned to speak English, although she did point out that Mass and prayers were in Latin, hence the necessity of the hours spent memorizing all those Latin verb conjugations. Studying secretarial skills as a part of her curriculum, my mother at least received an education that would theoretically prepare her to survive and earn economic independence in the white world.

Going on to earn an Associate's Degree from Haskell Institute, a former boarding school which is today a university, my mother managed to surpass the expectations non-Indian teachers and administrators usually had of Indian students. From the inception of the boarding school idea, however, federal officials generally held very low expectations of what Indian students might achieve professionally after they completed school. Secretary of the Interior Henry Teller had articulated a philosophy of education that had been adopted not only by Richard Pratt at Carlisle, but also by boarding schools everywhere up until the middle of this century. Within the curriculum of these schools, Teller declared, "more attention should be paid to teaching them to labor than to read" (qtd. in Prucha, *American Indian Policy* 271).

Students were expected to become laborers or domestic servants. In fact, policymakers envisioned Native people leaving their reservations to join the ranks of what was viewed at that time as a permanent underclass in white society. Captain Pratt's vision was that eventually tribal people would be swallowed up into the melting pot of immigrants that had become mainstream Euramerican culture. What he probably did not foresee, however, was that his philosophy would defeat the aspirations of some Indian people to use their education to secure more fulfilling professions than those in manual labor or domestic service.

Chief Standing Bear's situation is a case in point. Like so many others at the mercy of a paternalistic boarding school, he had little say in determining his own future. Standing Bear had wanted to spend his entire day in the classroom getting an education, rather than devote half of it working in the tinshop learning a profession that would be useless back at Rosebud. Eventually, after pointing out that the government was supplying his reservation with an abundance of tinware, he asked Captain Pratt if he could learn carpentry instead. Pratt refused his request. Standing Bear writes, "What worried me was the thought that I might not be able to work at the trade after I returned home. But Captain Pratt could not understand why I wanted to make a change, and so the matter was dropped" (*My People, the Sioux* 176). In this century, white educators' expectations of their Indian students clearly have not changed. In his 1992 autobiography, *The Gift of Power*, medicine man Archie Lame Deer states that his boarding school teachers held the opinion that "we Indians were only good at menial jobs. They did not prepare us to become teachers, lawyers, or doctors" (49).

According to the testimony of Native people and historians, boarding school students were essentially trained, then treated as indentured servants, not as scholars—a fact that students' parents were unaware of. Making the best of a difficult situation, parents such as those of Luther Standing Bear and Stay at Home Spotted Tail hoped that their sons' white education would afford them both professions and the knowledge they would need to protect and defend both personal and tribal interests. Unfortunately, this was not the case for Chief Spotted Tail's son. Visiting his son at Carlisle in 1880, Spotted Tail talked with the Lakota boys from Rosebud, learning that they were all generally "miserable and homesick" (Hyde 322). However, when he discovered that his son was working at harness making, rather than learning to read, write, and speak English, "the thunder began to roll," George Hyde explains, noting that ordinarily Spotted Tail's son would be back home at Rosebud, "training to become a chief," not a farmhand (322).

Although the students were there ostensibly to earn an education, child labor was vitally important to support the expense of maintaining the boarding school. Indeed, one-half of the pupils' day was devoted to the maintenance and upkeep of their prison, including farming, cooking, sewing their own uniforms, and making their own shoes. In his memoir, *Battlefield and Classroom*, Richard Pratt explains that even children too young to be put to work had to ". . . witness the productions of the older ones in harness making, tin ware, boots and shoes, clothing, blacksmith and wagon making . . ." (259). The prized jobs at his school were those in the kitchen, recalls Basil Johnston, because there students could eat the leftover food from their teachers' plates and at least satisfy their incessant hunger (49). Johnston's recollection of hunger echoes the testimony of students over a range of residential institutions. Not until the publication of the Meriam Report in 1928 and the subsequent investigations of the Red Cross was it widely known that children had to survive on "a diet that was the equivalent of slow starvation" (Szasz 19). The Meriam Report criticized the boarding school system on another charge, as well—the failure to demonstrate the practices they taught. Girls in home economics classes were lectured on the elements of proper nutrition and meal planning; yet, the schools themselves rarely provided milk, fruit, or vegetables in the children's diets (351).

A cruel irony, of course, was that graduates returning to the reservation might not find an opportunity to use the education or vocational training they received in these institutions. Robert Utley points out that "with the spoils system ascendant, the few government jobs available rarely went to Indians, and few Carlisle graduates found any occupation to utilize their newly learned talents" (xvi). As in the case of Standing Bear, who found no use for his training as a tinsmith, other students, such as those trained as hatmakers and tailors, found few opportunities to become independent and self-supporting once they returned home.

On the other hand, Indian graduates were not always successful in finding a place in the white world, either. My grandfather, Levi Prue, who graduated from Haskell Institute with a degree in accounting, could find only occasional, short-term employment at home—or within a Bureau of Indian Affairs office or other Indian agencies. After finding that white employers in Omaha were not anxious to hire an educated Indian, my grandfather, who loved to read and disliked the mind-numbing tedium of sheer manual labor, went to work in a cold storage company, then a sheet metal plant, before finally trading in his dreams for a bottle. On the advice of Uncle Moses Red Owl, who feared that she would not find a BIA (Bureau of Indian Affairs) job on the reservation, my mother decided not to return to Rosebud to look for work. Instead, she moved to a succession of white towns looking for some kind of meaningful employment. Unfortunately, she never had the opportunity to exercise her college degree or her shorthand skills (taking dictation at 120 words a minute). During the 1950s, racism against Indians had not abated much since my grandfather's day, so my mother also resigned herself to factory work.

At least my mother and grandfather did not have to face the type of racial discrimination that prevented them from securing a residence in the white world. In *My People, the Sioux*, Luther Standing Bear writes of his

Plate 3. Levi Joseph Prue, the author's maternal grandfather. Graduation photo from Haskell Institute, ca. 1915.

discouragement at facing racial discrimination in Philadelphia, where he wanted to work as a clerk in Wanamaker's Store. He explains, "I was to prove to all people that the Indians could learn and work as well as the white people . . ." (179). Unfortunately, he was denied the opportunity to prove his equality—white landlords refused to rent a room to him. Chief Standing Bear explains, "When I would find something that seemed suitable, and the people discovered my nationality, they would look at me in a surprised sort of way, and say that they had no place for an Indian boy" (189).

Sadly, many graduates returned to the reservation finding they did not belong there, either. A white education was an acquisition of dubious value for young people returning home expecting to reintegrate into their communities, earn a living, and move on with their lives. As Robert Utley points out, "The result was that they either existed in a shadow world neither Indian nor white, with acceptance denied by both worlds, or they cast off the veneer of Carlisle and again became Indians" (xvi). Commenting upon this predicament from a Native perspective, John Lame Deer writes, "When we enter the school, we at least know that we are Indians. We come out half red and half white, not knowing what we are" (27). For Sun Elk, a Taos Pueblo graduate, his homecoming would be a heartbreaking one. Soon after his arrival, tribal elders came to his parents' home, and, completely ignoring him, made the following pronouncement to his father:

> Your son who calls himself Rafael has lived with the white men. He has been far away. . . . He has not . . . learned the things that Indian boys should learn. He has no hair. . . . He cannot even speak our language. He is not one of us. (Qtd. in Josephy 436)

Alienated from home and family, culturally as well as emotionally, some Indian people have struggled with their ambivalence about claiming a relation to the people of whom they had been taught to be ashamed. Inculcated with white values and taught the Euramerican version of American history, Pequot minister William Apess, for instance, before he went on to work as an Indian rights activist, grew up "terrified" of Indians. LaVonne Brown Ruoff explains that "whites had filled him with stereotypical stories about Indian cruelty but never told him how cruelly they treated Indians" (1781). Albert White Hat, now a professor at Sinte Gleška University and spiritual leader at Rosebud, recalls having grown so alienated from his cultural roots that when he and his friends would watch western movies, "we cheered for the cavalry" (Beasley 41).

The emotional cost of the boarding school experience upon generations of Native families has been incalculable. When I was a child I would watch my mother brood for hours, chain smoking over memories that intruded insistently upon the present. Passed around from relative to relative, from orphanage to boarding school, she—like so many other Indian children—had to bear the consequences of her parents' shattered lives. Her life story and those of other boarding school survivors remind me of Basil Johnston's description of the youngest children at his boarding school, "the babies":

> They were a sad lot, this little crowd of babies; they seldom laughed or smiled and often cried and whimpered during the day and at night. . . . [T]hey were hunched in their wretchedness and misery in a corner of the recreation hall, their outsized boots dangling several inches above the asphalt floor. And though Paul Migwanabe and Joe Thompson and other carvers made toys for them, the babies didn't play with their cars and boats; they just held on to them, hugged them and took them to bed at night, for

that was all they had in the world when the lights went out, and they dared not let it go. (60)

Given such testimony, we must ask: What was to be the destiny of children like these? What were the experiences of children who grew up never feeling the nurturing of parents, who emerged from an institution without knowing how to function within a family, without possessing a sense of belonging to a particular group, of sharing a particular history, or of feeling pride in their ancestors? Whom were these individuals allowed to feel proud of? The Pilgrims? Christopher Columbus? These are the queries of the academic researcher, of course. Yet, they are also questions posed with bitterness by those who recognize that their own cultural heroes and tribal identities have been erased out of history by the Colonizers. We have been spiritually dispossessed with that erasure, bereft of our language and our pride in being Indian, diminished by the loss of the cultural knowledge that constitutes the psychic infrastructure of a people. My ancestors made this point more emphatically: A people without a history is like wind across the buffalo grass. A history, after all, is a narrative, a story. And the boarding school robbed generations of Indian children of the stories of their families and tribes, stories that would have otherwise empowered them with knowledge, wisdom, survival skills, and a spiritual foundation.

Aside from being an instrument of cultural genocide, another insidious effect of the boarding school system has been its effectiveness in eroding the foundation of tribal culture, the family. Since the inception of the boarding school system in the last century up to the present, Indian families all over the United States have struggled and are still struggling with healing the pain of generations of family dysfunction. The documentaries, *The War Against the Indians* and *The Native Americans*, both present testimony from Native people explaining that the years of institutionalizing did not foster in children the nurturing skills they would need to be parents. One of the producers of another well-known documentary on boarding schools, *In the White Man's Image*, Matthew "Sitting Bear" Jones, explains how the boarding schools have perpetuated generations of dysfunction within families: "They didn't teach us to be parents at the schools and we didn't have parents to teach us to be parents. When we had children we didn't know how to raise them" ("Boarding Schools" B2).

Healing Our Hoop

My approach to the subject of the boarding school system, as I have noted, grows out of my desire that the voices of adult children survivors be heard, and that the audiences which listen will understand how this important dimension of Indian history fits into the larger context of factors that have played a role in the attempted cultural genocide of the first Americans. For

Indian audiences, I hope that this testimony will bring the kind of healing shock I experienced after reading an interview with Carol Anne Heart Looking Horse in Sandy Johnson's *The Book of Elders*. Her story and those of others have helped me to construct the narrative of my family, as I hope they will for other people.

In her interview, Looking Horse discusses the "historical grief" we bear and its relation to not only the attempted eradication of our culture, but also the trauma our parents experienced as they were forced through this process. As tribal nations regain control over the education of their own children, she observes, Indian teachers have been able to teach our young people about the relationship between this history and our parents' personal experience. In doing so, we are able to help young people to make strides in recovering their culture, learning a history of America that does not demonize their ancestors, and regaining pride in tribal heritage.

An important key to this recovery lies in the tribal college. In sites such as Sinte Gleśka University on the Rosebud reservation, for instance, students have the opportunity to learn from Indian professors and to complete a core curriculum of Lakota studies that includes language, history, and traditional knowledge. At the same time, students can remain in proximity to their families and communities, sustaining the family bonds that have been so cherished within traditional families. A major challenge that tribal colleges all over the United States face, however, is financial. As always, the destinies of Native people have been subject to the seemingly capricious decisions of the federal government. For instance, although Congress had at one time authorized financial support of amounts up to $6,000 for each student attending college, the Reagan administration made cuts in allocations. By 1989 a student might receive only $1,900 of the funds Congress had originally allocated (Wright and Tierney 17). Even now, Congress continues to slash appropriations once promised to Indian tribes—funds which would enable Native people to pursue their dreams of economic independence and self-determination. Thankfully, a handful of tribal communities—not all—are experiencing an economic and cultural renaissance, due to gaming revenues that enable tribes to build new schools and hire qualified teachers to help bring the next generation proudly into the coming century. And, they will be proud, for they will have the choices our parents and grandparents were denied: to walk in either world, in the tracks and in the image not of the Colonizers, but of the ancestors.

Works Cited

Adams, David Wallace. *The Federal Indian Boarding School: A Study of Environment and Response, 1879–1918*. Diss. Indiana University, 1975.

Adams, Evelyn C. *American Indian Education, Government Schools and Economic Progress*. New York: King's Crown Press, 1941.

Annual Report of the Secretary of the Interior. Washington: GPO, 1879–1895.

Beasley, Conger, Jr. "The Return of the Lakota: An Indian People Thrive 500 Years After Columbus." *The Environmental Magazine* Sept.–Oct. 1992: 38+.

"Boarding Schools Likened to Concentration Camps." *Indian Country Today* (*Lakota Times*) 5 Oct. 1994: B2.

Bolt, Christine. *American Indian Policy and American Reform: Case Studies of the Campaign to Assimilate the American Indians*. London: Allen & Unwin, 1987.

Cowart, Fletcher J. "Reports of Agents in New Mexico." Secretary of the Interior. *Annual Report of the Secretary of the Interior*. Washington: GPO, 1886.

Crow Dog, Mary, and Richard Erdoes. *Lakota Woman*. New York: Harper Perennial, 1990.

Eadie, Betty J. *Embraced by the Light*. New York: Bantam Books, 1992.

Eastman, Charles. *From the Deep Woods to Civilization: Chapters in the Autobiography of an Indian*. 1916. Lincoln: U of Nebraska P, 1977.

Franklin, Benjamin. "Remarks Concerning the Savages of North America." *The Writings of Benjamin Franklin*. Ed. Albert Henry Smyth. Vol. 10. New York: Macmillan, 1907. 10 vols.

Fuchs, Estelle, and Robert J. Havighurst. *To Live on This Earth: American Indian Education*. New York: Doubleday, 1972.

Gibson, W. D. C. "Reports of Agents in Nevada." Secretary of the Interior. *Annual Report of the Secretary of the Interior*. Washington: GPO, 1887.

Hyde, George E. *A Sioux Chronicle*. Norman: U of Oklahoma P, 1956.

———. *Spotted Tail's Folk: A History of the Brule Sioux*. Norman: U of Oklahoma P, 1961.

In the White Man's Image. Prod. Christine Lesiak and Matthew Jones. Videocassette. PBS Video. 1991.

Indian Removal Act of 1830. 28 May 1830, c. 148, 4 stat. 411.

Johnson, Sandy. *The Book of Elders: The Life Stories of Great American Indians as Told to Sandy Johnson.* San Francisco: Harper Collins, 1994.

Johnston, Basil H. *Indian School Days.* Norman: U of Oklahoma P, 1988.

Josephy, Alvin M. *500 Nations: An Illustrated History of North American Indians.* New York: Alfred A. Knopf, 1994.

King Kong. Dir. Ernest B. Schoedsack. Perf. Fay Wray, Bruce Cabot, Robert Armstrong. Universal, 1933.

Lame Deer, Archie, and Richard Erdoes. *The Gift of Power: The Life and Teachings of a Lakota Medicine Man.* Santa Fe: Bear & Company, 1992.

Lame Deer, John (Fire), and Richard Erdoes. *Lame Deer, Seeker of Visions.* New York: Pocket Books, 1972.

Meriam, Lewis, et al. *The Problem of Indian Administration.* 1928. Introd. Frank C. Miller. New York: Johnson Reprint Corporation, 1971.

Milroy, R. H. "Reports of Agents in Washington Territory." Secretary of the Interior. *Annual Report of the Secretary of the Interior.* Washington: GPO, 1885.

The Native Americans. Narr. Joy Harjo. 3 episodes. TBS Productions. 1992.

Pearce, Roy Harvey. *The Savages of America: A Study of the Indian and the Idea of Civilization.* Baltimore: Johns Hopkins UP, 1953.

Powers, Marla N. *Oglala Women: Myth, Ritual, and Reality.* Chicago: U of Chicago P, 1986.

Pratt, Richard Henry. *Battlefield and Classroom: Four Decades with the American Indian, 1867–1904.* Ed. Robert M. Utley. Lincoln: U of Nebraska P, 1964.

Prucha, Francis Paul. *American Indian Policy in Crisis: Christian Reformers and the Indian, 1865–1900.* Norman: U of Oklahoma P, 1976.

———, ed. *Americanizing the American Indians: Writings by the "Friends of the Indian," 1800–1900.* Cambridge: Harvard UP, 1973.

Ruoff, A. LaVonne Brown. "William Apess." *The Heath Anthology of American Literature.* Ed. Paul Lauter. Vol. 1, 2nd ed. Lexington, MA: D. C. Heath, 1994. 1780–81.

Standing Bear, Luther. *Land of the Spotted Eagle.* Lincoln: U of Nebraska P, 1933.

——. *My People, the Sioux*. Lincoln: U of Nebraska P, 1975.

Szasz, Margaret Connell. *Education and the American Indian: The Road to Self-Determination Since 1928*. 2nd ed. Albuquerque: U of New Mexico P, 1974.

Thomas, Robert K. "On an Indian Reservation: How Colonialism Works." *The Way: An Anthology of American Indian Literature*. Eds. Shirley Hill Witt and Stan Steiner. New York: Alfred A. Knopf, 1972. 60–68.

Utley, Robert M. Introduction. *Battlefield and Classroom: Four Decades with the American Indian, 1867–1904*. Ed. Robert M. Utley. Lincoln: U of Nebraska P, 1964. ix-xix.

The War against the Indians. Narr. Harry Rasky. Canada Broadcasting Corporation. 1992.

Witt, Shirley Hill, and Stan Steiner, eds. *The Way: An Anthology of American Indian Literature*. New York: Alfred A. Knopf, 1972.

Wright, Bobby, and William G. Tierney. "American Indians in Higher Education." *Change*. March–April 1991: 11–18.

Zitkala-Ša. (Gertrude Bonnin). "The School Days of an Indian Girl." *Atlantic Monthly* Feb. 1900: 185–94. Rpt. in *American Indian Stories*. Washington: Hayworth Publishing House, 1921. 52–56.

RECLAIMING POWER

II

Educational Strategies

As Debra K. S. Barker's essay in Section I suggests, the issue of who controls Native American education is highly charged. The focus of the pieces in this section centers on Native Americans' struggle to regain control of their schools and to fashion curricula that reflect respect for their cultures. As we have seen, such respect for identity is not a politically correct nicety; without a clear sense of identity, Native communities experience dysfunction and individuals feel alienation.

Wayne J. Stein of Montana State University introduces the topic in his study, "American Indian Education." For Stein, the dilemma is clear: "Individuals must have strong formal educational preparation if they are to be able to compete in this society. Without formal education, individuals or groups can quickly become marginalized and thrust into lives of poverty." Following a brief history of Native Americans' experience with white educational institutions, Stein shows how the emergence of tribally controlled community colleges offers Native American students opportunities to learn in a milieu consistent with their values. Native Americans raised the issue of control over education after World War II; with the establishment of Navajo Community College in 1968, the movement blossomed. Currently, about 30 tribally controlled community colleges pursue a mission to serve Native communities by providing quality education, research on social issues, and vocational programs. Furthermore, strategic planning of the mission and the direction of many of the colleges is coordinated through the American Indian Higher Education Consortium (AIHEC), formed in 1973. As a result, Stein maintains, "The story of American Indian education is one of hardship, grief, and pain, but also one that may yet have a happy ending."

Jon Reyhner at Northern Arizona University describes the difficulties many Native American students face as they struggle to make the uneasy transition from reservation life to campus culture. His essay, "The Case for Native American Studies," establishes, both from a personal and academic point of view, that we do need Native American Studies programs and courses. Noting "the tragic connections that link education, a sense of identity, and dysfunctional behavior in young people," he asserts that "more needs to be done to keep . . . students in college." Reyhner's research shows that minority students face hurdles that mainstream students do not. Three factors, in particular, undermine Native American students' performance in college: first, a lack of academic preparation; second, uninformed expectations of college life, and third, unsupportive college culture. As Reyhner notes, Native American students are "ignored, overlooked, or actively face racism" on many campuses. A viable solution, Reyhner concludes, is found in Native American Studies programs because they help Native students to make the demanding transition to non-Native campuses, they sensitize non-Native students to the realities of Indian life, and they provide a base for academic studies which can benefit Native communities.

Finally, William Asikinack of Saskatchewan Indian Federated College provides an international view on Native Studies programs in "Why Native American Studies? A Canadian First Nations Perspective." Asikinack traces the first glimmerings and later development of Native Studies in Canada and the United States. He is in a unique position to do so; as an Anishinabe, Asikinack felt the discrimination typical of that experienced by First Nations people who sought academic training before the 1960s. He shows, like Reyhner, both the need for such programs and the benefits these innovations bring to academic life and beyond, building valuable bridges between campuses and Native American communities and between faculty from different disciplines.

4

American Indian Education

Wayne J. Stein

Introduction

Education is a defining aspect of all human beings' lives from the first breath they draw as infants. Formal education, which will be discussed in this essay, is that part of life which societies provide or impose on their young people. Mainstream culture in the United States demands that individuals must have strong formal educational preparation if they are to be able to compete in this society. Without formal education, individuals or groups can quickly become marginalized and thrust into lives of poverty.

American Indian people as a group have had a most difficult experience, both in their initial contact with Europeans and their cultures and in their dealings with subsequent generations of Euro-Americans. This experience includes contact with formalized education, one of the important institutions of modern Western society, where it has intruded and has been imposed on them by the majority non-Indian society. This chapter will give a brief history of that educational experience and will describe how contemporary American Indian nations are coming to terms with this foreign intrusion into their lives. The story of American Indian education is one of hardship, grief, and pain, but also one that may yet have a happy ending.

Colonial Efforts at American Indian Education

In the years both prior to and following first contact with Europeans, American Indian peoples had developed their own educational practices and systems. This simple fact is, no doubt, obvious to the student reading this text. Yet, surprisingly, it is an important fact that American Indian Studies scholars—even those who specialize in observing American Indians' interactions with contemporary educational systems—often overlook. Native educational practices varied from nation to nation, but were generally founded on oral traditions in which elders transmitted knowledge and skills to younger generations through methods such as storytelling, memory skills, hands-on experiences and practice, and prayer (Bill, 1990). The intrusion of Europeans, and, later, their Americanized descendants, into the world of

American Indians led to the breakdown of traditional American Indian educational practices. By the time of Wounded Knee in 1890, they had all but disappeared. The remnants of Native educational traditions were driven underground, to be carried forward into contemporary times by only a few American Indian elders who recall the old ways.

One of the most important factors leading to the destruction of American Indian educational systems was the invading Europeans' ethnocentric belief that their own Christian cultures offered the only legitimate path to the "good life"—the term anthropologists use to describe a people's sense of the proper way life should be lived. This ethnocentrism was the basic justification used by the Spanish, French, British, Dutch, and later, the Americans for their wars against indigenous American Indian nations. These wars and the introduction of harmful elements such as European diseases, weapons, trade goods, and liquor led to the eventual loss by American Indians of much of their lands, cultures, religions, languages, and control of the education of their children.

Initial efforts by European colonizers to educate Native children can be traced back to within a decade of the establishment of the first permanent European settlement at Jamestown (Wright, 1989). Over the next two hundred years, attempts to educate the children and young adults of American Indians were carried out by the churches of the European mother countries and their various colonies. On the eastern seaboard, English Protestant churches raised funds in Britain to support missions and even to establish colleges. Throughout the Southwest and California, the Spanish Catholic Church built missions, and, while teaching American Indians about Christianity, used them as slave laborers on mission farms and in silver and gold mines. In the far North, French colonizers had a much less structured approach to Christianizing American Indians. The Crown permitted missionary activities as long as they did not interfere with the fur trade.

Early on, several of the most famous colleges and universities in the United States today (e.g., William and Mary in Virginia and Harvard in Massachusetts) involved themselves in the education of American Indian youths. Their claims of pious intent often belied the profitable business elements of their educational missions. In 1765, for instance, the Reverend Eleazar Wheelock set out to build a college in New Hampshire dedicated to educating and Christianizing American Indians. In founding Dartmouth College, however, Wheelock's greatest successes came not in educating Native children, but in fundraising. Recognizing the powerful appeal of a "model Indian," Wheelock went so far as to send one of his own American Indian students, Samson Occum, to the British Isles to raise funds. Occum's visit was a huge success and raised thousands of pounds sterling for the express purpose of educating Indians. Upon returning to New Hampshire, however, Occum found that Wheelock had changed the charter of the new college to include the sons of British colonists "and others" as prospective students (Wright, 1989).

By changing the charter of Dartmouth College, Wheelock signaled an end to any authentic effort to educate American Indian youths. Indeed, when we compare the expressed purposes of colonial colleges to educate American Indian youths against the actual outcomes, we can have little doubt that these early efforts were failures. In the light of their half-hearted commitment and dismal records, it is difficult to believe that the founders and administrators of such institutions as Harvard, William and Mary, and Dartmouth sought anything but the funding to support the education of white children. Furthermore, given their founders' assumption that American Indians would see relevance in the religious and classical education the colonial colleges offered, should we have expected much success? The efforts of the early colonists to recreate American Indians in their own image only contributed to the overall failure of these early attempts to introduce Western education to American Indians (Wright, 1989).

American Indian Education in the United States

American Indian education in the United States has gone through a number of major phases. These phases can be inserted into chronological eras in American history and in federal Indian policy: Ongoing Contact and Conquest (1600–1776), Treaty-Making and Removal (1776–1887), Allotment and Forced Assimilation (1887–1934), Reorganization and Revitalization (1934–1946), Termination (1946–1961), and Self-Determination and Renaissance (1962-present).

Treaty-Making and Removal (1776–1887)

The federal government of the Early Republic viewed the idea of sharing the North American continent with American Indian nations with increasing trepidation. Early American leaders recognized that the fledgling United States was in no position to sustain an ongoing war with American Indian nations. The federal government then chose to deal with these nations through the treaty-making function of government, thus officially recognizing them as sovereign nations in their own right. As various tribes agreed to treaties of friendship and understanding, however, the seeds of destruction were being sown. The pattern began with the introduction of Western diseases and other factors, which decimated American Indian communities and substantively weakened their ability to defend themselves. When a tribe became weak enough, Congress would pass legislation to break the standing treaty or treaties between the U.S. and that "sovereign" nation. Federal troops then went in to remove the nation from its lands. If the tribe's leaders objected or resisted, Congress declared the existence of a "just war," then used military might to impose a forced removal.

During this period a number of treaties between various American Indian nations and the United States called for, as part of a treaty agreement, the provision for educating the children of the nations involved as payment for lands ceded to the United States. What little education was provided to American Indian youths by the federal government and its agents was based on these treaty provisions as the new nation of non-Indians rolled over one American Indian nation after another.

Congress relegated much of the responsibility for educating American Indian youths in the "arts of western civilization and Christianity" to various religious orders. Financial support for these mission schools was funded by both the federal government and church missionary charities. Moreover, as an interesting feature of this era, several of the Indian nations started their own educational systems based upon the Western European model. In New York, the Mohawk started and supported their own school. In Georgia, the Cherokee and Choctaw ran well-organized and very successful schools; these they had to re-establish after the administration of President Andrew Jackson forced their removal to Oklahoma during the 1830s (Eiselein, 1993).

An especially subversive form of Indian education was founded during this era—federally supported boarding schools. The roots of this style of education were in the manual labor schools and traditional boarding schools of the time. The founding of federal boarding schools for Indians is credited to Captain Richard H. Pratt. A former commandant of Ft. Marion prison in Florida, Pratt believed that, in dealing with his American Indian student charges, the Indian in them must be killed in order to save the man (or woman). Little regard was given to the damage such practices did to the American Indian children and the communities from which they came. Thus, federal boarding schools for American Indian students became little more than labor camps dedicated to the forced assimilation of the American Indian into the mainstream of the United States. Indian students in these schools frequently had their clothes and other personal possessions confiscated and burned. They were punished, often severely, for speaking their native languages or for practicing their traditional religions or other cultural customs (Eiselein, 1993).

Allotment and Forced Assimilation (1887–1933)

The period of Allotment and Forced Assimilation brought years of unrelenting catastrophe for many American Indian peoples. The Western tribes, in particular, suffered final subjection as the last of the free American Indian nations. They were witnesses to the abduction of their children, who were forcibly removed to the hostile world of federally run boarding schools. In addition, and no less disheartening, they watched as Congress, under various homesteading acts, reallocated 90 million acres of their remaining lands to white homesteaders, miners, ranchers, and speculators.

The release of the Meriam Report in 1928 (Meriam, 1928) slowed the pace of destruction of tribal communities. Documenting the shocking conditions and appalling despair into which the surviving Indian population had been forced, the Meriam Report's fierce censure forced a response. The public and national leaders agreed that major changes must be made in federal Indian policy. Of particular interest, a major section of the Report described the alarming practices associated with federally administered Indian education. The Report gave an especially scathing condemnation of the federal boarding schools and called for their termination.

Reorganization and Revitalization (1934–1946)
Yet another redirection of federal Indian policy came with the election of Franklin D. Roosevelt in 1932 and, in the following years, the ushering in of new administrators. The leadership of John Collier, controversial Commissioner of the Bureau of Indian Affairs, brought a dramatic turnabout in all phases of Indian affairs. Collier ended the official policy of forced assimilation, to be replaced with approaches that encouraged tribes to develop their own governments. The New Deal strategy sought to free Native peoples to again take responsibility for the revitalization of their cultures. Nowhere was this altered direction more apparent than in the federal government's new educational policy for American Indians. Many boarding schools were closed or changed radically, and community day schools were built. Collier's policies can be given much credit for laying the groundwork for the rekindled spirit which today pervades American Indian homelands (Bill, 1990).

Termination (1946–1961)
During the years following World War II, the federal government again shifted its policies for its American Indian citizens. Policymakers in the Eisenhower Administration (1953–1961), in particular, launched a major effort to reduce or eliminate the sovereign status of many American Indian nations. These policies succeeded, at least in part. The rationale given was that all citizens of the United States are created equal and all have the same opportunities. This principle, the conventional wisdom asserted, should include American Indians. The policymakers were supported by polls which showed that many voters believed Native peoples were coddled and that they received special treatment from the federal government. Underlying this rhetoric, deeper and less honorable reasons drove the termination policies of the era:

1. Congress wanted to get out of its treaty and legal obligations to the various Indian nations.

2. State governments deeply resented the semi-sovereign status which protected tribes within their boundaries.

3. Non-Indian neighbors wanted access to the remaining resources held by American Indians on their reservations (homelands) (Bill, 1990).

Yet, perhaps even more significant than the federal government's return to policies of retrenchment, the era produced new and positive results for American Indian nations. Native peoples organized to fight the termination legislation introduced by their enemies in Congress and the Eisenhower Administration. In a different realm, American Indian veterans of World War II (1941–1945) and the Korean War (1950–1953) benefitted from the Veterans' Readjustment Act of 1944, popularly known as the G. I. Bill, which encouraged and permitted several thousand American Indians to pursue higher education.

Beginning Self-Determination and Renaissance (1962-Present)

During the 1960s, many citizens awakened to the fact that the United States had to provide greater real opportunity to all of its citizens. American Indians were a part of the effort to realize that idea as they struggled to regain control of every aspect of their lives. No sphere of life was more important to them than education. Native peoples fully recognized that controlling the education of their youths would be their first major step back from the abyss toward which they had been pushed culturally, religiously, linguistically, and physically. During the 1970s and 1980s, Congress enacted major pieces of legislation which assisted American Indians in their attempts to regain control of the relevant educational systems.

Despite some successes, by the 1970s it became clear that overcoming educational problems would not be as easy for American Indian children as for their non-Indian friends. Formal educational achievement for American Indian children continues to lag behind that of non-Indian youths in too many areas. One important reason for these disappointing results stems from a fundamental fact of American Indian life—there is no single "Indian" culture. Rather, many different cultures—each as vibrant and authentic as the rest—exist side-by-side, yet in various phases of assimilation and acculturation. Each nation must find its own way to educate its people of all ages (Eiselein, 1993). For approximately thirty American Indian and Canadian First Nations communities, a most special and innovative answer has been found—the tribally controlled college.

Tribally Controlled Colleges—A Brief History

Tribally controlled colleges have been described as the homes of the "modern-day warriors" so needed by their respective tribes. Furthermore, many American Indian people see tribally controlled colleges as the embodiment of American Indian self-determination and the best long-term means of regaining control of their lives (Philion, 1995).

World War II had a major impact upon American Indian peoples. For the first time since the 1880s, large numbers of young men were exposed to a world away from their villages or communities. The scope of the conflict extended to include many Indian families on the homefront, which also left the reservations to work in the wartime economy. When these people returned to their reservations after the war, they had greater expectations from American society, were less inclined to endure overt or covert racism, wanted greater freedom from the authoritarian interference of the Bureau of Indian Affairs in their daily lives, and sought educational opportunities for themselves and their children.

Indian people returning to the reservations targeted education as the area of their lives most important and most amenable to change. Change began slowly with a number of veterans taking advantage of the G. I. Bill to pursue higher and vocational education. Young Indian leaders, newly elected to tribal councils, fought off the termination policies of the 1950s and demanded day schools for their children. The civil rights movement during the 1950s and 1960s, led by African Americans, spawned numerous social programs from which Indians also were able to benefit. National political leadership from Presidents Kennedy, Johnson, and Nixon set the tone and developed further educational opportunities through new laws which allowed Indians to gain a measure of self-determination over their daily lives.

While the movement toward Indian self-determination was taking place across the United States during the 1960s, events were moving even more quickly on the Navajo reservation. The Navajo people have the largest reservation in terms of land mass and population, giving them political power which other large tribes (e.g., Sioux, Chippewa) could not muster. Other tribes are separated on smaller isolated reservations great distances from each other, and all functions are under separate tribal governments. The Navajo also had special units in the Pacific conflicts during World War II known as "code talkers" (see, e.g., McLain, 1994). This service gave them an honored place in the non-Indian world on which to further build pride, leadership, and tribal government. These conditions led several young Navajo leaders in 1963 to ask, "Why don't we control our own educational system?"

Raymond Nakai, Navajo tribal chairman, was a leader in the drive to increase Native educational opportunities. During his 1961 election campaign, Nakai had promised to work toward Navajo control of education. When elected, he gave the go-ahead to several Navajo leaders who set out to fulfill those promises. In 1963, Allen Yazzie, Chair of the Education Committee of the Navajo Tribal Council, Guy Gorman, committee member, and other Navajo leaders started the long process of applying for federal grant funds to take over the Bureau of Indian Affairs (BIA) school in Lukachukai, Arizona.

The effort failed. Yet, the energy released in organizing this campaign only served to make Navajo leaders more determined to develop a school for Navajo children run by Navajos. The next opportunity came at Rough Rock, Arizona, when Allen Yazzie, Guy Gorman, and Dr. Ned Hatathli incorporated the Rough Rock Demonstration School. They had strong support in this effort from the Tribal Council and two unlikely allies— Graham Holms, BIA Navajo Area Director, and Buck Benham, Assistant Area Director for Education. The support of these two BIA officials was unusual during this period, as BIA endorsement for Indian self-determination was at best perceived as marginal. The unqualified support of BIA officials in this case made a great difference in the success of the Navajo venture (G. Gorman, personal communication, November 20, 1986).

A different Navajo educational strategy was developed through the efforts of an organization known as The Dine, Inc. This group established the Rough Rock Demonstration School, inviting Dr. Robert Roessel, whose strong ties to "the people" came through his Navajo wife, Ruth, to the reservation as school director. The two major goals of the school were: first, to provide a quality education to the children, and second, to prove that Navajos could run their own schools. During the mid-1960s, this effort was a success, and the group turned the school over to the local community for governance in 1967. Concurrently, Allen Yazzie, Guy Gorman, and Ned Hatathli, joined by the Roessels, began exploring the possibility of a community college for the Navajo people. Although the idea of a Native American college was not a totally new topic of discussion, never before had it been approached with such seriousness. A new era was about to begin in Indian education (G. Gorman, personal communication, November 20, 1986).

The 1960s were an era of exciting expansion in higher education, with community colleges playing a major role. Toward the end of the decade, a new community college opened its doors each week somewhere in the United States. In 1968, there were 739 public community colleges; by 1978, there were 1,047 such institutions, an increase of about 42%. It was within this historical tradition that tribally controlled colleges made their appearance in American higher education (Ramirez-Shkweqnaabi, 1987).

Despite the clear boundary separating non-Indian community colleges from tribally controlled colleges, their functions are much more similar than different. Both strive to serve their communities as comprehensive institutions providing programs which respond to community and student needs. Their differences lie in funding sources, jurisdiction, and cultural factors, not educational goals. The founders of the tribally controlled colleges deliberately chose the community college model of higher education as most appropriate to meet the needs of local Native American communities.

Where tribally controlled colleges have flourished, they have found state governments either supportive or, at least, passively benign. Arizona, California, Washington, Alaska, Montana, North Dakota, Wisconsin, Nebraska, and South Dakota all have deliberately stated policies which allow cooperation between their institutions and tribal colleges, but take no fiscal or policy responsibility. They have left it to the tribes and federal government to assume these important duties. In states such as Montana, which had an established community college system in place, there grew up a second system controlled by tribes. In states such as South Dakota, where no public community colleges existed previously, a system was instituted under tribal control.

After much hard work by the founders of Dine, Inc., the Navajo nation founded and chartered Navajo Community College in July of 1968. Though under-funded and breaking a completely new path in higher education, Navajo Community College survived and succeeded, encouraging a number of other tribes to found and charter their own colleges during the 1970s, 1980s, and 1990s. Today, the tribal colleges and their non-Indian counterparts remain separate in the political, educational, and fiscal arenas; yet, they are allied in spirit. An atmosphere of mutual trust and appreciation binds the two systems together in common purpose (Stein, 1992).

Currently, thirty tribally controlled colleges are scattered from the state of Washington to Michigan and from Saskatchewan to Arizona. These institutions serve a wide variety of tribes; yet, all adhere to a set of basic principles defined in their mission statements. Each has stated that the will to preserve, enhance, and promote the language and culture of its tribe is central to its existence. The colleges serve their communities as resources to do research on economic development, human resource development, and community organization. Each provides quality academic programs for students seeking two-year degrees for transfer to senior institutions. Wherever possible, each provides the vocational and technical programs which help assure that students can find decent jobs in their communities upon completion of their studies (The Carnegie Foundation for the Advancement of Teaching, 1989).

The American Indian Higher Education Consortium (AIHEC)

By 1972, founders of the fledgling tribal community college movement had begun to appreciate the need for a more united approach to common issues. These leaders recognized that such unity would enable them to more effectively promote higher education in the handful of tribal colleges as a viable option for Indian people seeking greater economic opportunity and political power. They saw, too, that unity among the tribal colleges would help them to stifle critics who would use tribal differences to create havoc within this unique movement. To this end, proactive leaders—Gerald One Feather of the Oglala Sioux Community College, David Risling of D-Q University, Pat Locke of the Western Interstate Commission for Higher Education (WICHE), and Helen Schierbeck of the U.S. Office of Education (USOE) among them—organized a meeting for those interested in creating a national organization (D. Risling, personal communication, November 20, 1986). Thus, the American Indian Higher Education Consortium was born of political necessity.

The October 1972 meeting produced agreement on several principles by which to form a national organization (D. Risling, personal communication, November 20, 1986; One Feather, 1974). Significantly, leaders of the colleges found they shared many traits, a discovery which further bonded them:

1. They were located on or near Indian reservations which were isolated geographically and culturally.

2. The institutions had Indian boards of regents or directors with a majority of Indian administrators and faculty.

3. Indian student bodies were small, serving a student population ranging from 75 to 800.

4. They suffered from chronic under-financing and funding unpredictability, affecting the stability of their programs.

5. Student bodies and the Indian communities surrounding the institutions were demonstrably from the lowest income areas in the United States (One Feather, 1974, p. 72).

Two other important decisions were addressed: First, the colleges formalized their organization, calling it the American Indian Higher Education Consortium (AIHEC), and second, with the encouragement of Helen Schierbeck, the newly founded organization would pursue Title III funds from the U.S. Office of Education to finance its operation. The decision to pursue federal funds meant that some colleges—those which are under federal supervision—would have to be excluded from membership in AIHEC. This understanding came about shortly after the meeting, when it was discovered that federal regulations prevent one federal program from financially benefitting another. Thus, schools such as Haskell, Southwestern Indian Polytechnic, and the Institute of American Indian Art, which were federally funded post-secondary Indian institutions, could not participate in AIHEC.

It is interesting to note that some members within the newly formed consortium did not view the exclusion of the federal institutions as a great loss. They believed that having BIA institutions in AIHEC would only give the BIA the opportunity to meddle in the tribally controlled colleges' business. Whether this was an accurate assumption cannot now be ascertained, but it can be noted that the bureaucracy within the BIA had not proven supportive of the tribally controlled college movement prior to the October 1972 meeting.

AIHEC's early founders realized the scope and difficulty of the task they were assuming. The creation of tribally controlled colleges on the depressed Indian reservations of the West was a daunting challenge. They intrinsically understood that a major spiritual uplift would be needed to see them through the many hard times ahead. The AIHEC board, therefore, consciously chose to honor traditional Indian ways by having prayers offered on AIHEC's behalf by Sinte Gleśka College board chairman and Lakota medicine man Stanley Red Bird (E. Wilke & P. Gailfus, personal communication, March 2, 1987).

In June 1973, AIHEC was formally organized when it received its incorporation certification from the state of Colorado; Denver was chosen as corporate headquarters for the non-profit organization. Once the Board of Directors received notice of federal funding through the Title III program, attorney Steve Little and Acting Executive Director Gerald Brown developed a set of articles and bylaws for the Board's approval (AIHEC, 1973). To implement its guiding principles, the Board chose to establish:

1. An American Indian Higher Education Accreditation Agency.

2. A Financial and Institutional Resource Office.

3. A Human Resource Development Program.

4. An American Indian Education Data Bank.

5. An American Indian Curriculum Development Program (One Feather, 1974, p. 73).

Did the national organization make any difference for tribal community colleges? Indeed. In particular, the AIHEC central staff provided valuable information on an as-needed basis—a resource the tribally controlled colleges had lacked—on a variety of issues, ranging from curriculum development to human resource development, administration, board training, fund-raising, and regional accreditation preparation. The benefits brought by AIHEC could be seen even more clearly as the organization expanded from six members to 16 by 1978. Many of the newer members of AIHEC had little or no funding, administration, or development experience, and little concept of what was needed to survive as a community college. So important was the support of AIHEC that consultant Jack Barden of Standing Rock Community College could state that, without AIHEC, several of the colleges he worked with would have failed (J. Barden, personal communication, February 28, 1987). Similarly, Carty Monette of Turtle Mountain Community College claimed that AIHEC was the glue that held the tribal college movement together from 1973 to 1978 (C. Monette, personal communication, November 21, 1986). Thus, AIHEC earned a reputation among the colleges as a first-class technical assistance agency, as it also gained a national reputation in Washington, DC.

As early as 1973, AIHEC's Board of Directors saw that they had to confront the single most difficult problem facing the tribal colleges—the chronic shortage of financial resources. Although tribal colleges pursued funding from every possible source, they often were denied support for reasons beyond their control. This constant shortage of funding retarded the natural growth and development the tribal colleges should have experienced in the early 1970s. The lack of funds led the board to choose as its number one task the securing of a solid, stable funding source for its membership. This decision set the course which would dominate AIHEC strategy for the next decade, often overriding other priorities set by the Board (AIHEC, 1973; L. Bordeaux, personal communication, February 26, 1987).

The culmination of AIHEC's success came with the Tribally Controlled Community College Assistance Act. In October 1973, the organization hired a staff and instructed them to work on legislation to bring fiscal stability to the tribal colleges. The process of developing the necessary legislation built AIHEC's legislative skills to a highly professional level. In addition, its dogged persistence, enduring long years of overcoming roadblocks, made the group highly respected in the difficult political atmosphere of Washington. Success came almost five years to the day when AIHEC began its campaign. On October 17, 1978, President Carter signed into law the Tribally Controlled Community College Assistance Act. This important legislation had two parts: Title I funded all the tribal colleges except Navajo Community College; Title II specifically funded Navajo Community College.

The American Indian Higher Education Consortium continues in the 1990s to do the important tasks in Washington which insure the survival of the tribal college movement. AIHEC also has recently undertaken a number of programs, such as the Tribal College Scholarship Fund and the Tribal College Institute, which had been envisioned by AIHEC founders, but postponed due to a lack of resources.

Without AIHEC, it is possible there would be no legislation, many fewer Indian post-secondary institutions, and poorer prospects of continued success for even the stronger tribal colleges. It is an organization that has met the challenges set before it, not always with total success; but, it has won the battles necessary to help secure the future of the tribally controlled colleges (Stein, 1992).

A Profile of the Tribally Controlled Colleges Today

Of all the factors that shape the tribal colleges—motivating the faculty, governing boards, administrators, and staff—the single most important element is the students. Tribal colleges are dedicated to the success of their students. Programs designed especially to serve students' needs, as well as the countless individual acts of caring by tribal college administrators, faculty, and staff, amply demonstrate this dedication.

American Indian students attend tribal colleges for many of the same reasons non-Indians enroll in higher education. They desire to better themselves intellectually, hope to improve their chances of securing good and rewarding employment, seek the skills to manage their own futures, and want opportunities to provide better lives for their families. What makes them different from non-Indian college students is their physical and spiritual situation. Many are older (30+ years); the majority are female single heads of households; and many have failed at non-Indian higher education institutions, have extended family obligations, and find college an unusually heavy burden. Virtually all are the first in their families to attend college (Boyer, 1990).

American Indian students attending a tribal college present their instructors and counselors with many challenging cultural, linguistic, and personal situations. Tribes in the western United States have existed for the past century in abject poverty; this is reflected by tribal members who attend tribal colleges. They bring with them a value system which is a hybrid of Native culture, mainstream culture, and welfare culture. Instructors and students often have to sort through this maze of cultural mixing to work out for the student a productive and healthy plan to get through the program of the college.

Tribal colleges also are in a position to carry forward unique programs for enhancing the chances that American Indian students will stay in school. Each tribal college has articulated clearly in its mission statement that it will work to help preserve, promote, and teach its tribe's culture and language. This important goal brings to students opportunities to learn more about their respective tribe's history and culture, which, in turn, helps them to build a sense of identity and pride in themselves—elements which are crucial to American Indian students as they struggle to overcome poverty, lack of self-esteem, and poor education in their quest for a higher education. The college, in turn, has to examine itself constantly to insure that its programs truly will assist students through the college experience (Stein, 1992).

This concern for the individual student has played an important role in the high retention rates within the tribal colleges. Retention for the tribal colleges can be measured in two ways: first, the conventional fashion, which counts as a dropout any student who leaves college before completion of a degree program—in which case tribal colleges have a retention rate of approximately 45 percent; or second, a more accurate method begun by the tribal colleges, which labels as "stop-outs" those who leave and then return within a quarter to continue their studies. By measuring in this fashion, the colleges' retention rate is approximately 75 to 80 percent. Students who "stop-out" generally do so because of financial difficulties or because they have been placed on academic probation (Three Irons, personal communication, December 3, 1991).

Further results of tribal colleges' special interest in the individual student can be found in testimony by AIHEC staff before appropriations committees of the U.S. Congress in 1983. AIHEC research studies found that Indian students who completed a course of study at a tribal college went on to complete a four-year degree program at a senior institution with a 75 percent greater success rate than Indian students who bypassed tribal colleges and went directly to four-year institutions. AIHEC research surveys also found that about 85 percent of tribal college graduates who stayed on the reservation were employed. The results are especially remarkable when we remember that many reservations experience unemployment rates from 45 to 80 percent (Stein, 1992).

Tribal colleges are successful at the approximately thirty sites where they have flourished and grown. This success has varied from college to college, and not every tribal college has survived. Several failed and had to close their doors, which is not uncommon among higher education institutions in the United States. Where tribal colleges have succeeded, American Indian students are making strides academically and are having a positive impact on their communities.

Although the tribal college movement has slowed in its overall growth and expansion across the reservations of the United States, it continues to make progress in numbers of colleges founded and quality of educational programs. This progress is most recently demonstrated in the successful effort to gain land-grant status for the tribally controlled colleges. President Clinton signed into law the Equity in Educational Land Grant Status Act of 1994, which was the culmination of three years of hard work by AIHEC, the tribal colleges, and their friends in higher education. The tribal college remains one of the most effective institutions for starting American Indian students on the successful pursuit of higher education (Stein, 1992).

Conclusion

There is little doubt that American Indian people have had a difficult journey along the educational trail since contact with the non-Indian world. The hardships suffered by generations of American Indian youths and their negative manifestations in tribal communities condemn in large part the use of Western education among American Indians. True, there are success stories of individual Indians becoming quite successful by Western standards after a mainstream education. However, these successes are far outnumbered by those Indian people who have been permanently damaged by that same educational system.

Today, the positive changes in how Western education is imposed upon American Indians can be attributed to the ever-increasing control American Indians are taking of those same educational systems in their communities. American Indians understand that today's world demands that they be able to function comfortably within their own cultures, as well as in relation to mainstream American culture. They recognize clearly that a good education, which takes their needs as a people into consideration, can be a wonderful tool with which to live life, as it also can be a terrible burden if imposed from outside with no regard to who they are as a unique people. In the words of Plenty Coups, a great Crow chief at the turn of the twentieth century, "With education, [we] are the white man's equal. Without education, [we] are his victim."

Wayne J. Stein

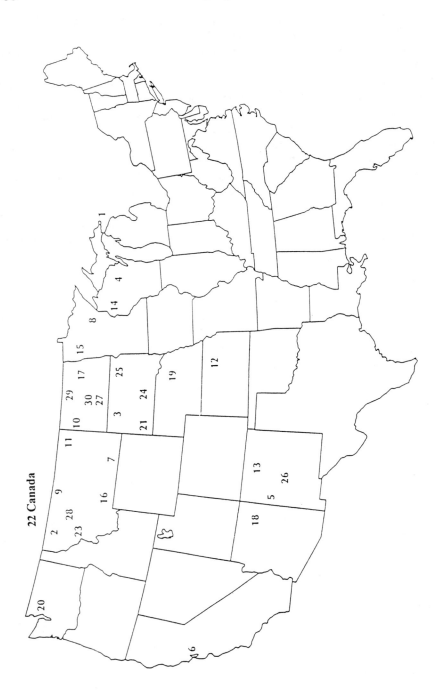

Figure 1. Map of Tribally Controlled Community Colleges in the United States. See membership listing for names and addresses of member colleges.

AIHEC Membership — 1995

1. Bay Mills Community College
Martha McCleod, President
Rt. 1, Box 315 A
Brimley, Michigan 49715
906-248-3354
FAX 906-248-3351

2. Blackfeet Community College
Carol Murray, President
P.O. Box 819
Browning, Montana 59417
406-338-7755
FAX 406-338-7808

3. Cheyenne River Community
College
Dawn Muir, President
Eagle Butte, South Dakota 57625
605-964-8635
FAX 605-964-1144

4. College of the Menominee
Nation
Dr. Verna Fowler, President
P.O. Box 1179
Keshena, Wisconsin 54135
715-799-4921
FAX 715-799-1308

5. Crownpoint Institute of
Technology
James Tutt, President
P.O. Box 849
Crownpoint, New Mexico 87313
505-786-5851
FAX 505-786-5644
EMAIL: jmtutt@aol.com

6. D-Q University
Dr. Francis D. Becenti, President
P.O. Box 409
Davis, California 95617
916-758-0470
FAX 916-758-4891

7. Dull Knife Memorial College
Dr. Alonzo Spang, President
P.O. Box 98
Lame Deer, Montana 59043
406-477-6215
FAX 406-477-6219
EMAIL:
uanet142@quest.osco.montana.edu

8. Fond du Lac Tribal and
Community College
Lester Jack Briggs, President
2101 14th Street
Cloquet, Minnesota 55720-2964
218-879-0800
FAX 218-879-0814
EMAIL:
ljbriggs@qasab.fdl.cc.mn.us

9. Fort Belknap Community College
Margarett Perez, President
P.O. Box 159
Harlem, Montana 59526
406-353-2607
FAX 406-353-2898

10. Fort Berthold Community
College
Karen J. Gillis, President
P.O. Box 490
New Town, North Dakota 58763
701-627-3665
FAX 701-627-3609

11. Fort Peck Community College
Dr. James Shanley, President
P.O. Box 575
Poplar, Montana 59255
406-768-5551
FAX 406-768-5552

12. Haskell Indian Nations University
Dr. Bob Martin, President
P.O. Box H-1305
Lawrence, Kansas 66046
913-749-8497
FAX 913-749-8411

13. Institute of American
Indian Arts
Dr. Perry G. Horse, President
Box 20007, St. Michael's Drive
Santa Fe, New Mexico 87504
505-988-6440
FAX 505-986-5543

14. Lac Courte Oreilles Ojibwa
Community College
Dr. Jasjit Minhas, President
R.R. 2, Box 2357
Hayward, Wisconsin 54843
715-634-4790
FAX 715-634-5049
EMAIL: lcooccl@aol.com

15. Leech Lake Tribal College
Larry Aitken, President
Rt. 3, Box 100
Cass Lake, Minnesota 56633
218-335-2828
FAX 218-335-7845

16. Little Big Horn College
Dr. Janine Pease-Pretty On Top,
President
P.O. Box 370
Crow Agency, Montana 59022
406-638-2228
FAX 406-638-7213

17. Little Hoop Community College
Dr. Merril Berg, President
P.O. Box 209
Fort Totten, North Dakota 58335
701-766-4415
FAX 701-766-4077

18. Navajo Community College
Dr. Tommy Lewis, President
P.O. Box 126
Tsaile, Arizona 86556
520-724-3311
FAX 520-724-3327

19. Nebraska Indian Community
College
Yvonne Bushyhead, J.D.
P.O. Box 752
Winnebago, Nebraska 86071
402-878-2414
FAX 402-878-2522

20. Northwest Indian College
Dr. Robert Lorence, President
2522 Iwina Road
Bellingham, Washington 98226
360-676-2772
FAX 360-738-0136
EMAIL: boblorn@aol.com

21. Oglala Lakota College
Thomas Shortbull, President
P.O. Box 490
Kyle, South Dakota 57752
605-455-2321
FAX 605-455-2787

22. Red Crow Community College
Marie Smallface Marule,
President
P.O. Box 1258
Cardston, Alberta, Canada T1K 4E2
403-737-2400
FAX 403-737-2361

23. Salish Kootenai College
Dr. Joseph McDonald, President
P.O. Box 117
Pablo, Montana 59855
406-675-4800
FAX 406-675-4801
EMAIL:
skcgw!joemcdonald@uugw.wmt.edu

24. Sinte Gleska University
Dr. Lionel Bordeaux, President
P.O. Box 490
Rosebud, South Dakota 57570
605-747-2263
FAX 605-747-2098

25. Sisseton Wahpeton
    Community College
Chris Cavendar, President
P.O. Box 689
Sisseton, South Dakota 57262
605-698-3132
EMAIL: cavendar@daknet.com

26. Southwest Indian Polytechnic
    Institute
Dr. Carolyn Elgin, President
Box 10146-9169
Coors Road NW
Albuquerque, New Mexico 87184
505-897-5347
FAX 505-897-5343
EMAIL: celgin@enan.unm.edu
celgin@kafka.sipi.tec.nm.us

27. Standing Rock College
David Archambault, President
HC 1, Box 4
Fort Yates, North Dakota 58538
701-854-3861
701-854-3861
FAX 701-854-3403
EMAIL:davida2058.@aol.com

28. Stone Child College
Luanne Belcourt, President
Rocky Boy Rt. Box 1082
Box Elder, Montana 59521
406-395-4313
FAX 406-395-4836

29. Turtle Mountain Community
    College
Gerald Carty Monette, President
P.O. Box 340
Belcourt, North Dakota 58316
701-477-5605
FAX 701-477-5028
EMAIL: cartym@aol.com

30. United Tribes Technical College
David Gipp, President
3315 University Drive
Bismarck, North Dakota 58504
701-255-3285
FAX 701-255-1844
EMAIL: dgipp@aol.com

Figure 2. List of Tribally Controlled Community Colleges. Numbers refer to map location.

References

American Indian Higher Education Consortium. (1973). *Board of Directors meeting minutes*. Denver, CO: Author.

Bill, W. (1990, January). *From boarding house to self-determination*. Olympia, WA: Office of Public Instruction.

Boyer, P. (1990, May). *Tribal colleges: Creating a new partnership in higher education*. Opening of the Montana Pipeline Conference, Bozeman, MT.

The Carnegie Foundation for the Advancement of Teaching. (1989). *Tribal Colleges*. Princeton, NJ: Princeton University Press.

Eiselein, E. B. (1993). *Indian issues: Blackfoot Nation*. Browning, MT: Spirit Talk Press.

Equity in Educational Land Grant Status Act of 1994. Pub. L. 103–382, 108 Stat. 4048 et seq.

McLain, S. (1994). *Navajo weapon*. Boulder, CO: Books Beyond Borders.

Meriam, L. (Ed.). (1928). *The problems of Indian administration*. Baltimore: Johns Hopkins University Press.

One Feather, G. (1974). American Indian Community Colleges. In V. Deloria (Ed.), *Indian education confronts the seventies: Vol. 5. Future concerns* (pp. 36–77). Oglala, SD: American Indian Resource Associates.

Philion, M. (1995, Summer). *The tribal college movement: Modern-day warriors*. Bozeman, MT: Montana State University.

Ramirez-Shkweqnaabi, B. (1987). *Roles of tribally controlled community college trustees: A comparison of trustees' and presidents' perceptions of trustees' roles*. Unpublished doctoral dissertation, University of Wisconsin, Madison.

Stein, W. J. (1992). *Tribally controlled colleges: Making good medicine: Vol. 3. American Indian Studies Series*. New York: Peter Lang.

Tribally Controlled Community College Assistance Act of 1978. Pub. L. 95–471, 92 Stat. 1325.

Veterans Readjustment Act of 1944, c. 268, 58 Stat. 284.

Wright, I. (1989). For the children of the infidels? American Indian education in colonial colleges. In L. F. Goodchild & H. S. Wechsler (Eds.), *The history of higher education* (pp. 53–59). *ASHE Reader Series*. Needham Heights, MA: Ginn Press.

5

The Case for Native American Studies

Jon Reyhner

The need for Native American Studies Programs in our public schools and colleges was brought home to me powerfully on a recent visit to a reservation school. Earlier that morning, the son of one of the Indian teachers had been thrown fifty feet through the windshield of his car after what was described to me as a "night of drinking."

One of his junior high school teachers told me about the boy's potential, as well as his problems. He had just graduated from the local high school the previous spring. Although the boy had gone to a large state university about one hundred miles away, where my daughter had met him at the Indian Center, he did not even finish out his first semester. Now, he was lying in a hospital, where the doctor noted how lucky the boy was to have not suffered any broken bones, although his face was cut up, and he had a major loss of memory, hopefully temporary. I was struck both by the senselessness of the boy's plight and by the tragic connections that link education, sense of identity, and dysfunctional behavior in young people such as he. I was reminded, as well, of how my own work as a professor of Native American Studies has been spent trying to understand and solve the problems of such students. Although this boy may well return to college and be successful sometime in the future, more needs to be done to keep such students in college and to prevent the type of dysfunctional behavior that led to his accident.

There always will be college dropouts. Even if we could fully prepare people for what they are getting into when they go off to college, it is only human to change one's mind periodically about what one wants to do with one's life. However, while dropping out cannot be eliminated, much can be done to reduce the chances that students will be pushed out because of their lack of academic preparation, their uninformed expectations of college life, and the unfriendly/impersonal environments of many universities. These are conditions that face all students at some time in their undergraduate careers. Yet, it is the case that especially for minorities—and perhaps, most especially for Native American students—what we might call "college culture" is distinctly alien and unfriendly. For these people, the message can be subtle, but clear: you are not welcome.

American Indian Dropout Rates in High Schools and Colleges

This essay can only begin to document the degree to which American Indians are ignored, overlooked, or actively face racism in America in general and at universities and in university curricula, in particular. It does, however, document how American Indian students are neglected and shunted aside in both K–12 schools and in higher education. Studies of the problem tell us that a lower than average percentage of American Indians enter colleges and universities and a lower than average percentage of those who do enter graduate (Scott, 1986). Research by Richardson and Pavel (1992), McEvans and Astin (1992), and Pavel and Padilla (1992) documents the fact that American Indian students are earning bachelor's degrees at less than half the rate of whites and Asians. Not only are American Indian students more at risk of dropping out when they get to college, but also, in fact, fewer get through high school even to be eligible to enter a university. When I compiled research on American Indian dropouts for the U.S. Secretary of Education's Indian Nations at Risk Task Force, I found that about one-third of Native students never finish high school, the highest dropout rate of any minority group (Reyhner, 1992). Furthermore, I discovered, a significant reason for this high dropout rate is the failure of schools and universities to reflect in their instructional approach and curricula any attention to American Indian history, culture, and current events. Indian students often report never having had a Native American teacher and/or being taught in school anything about Native American history, literature, or art.

Some Explanations of Student Failure

Several interesting American Indian dropout studies give us some insight into the sources of the problem. A 1986 study commissioned by the Navajo Tribe found that boredom was the top reason dropouts gave for leaving school (Brandt, 1992). This research reminds me of an old joke about why companies prefer to employ college graduates. The reason is that no matter how boring the job, they know that graduates can put up with it because they lasted through four dull years of college. Other studies also show that many dropouts, Indian and non-Indian alike, perceive their teachers as indifferent or uncaring (Reyhner, 1992; Brandt, 1992; Deyhle, 1992).

What accounts for this perception? High school teachers and university professors are trained to see themselves as teachers of subjects such as mathematics and history rather than as teachers of students. Relatively few high school teachers, and still fewer college professors, are taught methods of relating to their students—either as individuals or as members of cultural groups. This perceived lack of caring for students is often made worse by the large number of students, often several hundred, with whom teachers and professors must deal on a day-to-day basis. Even those who do care about their students have little time or energy left over to give them any personal attention. For Native American students, the feeling that they are deliberately ignored is acute. Deyhle heard the sense of rejection in one interview with an Indian high school student; as the student observed,

> It was just like they [teachers] want to put us aside, us Indians. They didn't tell us nothing about careers or things to do after high school. They didn't encourage us to go to college. They just took care of the white students. They just wanted to get rid of the Indians. (1992, pp. 24–25)

Typical high school and college texts set up another obstacle to students' success. Indians often find mainstream textbooks irrelevant to their lives or, to make matters worse, offensive. Too often, they present history as a process of civilizing a savage frontier. Messages such as these subtly reinforce the false stereotypes about Indians that prevail on and off campuses, such as the notions that all Indians get money from the government and that it is easy for any Indian to get money to go to college.

Through her interviews of dropouts and observations of classrooms, Donna Deyhle (1992) uncovered another barrier that Native students face. Too few Indian students show the fundamental academic language skills, specifically reading, that they need to do the work necessary to prepare for classroom discussion—reading the textbook and answering the discussion questions that come at the end of a chapter. This common type of class work bores television-addicted and mall-oriented mainstream students even when they have developed the academic language skills to perform it; it becomes even less interesting for students who must sit quietly at their desks doing nothing because they cannot read well enough to understand an assignment.

At this point—especially if the person reading this is not Native American —you might be asking if the phenomenon I am describing is an "Indian problem" or a "school problem." As an education scholar, I am trained to look for evidence in order to answer such questions. In fact, the evidence can be found in the experience of very successful American Indian graduates from small rural high schools. It is often the case that even these straight "A" students are shocked and offended when they enter a university and are instantly put in non-credit remedial courses. Suddenly, people who had been the proverbial big fish in a small pond, and who consequently felt high self-esteem, feel their self-esteem plummet and become dysfunctional when they find they are now small fish in a very big pond. This placement even can lead to their dropping out. Such was the case of the young accident victim I described when I began this essay.

However, students can react differently to their placement into remedial courses if they have social as well as academic support. With support, they may realize that they are not alone, and they may view their lack of preparation as a reflection on their previous schooling, not just on themselves. I can illustrate this point through a personal story. In 1962, I entered the engineering program at the University of California at Davis. At that time, engineering students who failed the "Subject A" exam would be placed in the non-credit course that we called—before the days of political correctness —"bonehead English." Curiously, it seemed to me that my fellow engineering students considered it almost a badge of honor to fail the "Subject A" exam. They were scientists, not men of letters. In fact, my passing the exam was one of my first indications that I was not meant to be an engineer—in effect, I did not belong.

So, from academic evidence and personal anecdote, we can see that the phenomenon of dropping out is not an "Indian problem" or even a "student problem." It does not apply just to American Indians from small rural high schools who are often inadequately prepared for university courses. Any student can face this problem—however, it is especially so for high school graduates from rural and inner-city areas. School achievement is highly correlated to family income. Thus, education scholars have found a consistent relationship between weak educational achievement and high rates of poverty. This poverty is not just a student or family problem: Jonathan Kozol (1991), a well-known education researcher, has documented how much better funded suburban schools are than many inner-city and rural schools. Better funded schools provide better teachers, better equipped classrooms, and a more challenging curriculum. What is significant for American Indians and for researchers who study American Indian education is the fact that reservation poverty has been documented time and again. Shannon County, South Dakota, home of the Pine Ridge Reservation and the 1890 Wounded Knee Massacre, as one example, has repeatedly held the dubious honor as the poorest county in the nation.

In fact, it is not just the schools, but the whole of American society that is weighted against the poor. The extremes of wealth and poverty in this country are unique. Industrialized countries in both Europe and Asia do not have the large numbers of homeless people we tolerate. This inequality is long standing, with beggars being a feature of nineteenth-century cities as the homeless are of twentieth-century metropolises. Some observers, such as Herrnstein and Murray (1994), argue that this is the natural order of things, with each individual getting what he or she deserves based on hereditary talents. However, Berliner and Biddle (1995), in their book, *The Manufactured Crisis: Myths, Fraud and the Attack on America's Public Schools*, do an excellent job of documenting on a large scale what Deyhle (1995) documents on a small scale: Minorities are failing because of racist policies such as school tracking. Both consciously and unconsciously, the economic elite in America works to make sure it is their children who are successful in getting the comparatively scarce higher paying jobs through better schooling.

The lack of concern for our fellow citizens that is found in unrestrained capitalism aggravates this country's high crime rate and the recurring instances of group violence such as racial and ethnic disorders. I have learned a number of things in my twenty-five years of relatively close contact with Native Americans that have led me to the view that our country's focus on individualism and capitalism is socially dysfunctional. I have learned about the importance of family—and not just the nuclear family—but also about the personal obligation to support one's extended family and also members of one's clan that is characteristic of Native American cultures. In addition, I have become convinced of the validity of characteristic Native ideas as the one I learned of recently while talking to a Hopi traditionalist and graduate student, who emphasized to me the Hopi concept that everyone is your brother or sister. The idea that "we are all related" crosses most tribes. In fact, it is closely linked to the equally prevalent belief in generosity which is also characteristic of Native cultures. If mainstream Americans practiced such Native American ideas more universally, I believe, we would create a better world. Instead, mainstream Americans continue to be dismayed about rampant crime, drug use, and other signs of social disintegration, without seeing how all these problems are linked to the extremes of wealth and poverty that we encounter in this country. Indeed, in our society, in which community responsibility is too often sacrificed for individual self-interest, we see even the elderly demand present economic entitlements at the future expense of their grandchildren.

I have learned something else, something more positive, in my work as an educational researcher. We can find solutions for some of these social problems. The studies my colleagues and I have completed demonstrate that we can compensate both for the lack of caring that universities show for Indian students and for the failure of a university's curriculum-at-large to focus on concerns of American Indians. By establishing Native American Studies departments, we can reduce the alienation that Native students experience when they enter colleges and increase their chances for present academic success—and future career and life success.

Obstacles to Native Student Success

Although the available research is somewhat limited, it does document the fact that teachers generally do not encourage Native American students to go to college (Davis, 1992). Any support teachers do offer pushes students toward a vocational curriculum (Deyhle, 1995). In her own study of ten successful Indian college students, Davis described the best behavior of their K-12 teachers as "benign neglect"; the only secondary-school encouragement they received was in extra-curricular activities (1992). The students who did go on to succeed did so in spite of their schools and teachers. Her students were "not from stable, financially comfortable, well-educated families" (p. 28), and successful students "were able to retain their Indian culture, to be Indian, and to be a successful student in the white middle class system" (p. 29).

A study (Dodd, Garcia, Meccage, & Nelson, 1995) of the support that 24 successful Indian college students had received and the barriers they had to overcome found the students tended to be above traditional college student age. Although many had dropped out of school for some time, obviously they were persevering persons. Most of them were married or had been married. Approximately as many spoke and understood their tribal language as did not. The majority of the students were from families in which they were first-generation college graduates. Most had returned to college after dropping out or had started college at an older than average age.

Most of these academically successful Native students identified their families as the factor that had most influenced their achievement. Participants also mentioned teachers, friends, religious faith, tribe, co-workers, and support services. When they were asked to indicate particular obstacles American Indian students face, the answers were again varied. Frequent responses were prejudice, finances, language, and alcohol. All but one of the 24 participants stated that prejudice exists on campus. When the students were queried about whether prejudice impeded success, 20 responded that it did. When the participants were asked with whom they would talk in case of difficulty with their school work, 18 indicated that they would go to support services and only seven indicated faculty. When asked if they had ever sought help from faculty members, eighteen participants said they had gone to a faculty member for academic help, but six indicated they had not received the help they sought. Finally, the students were asked to add any information that would help to identify the factors that support or inhibit academic success. Most listed the Intertribal Indian Club, the availability of tutors, and scholarship money (many mentioned the need for more) as helpful. Significantly, we believe, they also saw a clear need for better faculty understanding of American Indian cultures.

Theoretical Explanations of Minority Student Failure

Many commentators have offered explanations of why minority students in general, and American Indian students in particular, do not do as well in school, on average, as majority group students. Although the efforts to locate the causes of academic difficulty among minority peoples has followed a historical progression, the underlying line of thinking has not moved much beyond the racism that influenced earlier thinking. Most explanations have been of the "blame the victim" sort. These arguments claim to locate the causes of minority school failure in a supposed lack of intelligence among these minorities or in their presumed "dysfunctional" families. Such "explanations" are weak, however; they ignore the effects of white ethnocentrism and related prevalent racism on minority students. White America does not want to face up to the effects of its racism, as indicated by the current affirmative action backlash. But the effects of racism still haunt us today, and the attempt to ignore those effects is just racism in a new guise.

Late nineteenth-century explanations used a Social Darwinist line of thought, putting whites at the top of a mythical pyramid of social evolution. The development of intelligence (IQ) tests reinforced this explanation. Stephen Jay Gould (1981) has shown how Lewis Terman, the developer of the Stanford-Binet Intelligence Test, ignored compelling evidence that environmental factors greatly influenced student performance on his test in favor of a genetic explanation. However, when blacks did less well than whites, the test-makers simply assumed the explanation to be genetics rather than a mistake. Surprisingly, this genetic fallacy has resurfaced recently with the publication of best-selling books such as *The Bell Curve: Intelligence and Class Structure in American Life* (Herrnstein & Murray, 1994). It is clear from academic research, however, that supposed genetic weakness does not exist. Genetics certainly does not explain why Native American students with high Scholastic Aptitude Test (SAT) scores do not complete degree programs at the same rate as other racial and ethnic groups with similar scores (Pavel, 1992).

During the 1960s, the "cultural deficit" view became popular among social commentators. These writers claimed that minority students were culturally deprived and needed "compensatory" education to make up for the deprivation they faced in their homes. Anthropologists either laughed or cried at the simple-mindedness of this explanation, as they were acutely aware of the rich home cultures of different minority groups. During the 1980s, in an article in the *Harvard Educational Review*, Jim Cummins (1986) put forward a "cultural discontinuity theory" that identified the cultural differences between home and school as the root cause of minority school failure. When schools neglected to incorporate minority students' languages and cultures into teaching lessons and when administrators used culturally biased tests to determine what these students lacked, Cummins concluded, minority students were disadvantaged.

James Ogbu (1978) added the idea of resistance to the cultural discontinuity theory. In his research, Ogbu differentiated between "voluntary minorities"—peoples who had chosen to immigrate to this country—and "involuntary minorities"—peoples who had been overwhelmed by military might, such as American Indians and Hispanics in the Southwest, or brought here as slaves, such as African Americans. He observed that voluntary minorities did relatively well in school; peoples who had experienced conquest, however, showed disproportionate school failure. Underlying this difference, Ogbu concluded, was the long-standing heritage of resistance among involuntary minorities.

Resistance for American Indians is not new. Indeed, in 1932 a teacher reported,

> A few years ago, a primary teacher was about to punish a child who had been in school for three weeks without attempting to speak a word of English. But first she decided to find out all that she could about his apparent stubbornness. She sent out for two older cousins who could speak some English. "He say that his father say, 'You go there. Eat their food. Sleep in their beds. But you don't have to learn their talk or their books.'"
> (Lawhead, 1932, p. 132)

Mick Fedullo gives a contemporary account of resistance. He quotes an Apache elder's observation that Native students' parents

> had been to school in their day, and what that usually meant was a bad BIA boarding school. And all they remember about school is that there were all these Anglos [white people] trying to make them forget they were Apaches; trying to make them turn against their parents, telling them that Indian ways were evil.
>
> Well, a lot of those kids came to believe that their teachers were the evil ones, and so anything that had to do with "education" was also evil—like books. Those kids came back to the reservation, got married, and had their own kids. And now they don't want anything to do with the white man's education. The only reason they send their kids to school is because it's the law. But they tell their kids not to take school seriously.
> (Fedullo, 1992, p. 117)

Involuntary minorities resisted school because they were vehicles for the destruction of traditional languages and cultures. As Deyhle documents on the Navajo Reservation, they resisted also because "Navajos accurately perceive that they are shut out of the job market, and that their school success is not linked to their economic prosperity." In the eyes of these students and their parents, affirmative action is another "white lie" (1995, p. 407).

Deyhle, unlike Ogbu and others, does not see Navajo culture as a reaction to the dominant society. Rather she sees

> Navajo values—the communal nature of success and the primacy of the family—exist in well-developed institutional structures on the reservation independent of Anglo culture, and during social and economic crisis, help secure the Navajos' identity as a people.
> (1995, p. 408)

The point she is making is an important one to keep in mind for scholars trying to understand minority academic performance. Although border-town whites believe that non-Christian Indian religions, cultures, and languages hold Indians back, Deyhle (1995) and McLaughlin (1992) have documented Native American Church ceremonies that focus on getting children to work harder in school. In one ceremony described by McLaughlin, a student is advised to study hard, learn to read and write well, and above all, be neat and on time. . . . When you hand in papers, make sure they are clean. Do your homework. Listen to your teachers. Be careful with what you write, and do it neatly. (pp. 100–101)

During the ritual, children were given three hours of "encouragement and advice." Deyhle describes a similar Native American Church "peyote meeting," in which children were encouraged to pursue their education, but also to stay Navajo and to return home. In Montana, a Crow college student spoke to my class about a Sun Dance ceremony in which he had participated. He danced, he told us, for two reasons: to pray for the protection of his son who was fighting in the Desert Storm campaign against Iraq and to pray to find the strength within himself to finish college.

Non-Native Americans who have not bothered to understand the realities of American Indian cultures hold mistaken or exaggerated impressions of Native religions. Such views, too often based on nothing more than film and television distortions such as the Sun Dance scene from the movie *A Man Called Horse* (Howard & Silverstein, 1970), are essentially myths. These impressions distort the basically conservative focus of these religions on health and family. Moreover, just as non-Native Americans overlook the positive values of American Indian religions, so, too, do they either overlook the contributions that American Indians have made to modern society or reduce these contributions to simplicities such as the domestication of corn. Traditional Native American environmental values are overlooked in favor of shortsighted agricultural and mining policies that are destroying our top soil and rapidly depleting irreplaceable resources, leaving little for future generations.

Because of their own distorted views of American Indian community institutions, educators often do not draw on these institutions to support Indian students. For example, several research studies have demonstrated the fact that family support contributes to the success of Indian students, but educators still often see Indian families negatively, as drawing the students "back to the blanket" (Deyhle, 1995). Again, a personal anecdote: my wife was a college "stop-out"; it was members of her Navajo extended family that pushed her to return to college and to complete her degree.

Indian Students' Explanations of Success

There seems to be strong agreement between scholars and students about the sources of academic success. The research literature demonstrates that students succeed when faculty and families are supportive; they stumble when these supports are weak or absent. For instance, Coburn and Nelson (1989) conducted an interesting study of American Indian students in the Northwest who had successfully completed high school. They reported that teachers were the strongest influence in the students' educational experiences. This sample of students appreciated teachers who compliment students for doing well, provide evidence of respect for students, and who are caring persons. Most of the students in another study (Dodd et al., 1995) also indicated that their families were of primary importance in providing support. This finding supports Hall (1991), who wrote that the family is the most important unit in American Indian cultures. Most of these students indicated they would go to special support service programs rather than faculty for help with academic difficulties.

These surveys of American Indian students' perceptions of college life found that finances, family problems, alcohol, and a lack of acceptance by peers and faculty are common obstacles to academic success. Prejudice, also, was mentioned frequently. Successful students, however, indicated they had found ways to cope with it. Most had thought about leaving college and knew other American Indian students who had dropped out. The finding suggests that American Indian high school students should be prepared to encounter these problems when they enter college, and to develop strategies for dealing with them.

Can we draw any general conclusions from these research studies? I believe so. Because few of the reported obstacles to success were strictly academic, we can see that student support services are critical assets that contribute to the academic success of Indian students. Just as Coburn and Nelson (1989) reported that faculty are important in keeping high school students in school, these college seniors reported the importance of caring and concerned faculty to their academic success. Special activities and organizations such as Indian clubs and campus Pow Wows help students maintain their identities while embarking on new studies and careers. A study carried out by Wright (1985) supports this view. Wright reviewed the research literature related to various support services for American Indian college students, including academic support services, counseling support services, ethnic studies courses, student centers, and organizations. He concluded that support services are critical to the success of Native students and recommended that high school counselors evaluate the support service programs and commitment to American Indian students prior to recommending that students attend specific post-secondary education settings.

Of particular importance to the success of Indian college students, I have come to believe, is the establishment and maintenance of Native American Studies programs. Why, out of the possible range of solutions, do I emphasize Native American Studies programs? I have reached this conclusion through my own many years of research into this problem, as well as through my examination of the many other studies carried out by my colleagues in educational research. For instance, in an interesting (although somewhat limited) study of American Indian college student perseverance, Benjamin, Chambers, and Reiterman (1993) reported that American Indian students who persist in college commonly demonstrate an ability to adopt new traits while maintaining a sense of cultural integrity. They suggested that higher education's insistence on an inappropriate conformity to the values and norms of the dominant culture may contribute to the high dropout rate.

Likewise, Lin, LaCounte, and Eder (1988) reported that American Indian students frequently experience strong feelings of isolation based on a perception of hostility from the white campus community. Furthermore, Huffman (1991) found that American Indian college students commonly experience racism on campus—most often in the form of verbal attacks such as racial slurs and name-calling. Very few of us, of whatever culture, race, or ethnic group, are able or willing to accept such demeaning treatment for long. The consequence of this pervasive racism is often an early exit from academic institutions to return to more familiar and supporting settings within the home and family.

Hoover and Jacobs (1992) have studied the effectiveness of specific organizations and support services for American Indian students. They found that many of the colleges and universities that have substantial populations of Indian students provide intertribal clubs as well as academic support programs. Two strategies, they learned, enable the American Indian and Alaska Native students they interviewed to get around the high costs, large impersonal classes, inappropriate curricula, and long distances involved in attending large universities. Some students choose to enter higher education through tribal or community colleges; others choose to find a "university home" in the Native American Studies departments offered by some non-Native universities.

Why Native American Studies if Not White Studies?

Given the point I am arguing in this essay, it is important that we recognize the current conservative assault on multicultural education, minority studies, affirmative action, and bilingual education in this country. The powerful backlash downplays the "supposed" accomplishments of the civil rights movement. Many of these critics question why colleges and universities need Native American Studies departments when we do not have "white studies" departments. Moreover, some faculty members emphasize they should teach the academic disciplines in which they were trained rather than culture, which they believe should be left to the home. On the surface, these arguments make sense. Yet, such thinking contains an underlying fallacy. Cultural values and assumptions and societal norms permeate all facets of life, including university life. Thus, the curricula in American universities generally reflect "White Studies." College history courses, for instance, tend to concentrate on the development of white America and its European roots, not American Indian history; political science on federal, state, and county governments, not tribal governments; English on American and European literature, not tribal literature. Throughout American campuses, American Indian contributions to world civilization tend to be ignored.

This neglect of American Indian contributions in our educational institutions is not accidental. The historical role of mainstream schools in assimilating American Indians into the dominant culture is well documented—along with the catastrophic effects on American Indian societies (Reyhner & Eder, 1989). Government-sponsored studies such as the Meriam Report of 1928, the Kennedy Report of 1969 (U.S. Senate), and the Indian Nations at Risk Task Force Report of 1991 all document the conclusion that the pervading assimilationist effort to transform Indians into white people has been a failure. Assimilation strategies have shifted from the U.S. government's nineteenth-century efforts at direct "ethnic cleansing" through forced removal, as in the Cherokee Trail of Tears, to the twentieth-century strategy of an ethnic cleansing of the mind that included mouths washed out with soap for speaking Native languages. Such actions, while short of genocide, have left tragic consequences for American Indians. These systematic efforts to wipe out Native cultures deserve a response that, in the words of Sonia Nieto (1992), "affirms diversity" through programs such as Native American Studies departments. Indeed, as we have seen, a beneficial function of such programs would be to help both Native and white students unlearn the false, destructive myths that concerted efforts have sought to impose on our understanding of Native American life.

Native American Studies:
A Cultural Alternative to the Progressive Ideal

I have talked to Native people who can remember their reservation school bearing a sign at its entrance that read, "Tradition is the Enemy of Progress." Few American Indians I have met, however, believe this. Even the most traditionalist Native people, working to relearn their languages and cultures and pass them on to their children, also want their children to get the best education possible. In the same vein, the American Indian Science and Engineering Society, which promotes technologically oriented careers for American Indian students, advocates the idea that students should also learn about their Indian heritages. Studies conducted on the Navajo Reservation have shown that students who are more "traditional," who have held on to their language and culture, are more successful in school than their "progressive" peers (Deyhle, 1992, 1995).

Is it curious that the experience of these "traditionalist" students runs against the conventional wisdom of our educational system, which is based on a "progressive" or "modern" ideal? Not really. We can think of mainstream American culture as twin currents. One current is represented in our "modern" educational system. Educational administrators and teachers generally operate from the assumption that progress and change are automatically good, that individualism is automatically best, and that consumerism and materialism should be promoted. They do so, furthermore, at the expense of traditional values. It is a way of thinking, critics say, that "compartmentalizes" the human experience, preventing us from seeing the interrelationships between the different elements of social life, such as the connections that integrate education, environment, and consumerism. Through a second current swim the likes of Madonna, Snoop Doggy Dogg, and Texas Chain Saw Massacre videos. Television, radio, and videos are the great teachers of this aspect of American culture. The American culture they teach is not of the "family values" that former Vice President Dan Quayle called for. Nor are they quite the values of his nemesis, "Murphy Brown," either. They are the values of our popular culture—a hedonistic, consumption-oriented, entertainment-bound, drug-infested culture.

Ironically, for this situation the Dan Quayles and educational administrators must share some of the blame. We have worked in our schools to cut minorities off from their cultures and families through a quite explicit policy of assimilation, and the unintended results have been more alcoholism, drugs, and gangs. As it pertains to Native students, non-Indian missionaries, government officials, and teachers failed to recognize the strengths in American Indian cultures. They failed, as well, to see that their attempts to replace those cultures with an "American" culture often left a person caught between two worlds and thus susceptible to depression and other forms of personal and social disintegration, such as the appeal of gangs, alcohol, and drugs.

Scholars such as Chet Bowers (1995) offer an alternative approach. They lean towards a more "conserving" education, arguing that our current consumer-oriented culture is destroying our environment and is not sustainable in the long term. We hear a lot of concern about how the national debt is burdening our children and grandchildren. The national debt is only money; we would do well to be equally concerned with the pollution, degraded environment, and plundered natural resources we are leaving our descendants. It is ironic, then, that our society's educational leaders fail to recognize how the "traditional" values of many Native peoples can give us greater insight into these "modern" problems. Eastern Indian tribes such as the Iroquois, for instance, traditionally considered the consequences of their action on the next seven generations before making major decisions.

To counter the destructive "progressive" orientation in our schools, Bowers argues for a conservative move back from "student-centered" learning to "trans-generational" communication. In his more traditionalist approach, "the elders of the culture must be recognized as carriers of essential knowledge and values" who pass on both family and ecological values to the children (Bowers, 1995, p. 135). With such a move, students would be taught "how individuals are nested in culture, and culture in ecosystems" (Bowers, 1995, p. 176).

I argue in this essay that Native American Studies departments or programs are critical to providing a positive university environment for Native students, and to help educate non-Indians to the positive human values found in Native cultures. Native American Studies (NAS) departments help keep Indian students in school by providing them with a university "home." NAS faculty provide on-campus leadership for groups, such as the American Indian Science and Engineering Society, that provide academic and social support for American Indian students. NAS programs also provide cultural affirmation for Native American students and provide an entry-way into universities for Native American intellectuals. Lastly, NAS departments can provide the support for research into the many concerns facing Native Americans today, including research on the causes of Indian dropout rates, economic development on reservations, and ways to improve Indian education.

The worth of NAS programs is especially valid in the context of studies such as that of Huffman (1993). Huffman describes four types of American Indian college students—assimilated, marginal, estranged, and transculturated. Only the assimilated and the transculturated students, as described in the study, are generally successful in college. I would argue that the transcultural student may be in the optimal situation. This person can walk in both worlds—a goal that is preferable to either assimilation or Nativist isolation. Indeed, given the current trend towards a global economy, if not a global village, all Americans would do well to learn to understand and appreciate other cultures with the goal of becoming world citizens.

NAS departments can also play an important role for non-Indian students by dispelling myths about Native Americans, such as the old saw that "all Indians receive money from the government and have a free ride in college." It is important, I maintain, that NAS courses demonstrate to non-Native students that efforts to maintain or revive minority languages and cultures are not divisive, unpatriotic, or "un-American." Instead, such efforts embody the classical meaning of freedom, versus the false "freedom" to conform to conventional norms. They should seek to promote an ideal of tolerance—a hallowed ideal which has become lost among the harsh rhetoric of our times. In fact, they are more authentically conservative than many would realize, motivated by a sense of responsibility to conserve the cultural strengths of the past.

Minority enclaves in the United States need not threaten mainstream Americans. Amish, Hutterite, and Hasidic enclaves exist today without any threat to this country's stability. One need only attend an American Indian Pow Wow and see how the Stars-and-Stripes and Native American war veterans are honored to recognize this truth. When I have asked Native elders what they want for their grandchildren, the answer I most commonly hear is that they want their children to respect their elders, work hard, study in school, not to drink, and, of course, to remember their Native heritage—a set of very conservative values.

At the same time, care must be taken that NAS programs not attempt to impose guilt on non-Indians for the "American Indian holocaust." This does not mean we should gloss over the past. Rather, we might take care that in describing the history of past injustices, we do not idealize Indians or demonize whites. This has been an unfortunate tendency in similar programs, as seen in the trend in African-American Studies toward an extreme "Afrocentrism" that treats whites as cold, mean-spirited "ice people" and African Americans as warm, friendly "sun people." As an example of this historically inaccurate approach, it is sometimes argued that Europeans introduced scalping to the Indians, which tends to demonize Europeans and make Indians less "savage." Yet, historian James Axtell (1981), in his ground-breaking essay, "The Unkindest Cut, or Who Invented Scalping?" reviews the primary evidence to show rather conclusively that scalping was a pre-Columbian activity of some tribes. As Axtell demonstrates, the introduction of the practice of paying bounties for scalps was clearly an invention of the European colonists. Furthermore, Europeans, while only occasionally involved in scalping, certainly had equally horrific practices, such as burning heretics at-the-stake and drawing-and-quartering traitors. Indeed, the point we want to make in NAS courses may well be that no culture was pure, no culture was contemptible. Both Native and European, as well as the gamut of other peoples we encounter in world history, could inflict wrenching torture on hapless captives when the spirit moved them. Thus, while a simplistic approach that paints Indians as generous, spiritual, and natural environmentalists and whites as selfish, mean-spirited capitalists destroying Mother Earth might make a few non-Indians strong uncritical advocates of American Indians, it is more likely to add to the white backlash that is currently jeopardizing affirmative action and other minority support programs.

References

Axtell, J. (1981). The unkindest cut, or who invented scalping? In J. Axtell, *The European and the Indian: Essays in the ethnohistory of colonial North America* (pp. 16–35). Oxford: Oxford University Press.

Benjamin, D. P., Chambers, S., & Reiterman, G. (1993). A focus on American Indian college persistence. *Journal of American Indian Education, 32* (2), 24–39.

Berliner, D. C., & Biddle, B. J. (1995). *The manufactured crisis: Myths, fraud and the attack on America's schools.* Reading, MA: Addison-Wesley.

Bowers, C. A. (1995). *Educating for an ecologically sustainable culture: Re-thinking moral education, creativity, intelligence, and other modern orthodoxies.* Albany, NY: SUNY Press.

Brandt, E. A. (1992). The Navajo area student dropout study: Findings and implications. *Journal of American Indian Education, 31* (2), 48–63.

Coburn, J., & Nelson, S. (1989). *Teachers do make a difference: What Indian graduates say about their school experience.* Portland: Northwest Regional Educational Laboratory. (ERIC Document Reproduction Service No. ED 306 071)

Cummins, J. (1986). Empowering minority students: A framework for intervention. *Harvard Educational Review, 56,* 18–36.

Davis, J. (1992). Factors contributing to post-secondary achievement of American Indians. *Tribal College, 4* (2), 24–30.

Deyhle, D. (1992). Constructing failure and maintaining cultural identity: Navajo and Ute school leavers. *Journal of American Indian Education, 31* (2), 24–47.

Deyhle, D. (1995). Navajo youth and Anglo racism: Cultural integrity and resistance. *Harvard Educational Review, 65,* 403–444.

Dodd, J. M., Garcia, F., Meccage, C., & Nelson, J. R. (1995). American Indian student retention. *NASPA Journal, 33* (1), 72–78.

Fedullo, M. (1992). *Light of the feather: Pathways through contemporary Indian America.* New York: Morrow.

Gould, S. J. (1981). *The mismeasure of man.* New York: W. W. Norton.

Hall, M. (1991). Gadugi: A model of service-learning for Native American communities. *Phi Delta Kappan, 72,* 754–757.

Herrnstein, R. J., & Murray, C. (1994). *The bell curve: Intelligence and class structure in American life.* New York: The Free Press.

Hoover, J. J., & Jacobs, C. C. (1992). A survey of American Indian college students: Perceptions toward their study skills/college life. *Journal of American Indian Education, 32* (1), 21–29.

Howard, S. (Producer), & Silverstein, E. (Director). (1970). *A man called Horse* (Film). Twentieth-Century Fox.

Huffman, T. E. (1991). The experiences, perceptions, and consequences of campus racism among Northern Plains Indians. *Journal of American Indian Education, 30* (2), 25–34.

Huffman, T. E. (1993). A typology of Native American college students. In T. E. Schirer & S. M. Branstner (Eds.), *Native American values: Survival and renewal* (pp. 67–80). Saulte Ste. Marie, MI: Lake Superior State University.

Indian Nations at Risk Task Force. U.S. Department of Education. (1991, October). *Indian nations at risk: An educational strategy for action* (Final report of the Indian Nations at Risk Task Force). Washington, DC: Author.

Kozol, J. (1991). *Savage inequalities: Children in America's schools.* New York: Crown.

Lawhead, H. E. (1932). Teaching Navajo children to read. *Progressive Education, 9,* 131–135.

Lin, R. L., LaCounte, D., & Eder, J. (1988). A study of Native American students in a predominantly white college. *Journal of American Indian Education, 27* (3), 8–15.

McEvans, A., & Astin, A. (1992). *Minority student retention rates: Comparative national data from the 1984 freshman class.* Los Angeles, CA: Higher Education Research Institute, University of California at Los Angeles.

McLaughlin, D. (1992). *When literacy empowers: Navajo language in print.* Albuquerque: University of New Mexico Press.

Meriam, L. (Ed.). (1928). *The problem of Indian administration.* Baltimore: Johns Hopkins University Press.

Nieto, S. (1992). *Affirming diversity: The sociopolitical context of multicultural education.* New York: Longman.

Ogbu, J. (1978). *Minority education and caste: The American system in cross-cultural perspective.* New York: Academic.

Pavel, D. M. (1992). *American Indians and Alaska Natives in higher education: Research on participation and graduation.* Charleston, WV: ERIC/CRESS Appalachia Education Laboratory. (Digest EDO-RC91-2)

Pavel, D. M., & Padilla, R. V. (1992). *Assessing Tinto's model of institutional departure using American Indian and Alaska Native national longitudinal data.* Tempe, AZ: Program in Higher Education, Arizona State University.

Reyhner, J. (1992). American Indians out of school: A review of school-based causes and solutions. *Journal of American Indian Education, 31* (3), 37–56.

Reyhner, J., & Eder, J. (1989). *A history of Indian education.* Billings, MT: Eastern Montana College. (ERIC Document Reproduction Service No. ED 321 953)

Richardson, Jr., R. C., & Pavel, D. M. (1992). Better measures of equity in minority participation and enrollment. In American Association of State Colleges and Universities, National Association of State Universities and Land-Grant Colleges, *A challenge of change: Public four-year enrollment lessons from the 1980s for the 1990s.* Washington, DC: Authors.

Scott, W. J. (1986). Attachment to Indian culture and the "difficult situation": A study of American Indian college students. *Youth and Society, 17* (4), 381–395.

U.S. Senate. Committee on Labor and Public Welfare. (1969). *Indian education: A national tragedy, a national challenge.* Senate Report 80, 91 Congress, 1st sess. (commonly known as the Kennedy Report).

Wright, B. (1985). Programming success: Special student services American Indian college student. *Journal of American Indian Education, 24* (1), 1–7.

6

Why Native American Studies? A Canadian First Nations Perspective

William Asikinack

Background

In the not so distant past—during my lifetime, in fact—the very idea that a field of study or even a discipline called Native American Studies (as it is known in the United States) or Native Studies or Indian Studies (the terms used in Canada) could become an accepted part of academic life seemed to be not only unrealistic, but unimaginable.[1] At one time, both the secondary and post-secondary institutions that Native Americans were able to, or required to, attend in Canada and the United States were often parochial in nature and design, and there was no expectation that the status quo would change. Each discipline was—and frequently still is—self-contained. John Price articulated the problem when he wrote, "This historically insular nature of the disciplines makes it difficult even to recruit someone to teach Native studies because few people have ever had a chance to study aboriginal New World culture" (1978, p. 1).

Before 1951, status Indian people in Canada (those officially recognized as Indian by the Canadian government) faced a further barrier to becoming a part of this academic frontier. Through the legal procedures of the Canadian Indian Act, any status Indian person could become legally non-Indian when he or she graduated from a post-secondary institution. As the law stated,

> Every Indian who is admitted to the degree of doctor of medicine, or to any other degree, by any university of learning or who is admitted, in any province in Canada, to practice law, either as an advocate, a barrister, solicitor or attorney, or a notary public or who enters holy orders, or who is licensed by a denomination of Christians as a minister of the gospel may, upon petition to the Superintendent General, ipso-facto become enfranchised. (Canada, Indian Act, 1886, section 86)

Some Indian people who acquired a post-secondary education felt they had no choice but to accept enfranchisement under this law. The opportunity to exchange an Indian identity for a college education and become "enfranchised" prevented many talented Indian people from going beyond secondary school in their educational development. However, after World War II, a small number of Indian people did enter universities. For example, by 1958 five Indian people, including myself, attended teacher training institutions in Canada.

As a student in several post-secondary institutions, I found that the courses of study invariably were designed to prepare my fellow students and me for a role within North American middle-class society. When I enrolled in a history course, invariably it was oriented to Western European concepts, ignoring or minimizing the contributions of my people. When I took a course in religion, it was Christian-oriented, with my own Native religious belief system either ignored or belittled. This was the norm for almost all undergraduate courses in which I was enrolled.

Yet, one area appeared to depart from this convention. The discipline of anthropology, which Marvin Harris, a leading practitioner, defines as "the study of humankind, especially *Homo Sapiens* . . . the study of how culture, people and nature interact wherever human-beings are found," offered a more balanced approach (Harris, 1975, p. 1). It is within the discipline of anthropology that we are able to examine, analyze, and compare a variety of cultures and societies. Significantly, members of this discipline have displayed a keen interest in the cultures of aboriginal North America. Therefore, in a manner of speaking, it was within this discipline that Native Studies or Indian Studies was born. Yet, within a decade, and because of its own rapid development toward maturity, Native American Studies began to separate from the parent discipline. As it is with the birth of almost anything, this birth was quite painful to anthropology.

The Roots of Native Studies: 1960–1990

The Late 1960s

During the 1960s, there was growing awareness among Native American people that post-secondary academia could be used as an aid to foster a cultural renaissance. Indian Studies could be used as a means for increasing both self-respect and respect from the dominant society, we believed. According to Price (1978), the earliest program in American Indian Studies was started at the University of Minnesota in 1964 when the university appointed a multi-disciplinary university committee to examine and develop an American Indian Studies program. However, it was not until the fall of 1968 that the actual Department of American Indian Studies was formed. Beginning in the 1969–70 academic year, formal classes in Chippewa, as well as in Indian arts, Indian history, and contemporary issues relating to Indian people, were taught (Price, 1978). In Canada, the first Native Studies Department was created at Trent University in 1969 (Stonechild, 1992).

The scholars who organized these departments intended their courses to be consistent with the standards of other university courses and hoped that the students would be stimulated in their intellectual growth. Their more important assumption was that these departments needed to be, as well, a more accurate reflection of Native cultures. To this end, with the birth of Native Studies programs, Native American and First Nations people became more involved in the academic development of these programs. Furthermore, reflecting the interdisciplinary bent of these programs, non-Native academics from a variety of other disciplines, such as art, history, political science, psychology, and sociology, began to turn to Native American Studies.

The 1970s

In Canada during the 1970s, the Department of Native Studies at Trent University, the Saskatchewan Indian Federated College, the Native American Studies at the University of Lethbridge, along with Native Studies at the University of Saskatchewan, Brandon University, and the University of Manitoba, were established. In the United States, Arizona State University, Harvard, Dartmouth, the University of Arizona, the University of California at Berkeley and the University of California at Los Angeles, the University of Chicago, and the University of Minnesota implemented Native American Studies courses or programs. In addition, tribally controlled community colleges, on or near American Indian reservations, were founded.

As these programs, departments, and colleges became established, they were increasingly staffed by scholars of Native American or First Nations heritage. Accordingly, these programs were "influenced more and more by the Native people's own needs, beliefs and cultural ways and methods" (Blue, 1981, p. 180). Consequently, questions about the direction in which this newly emergent discipline should go arose.

At one of the seminal gatherings of academics in 1972, according to Price (1978), "two hundred Native scholars, professional people, artists, and traditional historians" came together at Princeton University. In his keynote address, Rupert Costo, a Cahuilla engineer, set the tone for linking academics to a social agenda, observing, "'We must begin to teach the true history of our people, and to the American public at large we should have had, long ago, practical schools for our children, to keep the languages alive, to keep the beauty of our heritage alive'" (qtd. in Price, 1978, p. 10). A Tewa anthropologist, Alfonzo Ortiz, reinforced the message of an academic-social issues linkage when he spoke on the place of American Indian philosophy in the modern world. "'Modern America is at long last ready to listen to the practical wisdom of the Indian People, as well as to share in our spiritual heritage,'" he observed. "'Indeed, modern America desperately needs to listen and to share. We anthropologists cannot continue year after year mindlessly reciting in the classrooms the litany of Indian exotica and assorted trivia'" (qtd. in Price, 1978, p. 10).

The major purpose for this and subsequent conferences was to send a message to non-Native academia. Native Americans and First Nations people wanted these non-Native academics to be less dominant in using their knowledge and skills primarily for their own advancement. Rather, Indian people wanted non-Native scholars to work more for the benefit of Indian people, and, furthermore, to follow the recommendations articulated by Native American and First Nations leadership.

In addition, such conferences became fora for young scholars to voice their concerns about the direction they saw for Indian or Native American Studies. They began a movement toward finding solutions to the practical, everyday difficulties that confronted Native Americans, issues they deemed as important for Indian peoples' future development. Thus, they targeted specific issues, such as education, health, land claims, social questions, and justice.

The 1980s

During the 1980s, continued growth characterized the field of Indian Studies. Many universities in both Canada and the United States had inaugurated area studies programs or departments. In fact, many of these universities built Native American Studies Departments with consultation from First Nations people (Stonechild, 1992).

In the United States, tribally controlled colleges continued to develop. They included Navajo Community College in Arizona, Bay Mills Community College in Michigan, Oglala Community College in South Dakota, and Blackfeet College in Montana. In the meantime, many more universities, too numerous to mention here, developed new departments and programs or offered courses in Native American Studies.

Formal and informal scholarly associations were formed throughout the decade. Such organizations served as fora in which Native American or First Nations scholars could exchange information and ideas. In Canada, for example, the Canadian Indian/Native Studies Association (CINSA) was established to promote Indian Studies on a national level. CINSA's bylaws can suggest the agenda which Native American academics sought to further during this period. They aimed to:

1. Foster the exploration, articulation and application of research and education grounded in Indian/Native philosophies and concepts.
2. Encourage and support:
   a. the development of Indian/Native Studies in Canadian universities and colleges; and
   b. the professional development of persons engaged in such programs.
3. Foster communication between Indian/Native Studies Departments and programs in Canada through the holding of meetings, conferences and symposia.
4. Promote research and publication of Indian/Native Studies.

5. Liaise with national, regional and local educational associations and Indian/Native communities.
6. Promote the immediate and long-range concerns of Indian/Native Studies departments and programs.

(Canadian Indian/Native Studies Association, 1986)

As the bylaws show, the major purpose for CINSA's formation was to aid, support, and act as a liaison for the scholarly development of both Indian/Native and non-Native students and scholars.

In the United States, the Native American Professors and Alaska Natives Association was formed. The members of this association meet annually to continue the communication process, to do networking, to encourage and stimulate research in issues pertaining to their field, and to promote the intellectual development of American Indian and Alaskan Native people.

Contemporary Thoughts on Native Studies in the 1990s

Have the strategies and concepts which were developed for Native Studies programs in the late 1960s and early 1970s continued to be applicable for the 1990s? In early 1996, I posed the question, "Why should we continue to have Native American Studies?" to a select group of colleagues and students.

An important response was offered by Jay Stauss, a member of the Jamestown S'Klallam Band in Washington State and Director of Native American Studies at the University of Arizona in Tucson. According to Stauss, "Native Studies provides a unique interpretation of Native/non-Native interaction." With Native American scholars such as Jay now in the halls of academia, we are able to present our philosophy and world view in a manner that is non-Euro based. Jay further stated, "Native Studies provides a safe haven for Native students to work. In the past, many Native students have been subjected to discrimination and prejudice in other academic disciplines" (personal communication, April 16, 1996).

Bryan Akiwenzie responded to the same question that Native American Studies offers "a method for passing on information about traditions and beliefs which were suppressed during the residential school era." Bryan continued, "It gives the current generation a vehicle for exploring a different truth from that taught by the dominant society about our heritage. Indian Studies is where we are correcting those western beliefs" (personal communication, April 17, 1996). Bryan is Ojibwa from the province of Ontario. He is a graduate of the Saskatchewan Indian Federated College with a major in Indian Studies. He is employed as a student counselor for a First Nations Band in Saskatchewan.

Don McCaskill, a professor of Native Studies in the Department of Native Studies at Trent University in Peterborough, Ontario, responded that "it is the study of the Aboriginal experience that is 80 thousand years old. [Native

Studies] is relevant to the Native student and provides a source for the establishment of a positive identity." Furthermore, according to Don, "Native Studies allows the student to have a critical reflection for contemporary political, social, and cultural rhetoric, [and] Native Studies provides a research resource for Native Organizations" (personal communication, April 19, 1996).

Joseph Laliberte, Swampy Cree from the province of Saskatchewan, stated, "Indian Studies is important for me to maintain my connections to my culture. It is important for my children so that they do not lose their heritage through the teachings of modern culture and technology" (personal communication, April 23, 1996). Joseph is a senior in the Department of Indian Studies, Saskatchewan Indian Federated College. His minor is in computer science.

Conclusion

In this essay, I have presented a synopsis of the inauguration and continued development of Native American Studies. The initial few courses in Native American Studies have blossomed into a valid transdisciplinary field of study which is presently attaining equivalent status to French, British, and Spanish history about North America. These courses present a view that First Nations communities in Canada and the United States have had and continue to have an impact on the development of North America. As an example, due to the environmental problems with which modern society is struggling, many non-Native people are turning, for solutions, to environmental concepts still held by traditional Native American people. With the continually expanding interest by both First Nations and non-First Nations people in the history, contributions and culture of Native America, I can say without hesitation that "Native American Studies is here to stay."

Note

1 For the purposes of this essay, the terms *Native American Studies* and *Indian Studies* will be used in an interchangeable manner. In the United States, the apparently preferred term is *Native American Studies,* whereas in Canada the term *Native Studies* or *Indian Studies* is used. To add to the confusion, now, in the latter part of the 1990s, *First Nations Studies* is beginning to be used by some post-secondary institutions in Canada.

References

Blue, A. (1981). Reflections on the direction of Native Studies Departments in Canadian universities." *Canadian Journal of Native Studies, 1* (1), 179–183.

Canada. The Indian Act. 1886. Section 86.

Canadian Indian Native Studies Association. (1986). *Bylaws*. Written by B. Stonechild, W. Asikinack, D. McCaskill, P. Chartrand, C. Morris, et al. Regina, Saskatchewan: CINSA.

Harris, M. (1975). *Culture, people, nature: An introduction to general anthropology* (2nd ed.). New York: Thomas Y. Crowell.

Price, J. (1978). *Native Studies: American and Canadian Indians*. Toronto, ONT: McGraw-Hill Ryerson Ltd.

Stonechild, B. (1992). The development of Indian/Native Studies in Canada. In D. Miller, C. Beal, J. Dempsey, & W. Heber (Eds.), *The first ones: Readings in Indian/Native Studies* (pp. 1–5). Regina: Saskatchewan Indian Federated College Press.

III

Economic Survival

Few factors shape the conditions of Native American life today as does the daunting fact of profound, pervasive poverty. Few elements dictate the status of Native Americans in the larger society as does economics. Yet, few mainstream politicians or political commentators find a place within their rhetoric for solutions to this ongoing dilemma. We can trace the struggles of Native American communities to develop economic strategies that will provide the means for sharing in America's bounty, however. The three essays in this section describe some of these strategies.

In "Taking up the Challenge: Fundamental Principles of Economic Development in Indian Country," Miriam R. Jorgensen describes the dimensions of Native American poverty. As a political economist, her focus is economic development. Jorgensen identifies U.S. government policies which caused or contributed to rampant poverty on reservations, assesses the flaws plaguing recent efforts at economic development, and shows how both have laid the foundations for "cycles of dependence." By analyzing past successes and failures and deriving lessons from these experiences, her work offers a good example of the contributions academics can make to the formulation of public policy. Jorgensen's analysis points to two fundamentals of economic development in Indian Country: First, development must be defined by the Native communities involved, and second, the development of sound institutions should precede other development efforts.

Wayne J. Stein, a member of the Turtle Mountain Chippewa and a Montana State University professor, focuses on the more specific strategy of gaming. In "American Indians and Gambling: Economic and Social Impacts," Stein raises the important question of whether the economic strategy of casino gaming has benefited Native American communities as much as many people believe. Connecting economic and social issues, he asks about gaming's effects on Native Americans' efforts to improve education, housing, and social/welfare programs. As he shows, gaming was a $330 billion industry by 1992, with each dollar turning over eleven times in the communities which sponsored it. Yet, he finds Native-controlled gaming enterprises both a blessing and a burden. Stein's research indicates that gaming has brought improvements in the standard of living to some Native communities; others, however, remain suspicious of this solution.

In "Native American Industry: Basket Weaving among the Wabanaki," Pauleena MacDougall of the University of Maine examines early newspaper reports, archaeological studies, travelogues, and Indian agent reports to trace the origins, development, and current status of basket making as an economic strategy among the Wabanaki peoples of Maine. She shows how the Wabanaki developed this niche market of the tourism industry during the nineteenth century, forging strategic alliances with fashionable resorts and modifying tools, techniques, and marketing to adapt to changing economic conditions. MacDougall's interest is in the usefulness today of this traditional Native craft. She concludes that basket weaving serves as a strategy that not only provides a viable economic opportunity, but also serves as a path toward cultural renewal.

7

Taking up the Challenge: Fundamental Principles of Economic Development in Indian Country

Miriam R. Jorgensen

The U.S. Government Census of 1990 is a profound snapshot of American life in the last decade of the twentieth century. For one trained in economics, as I am, the most striking element of this picture is the stark economic difference it shows between various subgroups of our larger society. In particular, statistics from that census, which is arguably the most complete census of the American Indian[1] population for decades, reveal the difficult circumstances in which many Natives live: 47 percent of all Native American families living on reservations or trust lands (that is, in "Indian Country"[2]) reported a 1989 income below the poverty level (U.S. Bureau of the Census, 1993, p. 82). By comparison, 26 percent of African American families and 7 percent of white American families reported 1989 incomes in this range (U.S. Bureau of the Census, 1992, p. 49). The statistics are even more alarming for the most vulnerable members of Native society, children and the elderly, 55 percent of whom are classified as poor. Without question, American Indians are one of the poorest sub-populations in the United States. This poverty is connected to—and often caused by—an array of other socio-economic problems, such as high unemployment, heavy reliance on government transfer programs, low educational attainment, and poor health status (see Table 1). For those who research Native American economic issues and who care about the effect of economic conditions on the lives of Native Americans, the significance of the Census is clear: At the close of the twentieth century, one of the most daunting challenges Native Americans face is that of improving their economic welfare. How that task can be accomplished is the subject of this essay.

The Context for American Indian Economic Development

American Indian poverty is not a new phenomenon. During the mid-1800s, under the express political justification of "Manifest Destiny," the U.S.

Miriam R. Jorgensen

Table 1
Comparative Socio-Economic Status of American Indians and Alaskan Natives, 1990

Employment Statistics	American Indians[1] (on reservations)	US All Races	US Whites	US Blacks
Unemployment Rate[2]				
Males, age 16 & over	29.5	6.4	5.3	13.7
Females, age 16 & over	21.1	6.2	5.0	12.2

Education	American Indians (on reservations)	US All Races	US Whites	US Blacks
Percent of persons 25 years & older having				
Completed less than 9th grade	21.7	10.4	8.9	13.8
9th-12th grade, no diploma	24.4	14.4	13.1	23.2
Completed high school	49.9	75.2	77.9	63.1
Completed bachelor's degree or more	3.9	20.3	21.5	11.4

US Gov't Transfer Program Support	American Indians (on reservations)	US All Races	US Whites	US Blacks
Percent of families receiving				
Public assistance income in 1989	31.6	7.7	5.5	21.0
Social security income in 1989	17.5	22.5	23.8	18.9

government intensified its policy of forced Native relocation to reservations. Since at least that time, there has been a notable differential between the economic welfare of Native Americans and that of the encroaching Anglo-Europeans. As one visitor to Pawnee Country (present-day Nebraska) wrote in the 1840s: "one third of them had, neighter [sic] a kernel of corn nor a mouthful of meat in the world" (Milner, 1982, p. 32). Even in the "Roaring Twenties," as this century's first American Indian policy reform movement took shape, numerous reports to the U.S. government emphasized the desperate conditions in which Indians lived. These reports exposed economic hardship, a high incidence of treatable disease, the inadequacy of primary schooling, and elevated crime rates. Then, as now, care-

Table 1 (continued)

Health Indicators	American Indians (entire population)	US All Races	US Whites	Ratio AIAN to US All Races
Deaths per 100,000 population from				
Major cardiovascular diseases	163.7	189.8	182.1	0.9
Malignant Neoplasms	94.5	135.0	131.5	0.7
Accidents	86.0	32.5	31.8	2.6
Chronic liver disease and cirrhosis	30.3	8.6	8.0	3.5
Diabetes mellitus	29.7	11.7	10.4	2.5
Pneumonia and influenza	20.5	14.0	13.4	1.5
Suicide	16.5	11.5	12.2	1.4
Homicide	15.3	10.2	5.9	1.5
Chronic obstructive pulmonary disease	13.8	19.7	20.1	0.7
Tuberculosis, all forms	2.7	0.5	0.3	5.4

Sources: U.S. Bureau of the Census (1992, 1993); Indian Health Service (1994).

Notes:

1. Technically, these numbers are for the "AIAN," or American Indian and Alaskan Native population.

2. Different data collection and rate calculation methods can lead to substantial differences in reported American Indian unemployment rates; in particular the rate calculated from Census statistics (as here) differs from the rate calculated by the Bureau of Indian Affairs (which uses a method similar to that of the Bureau of Labor Statistics). Thus, these rates should be interpreted as an indication of severe unemployment, but not as an accurate measurement of its precise level. In fact, reservation unemployment rates are probably even higher (up to 80 percent, for example) than any of these official statistics suggest, since "discouraged workers" (those who have given up looking for a job) are not included in the calculations.

ful observers of American Indian life saw an intimate connection between harsh economic conditions and wider negative outcomes (Deloria & Lytle, 1984). One specific example is provided by a former Superintendent of the Bureau of Indian Affairs agency at Pine Ridge (a reservation in South Dakota).[3] In 1925—well before the ravages of the Great Depression—the Superintendent reported to his superiors in Washington that even with U.S. government rations, "There is no question but that the Pine Ridge Sioux have suffered considerably during the winter and spring on account of insufficiency of food" (U.S. Bureau of Indian Affairs, 1925, roll 106). Anthropologist Thomas Biolsi, who quotes this account, adds that these conditions "no doubt contributed to the high mortality rate ascertained by the Meriam commission for South Dakota reservations in 1925. The rate was 23.5 deaths per 1000 population" (Biolsi, 1992, p. 29). In the same period and among all races, there were approximately 8.6 deaths per 1000 population in the entire state (estimated from the South Dakota Department of Health mortality rate records for 1920 and 1930, provided by M. Gildemaster, personal communication, April 10, 1996).

Throughout the last century, private reformers and U.S. government policymakers have advocated a wide variety of policies in response to these welfare issues—responses which have ranged from the strongly assimilationist ideas of "allotment" and "termination" to the more separatist statements of "Indian Reorganization," "self-determination," and "self-governance." Resulting U.S. policy has been inconsistent and, in turn, relatively ineffective at improving Natives' welfare. For instance, the General Allotment Act of 1887 (often called the Dawes Act after its sponsor, Senator Henry L. Dawes of Massachusetts) subdivided reservation land and gave individual Indians title to it. Allotment supporters believed that Natives could earn a reasonable subsistence income through farming. Most did not; in fact, the policy only further impoverished Indians by promoting the transfer of valuable Indian land assets to non-Indians (Canby, 1988; Cornell, 1988).[4] The U.S. government acknowledged the failure of allotment policy in the 1930s and reversed course with the Indian Reorganization Act (IRA) of 1934. The IRA encouraged tribes to restructure themselves as business corporations capable of promoting reservation-based, tribal government-led business development.[5] Programs providing federal loans and grants as start-up funding for agricultural operations, resource extraction industries, and local retail enterprises followed (Deloria & Lytle, 1984). By the 1950s, however, Indian policy reformers sought to free Natives from what they saw as "rural ghettos," and the official U.S. stance changed again. The new policy of relocating Native individuals to cities, where they would have broader opportunities and better economic prospects, went hand-in-hand with congressional desires to terminate the U.S. government relationship with tribes. Relocation was partially successful in that urban Indians reported higher incomes than their reservation-based counterparts; yet this "success" can be attributed largely to the fact that economic conditions in Indian Country were dire (Cornell, 1988). Explicit termination had more obvious negative consequences for Natives' welfare, and in this case, the Menominee Tribe's experience is instructive. They endured an interlinked loss of community and economic wherewithal as termination drove them from near self-sufficiency into extreme poverty (Debo, 1974). By the mid-1970s the pendulum had swung fully in the other direction. Especially after passage of the Indian Self-Determination and Education Assistance Act of 1975, U.S. government policy has emphasized tribal sovereignty and Native empowerment. Moreover, reservation economic development (defined narrowly here as the creation and sustenance of income-generating activities) has become a centerpiece of long-term welfare improvement for American Indians. In addition to the agricultural and resource-based enterprises popular with the BIA in the IRA-era, modern projects and programs also attempt to capitalize on tribes' special status as "domestic dependent nations."[6] For instance, U.S. government procurement guidelines have been amended to give Natives minority preference, and federal Indian administrators have encouraged tax-advantaged joint ventures. Table 2 summarizes this history.

Through all of these policy changes, several consistent threads characterize the endeavors which focused on economic development in Indian country. The large majority were U.S. government-inspired, and most concentrated on narrowly defined projects or programs alone with paradoxical results. Almost all efforts posted poor track records. Many plans never came to fruition, and many of those that did eventually failed; one study conducted in the late 1980s at the Standing Rock Sioux Reservation (in North and South Dakota) found that 18 of 19 businesses started by the tribal government over the previous 20 years had failed (R. McLaughlin, personal communication, December 27, 1989). Instead of promoting economic vitality, the attempts at economic development pushed Native Americans deeper into a trap—what economists term "cycles of dependence." Indeed, government itself became the only reliable source of employment opportunity for many Native Americans; in 1990, nearly 50 percent of all reservation-based, employed Indians age 16 and over worked in the public sector, for either the tribal, state, or federal government (U.S. Bureau of the Census, 1993, p. 924). Such overwhelming dependence on public service jobs is neither economically healthy nor prudent within the larger context of American politics.

More pointedly, economic development failures of the past stand out not only against the backdrop of American Indian poverty, but also in the face of new pressures for reservation development. The U.S. government is the most important source of external pressure, and modern political history suggests that without increased reservation-based economic development, the vagaries of U.S. politics will cast a shadow on Natives' future welfare. One ominous sign is that recent Congresses have become ambivalent about Natives' special status as domestic, but semi-sovereign nations. The Indian Gaming Regulatory Act of 1988 (IGRA) is a premier example. By forcing tribes to negotiate gaming compacts with state governments, Congress actively violated the promise—implicit in the Constitution and treaty law— that the United States would maintain *national* government-to-government relationships with Indian nations within its borders. The U.S. Supreme Court's March 1996 ruling in the *Seminole Tribe of Florida v. Florida* complicated the issue further. The State of Florida challenged IGRA's enforcement provision by arguing that Congress could not authorize tribes to sue states in the U.S. District Courts. In a 5–4 decision, the Court agreed that

Table 2
Historical Changes in the U.S. Government's Indian Policy:
Late 1700s to the Present

Period	Implication for Economic Resources	U.S. Government Approach to Native Welfare Improvement
Conflict (c. late 18th to late 19th centuries)	Forced expropriation of Indian lands; exclusion of Indians from the larger U.S. economy.	None.
Reservation & Allotment (c. late 19th century to 1930s)	Continued land loss through allotment; welfare dependency; eventually declining demand for Indian resources.	Individualized; desire to create self-sufficient family farmers.
Indian Reorganization (1930s to late 1940s)	Efforts to stabilize land base and to develop reservation economies; support for reservation communities.	Corporate; desire to create self-sufficient, "Americanized" Native communities.
Termination & Relocation (late 1940s to early 1960s)	Some demand for Indian lands; federal promotion of urban migration; withdrawal of support for reservations.	Individualized; desire to provide access to the modern, urban labor market.
Self-Determination (mid–1960s to present)	Resurgent demands for Indian resources (particularly water and minerals); major efforts to develop reservation economies.	Corporate; desire to create self-sufficient Native communities in which individuals also have access to U.S. government social safety net services.

Note: The period names and effects on Native resources derive from Cornell's (1988) similar chart (p. 14).

such action was unconstitutional. On the one hand, this decision can be seen as freeing tribes to act as they please on gaming, without approval from the states in which they are located. On the other hand, by affirming states' rights and leaving tribes' rights undefined, the Court's decision can be also interpreted as slippage, similar to that in Congress, in the regard its members have for Native rights. If so, the ruling is *one more* U.S. political pressure that serves to focus tribal leaders' attention on economic development as a means of reducing reliance on fickle federal promises.

Similarly, in the current climate of budget reduction, Congress is increasingly willing to cut Native program funding. These cuts are controversial. Members of Congress justify their actions with the statement that all citizens must bear the pain of federal budget cutting. But many Natives argue that Indians have already borne their pain, and that the services they receive are annuity payments for past land cessions. As such, budget allocations to Native programs are different from those to other U.S. government transfer programs, and to cut them proportionally threatens fragile reservation economies and abrogates Native rights. The U.S. government always has been the most important external source of financial support for social service spending, tribal operating expenses, and start-up capital for reservation development initiatives, and while these U.S. government programs have not always helped, it would be disastrous to significantly reduce federal funds without the cushion provided by vibrant Native economies.

Internal events cause concern for the future, as well. In particular, population growth may strain the ability of reservation economies to provide adequate incomes for tribal citizens even if changes in federal spending policy do not. Growth of the population overall has been robust: "In 1950 the United States Census counted 377,000 American Indians and Alaskan Natives. By 1990, the Indian population had increased more than five-fold to 1.96 million" (Eschbach, 1995, p. 89). As demographers (those who study population growth) have pointed out, of course, a significant portion of this growth can be attributed to "re-identification" (Harris, 1994).[7] Yet, most re-identification has occurred in regions which, historically, have not had large Native populations and among individuals who probably are not enrolled as tribal members; in reservation areas, high fertility rates remain the most important cause of Indian population growth (Eschbach, 1993).

In other words, the population growth observed in designated tribal areas *will* put pressure on reservation economies both to keep pace and to grow in per capita terms.[8] For example, the census-estimated population at Fort Apache (home of the White Mountain Apache in Arizona) grew from 6,880 in 1980 to 9,902 in 1990, which translates to an annualized population growth rate of 3.7 percent; from 4,159 to 5,717 at Wind River (in Wyoming), or 3.2 percent growth per year; from 613 to 792 at Cochiti Pueblo (in New Mexico), or 2.6 growth per year; and from 5,525 to 7,031 at Blackfeet (in Montana), or 2.4 percent growth per year (rates calculated from U.S. Bureau of the Census, 1986, 1993).[9] Tribes such as these will continue to grow; the median age of Natives living in designated American Indian and Alaskan Native areas is 22 (calculated from U.S. Bureau of the Census, 1993), which means that most tribal members have not even begun to bear children and raise families. On the one hand, these population growth figures demonstrate the resiliency of Indian nations; on the other, they warn that Native national income generation will be of even greater importance in the future than it is today.

As I suggested at the beginning of this essay, one of the most daunting challenges Native Americans face at the close of the twentieth century is that of improving their economic welfare. How can that task be accomplished? Two important resources provide at least the outlines of an answer to this difficult question—the anatomy of past project failures, and, more optimistically, lessons derived from Native development successes. Particularly since 1975, when changes in U.S. law permitted tribes to assume control over many U.S. government-sponsored programs on reservations, some Native nations have begun to diverge from the rest of the pack.[10] Greater scope for true self-determination has allowed the White Mountain Apache Tribe, the Mississippi Band of Choctaw, and the Confederated Salish and Kootenai Tribes, among others, to make remarkable progress toward implementing their development goals.[11] Two fundamental principles of American Indian economic development emerge from reflection on past failures and on the nature of earlier successes, and they structure a new way of thinking about development as a response to American Indian poverty. The next sections of this essay highlight these essential ideas: first, that development must be self-defined and, second, that the development of institutional capacity should precede other development efforts.

Development Must Be Self-Defined and Culturally Appropriate

Judging by the number of books on Native religion, mail-order catalogs selling American Indian (or American Indian-inspired) products, and even the presence of Native staples in supermarkets' ethnic food aisles, American Indians have become fashionable. Consequently, it is tempting to say that mainstream America is finally beginning to understand "Native culture." In reality, mainstream Americans are probably only aware of some distillation of Native beliefs and practices, pulled from a variety of sources, and quite unaware that "Native culture," discussed in the singular, is a misnomer which masks great diversity. Despite some spillover of pan-Indian activities into individual tribes' lifeways, the present Native American population is composed of dozens of distinct linguistic and cultural groups, as even a brief look at the many tribal "nationalities" recorded by American Indians and Alaskan Natives in the last census would attest. Even tribes living nearby each other might have cultural traditions as different from one another as those of Greece are from those of Vietnam. As Native American people are happy to point out, there is not *one* Native culture or *one* Native world-view, but many (Jorgensen, 1995). Writ small, each group has a different way of conducting the nitty-gritty activities of day-to-day life; writ large, each group has a different vision of and for itself. The implication for economic development is that there cannot be *one* kind of development which suits every tribe.

Many past attempts to develop American Indian reservations ignored this diversity. Well into the self-determination period, Washington-based administrators promoted "one size fits all" economic development projects. Therefore, they made the implicit (and bureaucratically convenient) assumption that all Indian areas and all Native cultures were ripe for farming, or motels, or assembly plants. The obvious result was that few of the economic development projects undertaken in Indian Country were self-defined; they were not conceived and implemented through community-appropriate decision-making processes, nor were they pursued with attention to a group's specific market niches or prioritized national needs. Frequently, these rote-response federal projects were inappropriate for individual tribes' unique economic and socio-cultural conditions, and just as frequently, they failed.[12]

In contrast, successful Native development efforts—the wildlife program at Fort Apache, the wire harness assembly plant at Mississippi Choctaw, and the Kah-Nee-Ta Resort owned by the Confederated Tribes of Warm Springs (Oregon), for instance—cohere with their nations' economic settings and living cultures. To secure that fit, tribes have taken positive actions to pursue projects which they defined as appropriate, both in substance and in scope. Sovereign, self-determined development arises from nothing less. The principle is important enough to state in another way: Despite the allure of phrases like "self-determination" and "self-governance" (two modern policy expressions of Indian sovereignty), tribal economic development efforts embody neither policy unless the tribe has previously addressed the question, "What is our vision for ourselves?" Asking, answering, and implementing the answer to this question is the strategy that puts Native development efforts on the right track. The exercise of sovereignty (here, the exercise of decision-making authority) is a necessary precursor to all effective development efforts.

Several extremely important points follow from this. Significantly, Native nations which have not faced up to the challenge of self-definition may find it wiser to defer all development activity rather than react to externally defined programs and accept externally approved projects. These projects are prone to failure and, therefore, contribute to situations in which successive failures erode confidence, heighten feelings of desperation and despair, and make subsequent development decisions not only more necessary, but also more difficult.

The Oglala Sioux Tribe's 1986 decision to invest in the Nebraska Sioux Lean Beef slaughterhouse and meat-packing plant is one example of this negative progression.[13] No process of self-definition had occurred at Pine Ridge around the appropriate role of the central tribal government in large-scale investment. Yet, pressure from a number of sources led the Tribal Council to vote in favor of the plant. First, officials from the U.S. Department of Housing and Urban Development had told the Tribal Council that if they did not invest in the packing plant, they would lose their Community Development Block Grant; the Council, in response, feared that the loss of this grant would jeopardize the future flow of federal funds. Second, their joint venture partner had threatened to pull out if they did not act soon. Finally, the Oglala Sioux Tribe's leaders knew that tribal members living on the reservation were the poorest people in the United States (Johnson, 1987) and that they desperately needed jobs. Once the Council made the go-ahead decision, the Tribe financed the plant with their block grant and several large loans. Unfortunately, after only twenty months of operation, and without ever generating significant tribal employment, the plant's non-Native managers abruptly closed its doors. In the end, the plant's large, lingering debt and the suspicious circumstances of its closure left the Tribe in an even more precarious financial and political situation than it had been in before the investment debacle. The example of Sioux Lean Beef suggests that despite a desperate need for income and jobs, it might be better for a tribe to do nothing and to be in control of that decision than it would be to act in a policy vacuum and lose control, money, and pride. If a tribe's journey toward self-defined economic development cannot begin with a strictly positive step, a non-negative one might be the next best choice.

Next, it is worth noting that the logical result of the concept of "self-defined, culturally appropriate development" is that different tribes will make different choices. What is acceptable to and desired by some Native nations may not be acceptable to and desired by others. For example, unlike the White Mountain Apache, members of the Confederated Tribes of the Warm Springs Reservation (in Oregon) decided against development of a ski resort on their land, and the Yakama Indian Nation (in Washington State) decided not to pursue a commercial wildlife harvesting venture—even though both of these were profitable options available to the tribes. Likewise, in the mid-1990s, both the Hopi and Navajo Nations decided not to develop reservation-based gaming. These choices reflect previous deliberation of the questions, "What do we want?" and "Does that kind of thing belong here and work here?" By their very nature, these questions lead to answers which vary across groups.

Finally, the process of self-definition will make it clear that within many Native world views, "economic development" means more than increasing the financial strength of a tribe or the incomes of its members (Jorgensen, 1995). Traditional Native ways of knowing may not distinguish between the economic, religious, political, educational, social, and personal spheres, as mainstream American culture does. Thus, self-defined Native economic development plans may incorporate issues as diverse as housing, crime, education, laws, and ceremonies. Natives may also be more attuned to the ways in which development, even the latest proposal for an assembly plant or product finishing facility (usually considered to be "low impact" development), spills over into all areas of life. Besides being "self-defined and culturally appropriate," this recognition of the connectedness of different aspects of social life may be an extremely reasonable way of responding to the challenges that each tribe faces. As I noted at the outset, poverty is related to an array of other social problems; a broader vision of economic development automatically takes account of and wrestles with those ripple effects. Moreover, this is a point on which we economists can learn both from Natives and from the practitioners of other academic disciplines (especially anthropology and sociology), and in so doing, change our language and outlook: the socio-economic vitalization of Indian Country is not *economic development* alone, but simply *development*, broadly conceived.

Many excellent examples of this richer view of development can be given. The Brotherhood Health Clinic in Porcupine, a small town on the Pine Ridge reservation, serves both as a health facility and as a forum for community meetings; it is *Native development*. American Indian efforts to protect Bear Butte (a sacred site in the Black Hills of South Dakota) from disrespectful tourists are a form of Native development, as are all efforts to protect sacred sites. The approximately thirty tribal colleges are development, and so, too, are their new or expanding programs in nursing, counseling, education, management, and Native languages. A final, dramatic example of holistic development is the restoration of physical and mental health to members of the Alkali Lake Shuswap community in British Columbia. There, religious and cultural revival combine to promote personal and social life changes (particularly freedom from alcohol) and to invigorate overall political and economic change. These development efforts, none of which are strictly income-generating in intent, have nonetheless moved Native American communities closer to their chosen futures. Moreover, they are an encouraging sign that some American Indian groups have accepted the true challenge of self-determination and are actively engaged in self-defined development.

Yet, that process is neither ubiquitous nor complete, as Natives themselves make clear. Two eloquent summaries of the points raised in this section come from columnists Tim Giago and Gemma Lockhart, whose syndicated editorials have made them opinion leaders in Indian Country. Giago's tone is challenging and direct:

> It took a lot of help from a lot of well-meaning do-gooders and short-sighted bureaucrats to nearly destroy the economy of the Indian nations. Instead of asking the tribal leaders "what is it you want?" the government and the do-gooders said "here's what we are going to do for you." (Giago, 1994, p. A9)

Lockhart's version of the same idea is less confrontational, but no less biting:

We need a future for our people and prosperity across our lands. We need development that is not just any development. We need an effort that sings out loud about who
we are. (Lockhart, 1993, p. A8)

Why is it that these mistakes and deficiencies continue for some tribes? The
harsh reality in which many American Indians live is this: Accurate diag-
noses of problems and ardent desires for change are impotent in the
absence of a policy structure capable of supporting sovereign, self-determined economic development. These structures are the topic of the next
section.

Economic Development Includes and Is Founded on Institutional Development

Because self-defined Native development encompasses many areas of
change, it should not be surprising that institutional reform appears on the
list of possible policy actions. Instead, the surprising research finding is how
central institutional development is to all other kinds of development in
Indian Country. It is in such discoveries that the economist crosses into the
domain of the political scientist; it is here, as well, that political economists
like myself can bring insights into our research that are based on the
connections we see between politics and economics—insights that often
elude the standard approaches of economics or political science alone.
Through the lens of political economy, a society's socio-economic performance appears to depend intimately on its social and political institutions (or, more colloquially, on that society's "rules of the game"). Boldly
stated, positive socio-economic progress can occur only in the presence of a
policy infrastructure which supports and promotes development in a virtu-
ous cycle.[14] Institutions are the key to generating appropriate, long-term
development success. Consequently, if a tribe's present institutions are
incapable of performing the task, institutional reform should be the first
focus of development.

This is another point on which the U.S. government's Indian policymakers have often stumbled. By and large, they have concentrated on limited
projects. They have assumed that structural changes—changes in the way a
group organizes, or structures, its political institutions—would occur as
economic success demanded greater institutional sophistication. But, by
pursuing projects ahead of the institutional changes which could have
provided a supportive social and political atmosphere for project implementation, they put the "cart before the horse." To be fair, Indian affairs
administrators were not alone in getting this progression wrong; only in the
last decade has the focus in international development been as much on
"capacity building" as on specific income-generation projects (Grindle,
1996). Rather than excuse federal administrators' actions, however, the
focal shift by other development experts should influence actions taken in

Indian Country. Capacity building, particularly institutional capacity building, must occur there, as well.

So, in theory and in practice, what kind of institutional infrastructure is needed to support and promote development? Logic and experience suggest that Native nations' social and political institutional structures must be capable of three things: generating support for development strategies, making and implementing strategic choices, and providing a political environment in which investors feel safe.[15] These points are covered in turn below.

Generating Support

The institutional structure of a Native nation should give its citizens confidence that their agents (tribal politicians and planners) are making appropriate choices about the path of development. Citizens should be comfortable either with the specific efforts undertaken or with the authority of the decision makers who have made those choices. Clearly, these impressions of tribal governmental action are bound up in Native citizens' beliefs about the legitimacy of their own governments and about the support they owe them. But where do beliefs about legitimacy come from?

In most "western" societies, democratic processes legitimize governments. Democracy provides for the direct popular choice of policymakers, and through this means, citizens also have an indirect choice over policy. Their choice of representatives legitimizes government because, as voters, they either have the government they want or, in the classical liberal sense of "legitimate government," the opportunity to remove governments they do not want. Furthermore, this method of legitimization appears to matter just as the political economist would expect—democratic principles are often positively correlated with desirable socio-economic outcomes (Goldsmith, 1995).[16] Significantly, representative democracy appears to promote desired outcomes in Indian Country, as well. Generally, tribes whose citizens elect their tribal chairmen[17] directly and delegate legislative decision making to tribal council representatives perform better both on macroeconomic measures, such as unemployment and average incomes, and on microeconomic measures, such as returns to timber enterprise investments (Cornell & Kalt, 1991; Jorgensen, 1996).

Though these results are important, they may not describe the legitimization process used by every tribe. Why should all cultures breed democrats? Although it may be the case that many cultures rely on democratic processes to legitimize government, at least some others will have alternative means. Sociologist Stephen Cornell and economist Joseph Kalt examined this question by comparing the experiences of the Oglala Sioux and White Mountain Apache under their nearly identical, "single and popularly elected strong leader" forms of government (Cornell & Kalt, 1995). Their

evidence suggests that legitimacy flows from the "match" between formal
institutional structure and culturally sanctioned means of governance. What
this means is that if formal structures (the tribe's constitution and other
legal documents which expressly delineate government powers) do not
match tribal members' culturally constructed concepts of legitimacy, then
the government and all the actions it takes are insupportable. Thus, the first
challenge of institutional development is to refine the over-arching political
system in such a way that it can generate support for other chosen development strategies.[18]

Making and Implementing Choices

Popular support is crucial, but sound institutions are also defined by their
capacity to direct and implement strategic choices. Democracy alone (or its
legitimate alternative) is too unwieldy for this task, and thus, a certain
amount of administrative infrastructure is necessary. An institutional structure that is equipped to make overall policy, pick projects, and see those
projects through must contain rules of choice, procedural guidelines, and a
bureaucratic apparatus both sophisticated enough to meet the tribe's development needs and strong enough to insulate day-to-day decisions from
political interference (including the interference of tribal politicians).
Therefore, the second challenge to institutional development is to
construct these capabilities where they do not already exist.

How do these technocratic structures work to promote good development policy? For starters, "choice rules" are institutional structures
designed to provide explicit policy guidance and to pick projects. They
specify who makes what decisions and how. For example, tribal councils are
often vested with the power to make overall development policy, using
some system of majority rule. After the tribal council has made its policy
recommendation, it might then be the responsibility of a tribal planning
department to narrow the field of possible project choices. Political and
technical experts might next be asked to rank projects by consensus, and
perhaps the tribal chairman must give final approval to the top-ranked
choice. While there is obviously a menu of possibilities at each step, some
explicit set of rules for choice-making must be used. If institutions do not
clarify both responsibility over choice and the methods for choice, members
of tribal government will have difficulty deciding what development activities to undertake, and citizens will have difficulty supporting the activities
which do occur.[19]

Once a strategic development choice is made, effective bureaucratic
structures help ensure its smooth implementation. Financial systems oversee budgeting, invoicing, and bill payment. Personnel systems supervise
hiring, conduct training, hear grievances, and set standards for promotion.
Record-keeping systems clarify and make apparent the details of decisions

and create institutional history. Each of these operations should follow known, accepted, and standard procedures. All together, they should constitute an efficient bureaucracy and professional civil service, systems able to support development projects over the long haul and through election cycles.[20]

Maintaining Investor Confidence

The third requirement of social and political institutions is that they must provide an environment in which investors (both inside and outside the tribe) feel confident that their investments are secure. Significantly, investor confidence is based less on rules of procedure than on investors' perceptions of politicians' behavior (Brunetti, 1995). In the absence of enforcement, it will usually be rational to break rules,[21] a fact which makes observed behavior a stronger indicator of the institutional capacity to protect investors than the mere existence of laws requiring government officials to behave honestly. For example, investors feel safe when they see that tribal officials are trustworthy and that they are not "rent seekers" (who use their positions of power to extract personal gain). Investor confidence is boosted when they see that politicians will give policy guidance, but will not micro-manage development efforts. Investors are encouraged when they see that officials refrain from mixing politics with business. Finally, investors gain confidence when they see that politicians' electoral cycles are not allowed to disrupt bureaucratic procedures. Consequently, the third task of institutional development is to create a structure in which there are incentives for government officials to behave honestly.

As noted above, rules that ban "bad behavior" are not incentives, but the active enforcement of those rules can be. Several possibilities for enforcing good behavior exist. For one, since following rules is a type of moral behavior, some Native groups may be able to draw on indigenous traditions for rule enforcement. These tribes may be able to police inappropriate (in this case, investor confidence-eroding) actions with culturally based social sanctions. They may say, for instance, "We Choctaw don't do that kind of thing." A tribal official's desire to avoid ostracism can then be a powerful motivation to toe the line. In other cases, tribes will find it necessary both to write rules against behavior which erodes investor confidence and to design a system of formal checks and balances on government power. The most common type of formal institutional check on the power of politicians is the "third party enforcer," or independent judiciary. Truly independent judiciaries have the capability of censuring politicians and government administrators if their behavior is inappropriate and of enforcing some kind of punishment. Investors can operate with confidence in nations with third-party enforcement because they know judicial safeguards give politicians an incentive to behave.

Notably, Indian governments are ripe for this kind of development. Many tribal constitutions do not yet provide for an independent judiciary. Of the 50-plus tribal constitutions I have studied in my research, only two have any such provisions. Instead, the old Indian Reorganization Act constitutions, under which many tribes still operate, provide for a judiciary controlled by the tribal council and do not specify precise function or form. In practice, this plank has meant that tribal courts operate under sufferance from the council and tribal chairman, and if judges make decisions with which politicians disagree, they are often dismissed. Of course, establishing an independent tribal judiciary may not be easy. Perhaps more so than other kinds of institutional development, establishing a truly neutral and authoritative court threatens tribal politicians who have benefited from the lack of checks and balances. Furthermore, if the birth of such guarantees is a difficult one, the reputation (and perhaps even personal safety) of those tapped to be its first judges may be put in danger. Given these difficulties, several new and innovative attempts to build independent judiciaries may be important harbingers of change in the prospects for economic development in Indian Country. For example, some Montana tribes use an inter-tribal court of appeals, and the Rosebud Sioux (whose reservation is located in South Dakota) have experimented with both an "Ethics Board" and a tribal supreme court with some non-tribal judges (Cornell & Kalt, 1992; Pommersheim, 1995).

In closing, it is worthwhile to state directly the foundation upon which these recommendations are made: Strong governing institutions are the key mechanisms of sovereignty, and their absence has wide-reaching implications. Lacking legitimate and effective governing institutions, a Native nation is limited in its ability to exercise independent authority over virtually any issue that it faces—whether that issue concerns the nation's land, resources, citizens, or citizens' ideas. Pommersheim (1995) summarizes the breadth of impact of strong institutions by noting, "It is important not to lose sight of the fact that all significant public values are realized through institutions. Better institutions are essential to better lives" (p. 131). The first fundamental principle mentioned in this essay is that economic development in Indian Country must be self-defined and culturally appropriate. The statements above make the second fundamental principle clear—the development of institutional capacity should precede other development efforts. In fact, these principles combine in a fruitful way. Effective institutions promote sovereignty, and it is from the active application of sovereignty that self-determined economic development flows.

Conclusion

Most American Indian tribes are deeply committed to improving the economic welfare of their peoples. But, forward progress is not easy—it must occur against a backdrop of extreme poverty and under political and population pressure. Additionally, attempts at forward progress cannot be desperate responses to these difficult circumstances. Economic development efforts must occur in ways which promote rather than jeopardize Native nations' political and social sovereignty. In other words, development must enhance Native Americans' control over their own affairs and over the quality and nature of reservation life. This essay has highlighted two ingredients of the development process which are fundamental to achieving these ends, principles which help ensure self-determined, sovereign, and successful forward progress. In fact, the argument of this essay is that those ideas are intimately linked.

In particular, the challenge for American Indian economic development is for it to be indigenously defined and institutionally based. As such, development will be a process which takes account of Native assets and goals and incorporates them into specific plans for the future. It will be capable of addressing welfare issues generally, and not income issues alone. Because it concentrates on institutional development, it will not put limited projects ahead of broader policy-making. It will create a political-economic environment which is conducive to investment by tribal members and non-members alike. Furthermore, its political and social institutions will together promote the continued success of these designated welfare-improving investments. Clearly, development that succeeds at combating poverty and its concomitant ills is not narrowly "economic."

Finally, if Native nations achieve this kind of development, their success will be a beacon not only to other indigenous peoples whose colonizers allow a measure of political independence, but to all nations which are restructuring their development outlook. American Indian nations have the potential to show other countries—from Eastern Europe to Asia and beyond—how development can be done "right."

Notes

The author would like to thank Delores Jorgensen for essential research assistance and Sousan Abadian, Manley Begay, Stephen Cornell, and Karl Eschbach for helpful comments on earlier drafts of this essay.

1   The essay uses the terms "American Indian" and "Native American" interchangeably, since little consensus exists among Natives themselves as to appropriate terminology. Many Natives feel comfortable with the older designation "Indian," although they might feel most comfortable with their own linguistically appropriate appellations, such as "Dine" or "Lakota."

2   "Indian Country" is a phrase used throughout this essay, which refers somewhat loosely to all Indian land recognized as such by the U.S. national government or by individual state governments. This may include reservation land, Alaskan Native villages, other lands held in "trust" for Natives by the U.S. government, and areas not strictly owned by tribes, but over which they have a measure of jurisdiction.

3   Throughout this essay, I have identified Indian land areas by referring to the U.S. state by which they are encompassed, as here, "Pine Ridge, a reservation in South Dakota." However, there is an unfortunate distortion implied by this description—it suggests an authority relationship between tribes and states that does not exist. While tribes and U.S. states have a geographical relationship, they do not have a political relationship.

4   The Dawes Act both directly and indirectly diminished the Native land base and tribes' productive capacity. Direct loss occurred because each eligible tribal member received an allotment of a designated size; thousands of reservation acres were then declared "surplus" and made available for further non-Native settlement. Oftentimes, the "surplus" lands were also the most productive. Indirect losses occurred when tribal members could not meet their immediate needs through farming and were forced to sell their allotted land holdings. Canby (1988) emphasizes these points in his description of the effects of allotment: "The primary effect of the Allotment Act was a precipitous decline in the total amount of Indian-held land, from 138 million acres in 1887 to 48 million in 1934. Of the 48 million acres that remained, some 20 million were desert or semi-desert. Much of the land was lost by sale as tribal surplus; the remainder passed out of the hands of allottees" (p. 21).

5   As Cornell (1988) notes, even the IRA was essentially assimilationist, although at the community, rather than individual, level: The U.S. government's assumption was that, "as Indian tribes voluntarily formed constitutional governments, undertook the development of their own resources, and joined with the federal government in the assault on poverty and ignorance, assimilation would necessarily follow. American economic and political institutions would be reproduced within Indian societies. . . . The tribes, as a political construct, might well survive and, conceivably, at least some of what remained of Native American cultures along with it, but survival would take place within the institutional structures of American society, newly realized in the tribal context" (p. 95).

6   This term originated in Chief Justice John Marshall's opinion in *Cherokee Nation v. Georgia* (1831).

7   Individuals who had not identified themselves as Native Americans in previous Census counts, but now do, are said to have "re-identified" with their Native ethnicity.

8   Mathematically, economic growth must occur at the same rate as population growth just to keep per capita incomes constant; this is usually described as the requirement of "having to run just to stay in place." Thus, if individuals are to make real economic gains, overall economic growth must occur at a *higher rate* than population growth. When inflation (price growth) is also present, real progress occurs when the nominal economic growth rate exceeds the sum of the population growth and inflation rates.

9   Historically, all of these states have had large Native populations.

10   The fact that the Self-Determination Act of 1975 allowed tribes to re-assume management control over their own resources appears to have been especially important for successful economic development (Krepps, 1992).

11   The book, *Tribal Assets*, by Robert White (1990) and the paper, "Pathways from Poverty," by Stephen Cornell and Joseph P. Kalt (1990) are two excellent sources on successful Native development efforts; Bordewich (1996) updates the Mississippi Choctaw Tribe's progress.

12   Motels founded by the Economic Development Administration of the U.S. Department of Commerce, the shells of which dot Indian Country, are probably the classic example of this kind of U.S. government development effort. Furthermore, while this essay emphasizes the generic solutions proposed for Indian Country by federal administrators, it should be recognized that they are not the only development proponents with rote responses to individual tribes' needs. For instance, it is worth asking whether or not the rush to develop casinos is an example of self-determined American Indian economic development or the reaction to another generic prescription offered by non-Native (or even Native) developers.

13   The sources for this case description are personal interviews conducted by the author in June 1990 and the teaching case studies, "Nebraska Sioux Lean Beef, Part A" and "Nebraska Sioux Lean Beef, Part B" (Jorgensen, 1990a, 1990b).

14   While many theoretical and empirical papers make this argument, one of the most lucid explanations is made by Douglass North (1990) in *Institutions, Institutional Change, and Economic Performance*.

15   This section follows Cornell and Kalt (1992) quite closely, but updates their conclusions.

16   See, especially, the summary on pages 158–159 and Table 2, regression (b), page 168. Goldsmith (1995) also argues that, in the developing world, property rights augment the connection between democracy and economic growth. This particular argument is probably not applicable to Indian Country, since, as Singer (1991) writes in his discussion of American Indian property rights, "the model of individual ownership is often not an appropriate basis for understanding property rights held by large organizations, such as business corporations, non-profit institutions, public authorities and government entities" (p. 49). In fact, even in the developing world context, secure individual property rights are probably a proxy for an entire institutional structure which secures and protects investment—the elements of which are discussed in the remaining sub-sections of this essay.

17 This term is used for convenience; it is worth acknowledging that many tribes' principal leaders are women and that different tribes used different terms for this office, such as President, Governor, or Chief.

18 There are some cases in which the entire system of government may be deemed illegitimate, making wholesale institutional reform necessary. Because that may be too daunting a task, and one which then serves to stymie all other development efforts, another approach may be possible: It may instead be possible to change, mobilize support for, and therefore legitimize "policy islands" which nurture development. At Pine Ridge, for example, little attempt has been made to change the system of government overall, but some positive developments have occurred at the district level and with the support of district governments, which have both carved authority out of the IRA constitution and built it up from cultural norms.

19 The idea of "match" between culturally inspired norms of appropriateness and formal institutional structures probably applies here, as well; if the choice rules are not congruent with the culturally appropriate loci of decision-making power, citizens will probably not support the ideas which emerge.

20 After this description, it is tempting to think that an institutional structure equipped to make and implement strategic development decisions will be an *unwieldy* institutional structure. Effective institutions should not be so; they should structure decision-making without impeding it and facilitate implementation without slowing it down. In the right cultural context, flat or lean institutional structures may be perfectly capable of these tasks.

21 Whenever it is possible for someone to gain by breaking rules, and there is no enforcement of the rules, those rules will be followed only out of "goodness." In general, the result is that noted in the text—rules are broken in order to serve individual interests. (The best way to think about this problem is as a "prisoners' dilemma"; interested readers should consult a basic game theory text.) In the context of economic development in Indian Country, poor enforcement can lead to misbehavior by both tribal politicians and investors, although this essay stresses the former.

References

Biolsi, T. (1992). *Organizing the Lakota: The political economy of the New Deal on the Pine Ridge and Rosebud Reservations*. Tucson, AZ: University of Arizona Press.

Bordewich, F. M. (1996, March). How to succeed in business: Follow the Choctaws' lead. *Smithsonian, 26*, 71–82.

Brunetti, A. (1995). *Perceived political instability and economic growth: Development and cross-country tests of a new set of political indicators*. Unpublished manuscript, Department of Economics, Harvard University.

Canby, W. C. (1988). *American Indian law in a nutshell*. St. Paul, MN: West.

Cherokee Nation v. State of Georgia, 5 Pet. 1 (U.S. Sup. Ct. 1831).

Cornell, S. (1988). *Return of the Native: American Indian political resurgence*. New York: Oxford University Press.

Cornell, S., & Kalt, J. P. (1990). Pathways from poverty: Economic development and institution-building on American Indian Reservations. *American Indian Culture and Research Journal 14*, 89–125.

Cornell, S., & Kalt, J. P. (1991). *Where's the glue? Institutional bases of American Indian economic development* (Harvard Project on American Indian Economic Development Rep. No. 91–1). Cambridge, MA: JFK School of Government.

Cornell, S., & Kalt, J. P. (1992). Reloading the dice: Improving the chances for economic development on American Indian reservations. In S. Cornell & J. P. Kalt (Eds.), *What can tribes do? Strategies and institutions in American Indian economic development* (pp. 1–59). Berkeley: University of California Press.

Cornell, S., & Kalt, J. P. (1995). Where does economic development really come from? Constitutional rule among the contemporary Sioux and Apache. *Economic Inquiry, 33*, 402–426.

Debo, A. (1974). *A history of the Indians of the United States*. Norman, OK: University of Oklahoma Press.

Deloria, V., & Lytle, C. (1984). *The nations within: The past and future of American Indian sovereignty*. New York: Pantheon Books.

Eschbach, K. (1993). Changing identification among American Indians and Alaska Natives. *Demography, 30*, 635–652.

Eschbach, K. (1995). The enduring and vanishing American Indian: American Indian population growth and intermarriage in 1990. *Ethnic and Racial Studies, 18,* 89–108.

General Allotment Act of 1887, 24 Stat. 388.

Giago, T. (1994, February 20). Like the Constitution, old treaties haven't lost validity. *Sioux Falls Argus Leader,* p. A9.

Goldsmith, A. A. (1995). Democracy, property rights, and economic growth. *Journal of Development Studies, 32,* 157–174.

Grindle, M. S. (1996). *The good government imperative: Human resources, organization, and institutions.* Unpublished manuscript, Harvard Institute of International Development, Harvard University.

Harris, D. (1994). The 1990 census count of American Indians: What do the numbers really mean? *Social Science Quarterly, 75,* 580–593.

Indian Gaming Regulatory Act of 1988, 25 U.S.C.G. §2710.

Indian Health Service, U.S. Department of Health and Human Services. (1994). *Trends in Indian health: 1994.* Washington, DC: Government Printing Office.

Indian Reorganization Act of 1934, 25 U.S.C.G. §461.

Indian Self-Determination and Education Act of 1975, 25 U.S.C.G. §450.

Johnson, D. W. (1887). *A study of the twenty-four poorest counties in the continental U.S. in 1986.* New York: United Methodist Church.

Jorgensen, M. (1990a). *Nebraska Sioux lean beef: Part a.* (Harvard Project on American Indian Economic Development Teaching Case C–2). Cambridge, MA: JFK School of Government.

Jorgensen, M. (1990b). *Nebraska Sioux lean beef: Part b.* (Harvard Project on American Indian Economic Development Teaching Case C 3). Cambridge, MA: JFK School of Government.

Jorgensen, M. (Rapporteur). (1995). *Linking education and research for self-determined Native American development: What can be done?* (Harvard Project on American Indian Economic Development Rep. No. 95–2). Cambridge, MA: JFK School of Government.

Jorgensen, M. (1996). *The constitution of good government.* Unpublished manuscript, JFK School of Government, Harvard University.

Krepps, M. (1992). Can tribes manage their own resources? A study of American Indian forestry and the 638 program. In S. Cornell & J. P. Kalt (Eds.), *What can tribes do? Strategies and institutions in American*

Indian economic development (pp. 179–203). Berkeley: University of California Press.

Lockhart, G. (1993, April 26). Gambling is not Indians' future. *Sioux Falls Argus Leader*, p. A8.

Milner, C. A. (1982). *With good intentions: Quaker work among the Pawnees, Otos, and Omahas in the 1870s*. Lincoln: University of Nebraska Press.

North, D. (1990). *Institutions, institutional change, and economic performance*. Cambridge, UK: Cambridge University Press.

Pommersheim, F. (1995). *Braid of feathers*. Berkeley: University of California Press.

Seminole Tribe of Florida v. Florida, decided March 17, 1996 (U.S. Sup. Ct. 1996).

Singer, J. W. (1991). Sovereignty and property. *Northwestern University Law Review, 86*, 1–56.

U.S. Bureau of the Census, Department of Commerce. (1986). *1980 census of the population: Vol. 2. Subject reports: American Indians, Eskimos and Aleuts on identified reservations and in the historic areas of Oklahoma*. Washington, DC: Government Printing Office.

U.S. Bureau of the Census, Department of Commerce. (1992). *1990 census of the population, social, economic and housing characteristics: U.S. summary*. Washington, DC: Government Printing Office.

U.S. Bureau of the Census, Department of Commerce. (1993). *1990 census of the population, social and economic characteristics: American Indian and Alaska Native areas*. Washington, DC: Government Printing Office.

U.S. Bureau of Indian Affairs, Department of the Interior. (1925). *Superintendents' annual narrative and statistical report: Pine Ridge*. Microfilm Publication No. 1011, National Archives, Roll 106.

White, R. H. (1990). *Tribal assets: The rebirth of Native America*. New York: Henry Holt.

8

American Indians and Gambling: Economic and Social Impacts

Wayne J. Stein

Introduction

Many American Indian nations have discovered for themselves a new economic tool which has been both a blessing and a burden: tribally controlled gaming. Put more bluntly, for economic success, they have tapped into that most American of urges, gambling. Has this been a good choice—economically, legally, or culturally—on the part of American Indians? It is still too early to come to a decisive conclusion about the total or partial success or the impacts on Native people of tribally controlled gaming.

Too often the arguments about the positive or negative effects of tribally controlled gaming ventures on Indian communities or on nearby non-Indian communities are based on mere anecdotal information rather than on solidly researched fact. One of the sources for this essay is a survey, completed in June of 1995 (Stein, 1995), which investigated the positive and negative impacts of tribal gaming on tribal education, housing, and some social/welfare programs. The study revealed much useful information. The survey was sent across the lower 48 states and was answered by 25 American Indian nations and tribes, representing all the major regions of the country. The respondents included the tribes with the largest gaming facilities, as well as several of the newest and smallest gaming operations. The surveys were answered by individuals in a wide range of positions serving their respective tribes, e.g., tribal chairpersons, education directors, attorneys, gaming commissioners, and economic planners.

This essay will examine some fundamental issues of Indian gaming in an effort to bring clarity to the reader. Questions to be answered include: What are the roots of gaming in the United States and among Indian peoples? Has it been a wise move—economically, legally, and culturally—to implement gaming on Indian reservations? What are some of the conflicts now being experienced by Indian nations because of their use of gaming as an economic tool? Finally, what are some of the impacts of Indian gaming on American Indians themselves?

Historic Traditions

The United States has an interesting and colorful historical tradition of gambling, dating back to the founding of its first colonies. Even before European contact, the Native peoples of North America also had developed vital social traditions of recreation and play which included gambling. These two streams have come together in the past decade to create a gaming industry that has swept the nation and many of its American Indian citizens into a cauldron of controversy and opportunity.

During the colonization of North America, enterprising English entrepreneurs used lotteries held in England to raise the necessary capital to build colonies in North America. In fact, Virginia's colonists and their backers looked to a lottery held in England to raise most of the funds they needed to settle the Chesapeake. Lotteries were widely used to finance many public works projects carried out by the early colonial and American governments. Benjamin Franklin even organized a lottery in 1748 to finance the defense of Philadelphia during the so-called French and Indian wars, while the fledgling government of the United States used a lottery in 1777 to pay many of its revolutionary war debts (Jaeger, 1994). By 1831, lotteries were being sponsored by eight states, and wagers exceeded $66 million, five times the then current national budget. The lotteries organized by the state governments of the early Republic were not considered gaming at all, but rather a form of voluntary tax collection (Deloitte & Touche, 1994).

Gaming has flourished and waned during several periods since the founding of the United States in 1776. In particular, it was prevalent during the colonial/pre-Civil War, post-Civil War, and early twentieth-century eras, as well as the period inaugurated with the New Hampshire lottery in 1964. The fate of gaming has been tied to the periodic outcries of citizenry outraged by moral conditions and the mis-adventures of gaming officials. Americans continue to struggle with the dual personality of a mainstream culture which combines strict moral conduct in the tradition of the Judeo-Christian religions and the attitude that "anything goes" in a young, exuberant nation on the rise. Nowhere is this conflict more evident than in our society's relationship with gambling.

By 1931, after one of the periodic shut-downs of gambling in the United States, Nevada remained the only state which offered legalized gaming. In 1964, however, New Hampshire legalized its lottery, ushering in a new "boomer" era of state-sponsored gambling. Today forty-eight of the fifty states, plus the District of Columbia, provide formal opportunities for some form of gaming. Hawaii and Utah are the sole exceptions (Deloitte & Touche, 1994).

Native traditions and historical records tell us that the attitudes of the various American Indian cultures toward gaming have been more supportive—and more consistent. Native gaming traditions developed well before contact with Europeans, and early records describe these traditions for every region of the country and within almost every nation of Native people. Gaming was an accepted part of the social life of American Indian nations, with many Native societies setting aside specific times of the year when important celebrations of life included gambling. By 1907, Steward Culin found dice-like games among 130 tribes, and 81 Native peoples played some form of the "button game," better known among American Indians as the "stick game" or "hand game." These games varied from nation to nation, but all focused on chance and wagering. Tribal members would gather around the players on each team and wager on the outcome. Other games of chance centered around horse-racing, archery, and other athletic contests (Lowie, 1954).

The Native nations of the eastern and southeastern United States traditionally featured a sport known as "the ball game"—what we know today as lacrosse—which reaches far back in time. Played throughout the summer and into the fall months, "the ball game" integrated fundamental social, political, and ceremonial elements. Each nation, as well as its villages and towns, had its own team. The rules might vary from nation to nation, but the one common denominator was the furiously competitive nature of "the ball game." Warriors played for honors, pride, and the pure joy of playing. An important element that enabled the audience to participate indirectly was the intense wagering surrounding the outcome of each game. Individuals as well as whole towns wagered farm produce, craft goods, and other valuables, betting that their team would win the contest (Hudson, 1976).

It comes as no surprise to American Indians, then, that gambling could be and is big business in the United States today, for most tribes have traditionally viewed gaming with great interest and seriousness. What is surprising to many American Indians is the ignorance of the shared history of gaming in the United States demonstrated by their fellow non-Indian citizens. Today, taking advantage of their special legal treaty relationship with the federal government, many Native nations are once again gaming, but now as part of a broad economic strategy to improve the conditions in which their people live on their homelands. These efforts, however, have a price—one that has sparked controversy among tribal members within Native nations, and among tribes, their non-Indian neighbors, and the state governments which seek to dominate them.

Gaming in Indian Country: A High Stakes Controversy

The tragic events of 1890 marked the end of a way of life for the original peoples of the United States, now known collectively as American Indians. Beginning on the Atlantic coast during the fifteenth century and ending on the Great Plains and in the Southwest in the late nineteenth century, nation after nation of American Indians experienced the disintegration of their cultures and the accompanying destruction of their economic systems. A land-hungry United States systematically destroyed the economic foundations of each nation, whether farming, fishing, or hunting, as white settlers, ranchers, and railroaders plundered and confiscated the land and natural resources supporting a once-vital and established way of life. Most American Indians were forced onto isolated, hard-scrabble reservations—which offered little chance to refashion viable economic strategies capable of replacing those destroyed by their non-Indian conquerors. Even so, these survivors were fortunate by comparison. Vicious frontier wars wiped out many nations, while others were simply shunted aside and left to fare as well as they could in a country which preferred to forget them.

The years between 1890 and 1970 proved to be difficult in the extreme for American Indian peoples. Most tribes—relegated to reservations virtually devoid of resources—faced the daunting prospect of fashioning economic strategies marked by the need to simply make a living of some sort to support families and communities. The tribes confronted, as well, the efforts of non-Indian institutions, both organized and informal, to suppress their cultures, languages, and religions. The lasting legacy of those decades still haunts Indian peoples in the poverty and despair which can be found on many American Indian reservations. The legacy of economic deprivation, in particular, manifests itself in the 1990 U.S. Census Bureau report (U.S. Bureau of the Census, 1991), which identifies eight of the poorest counties in the United States as American Indian reservations.

Although the decades between 1890 and 1970 were difficult for American Indians, events occurred within the United States and the world which allowed Indian peoples to begin regaining and repairing their shattered world. The passage of the Indian Reorganization Act of 1934 allowed Native nations to formalize their governmental structures. Franklin D. Roosevelt's administration (1933–1945) shifted federal policy from a strategy of forced assimilation to one of limited accommodation. The New Deal experiments of the Depression Era introduced many self-help programs to Indian Country. World War II brought Indians onto the world scene as servicemen and women. The post-war civil rights movement sensitized the American public to the needs of minority peoples in the United States.

Few white Americans understand the unique relationship that governs affairs between American Indian peoples and the federal and state governments of the United States. Almost all of the federally recognized tribes of the United States have formal, congressionally ratified treaties with the federal government. In addition, American Indian nations are specifically mentioned in the U.S. Constitution as answerable in principle only to the federal government. State governments must treat these federally recognized nations of American Indians as fellow semi-sovereign political entities. American Indians are the only people in the citizenry of the United States to have this special political status guaranteed through treaty rights. Once this fact is grasped, it is much easier to understand the idea that American Indian nations can stand against states and develop their own legal and economic systems. A government-to-government relationship does exist today between American Indian tribal governments and the United States. The relationship is constantly being redefined by Congress, the Supreme Court, and challenged by state governments. These re-definitions do not change the underlying fact, however, that the government-to-government relationship is still very much in existence. American Indian tribal government sovereignty is a vital and central issue in examining the genesis of Indian gaming and its subsequent tremendous growth in this past decade (Wilmer, 1994).

All of these issues were brought together for American Indian nations in 1970 in the famous "self-determination speech" of then-president Richard M. Nixon. In this speech, Nixon declared that the century-old policy of constant federal and state intrusion in Indians' lives and institutions would come to an end. He further stated that Indian nations had the right to determine their own futures. Many Native people took this message to mean that they could seek out and develop their own economic destinies. It was not long before one aspect of this economic development appeared on an Indian reservation in Maine: bingo!

In 1976, the Penobscot of Maine were among the first American Indian nations to institute gaming as an economic tool to improve the lives of their people. Like many tribal governments since, the Penobscot understood that the transfer payments they and other American Indian nations receive from the federal government (e.g., program subsidies and individual welfare payments) were not working to lift their people out of the grinding poverty and unemployment in which they had been stuck for decades. If their communities were ever going to grow and prosper economically, they had to find a source of revenue other than federal transfer payments. The Penobscot instituted modest bingo games, held on Sundays only, with substantial prizes of up to $5,000 a pot for the first several years. In 1980, however, the Penobscot agreed to renounce their status as a sovereign nation, and to live within the laws of the state of Maine. This decision cost them their legal right to set the rules and prize limits of their bingo games. The state quickly forced the tribe to limit the size of their prizes to $200 a pot, thus effectively reducing the appeal of their games ("Indian War Cry," 1984, p. 58). This action was a warning to other American Indian nations interested in gaming as a source of economic development: state governments could not be trusted not to interfere with American Indian rights to implement their strategies for economic independence.

A similar example of state interference threatened the economic development efforts of the Seminole in Florida. In 1979, the Seminole opened their own bingo operation; within five short years they had a $4.2 million business operating on their reservation. James Billie, the tribal chairman of the Seminole, stated, "We used to make trinkets, but we really didn't have the marketing skills to make a go of that" ("Indian War Cry," 1984, p. 58). In response, Florida state officials quickly tried to impose criminal and civil jurisdiction over the Seminole by attempting to close down their bingo operations. The Seminole fought back by taking the case to the higher authority of the U.S. Supreme Court. In the subsequent legal battle—won by the Seminole—the Court found that a state could prohibit gambling within its boundaries only if that form of gambling was against the laws of the state for all of its citizens. In addition, the Court made two other equally important declarations: First, states may have some criminal and civil jurisdiction on Indian reservations, but they do not have regulatory powers—only tribal governments have those powers. Second, if a state permits a form of gaming, such as bingo, in any form, then American Indian nations within that state's boundaries have the right to organize and manage their own gaming ventures as they see fit within the legal parameters pertaining to that state (Wilmer, 1994). This ruling is the cornerstone for the explosion of tribally controlled bingo operations across the United States that American Indian nations are now using as an economic tool to improve the lives of their people.

A second U.S. Supreme Court case in 1987, *California v. Cabazon Band of Indians*, opened the doors for casino-style gaming on Indian reservations. In this landmark 1987 case, the Court guaranteed American Indian nations the right to operate any form of gaming already permitted within the states in which they reside. State officials in California, citing their concern in preventing organized crime from taking advantage of tribal governments in the fledgling Indian gaming industry, had attempted to use a 1953 federal law known as PL-280, which granted six states some degree of criminal jurisdiction over reservations within their boundaries, to stifle the growth of Indian gaming on California reservations (Wilmer, 1994). Because there was no evidence that organized crime was actively making inroads in Indian gaming, the argument was disregarded by the Supreme Court. The successes of the Seminole and Cabazon nations in federal court cases had two important additional consequences. First, the legal victories opened a boom in Indian gaming as other American Indian nations launched their own bingo and casino-style operations. Second, state officials, non-Indian gaming businessmen, and some members of Congress began a campaign to pass congressional legislation that would kill, or at least handicap, the growth of Indian gaming. Viewing gaming by American Indian nations as a threat to their narrow self-interests, rather than as a viable economic strategy for American Indian economic development, these forces preferred to squelch it.

After much contention and political jockeying in Washington, in 1988 Congress passed the law which signalled defeat for the anti-Indian forces. The Indian Gaming Regulatory Act of 1988 (IGRA), signed by President Ronald Reagan, had three stated purposes: to provide a statutory base for Indian gaming so that tribes could enjoy the benefits of economic development, self-sufficiency, and strong tribal government made possible by revenues generated from gaming enterprises; to provide protection from unlawful outside forces so as to ensure that tribes would be the principal beneficiaries of gaming revenues, and that fairness would prevail for both operators and players, and to establish a national Indian gaming commission with federal regulatory authority which would set standards to answer congressional concerns about Indian gaming (Wilmer, 1994).

The Indian Gaming Regulatory Act also divided Indian gaming into three classes or areas of activity. The law defines Class I as "social games solely for prizes of minimal value or traditional forms of Indian gaming engaged in by individuals as part of, or in connection with, tribal ceremonies or celebrations." Significantly, this classification places authority for Indian gaming solely within the jurisdiction of tribal governments and requires no input from state officials.

Class II games are gambling activities explicitly authorized by state law or not explicitly prohibited by state law and are played in conformity with state law. These types of gambling include all forms of bingo and card games; they exclude baccarat, black jack, and the highly profitable slot machines. Again, Congress allows state governments little say in this class of gaming; regulation rests with tribal governments.

Class III gaming activities carry a host of complicated requirements. These games are legal only with passage of specific tribal ordinances, if the pertinent state permits such gaming, and specific tribal-state compacts allow it. This classification is known as casino gaming, and it is at the heart of most of the current gaming controversies between American Indian nations and state governments (National Indian Policy Center, 1993).

Class III gaming, in effect, requires American Indian nations to negotiate with state governments. Currently, such efforts to craft tribal-state compacts have had mixed results across the country. Several states have recognized the potential for great economic growth from reservation-based casino gaming, and have negotiated compacts to that end. Other states have stubbornly resisted any gaming ventures proposed by the American Indian nations within their state boundaries, and they have defied the IGRA's requirements for good faith negotiations between states and tribes when a compact is in question. The states that have defied the IGRA requirements have made their Tenth and Eleventh Amendment rights the basis of their arguments to keep the federal government and Indian nations from forcing them into negotiated gaming compacts.

The Tenth Amendment to the U.S. Constitution was designed to protect states from the awesome power of a large national government. As the amendment asserts, powers not specifically delegated to the federal government by the Constitution are reserved to state governments. Thus, the federal government cannot require states to do anything not specifically described in the Constitution. The Eleventh Amendment guarantees to state governments sovereign immunity from lawsuits brought by any individual or entity unless this immunity is explicitly removed by federal legislation (Deloitte & Touche, 1994). As clear as these principles appear, their interpretation by federal judges has been confused. A number of conflicting federal court rulings are now winding their way through the federal court system to final resolution in the Supreme Court. In different regions of the country, individual federal courts have sometimes found in favor of state governments, and at other times in favor of the American Indian nations suing the state governments to force them to negotiate gaming compacts.

There are two possible outcomes to these conflicts. One is that the Supreme Court will agree to hear all the cases at once and to rule on the states' use of the Tenth and Eleventh Amendments to protect themselves from IGRA. The other possibility is that, even before the Supreme Court hears the cases, Congress will pass amendments to IGRA which will clear up the disputed language in the Act. No matter how these conflicts are settled between American Indian nations and those state governments fighting the growth of Indian gaming, the outcome will have a profound effect on everyone involved in Indian gaming.

As American Indian leaders, scholars, tribal members, and supporters anxiously await the outcome of this crucial legal struggle, their underlying ambivalence about gaming as a strategy for economic development has surfaced. Many have expressed concerns. Perhaps their greatest fear lies in their ambivalent feelings over the practice of Indian gaming. Many fear that gaming, with all of its attendant baggage, will further erode the grip American Indian nations have on their retained sovereign treaty rights. Many argue that the passage of the Indian Gaming Regulatory Act was a major blow to American Indian governmental sovereignty because the Act allows state governments a say in what should be strictly a tribal government decision; that is, whether a tribe should become involved in gambling. In the expedient quest for economic development, the skeptics complain, gaming's supporters have been too willing to compromise a far more important principle—the political independence carried in the critical sphere of tribal authority. Critics of the IGRA's political dimensions are concerned that states might flex their legislative and judicial muscle over a tribe negotiating for a Class III gaming compact. Significantly, this interference would weaken tribal sovereignty in the view of American Indians opposed to gaming as an economic tool.

Critics point out the prospect of other negative consequences of Indian gaming. Some fear that criminals who follow gaming will gain entrance into Native communities, bringing the prostitution and drugs that often accompany this activity. Others are concerned that the divisions between pro-gaming and anti-gaming factions within a community will erode tribal unity. These critics point to several cases in which such divisions have even become violent, and tribes have been caught in a whirlwind of controversy. Whether these divisions arise from traditional cultural values or acquired Christian moral values, they are destructive to the often fragile social environments of American Indian reservations (Thompson & Dever, 1994b).

Conversely, supporters of American Indian use of gaming as an economic tool to strengthen tribal sovereignty point to the potential for some distinctly positive outcomes. The most obvious benefit lies in the fact that "money talks" in the contemporary world. Wealth equals power, especially the power to invest in the ways specific groups may want their world to operate. In this frame of reference, money equals sovereignty, whether in the American Indian world or the dominant Euro-American society in which Indians live in the United States.

Gaming, as its supporters contend, can bring the revenues that would enable an American Indian nation to build a strong, independent economic base. Organized gaming is a major job-producer in any community. It has put thousands of Indian and non-Indian people to work in American Indian communities and surrounding non-Indian communities. Furthermore, according to this argument, wisely used, gaming's own revenues will provide the foundation to gradually lead Native nations away from dependence on a single revenue-generating institution to a fully diversified economic structure (Thompson & Dever, 1994a).

Does a clear answer emerge from this debate? The issue finally comes down to each American Indian nation deciding for itself whether the potential economic benefits outweigh the challenges to tribal sovereignty that gaming poses. Even so, the historical consequences will continue to affect all American Indian people, regardless of their decisions. Why should this be? Even if a tribe should decide not to participate in gaming as an economic development strategy, the issues of tribal sovereignty remain in the hands of Congress because of the controversy raised by tribes that have chosen to become involved in gaming since 1980. Unless many states opposed to Indian gaming retreat from their position or American Indian nations presently operating gaming enterprises close them down—and either scenario is unlikely—the debate over tribal sovereignty will continue into the next century.

American Indian Gaming: What's the Big Deal?

The impact of the gaming industry in the United States is of major importance to the overall economic well-being of the country. From modest roots as small bingo games held on Sundays through the boom which began in the 1960s, the gaming industry had become a $330 billion economic phenomenon by 1992 (Deloitte & Touche, 1994). The industry realizes an average 9% return on the wagers placed by bettors in all forms of gambling. Gamblers lose the highest percentage of their wagers—47%—on the many lotteries currently operated by state governments. The lowest return on gaming wagers—a 2.2% rate—is realized by casino tables. When it is prorated, gambling realizes about $30 billion in revenue (Worsnop, 1994). From these revenues, the gaming industry extracts its operational capital and profits.

Even more impressive is the conventional economic wisdom of gaming—every dollar earned generally turns over eleven times in the community in which it is generated, through wages spent and earned as it makes its way through the community. It is no wonder that American Indian leaders recognize the potential of gaming as an economic tool to boost their poverty-stricken communities into stability and prosperity. In defense of gaming as an economic strategy, many American Indian leaders are fond of quoting President Reagan, who, during the years of his administration (1981–1989), told them to "pull themselves up by their bootstraps." In other words, Native leaders point to tribally controlled gaming as their "new boots." In the same vein, Indian leaders recall the phrase often attributed to Leonard Prescott, former chairman and chief executive of Little Six, Inc., of Prior Lake, Minnesota, the second-largest Native-owned casino. Prescott is said to have described Indian gaming as the "new buffalo" of Indian Country (Prescott, 1992). The significance of the "new buffalo" becomes clearer when we recall that the buffalo was a sacred animal to the Plains Indian peoples who once hunted its vast herds as a way of life. In Plains culture, the Creator provided the buffalo as a source of life and livelihood, so that the people of the Earth could prosper. Native people used virtually every part of the buffalo from the tips of its horns to its hooves. To extend the metaphor to gaming, many Indian leaders today see gaming as offering similar potential to better the economic situation in which American Indians find themselves.

The economic phenomenon of Indian gaming—earning annual revenues of $2.6 billion in 1993—has had a profound impact on Native American communities and their neighbors (Deloitte & Touche, 1994). Whether planned or happenstance, these results have altered economic and social life in those American Indian communities in which gaming has been instituted. Of wider significance are the influences Indian gaming has had on neighboring non-Indian communities surrounding the gaming Indian nations. These influences also have reshaped the political and legal assumptions of other, non-gaming American Indian nations.

In assessing the effects of gaming on contemporary American Indian ways of life, we should keep in mind that gaming nations have experienced a wide spectrum of economic success. A dozen or so Native nations, such as the Mashantucket Pequot, the Shakopee Mdewakanton Dakota, the Oneida of Wisconsin, and the Sycuan Mission Indians, have realized great economic success through gaming, as well as through their own hard work, perseverance, and luck of geographical location. However, the majority of the two hundred American Indian nations involved in gaming are realizing more modest success. For these groups, the principal factor in more moderate economic gains has been their more remote locations from large centers of population. Here again, federal government policy crafted during the nineteenth century plays a role. Washington policymakers placed most reservations (federal trust homelands) in isolated locations in an attempt to reduce friction between American Indians and Euro-American settlers. A completely different attitude can be identified in American Indian nations such as the Navajo. The largest of the Indian nations, the Navajo have rejected gaming as an economic development tool for cultural and religious reasons, and other Indian peoples have followed their lead. From these examples, we can see the need to use discretion in examining the effects of Indian gaming to avoid gross and inaccurate generalizations. Such discretion becomes particularly important when discussing gaming's impacts for such purposes as developing federal policy or assessing general educational gains.

The economic success of Indian gaming has brought both tangible and intangible results. An examination of the positive and concrete economic, social welfare, and educational benefits reveals why many American Indian leaders are so enthusiastic about continuing to ride this economic wave to its peak.

The arena of education offers a telling example. Gaming revenues have provided greater educational opportunities for members of tribes which have chosen this strategy for economic development. Approximately 10.5% of net gaming revenues are being invested in new higher education scholarships, K-12 facilities, curriculum development for culture and language preservation and enhancement, or as contributions to existing educational institutions. Seventy-five percent of the tribes which responded to a survey I conducted reported some investment of gaming revenue in new or existing tribal education programs or institutions (Stein, 1995). Sixty-four percent of the tribes responding to the Stein survey reported overall positive educational results from gaming revenues.

The tangible results included:

1. More tribal members are able to take advantage of higher education opportunities.
2. The quality of facilities for students has improved.
3. Gaming revenues have supplied additional funding for existing educational programs.

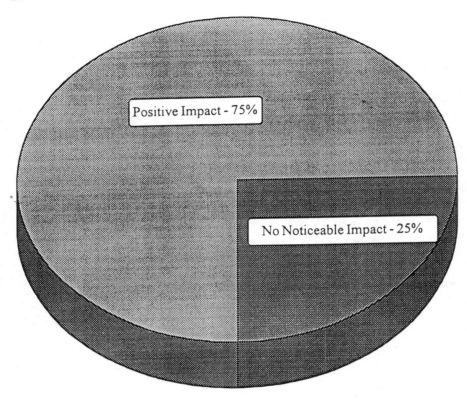

Figure 1. Impact of tribal gaming. Tribes reporting positive impacts have a wide array of programs that were instituted as a result of gaming revenues. Most frequently were reported (60%) new funds for tribal higher education scholarships. Figure 1 and subsequent figures are taken from Stein and Fleming (1995).

As for the intangible results, I found:

1. Students' and parents' self-esteem has increased because of participating in and identifying with an obviously successful tribal venture.

2. Tribal members' self-esteem has improved because of the presence of hope, the promise of jobs, and hence new revenues for the tribe.

Gaming revenue has produced direct economic improvement for those nations involved. It has also greatly increased opportunities for diversifying into new business ventures unrelated to gaming or to expand business enterprises which are in direct support of reservation gaming industries.

Another domain of significant economic success derived from gaming has been the immense growth in new employment opportunities. Most reservations historically have experienced crippling unemployment rates, with some western reservations experiencing as much as 80%. These rates often extend into the non-Native populations surrounding reservations, although never in the same devastating percentages as experienced by the American Indian population. For many gaming nations, these appalling

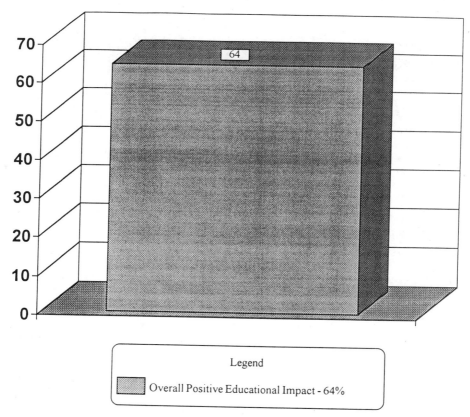

Figure 2. Positive educational impacts. Sixty-four percent of the respondents indicated that gaming had a positive impact, in terms of finances, on education.

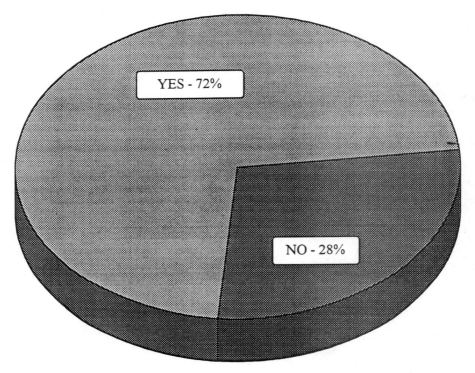

Figure 3. Economic growth in other areas? Seventy-two percent of the respondents reported that gaming had a positive effect on economic growth in other areas, whereas twenty-eight percent reported that it was not the case for their ventures.

unemployment rates, both among tribal members and among surrounding non-Indian populations, have been erased.

One tribe created 11,500 new jobs (employing 200 tribal members); another brought 250 new jobs (40% to tribal members and 60% to non-tribal members).

In a third arena of development, the ability of gaming nations to increase social welfare benefits to tribal members is illustrated by new programs in housing and other services made possible by gaming revenues. Fifty-two percent of the tribes responding to the Stein survey (1995) reported investment of gaming revenue in new services for their respective tribes' children. Sixty percent reported investments in tribal housing or housing improvement programs. Forty-six percent have used gaming revenues to develop or expand nutrition programs for their elderly tribal members.

So strongly do most gaming nations feel about the economic strength and the sense of self-control of economic destiny that gaming enterprises

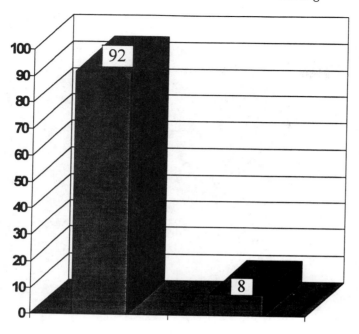

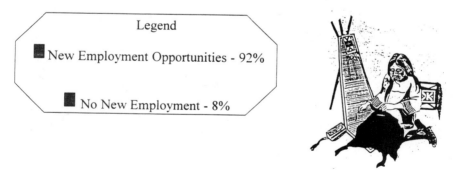

Figure 4. New employment opportunities. Ninety-two percent of the respondents indicated that gaming offered new employment opportunities. Eight percent reported that that was not the case for them.

have given them that they do not hesitate to recommend serious study of the subject for possible entry into gaming ventures to non-gaming tribes.

Eighty-four percent of gaming tribes would recommend to other tribes a serious look at gaming ventures as revenue-generating opportunities.

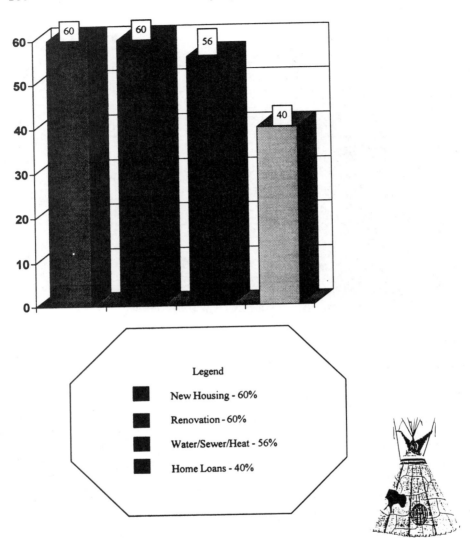

Figure 5. Housing improvements from gaming. Gaming revenues have made it possible to improve the housing situation.

Seventy-six percent of responding tribes stated that gaming has helped them to gain more control of their own futures as a people.

There can be little doubt that tribally controlled gaming has had profound tangible benefits for American Indians in economic gains, in improved social welfare programs, and in enhanced tribal sovereignty.

Percentage of Increase

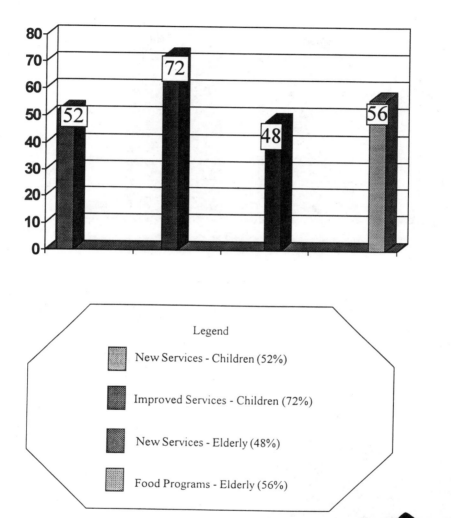

Figure 6. Services to children and the elderly. Tribes with gaming revenues are substantially increasing important services for their youngest and oldest tribal members.

Wayne J. Stein

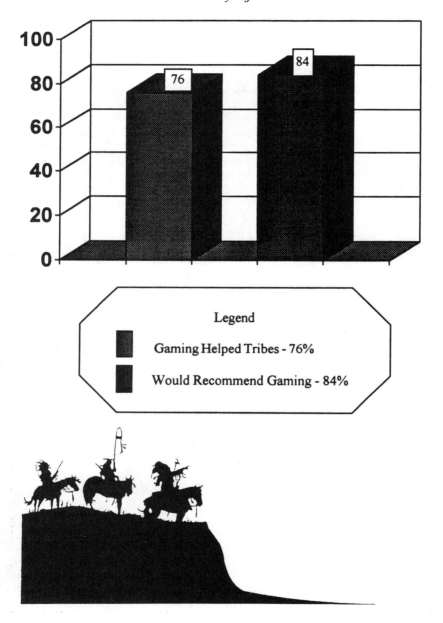

Figure 7. Conclusions. Seventy-six percent of the respondents indicated that gaming was helpful to tribes; eighty-four percent would recommend gaming.

Indian gaming also has had more intangible impacts, which, of course, are harder to measure.

Perhaps the most profound effect of the economic development issues we have discussed can be best understood through the lens of "ethnostress." Gregory Cajete coined this poignant term in 1994 to describe the experience of a culture or society that is under extreme pressure to change radically or is even threatened with extinction. American Indian peoples have suffered ethnostress in one form or another since contact with aggressive European societies. Since the complete political subjugation of Indian nations in the United States in the 1890s, ethnostress has manifested itself in many guises among American Indian peoples and communities. Dysfunctional relationships, divisive behavior, cynicism, distrust of one's own judgment and thinking, and other forms of destructive behavior and attitudes represent some of the symptoms of the ethnostress which has plagued Indian people. These manifestations present real barriers to attaining authenticity, both for individuals and for the communities which they poison (Cajete, 1994).

Advocates of Indian gaming claim that gaming-based economic successes have reduced the debilitating effects of ethnostress. Pride and empowerment seem to be the by-products of successful gaming ventures controlled by American Indian nations. Individual Indian children and youths are beginning to improve their grades and enhance their skills in school, are more willing to challenge misrepresentations they see in curricula and textbooks, and are beginning to carry a sense of pride in their identity as American Indians. When asked about this new sense of empowerment, young Indian people point with pride to their nations' successes in using gaming ventures as an economic tool. The very ability of tribal leaders to successfully run a major business enterprise to their tribes' benefit seems to empower individual tribal members with a sense of success. This empowerment is evident also in adults who, often for the first time in their lives, are earning a good living and providing comfortable lives for their families (Stein, 1995).

Conclusion

For many American Indian nations, gaming has created a "new world" of opportunity; yet, it has carried a price that must be paid. Gaming has brought serious divisions within some tribes. They must struggle to resolve conflicts between traditional cultural forms and modern influences. They face, as well, disagreements over how to handle the new funds made available. Gaming also has increased threats to treaty rights and tribal sovereignty from state governments attempting to negotiate away independence in return for gaming privileges or bringing direct legal challenges in federal courts.

In addition, the success of tribally controlled gaming has further contributed to the specter of white racism, although in a somewhat new and unaccustomed form. A glaring misconception has been promoted in the media, in Congress, and in mainstream non-Indian society, supporting the fiction that all American Indians are becoming rich from Indian-controlled gaming, and doing so at the expense of their non-Indian fellow citizens. As we have seen, the majority of Indian nations and individuals are not realizing riches from gaming, but are living their lives much as they have in the past. Yet, the falsehood has fostered a form of economic racism, and recently it has led to attempts by members of Congress to impose special taxes or responsibilities on Indian nations involved in gaming. This kind of economic discrimination has put American Indians again on the defensive, and has challenged Indian leaders to set the record straight. A representative response can be seen in the statements of Rick Hill, Chairman of the National Indian Gaming Association. Hill has had to remind Congress that American Indian nations are independent entities that do not share gaming revenues across the board with each other (e.g., Hill, 1996). Furthermore, a congressionally imposed revenue-sharing policy could be analogous to expecting New York to share its tax revenues with Hawaii. Hill and other Native leaders have had to fight a second initiative from uninformed Congress people. Some representatives have proposed that Congress reduce federal dollars to tribes in direct proportion to their income from gaming. This plan borders on racist policy. After all, it is not generally suggested that states will have federal dollars reduced in direct proportion to their lottery profits or tax revenues generated from other forms of state-sanctioned gaming.

Troublesome problems and potential for mishap characterize gaming in Indian Country. However, the significant benefits already realized by most gaming tribes and the newfound pride among all Indian people because of the success of tribally controlled gaming seem—so far—to vastly outweigh these concerns. An economic tool such as Indian gaming may come only once to American Indian people, and they do desperately need such a tool. Many American Indians believe they must use this economic tool now, but also that they must keep vigilant to the problems its use can bring. Their fellow citizens and the federal and state governments must also view this economic phenomenon for what it is—a rare opportunity coupled with risks for American Indians—rather than as simply a threat to non-Indian sovereignty or another resource to steal from Indian people. If the non-Indian people of this country attack Indian gaming and destroy it, would that not be just another form of treaty-breaking? Mainstream American society must move past such behavior and treat its Indian citizens with fairness and good will.

References

Cajete, G. (1994). *Look to the mountain*. Durango, CO: Kivaki Press.

California v. Cabazon Band of Mission Indians, 107 S. Ct. 1083 (1987).

Deloitte & Touche [Law firm]. (1994, April). *A historical review of gaming in the United States. A report*. Washington, DC: National Indian Gaming Association.

Hill, R. (1996, January). Past experience guides future efforts. *Indian Gaming Magazine*, 3.

Hudson, C. (1976). *The Southwestern Indians*. Knoxville: University of Tennessee Press.

Indian Gaming Regulatory Act of 1988, Pub. L. No. 100–497, 102 Stat. 2467.

Indian Reorganization Act of 1934, c. 576, 48 Stat. 984.

Indian war cry: Bingo! (1984, January 2). *Time*, 58.

Jaeger, C. (1994, July). Playing in America. *Casino Magazine, 4*, 105–107.

Lowie, R. H. (1954). *Indians of the Plains*. Garden City, NY: McGraw-Hill.

National Indian Policy Center. (1993). *Reservation based gaming: A report for the National Indian Policy Center*. Washington, DC: The George Washington University.

Nixon, R. M. (1970, July 8). The American Indians—Message from the President of the United States (H. Doc. No. 91–363). *Congressional Record, 116* (117), 23131–23136.

Pub. L. No. 83–280, 67 Stat. 588 (1953).

Prescott, L. (1992, July 6). *New white buffalo*. Speech given at the NIGA Conference & Trade Show, Minneapolis, MN.

Seminole Tribe of Florida v. Butterworth, 102 S. Ct. 1717 (1983).

Stein, W. J. (1995, Summer). *American Indian gaming impacts: Survey analysis of Indian gaming*. Bozeman, MT: Center for Native American Studies, Montana State University.

Stein, W. J., & Fleming, W. C. (1995, Summer). *Impact facts on Indian gaming. Fact sheet/report.* Washington, DC: National Indian Gaming Association.

Thompson, W., & Dever, D. R. (1994a, April). A sovereignty check on Indian gaming. *Indian Gaming Magazine,* 5–7.

Thompson, W., & Dever, D. R. (1994b, May). A sovereignty check on Indian gaming: Part II. *Indian Gaming Magazine,* 8–9.

U.S. Bureau of the Census. (1991). *American Indian and Alaska Native areas* (1990–CPH–L–73). Washington, DC: U.S. Government Printing Office.

Wilmer, F. (1994, January). *Indian gaming: Players and stakes. Monograph for the local government center.* Bozeman, MT: Montana State University.

Worsnop, R. L. (1994, March 18). Gambling boom. *The CQ Researcher, 4,* 246.

9

Native American Industry: Basket Weaving among the Wabanaki

Pauleena MacDougall

Every man, as long as he does not violate the laws of justice, is left perfectly free to pursue his own interest his own way, and to bring both his industry and capital into competition with those of any other man or order of men.

—Adam Smith, *An Inquiry into the Nature and Causes of the Wealth of Nations*, 1776

Introduction

Basket making has been an important source of income for Native Americans in the Northeast since the early nineteenth century. However, the tradition fell into decline after World War II and was replaced by other forms of income. Its revival in the 1980s emerged as young people began to ask their elders to teach them the craft. Yet, they soon found themselves facing a crisis. For unknown reasons the primary raw material, the brown ash tree, was disappearing. In response, basket makers from several tribes came together to save dwindling brown ash resources. They also learned to cooperate by combining forces in the marketplace. Today, Wabanaki artists make baskets that are in demand by collectors of Indian art and museums, and thus earn a good price for them.

A Tradition of Cooperation

During the nineteenth century, the peoples of the Wabanaki Confederacy eked out a meager existence making baskets that at first sold for pennies.[1] The Micmac, Maliseet, Passamaquoddy, and Penobscot who made up this loose alliance gradually created a successful basket making industry during the nineteenth century out of necessity. Traditional ways of making a living were undermined as white settlers moved onto their land and stripped it of lumber and wild game. In response, the Wabanaki transformed an existing basket making technology, integrating their traditions of cooperative work with capitalist ideas they learned in the marketplace, such as hiring labor, using division of labor to perform basket making tasks, inventing labor-saving devices, and marketing their products in high demand areas.

Cooperation among Wabanaki was not a new idea. Wabanaki peoples have long spoken related languages (although some languages are now extinct), and continue to live throughout Quebec, Vermont, New Hampshire, Maine, and the Maritime Provinces of Canada. The group includes modern tribes known as Abenaki, Penobscot, Passamaquoddy, Maliseet, and Micmac (see Figure 1).[2] Early in their history, these tribes banded together to fight common enemies. During the French and Indian Wars of the eighteenth century, a Wabanaki confederacy made up of tribes already mentioned, together with Mohawks, allied themselves with the French and successfully fought off the English.[3] However, the common enemy for the tribes in the nineteenth and early twentieth centuries was economic deprivation.

The people of this region traditionally made their living through hunting large and small game, fishing, trapping, and gathering wild foods. Gardening was practiced only in the southern areas of present-day Maine, and people moved their residences according to the season in order to take advantage of the game or fish that were available. For example, in the spring people moved to areas where they could capture migrating fish and collect eggs from waterfowl; during the winter months they might camp where they could capture beaver and deer.

The arrival of Europeans throughout the seventeenth and eighteenth centuries brought new trading partners with novel technologies and exotic goods for both cultures. For example, guns and steel tools from Europe were exchanged for snowshoes and canoes from America. Each culture enjoyed the other's technology as well as the trinkets—European glass beads delighted Native Americans, while wampum and birchbark baskets entranced Europeans. Even so, the relationships that developed during these early contacts set the stage for two centuries of conflict between the Native Americans, the English, and the French. Additionally, English and French forces carried their wars into Wabanaki territory, with both sides seeking Native allies. Caught between these forces, some tribes fought with the French, while others, notably the Penobscot, tried to remain neutral. Still, the results were the same for all. Following the French defeat in 1763, the British flag flew over New England. Settlers from Massachusetts and New Hampshire moved onto the territory of the Wabanaki in great numbers.

The story was the same throughout the 1800s. By this time, settlers had swarmed over Native lands east of the Mississippi, and the Native Americans of this area were forced onto much smaller plots of land "reserved" for their use. The integrity of Native styles of living were a memory. In response, Native Americans learned to adapt by engaging in the emerging industrial economy in various ways. Some worked for wages in factories and

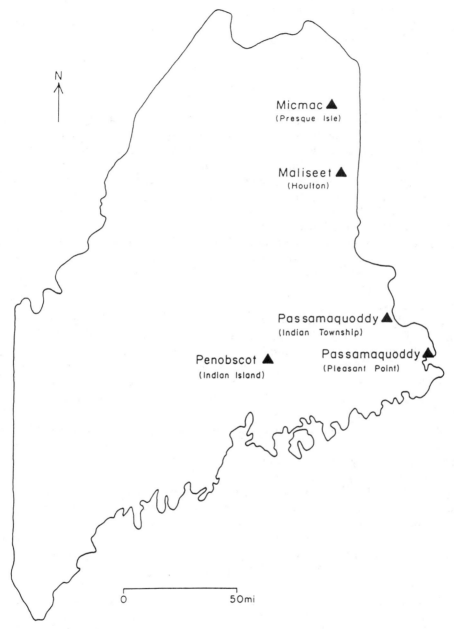

Figure 1. Wabanaki communities located within Maine. Map by Stephen Bicknell.

stores, some farmed the land, and others began to develop arts and crafts into money-making ventures. One item that found great demand in the marketplace was the Indian basket.[4]

Baskets

Archaeologists and amateur "pothunters" have uncovered baskets in ancient cemeteries, mounds, caves, and ruins throughout North and South America, as well as in Europe, Africa, and Asia. They have identified, as well, two techniques that dominate the craft: hand-woven baskets are built on a foundation of warps; coiled baskets are built on a foundation of rods. Evidence of early twining has been found in the western United States in archaeological sites dating 9,700 years ago, while coiled basket materials have been dated to 6,600 years B.P.[5] Woven baskets are made by weaving materials of various kinds, and they take many forms. They may be flat, as in mats or wallets, or slightly concave, such as dishes or sieves, or bowl-shaped, cylindrical or square, conical or jar-shaped. It is in woven basket making that the indigenous peoples of the Northeast, including the Wabanaki, excel.

The earliest baskets were woven freehand without a mold using hand-cut splints of slightly irregular widths. Some scholars have stated that wood-splint baskets were not invented by Native Americans. However, archaeologists excavated fragments of splint baskets at the Marsh and Steel sites in New York dating 1640–60.[6] Such evidence suggests that Native Americans in the Northeast used the technology of splint basket making prior to European contact.

Many different materials have been used throughout the Americas to make baskets. Some baskets are made from the skins of animals, and some are lined with clay. However, most are made from plants of various kinds. The Wabanaki traditionally have preferred wood from the brown ash tree for basic basket weaving material, a resource they used also in the manufacture of canoes and snowshoes.[7] Sweetgrass—a nineteenth-century innovation—and dyes are used to embellish and color the basket.

Colonists made their own baskets for storing food, to hold harvested potatoes and corn, to carry clothing while traveling, and to sift grain and meal. Some kind of basket stored almost all ordinary household and family goods. Square baskets served to separate the curds from the whey in cheese making, and many large baskets were needed for farming. As a result, during the nineteenth century, itinerant basket makers—of both European and Native American extraction—traveled from town to town peddling their crafts. In the Northeast, Wabanaki people first sold their birchbark baskets and other trinkets. Demand for the woven baskets was much greater, however, and the Wabanaki responded by creating many different shapes and sizes of these items for the market. Later, they found a ready market for the famous large woven pack basket and other utility baskets.

Early Adaptations

When Europeans came to North America, the Wabanaki traded the skins and hides they collected from their winter hunts for various goods, such as steel knives, guns and ammunition, pots and pans, and other European manufactured items. After the Revolutionary War, thousands of settlers from Massachusetts and New Hampshire moved into Maine and claimed homesteads on lands previously owned by Wabanaki people. The settlers cleared previously forested land and built farms, put up fences, grew crops, and raised cattle. Settlers spent their winters hunting game and logging in the forests. Soon, many of the resources that the Wabanaki had relied upon, especially wild animals, became scarce. As more and more settlers moved into their territory, the Wabanaki found making a living by hunting and trading furs and skins much more difficult. They often returned from the winter hunt without enough furs to trade for the goods they needed to support their families. Although hunters shared their wealth with all of their extended families, it was increasingly a meager existence. Among the Wabanaki, the Penobscot were the first to lose their territory to settlers and to find it necessary to develop new sources of income, but it was not long before the Passamaquoddy, Maliseet, and Micmac found their own territories and game resources shrinking. As a result, the Wabanaki peoples sought new ways to make a living. One way they found to raise money to purchase food and other supplies was by selling home-made items.

As early as the eighteenth century, Wabanaki women, children, and elderly men were supplementing family income by making crafts to sell to white people. By the middle of the nineteenth century, Wabanaki men took work as guides for scientific expeditions and for sports hunters.[8] Others worked on the river drives or as boat handlers in the lumber industry. Still other men, and almost all of the women, began to develop the cottage industry that would eventually become the mainstay of their livelihood. Basket making was a family enterprise, with established yet flexible roles for men, women, and children. Women played an important leadership role not only in the manufacturing of baskets, but in determining what baskets to make. The women were also responsible for packing and moving family and materials to summer resorts and for hiring help. At the same time, they continued their everyday subsistence activities, including caring for their children, cooking, sewing, and carrying water.

The Wabanaki basket making industry developed out of an existing birchbark utensil making technology. As one early writer observed, the eastern Algonquian peoples impressed Europeans with their ability to transform birchbark into "several sorts of baskets, great and small. Some will

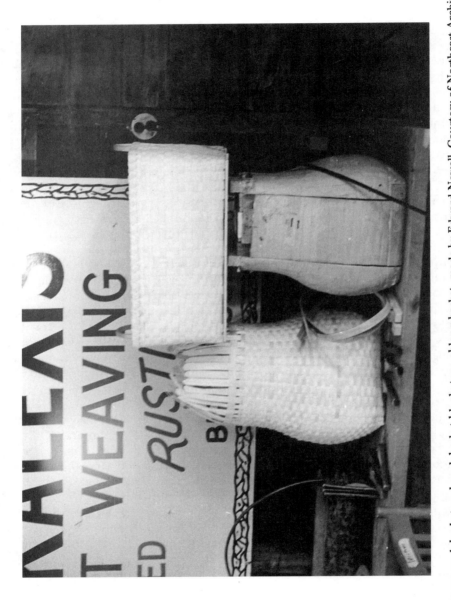

Plate 1. Bottom: pack basket and pack basket block; top: oblong basket, made by Edward Newell. Courtesy of Northeast Archives. Photo 4042. Maine Folklife Center, University of Maine, Orono.

hold four bushels, others more, and so downward to a pint."[9] Yet, by adapting the technological tradition to a capitalist framework, they learned to modify their manufacturing techniques, styles, and marketing practices in response to changes in customer demand. These finely made baskets, the precursors to modern ash tree basketry, were often decorated with carved and painted designs. Building on this tradition, nineteenth-century Wabanaki peddlers found a market for birchbark containers among middle-class Americans who sought baskets as decorative items for their homes. Thus, the Wabanaki began to make baskets that mimicked the size and shape of containers of various kinds. The large cylindrical band basket was a version of the band and hat box and served as a trunk for traveling purposes. Large baskets for carrying personal items in a canoe (pack baskets) and other large baskets for harvesting potatoes and storing materials were manufactured and peddled in the early nineteenth century (see Plate 1).

In time, basket making emerged as an industry that was essential to Wabanaki survival. The exceptional quality of their baskets, combined with limited opportunities elsewhere, enabled the Wabanaki to carve out a niche in the changing economic conditions. Even during economic depressions, when work was nearly non-existent and markets for fancy baskets declined, the continued demand for utilitarian baskets, such as those needed for potato harvesting, provided Wabanaki communities a measure of security.

Adapting Baskets to an Industrialized Society

Over the course of the nineteenth century, contact with the larger marketplace altered the design of baskets, the methods and technologies used to manufacture them, and the marketing strategies used to sell them. One early technological innovation came through the adoption of gauges. Wabanaki artisans traditionally used crooked knives to cut strips of ash to shape their baskets. The knife carved strips that were slightly irregular and made the process quite time-consuming. The introduction of the gauge not only facilitated this painstaking task, but also made it possible to cut strips of ash into even-width pieces (see Plate 2). Its origins are uncertain. One of the northeastern tribes may have invented it. Conversely, the Shakers used a similar tool to make the splints from which they wove their distinctive hats. Whatever its beginnings, by 1850 virtually all Wabanaki artisans were using the gauge. In the earliest examples, the "teeth" of the gauge were made from ordinary clock springs set into the wooden handle and then cut into blades. Later, old razor blades replaced the clock springs. The teeth were held in place with various materials, including brass, wood, copper, or tin sheets laid horizontally across the top of the gauge.[10] Generally, a Wabanaki basket maker owned several gauges of different sizes to make splints of various widths (see Plate 3).

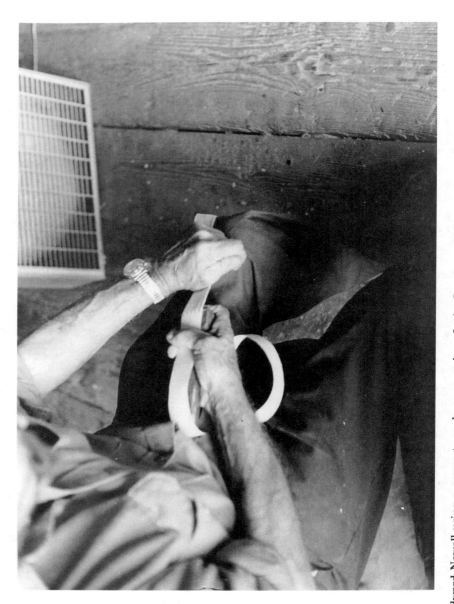

Plate 2. Edward Newell using a gauge to make even strips of ash. Courtesy of Northeast Archives. Photo 4049. Maine Folklife Center, University of Maine, Orono.

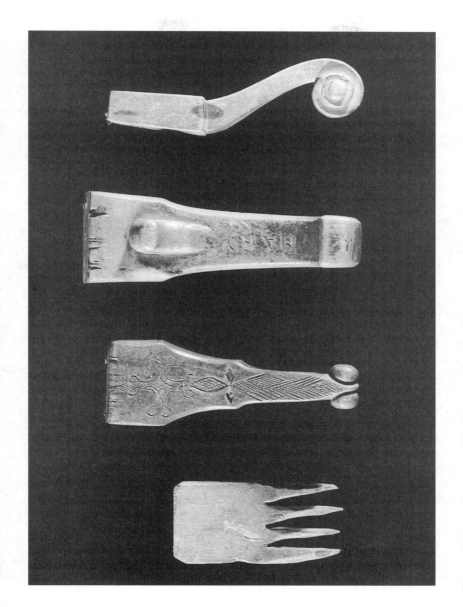

Plate 3. Gauges. Courtesy of the Hudson Museum, University of Maine, Orono. Photo by Stephen Bicknell.

The other significant technological innovation was the use of the form or block. As with the gauge, the origins of basket blocks is open to question. Both Native Americans and Shakers in the Northeast formed their baskets around molds or blocks. Indeed, a comparison suggests a continuing exchange of ideas between these cultures. However, early industrialization undoubtedly influenced these new inventions. As Joan Lester, a student of Northeast material culture, has observed, "In the mid-nineteenth century the entire country was being transformed by a technological revolution. Indian people who worked in the mills and factories may have been inspired by examples of labor saving devices, including molds and cutting tools."[11]

Wabanaki artisans made their blocks either from a single piece of hand-carved wood or from several pieces of wood fitted and nailed together (see Plate 4). Blocks often had handles so that they could be easily pulled out of the basket. The bottom of the mold was used to center the base of a basket. The base was sometimes pinned on as work commenced. Some blocks were composites, held together with a piece of string—necessary because a basket with a small opening required that the block be removed in pieces at the end of the weaving process.

Different shapes of blocks developed as Wabanaki artisans sought to satisfy consumers' ever-changing demand for new basket styles. About 1920, for example, John Lewey invented a block to shape "shoulder pocketbook" baskets and a two-part block to manufacture "shopper" baskets. Lewey used machines to make some of his blocks at the Old Town Canoe Factory, where he worked. His name continued to be associated with this form, and he was called upon to make these forms for other basket makers.[12] The form determined the shape of the basket and its diameter, but the artisan could vary the height of the basket.

In addition to adopting new inventions, Wabanaki basket makers also incorporated one organizational feature from early American industry—a task-based division of labor. The production of baskets continued to be conducted in family groups and in larger, extended clan groups. However, while previously one person would make a whole basket, by mid-century groups of women would work together, some making the bases, some weaving the sides. Older children sometimes were allowed to bind the rims of nearly completed work baskets. Penobscot and Passamaquoddy basket makers in Maine even imported "immigrant" labor, hiring young Maliseet women from Canada for their skilled assistance in filling large orders. Wabanaki artisans did not adopt the changing view of work that was emerging in the factories of Lowell and Lawrence, however. Where factory managers were redefining work as mindless tasks and workers as interchangeable "hands," the Wabanaki concept of work remained vested in traditional meanings of community ritual. Families held basket and braiding parties in which everyone would bring food and talk and laugh and tell stories while

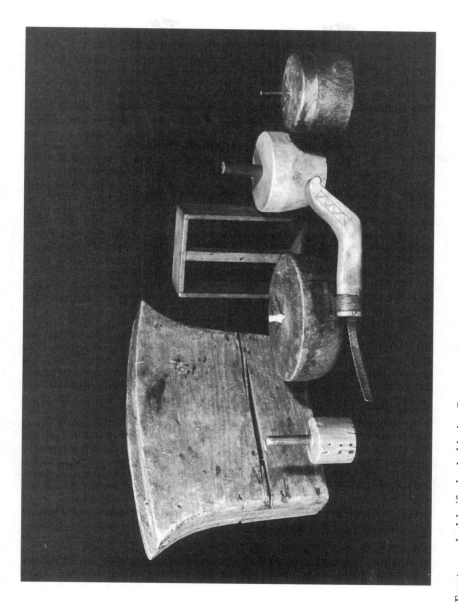

Plate 4. Front: crooked knife; back: blocks. Courtesy of the Hudson Museum, University of Maine, Orono. Photo by Stephen Bicknell.

they braided the sweet grass or made additional baskets when consumer demand increased (see Plate 5).

The development of novel tools and techniques for making baskets grew out of the response to consumers' demands for new styles. Increasing demand was the result of an emerging middle-class culture as industrial capitalism spread throughout the United States after 1815. Especially after 1860, more and more members of this rising middle class—the managers, shopkeepers, salesmen, and clerks of the factories and department stores, railroads and steamships that were transforming the American economy— acquired greater wealth and leisure. Within the blossoming middle-class culture, it was said, "a woman's place is in the home." This "cult of domesticity" or "cult of true womanhood," as historians such as Nancy Cott and Barbara Welter describe it, prescribed that middle-class married women focus their attention on making the home a temple of family virtues.[13] Such homes symbolized both a refuge from the overwhelming, often frightening changes brought by the marketplace revolution and a sign of the family's status in the community. As Americans became infatuated with the Victorian styles made fashionable in nineteenth-century England, then, elaborately adorning the home with an array of knickknacks became a preoccupation for middle-class American women.

In response, Wabanaki artisans devised novel shapes for their baskets, often cleverly copying articles made from remarkably different materials, furnishing them with innovative functions and adorning them with fresh designs of fancy work. Their baskets, for instance, imitated cloth, china, or glass items such as work boxes, glove boxes, napkin rings, scissors' cases, candy dishes, and creamers. Victorian women found these items intriguing perhaps because they were so cleverly and prettily constructed by their "primitive" sisters, as well as because they were very inexpensive. Thus, the representative form of these innovations emerged as the famous nineteenth-century fancy basket.

In developing the fancy basket, Wabanaki basket makers particularly recognized and responded to Victorian America's fondness for elaborately embellished baskets which featured elegant handles, decorative weaves, dyed splints, and sweet grass. Many original and peculiar designs came out of these innovations. In 1860, a new ornamental weave in which a strand of weft was twisted became a hallmark of Penobscot baskets. Later, basket makers learned to delight customer tastes by doubling the twists. (In the Penobscot language, each twist is called *čákiẅis*, or "little wart;" in English, this is "porcupine work.")[14] Additional embellishments were added by braiding the sweet grass.

It appears that all of the northeastern tribes manufactured some of the basic styles of baskets, with slight variations in design. The "flat," a basket that measured from six to thirteen inches in length, and most commonly ten inches, was used as a catchall for sewing tools. The "shopper" featured a

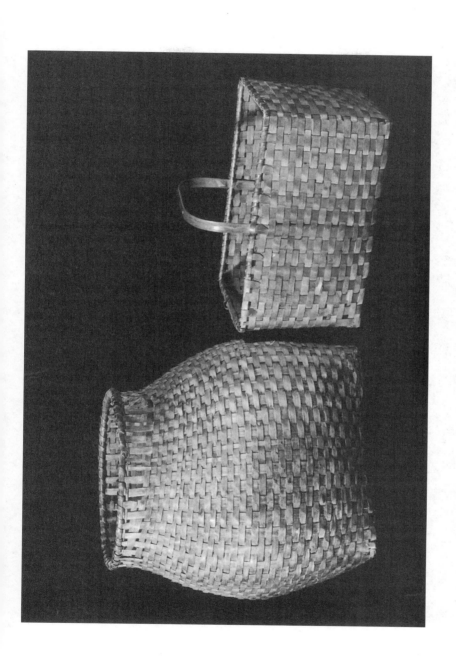

Plate 5. Wastebasket and picnic basket. Courtesy of Bicknell Collection. Photo by Stephen Bicknell.

Plate 6. Left: fancy baskets; right: acorn basket. Author's Collection. Photo by Stephen Bicknell.

satchel design. Small, footed vessels became popular as "jewelry baskets." Covered baskets, some with bases, were made in various sizes and offered practical handles. Open work baskets, a feature of outdoor life, evolved into wastepaper baskets for offices (see Plate 6). By the end of the century, the range of uses had expanded to include popular items such as bookmarks, placemats, button baskets, flat handkerchief baskets, purses with folding tops, pin cushions, napkin rings, and thimble, scissors, and portfolio cases. In addition, Victorian America sought acorn-shaped yarn baskets; fruit or comb baskets; pack baskets; filing baskets and creels; bushel, clothes, hamper and potato baskets, glove, knitting, and needle cases, as well as the basic picnic basket (see Plate 7). Wabanaki men and women also crafted bark and wood model canoes, trays and fans, quill-decorated boxes, bark picture frames, bows and arrows, Indian dolls, model wigwams, snowshoes, sweet grass whisks, model toboggans, and moccasins for the emerging tourist trade.

Adapting Baskets to Emergent Tourist Markets

As we have seen, the spread of industrial capitalism throughout the United States after 1815 laid the foundation for a middle-class culture. Some of the newfound prosperity was channeled into a budding American ritual—the summer vacation. The travelers sought to escape steamy cities by visiting resorts in the more rural areas of New England. They found the coasts and forests of Maine especially appealing. One favorite resort that continues to draw vacationers today is Mount Desert Island. Prominent artists began to visit the resort during the 1840s. Following a hiatus brought by the Civil War, in 1865 the island's hotels enjoyed a great spurt in business. The spurt became a trend, so that by 1887, 17 hotels drew summer guests.[15] Likewise, within the nestling green forests of Maine's northwestern interior, the Rangeley Lake House advertised itself as "The Adirondacks of New England: fine scenery, excellent trout fishing, steamboat excursions, delightful rides, good accommodations, and moderate prices."[16] Hiram Ricker established yet another popular spa at Poland Springs. Capitalizing on his 1844 discovery of the "medicinal water" of the spring, Ricker marketed his first shipment of bottled water in 1859 and exhibited the product at the Colombian Exhibition of the World's Fair in 1893. The publicity clearly worked, as hundreds of guests traveled each year to partake of the "powerful cathartic" waters of Poland Springs, the shining lakes, forests, and hills of Maine, and the 450 rooms and beautifully landscaped lawns of Ricker's hotel.[17]

Summer resorts offered a stable, if seasonal, market for basket sellers. In fact, Indian agents reported good returns on basket sales and other wares until the four-year business depression brought on by the Panic of 1873.

Plate 7. Basket makers from Indian Island, Maine, ca. 1850. Courtesy of Special Collections, Fogler Library, University of Maine, Orono.

For example, Indian Agent George Dillingham reported in 1872, "Many of the tribe have during the fall made improvements in their houses. This they are enabled to do from their savings in the result of their labor and profits in selling baskets and their other wares at the different watering places."[18] Home crafts brought in seasonal revenues large enough to make continued production throughout the winter not only possible, but necessary to fill the large demand of the summer trade. The corresponding demand for materials increased, also. Although families collected their own ash and sweetgrass, at times demand grew so high that they had to purchase materials from other basket makers who had a surplus. Thus, by the end of the century the home-production of baskets and related domestic goods had become the most important source of income for the Wabanaki.

Sagely adjusting to the developing tourism market, Wabanaki families likewise congregated at these "watering places." Setting up camp in the late spring and early summer, they sold souvenirs until vacationers returned home in the fall. They did not limit their travels to Maine, however. For many years, Native basket makers from Maine, New Brunswick, and Quebec traveled to resorts throughout New England during the summer months. Souvenir stands were occupied year after year and generation after generation by the same family on the same spot. By the 1930s, great-grandchildren of the first tourists could find the great-grandchildren of the first resort-based basket makers plying their trade at the same family stands.

Some families became associated with specific sites. Julia (Saul) Newell, for instance, established her family's long-standing summer camp at Rye Beach, New Hampshire.[19] Mary Swasson, wife of Sockbesin Swasson, continued her craft at Narragansett Pier in Rhode Island, "her usual summer rendezvous for the basket trade," until her death there in 1888.[20] Other well-known families concentrated their efforts at Belgrade Lakes and Bailey Island, Maine. The craft work of John Ranco was a feature of Deer Island, Maine, as Mitchell Attean's goods were at Bar Harbor.[21] Tourists who frequented Lock's Mills purchased Native crafts from Ed Newell, a member of the extended Sockalexis family. Settling near Norway, Maine, around 1898, Newell built a camp beside North Pond, where he sold baskets and rustic furniture to passing motorists.[22] At the turn of the century, then, about one hundred Wabanaki people left from each reservation every spring to sell their wares at summer resorts. Others set up stores on their reservations or sold to local retailers.

Native artisans and resorts cooperated in drawing tourists. When the Newell family moved to Poland Springs and built a cabin that they covered with sheets of birch bark, for instance, the resort was happy to have them. Resort managers recognized they were a great draw for tourists. In an article proclaiming "Indian Visitors Arrive," a local paper reported:

The Indians—members of the Penobscot tribe of Old Town, Me.—are here for their annual visit.

We have spoken of Poland Spring as a place of many picturesque touches and of vivid contrast. In a corner of the great office of the Poland Spring House, for example, one often finds a little group of visitors in gray, quaint gowns, presiding over tables on which are baskets woven of poplar-wood fiber, curious Polly-Prim aprons, and many other novelties. They are Shakers from the near-by colony—members of a kindly, little-known religious sect, who believe in doing good.

Follow one of the winding paths, leading past the golf links, past the spring, into one of the sylvan lanes with which Poland Spring abounds, and you find—the Indians! Here, also are tables piled with baskets, but of a type very different from those the Shakers offer. For these are Indian baskets, exquisitely woven—and differing little in workmanship and pattern, probably, from those in the days when America's forests swarmed with red men, and Pocahontas, John Smith and their friends wove romances that poets have immortalized.[23]

The denizens of the "sylvan woods" captivated white visitors from the larger cities, who taught their children the imagery of "the bright, black-eyed little Indian maid from the cabin down the winding trail into the grove."[24] In short, the romance of the "noble savage" had great appeal for the city-dwelling middle class and well-to-do who came to rusticate at Poland Springs and other New England resorts. From the Wabanaki point-of-view, such curiosity was good for the basket business.

Problems of Production

Wabanaki artisans adapted to the economic changes brought by white encroachment and industrialization; they remained, however, on the margins of mainstream society. Consequently, their efforts to survive, in terms of both economic welfare and ethnic integrity, were a constant struggle. One obstacle can be traced, in part, to the seasonal nature of the basket making industry. A great deal of time and work was required to move family and belongings to resort areas each spring. As Indian Agent John H. Stowe reported in 1888, "The preparations for these yearly trips often-times involve the labor of months and no little self-denial."[25] In an oral history interview, an elderly member of the Penobscot tribe recalled living conditions:

They all had big tents. They pitched these big tents. They would have one to live in and the other one would be for the display of their baskets. They made baskets all summer right there, the women made baskets all summer, and the men helped some. The men worked on some of the boats, fishing boats in the summer.

They took all their belongings in boxes when they went. In those days they would go by train and I remember there was a steamboat that used to run out of Bangor. They would go on that steamboat down to Bar Harbor and along the coast.[26]

The reception Wabanaki artisan families received from their white neighbors mirrored the ambivalence white society demonstrated toward

Native peoples. A visitor's 1894 description of the Passamaquoddy encampment at Bar Harbor provides a window into the treatment with which local businesses responded to Native Americans. They were both attracted to and repulsed by the Indian basket makers.

> An element of the picturesque is supplied by an Indian Camp, which used for years to be pitched in a marshy field known as Squaw Hollow; but with the advent of a Village Improvement Society certain newfangled and disturbing ideas as to sanitary conditions obtained a hearing, and the Indians were banished to back roads out of the way of sensitive eyes and noses. They claim to be of the Passamaquoddy tribe, speak their own language, and follow the peaceful trades of basket-weaving and the building of birch bark canoes. Their little dwellings—some of them tents, some of them shanties covered with tar-paper and strips of bark—are scattered about.[27]

Members of the Village Improvement Society wanted the basket makers located nearby as an asset to tourism, but they were not quite comfortable about seeing them in the forefront of their village (see Plate 8). Economic rewards brought both parties together, albeit reluctantly.

Complicating travel arrangements, artisan families would bring not only all of their belongings, but also all of their tools and a supply of ash for summer basket making. Getting the ash was not a simple matter—hiking into the forests, cutting, tying up, and loading the branches, and hauling the materials back home could be arduous work. The Bangor and Aroostook railroad eased the difficulties for those who lived on nearby reservations. Men travelled to the Brownville area, cut the ash, and brought home a supply on flat cars that would be unloaded across the river from the reservation (see Plate 9). Sometimes whole families moved into the wooded areas to obtain their ash:

> Sometimes they'd stay there all winter. Or at least part of the winter. My dad would come and my grandfather. They had a big sled which all Indians had and he could take his ax and saw and sled and he'd go out and come back with a couple of logs on there. They'd pound them. Some of them would go into the woods and pound them right there.
>
> And they'd take a potato barrel and roll them in. So probably in two big tubs they could probably carry ten to fifteen pounded logs in there which would be simple to handle [pounded and separated into strips]. Because a couple of those big tubs full would last them all winter. . . . There were some men who specialized in going after ash and selling ash to the basket makers.[28]

Weather conditions also complicated the prospects of a successful basket trading year. For instance, Indian Agent Charles Bailey reported that during the 1881 summer season there was

> a failure of the revenues usually resulting to the tribe from a mid-summer visitation to the various watering places along the Atlantic Coast. Owing to the unpropitious weather, it is well known there was a greatly diminished attendance at these resorts; many were brought to need who had before been able to care for themselves and their families.[29]

THE INDIAN VILLAGE,
BAR HARBOR, ME.

Arthur Livingston, Publisher, New York 113

Plate 8. Passamaquoddy basket makers at Bar Harbor. Postcard. Courtesy of Abbe Museum, Bar Harbor, Maine.

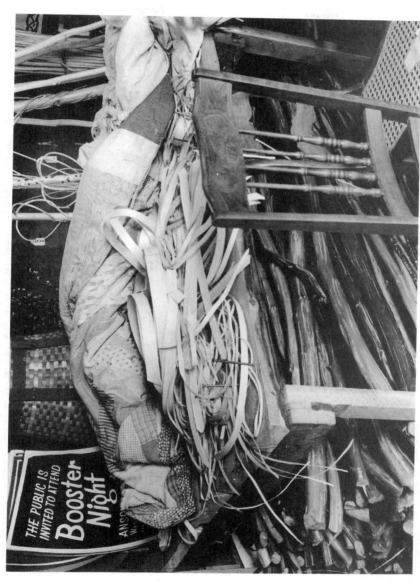

Plate 9. Ash logs and strips in Edward Newell's workshop. Courtesy of Northeast Archives. Photo 4043. Maine Folklife Center, University of Maine, Orono.

Then again, in 1888, Agent John Stowe reported that the summer trade was "long continued and poorly remunerative. Owing to the backwardness of the season, the Indians found themselves on the ground long before many of the visitors arrived; and the numberless rainy days that followed proved, in may ways, a severe setback to their business."[30]

Another cold, wet season was reported in 1889. However, some families were able to make up for the poor summer by taking orders for Christmas gifts from patrons of the resort or by filling orders from abroad. In 1891, several families tried a new course of action. As Agent Stowe reported, "A few families having homes here were absent in Portland and vicinity, trying the now unusual experiment of living away from the reservation, while filling basket orders for the Christmas trade."[31]

Maine Indians blamed other events, as well, for reducing the basket trade. These included the Paris Exposition of 1889, which drew away patrons, and the presidential election campaign in 1888. However, during the 1890s the greatest complaint was competition from other Indian tribes.

The first mention of this problem is found in the Indian agent's report of 1892. Agent George Hunt reported that summer basket sales were not so profitable, "owing chiefly to the sharp competition they meet at the hands of the Canadian Indians who bring in their cheaper wares free of duty."[32] The problem is mentioned again in the agent's reports for 1899 and 1901. In fact, in 1901 George Hunt wrote, "the Indians have had a fairly successful business year though the competition of the Canadian tribes in the making and selling of fancy baskets is severely felt. They pay no duty."[33] Most of the time agents were able to report good returns on basket sales. Even in 1914, when "the outbreak of the European war checked very perceptively the sale of baskets," Agent Ira Pinkham reported that the Christmas holiday trade was very good.[34] In some ways the war helped the domestic basket business: Since imports of baskets ceased, Wabanaki baskets were in demand more than ever before. However, very high prices for necessities offset the temporary boom in basket sales.

In 1919, Agent Pinkham reported a very prosperous year for both Native men and women who worked in factories. In addition, he reported that the summer trade was excellent. Again, however, he remarked, greatly inflated prices for their own purchases were making life difficult for the basket makers.[35] Even so, business continued to boom. Canadian Abenaki made baskets for catalogue dealers, but the Maine Wabanaki did not at this time. However, they did manufacture one thousand work baskets for the Red Cross during the 1920s. In addition, they conducted some business with Gypsies, who ordered Indian baskets and peddled them elsewhere.

Decline and Renaissance

During the 1920s and 1930s, economic crises and social change disrupted the basket making industry. The Great Depression (1929–42) devastated

American business, including niche markets such as crafts. As the nation's unemployment rate rose to nearly 25 percent of the workforce by 1933, the resort business waned. Consequently, the market for fancy baskets plummeted. Further complicating their opportunities for survival, wage work, especially for men, whose wages were significantly higher, became very scarce. Most Wabanaki eked out a living in whatever way they could. Those basket makers living on reservations were able to market their goods to declining groups of tourists. One clever strategy was a summer pageant on Indian Island, organized by several woman artisans, which drew in some summer visitors. Through such means, a few basket makers could continue their craft. Used to living on very little, many families were able to survive in large part by bartering their home production. Families who moved into the woods to collect ash and make baskets in the wintertime got by in this manner. As Theodore Mitchell, a Penobscot man who experienced the difficulties of this time, described in an interview, "They swapped, and bartered. They'd go to the farms around and swap for potatoes and different kinds of produce or maybe a ham shoulder or something. Of course, they were very, very frugal."[36]

World War II brought prosperity, but at a high cost to Native communities. Many Wabanaki people moved away to Massachusetts and Connecticut to work in wartime industries. Others, both men and women, left to serve in the military. Those who relocated often continued to make baskets to supplement their wages. Yet, the decline in the basket making industry continued even during the post-war era, threatening the cultural integrity of the people. To the lament of older basket makers, young Wabanaki were less interested in learning the craft. By 1950, few were training to carry on the tradition, instead rebelling against the rigors of such hard work and long hours. In a world of abundant work and high wages, the new generation disdained a craft used by marginal people to scratch up a meager income.

The dramatic social upheavals of the 1960s and 1970s reversed the decline. The political protests of the Red Power movement spawned a resurgent interest in Native American culture among Native (and often white) young people. Many young Native Americans throughout the country expressed a desire to learn about and to restore a way of life that seemed to be vanishing. In the Northeast, basket making and related crafts emerged as a major symbol of Wabanaki culture. As they began to understand the place of basket making within a larger cultural context of values and institutions, of language, dancing, and song, of kin network and religious belief, this generation increasingly recognized the craft as a highly skilled art form which integrated the culture at many levels. By 1990, with the help of funding from the Maine Arts Commission and the National Endowment for the Arts, Maine instituted a Traditional Art Apprenticeship Program to support efforts to rediscover such traditions. The Program enables a master basket maker to take on an apprentice. The result was not only ten new well-trained basket makers in Maine, but a true resurgence of interest among young people to continue the craft.

The renaissance in Wabanaki basket making can be seen today in a wide-ranging variety of initiatives. To preserve the dwindling brown ash resources, for instance, basket makers in several Wabanaki communities combined their efforts in 1991 to develop a Brown Ash Task Force. Presently, the Task Force is propagating brown ash seedlings in greenhouses and is preparing a brown ash plantation on Passamaquoddy lands.[37] The Maine Basketmakers Alliance, a related organization, assists members by combining forces in the marketplace. Through such sophisticated examples of cooperation, contemporary Wabanaki artists make baskets that sell for much better prices than the baskets of the nineteenth century. Individual collectors of Native American art and museums seek these fine baskets for their collections and exhibits. Today, members of the Wabanaki communities in Maine and the Maritimes are proud of and support their basket making and basket makers.

Notes

1. Historical sources describe the Wabanaki or Abenaki as a loose confederacy of tribes.

2. Tribes which were once part of the Wabanaki, previously known as the Aroosagunti-cook, Pigwacket, Caniba, Pennacook, Cowasuck, Sokoki, and perhaps some others, are now extinct.

3. David Lynn Ghere, "Abenaki Factionalism, Emigration and Social Continuity: Indian Society in Northern New England, 1725 to 1765" (Ph.D. diss., University of Maine, Orono, 1988), 46–50.

4. Native peoples succeeded in adapting to industrialization in areas where this alternative was available. For example, in the Old Town area of Maine, Native Americans gained employment in lumber mills, shoe factories, and later in the Old Town and White Canoe factories. See, for example, Fannie Hardy Eckstorm, *Penobscot Man* (Boston: Houghton Mifflin Co, 1904). Also, "Machias Log Driving Record Book, 1859," 47–48 and "Penobscot Logging Association Record Book 1854–1916," Special Collections, Fogler Library, University of Maine, Orono.

5. Jesse D. Jennings, "Danger Cave," *University of Utah Anthropological Papers*, no. 27 (1957).

6. Russell G. Handsman and Ann McMullen, "An Introduction to Woodsplint Basketry and Its Interpretation," in *A Key Into the Language of Woodsplint Baskets*, ed. Ann McMullen and Russell G. Handsman (Washington, CT: American Indian Archaeological Institute, 1987), 23.

7. Brown ash: Penobscot, ákawəl; Latin, Fraxinus nigra. Sweetgrass: Penobscot, wəlí-mskihko; Latin, *Savastana odorata* or *Hierochloe odorata* Beauvois.

8. Wabanaki men served as guides to the earliest explorers, such as Samuel de Champlain, in Benedict Arnold's expedition during the Revolutionary War, for government surveys, and for private citizens. For an example of the latter, see Henry David Thoreau, *The Maine Woods* (1864; reprint, New York: Thomas E. Crowell Co., 1966).

9. Daniel Gookin, "The Historical Collections of the Indians of New England" (1674; reprint, Boston: Massachusetts Historical Society Collections, 1806).

10. Joan Lester, "'We Didn't Make Fancy Baskets Until We Were Discovered': Fancy-Basket Making in Maine," in *A Key Into the Language of Woodsplint Baskets*, ed. Ann McMullen and Russell G. Handsman (Washington, CT: American Indian Archaeological Institute, 1987), 53.

11. Ibid., 47.

12. Ibid., 48.

13. Nancy F. Cott, *The Bonds of Womanhood: "Woman's Sphere," in New England, 1780–1835* (New Haven: Yale University Press, 1977); Barbara Welter, "The Cult of True Womanhood: 1820–1860," *American Quarterly* 18 (1966): 151–74.

14. Lester, "We Didn't Make," 42; Fannie Hardy Eckstorm, *The Handicrafts of the Modern Indians of Maine* (1932; reprint, Bar Harbor, ME: Robert Abbe Museum, 1980), 24;

Frank T. Siebert, Jr., and Pauleena MacDougall Seeber, Kəlósəwɑkanal *Book of Illustrated Words* (Indian Island, Old Town: University of Maine, n.d.), 32.

15. Samuel Eliot Morison, *The Story of Mount Desert Island* (Boston: Little, Brown & Company, 1960), 46.

16. J. Sherman Hoar, *Pioneer Days of Rangeley, Maine* (Lewiston, ME: J. Sherman Hoar, 1928), 11.

17. Mary E. Bennett, ed., *Poland: Past and Present 1795–1970* (Lewiston, ME: Poland Anniversary Committee, 1970), 71–73.

18. George F. Dillingham, *Report* (Augusta, ME: Sprague; Owen & Nash, 1873), 5.

19. Madeline Shay, interview by author, tape recording, at Indian Island, 28 January 1993, Northeast Archives of Folklore and Oral History, Orono.

20. J. N. Stowe, *Report of the Agent of the Penobscot Tribe of Indians for the Year 1888* (Augusta, ME: Burleigh & Flynt, 1889), 7.

21. Joan Lester, "We Didn't Make," 53.

22. A. Hyatt Verrill, *Romantic and Historic Maine* (New York: Dodd Mead & Co., 1938), 111–12.

23. "Indian Visitors Arrive," *The Hill-Top*, 22 July 1922, 1–2.

24. Ibid., 4.

25. Stowe, *Report . . . for . . . 1888*, 8.

26. Theodore Norris Mitchell, interview by author, tape-recorded, Orono, Maine, 19 August 1993, Northeast Archives of Folklore and Oral History, University of Maine, Orono.

27. F. Marion Crawford, *Bar Harbor* (New York: Charles Scribner's Sons, 1894), 12.

28. Mitchell, interview.

29. Charles Bailey, *Report of the Agent of the Penobscot Tribe of Indians* (Augusta, ME: Sprague & Son, 1882), 8.

30. Stowe, *Report . . . for . . . 1888*, 8.

31. J. N. Stowe, *Report of the Agent of the Penobscot Tribe of Indians for the Year 1891* (Augusta, ME: Burleigh & Flint, 1892), 9.

32. George Hunt, *Report of the Agent of the Penobscot Tribe of Indians for the Year 1892* (Augusta, ME: Burleigh & Flint, 1893), 8.

33. George Hunt, n. p. "Report of Agent, December 31, 1901," handwritten ms. Special Collections, Fogler Library, University of Maine, Orono, 6.

34. Ira E. Pinkham, "Report for 1914," typed ms., 3 (Augusta: Legislative Graveyard, Maine State Archives).

35. Ira E. Pinkham, "Report for 1919," typed ms., 4 (Augusta: Legislative Graveyard, Maine State Archives).

36. Mitchell, interview.

37. Kathleen Mundell, *Basket Tree Basket Makers* (Augusta: Maine Arts Commission, 1992), 12.

IV

Spirit and Power

In the long, conflictive history of relations between Native Americans and Euro-Americans, few arenas have been as sensitive or as contested as religion. In Native cultures, religious belief and practice are bound up in the people's sense of place, history, and identity. Spirit is understood as both knowledge and power, as in the belief in manitou held by many eastern tribes. In Western thought, however, and especially in the modern world, power is a more secular concept. Power lies more in the domain of politics, of using laws or force, if need be, to promote preferred behaviors. From the beginnings of this country, as historians document, Euro-American missionaries and politicians have directed their power toward undermining the legitimacy of Native American religions. Most scholars today are critical of these efforts, decrying them as part of the Western attempt to dominate American Indians. The essays in this section, however, present differing pictures of the relationships between Native religion and mainstream institutions.

In "The Catholic Mission to the Native Americans," Ross Enochs traces an important aspect of the roots of this history. Departing from the critical revisionist interpretations that became popular during the 1960s, Enochs describes the Catholic missionaries in the Spanish, French, and British American colonies and in the United States in a much more positive light. Although Catholic missionaries from Europe and the United States maintained the conceit that Western ways were superior to the cultures of Native North and South America, they generally were tolerant of Native practices and often worked to incorporate indigenous ways into the religious programs they established. He tells us that Catholic missionaries sought to protect Indians from rapacious colonists and, although the churchmen attempted to proselytize, they respected many Native beliefs and practices. Enochs's study presents the Catholics' work among the Lakota people as particularly just and mild.

Tension between religious practice and governmental order is also the theme of "Stolen Spirits: An Illustrative Case of Indigenous Survival Through Religious Freedom," Gabrielle A. Tayac's essay. As a Piscataway woman and Harvard University doctoral candidate in sociology, Tayac shows how Native American scholars can use their academic skills to shed light on issues that involve their people. Her essay is a case study of the efforts of the Piscataway of Maryland to conduct religious ceremonies and burials on their ancestral lands—lands now in the hands of whites. She describes how archaeologists desecrated the Piscataway ceremonial center of Moyaone, digging up burial remains throughout the last century. In our time, white property owners and the National Park Service have refused her people access to their traditional burial grounds, while freely providing entry for white visitors. Even when the property owners have accommodated Native American requests, they have made visits inconvenient and uncomfortable. Tayac observes that the Piscataway's continuing efforts to conduct ceremonies at Moyaone are symbolic of Native Americans' "ongoing struggle to protect their community against the dominant majority."

A similar point is made by Eric Mazur in "'The Supreme Law of the Land': Sources of Conflict between Native Americans and the Constitutional Order." The University of California at Santa Barbara religious studies scholar describes the conflict between Native American efforts to achieve religious freedom and the political order based on the United States Constitution. Mazur asks, "How can different sources of authority be reconciled in a democracy which promises every citizen the right of religious free exercise?" Drawing upon federal law and judicial decisions, news accounts, and histories, he reveals a conflict within our constitutional structure which pits the idea of pluralism—a belief that the values and practices of different groups must be respected—against the concept of particularism—an idea that emphasizes the needs of a particular group within society. A chief victim of this conflict, Mazur contends, is Native religious freedom. At issue is Native Americans' insistence on following traditional practices such as the use of eagle feathers or peyote on their own lands. Mazur analyzes recent judicial decisions to show how "Native traditions, centered . . . on the cultural orientation toward land, cannot but conflict with the American constitutional order's orientation toward the same land." Native Americans "may not accept" the authority of the constitutional order of the United States, he concludes, but "in the face of overwhelming power, they may have had no choice" but to accommodate themselves to it.

10

The Catholic Missions
to the Native Americans

Ross Enochs

Missionaries to the Native Americans have suffered a tainted reputation in recent accounts of American history. Critics such as Vine Deloria, Jr., have claimed that the missionaries had a low regard for the cultures and religions of the Native Americans they evangelized.[1] Others, including Harvey Markowitz, have argued that the missionaries tried to eradicate Native American cultures and substitute Western culture in its place.[2] Others, still, have asserted that the missionaries wanted to make Native Americans conform completely to the Western culture that was steadily encroaching on their lands. Many of those who are critical of the missionaries often assume that the missionaries believed that Westerners were in all ways more civilized than Native Americans and used the power of the state or the military to help coerce Native Americans to become Christian. Although this conception of the missionaries is common among some historians and activists today, it was never accurate. The actual views of the missionaries concerning Native American cultures and religions were far more complex than many have recognized. Although the missionaries in some cases had little respect for the indigenous cultures and though they did try to eradicate certain aspects of Native American cultures, many missionaries, as this essay will show, sought to preserve aspects of Native American cultures and to protect Native Americans from the exploitation of the colonists. To this end, the essay will examine the Catholic missions to Native Americans.

The Legacy of Spanish Catholicism

During the conquest of Mexico in the sixteenth century, Spanish conquistadors and colonists brutally suppressed or enslaved the indigenous peoples. While this was occurring, the only organized resistance to unrestrained oppression came from Catholic missionaries who steadfastly opposed the tactics and methods of the conquistadors and colonists. One of the most prominent of these early Catholic missionaries in the New World was

Bartolomé de Las Casas. He arrived in Cuba in 1513 as the chaplain of the force that conquered this island. After living in Cuba for a year, he began to oppose the Spanish settlers for their treatment of the indigenous peoples. The colonists had set up an *encomienda* system in which Spanish families took control of tracts of land in Cuba and Mexico for farming or for mining gold and silver. Although they were in theory obligated to guard the interests of the Native Americans, the Spanish, led by their greed and disregard for the indigenous peoples, instead enslaved them. Las Casas traveled back to Spain in 1515 to speak out against the brutality he had witnessed. In 1522, he joined the Dominicans, the religious order whose members were most vocal in their denunciations of the Spanish conquistadors. As a Dominican friar, Las Casas dedicated the rest of his life to eradicating the enslavement of the Native Americans.

Las Casas gave voice to the horrors he had witnessed in several books, including the highly influential *In Defence of the Indians*, originally published in Spanish in 1552. This book denounced the Spanish colonists for their campaign against the indigenous peoples and stated that the Spanish had no right to attack or enslave them. Dismissing the colonists' argument that they must subdue indigenous peoples by force before they could be Christianized, Las Casas argued that no hostile actions against the Native Americans could be justified, and he accused the Spanish of using the Native Americans to gain wealth:

> It is the height of effrontery and rashness for [the Spanish conquistadors] to attribute publicly to the Indians the gravest failings both of nature and conduct condemning *en masse* so many thousands of people, while as a matter of fact, the greater number of them are free from these faults. All this drags innumerable souls to ruin and blocks the service of spreading the Christian religion by closing the eyes of those [the Spanish conquistadors] who, blinded by ambition, bend all their energies of mind and body to the one purpose of gaining wealth, power, honors, and dignities. For the sake of these things they kill and destroy with inhuman cruelty people who are completely innocent, meek, harmless, temperate, and quite ready and willing to receive and embrace the word of God. . . . What will these [Native American] people think of Christ, the true God of the Christians, when they see Christians venting their rage against them with so many massacres, so much bloodshed without any just cause, at any rate without any just cause that they know of (nor can one even be imagined), and without any fault committed on [the Native Americans'] part against the Christians?[3]

Las Casas asserted that neither the non-Christian status of Native peoples nor their practices of human sacrifice and cannibalism justified the Spanish attacks on their civilizations and their subsequent enslavement. Since the slavers' actions were wholly opposed to the Gospel, he maintained that the Spanish settlers' brutal treatment would only hinder the spread of Christianity among Native Americans. Las Casas argued that because the latter recognized the contradiction between Christian morality and the settlers' actions, the missionaries could not hope to convert people preaching the

"Gospel of love" while the settlers captured them, drove them into mines, and worked them to death. Las Casas petitioned Pope Paul III on behalf of the Native Americans. In response to his pleas, the Pope in 1537 wrote *Sublimis Deus*, in which he stated that the Native peoples were true human beings who could not lawfully be made slaves. Paul III also stated that they had the right to hold governmental offices. Most Spanish settlers, however, ignored the papal statement and continued their practices. Although the missionaries were a thorn in the sides of the slavers, the only power the former had was to deny them the sacraments—an ineffective deterrent to those who had no regard for the lives of Native peoples. Since the Spanish officials and settlers profited a great deal from the slave trade, they did little or nothing to stop it.[4]

The Society of Jesus (a Catholic religious order commonly called the Jesuits), also, actively opposed Spanish and Portuguese slave traders. In 1610, they began to found havens in Paraguay for the Guarani, the indigenous people of that region. Because the Jesuit missionaries believed the Guarani should be protected from the ravages of the slavers and diseases from the West, they established missions hundreds of miles away from colonial cities. For the next 150 years, these missions, known as reductions, proved to be one of the great accomplishments of the Church in the New World. Traveling into the interior in small groups without any military escort, the Jesuits lived among the Guarani, learned their language, and won their trust. Through Jesuit guidance, the Guarani built churches, schools, bridges, roads, masonry houses with tiled roofs, and large farming communities in the jungles.[5]

Introducing the concept of private property to the Guarani, the Jesuits assigned each family a plot of land for them to cultivate. They organized, as well, communal plots of land that everyone at the reductions had to work. Privately or communally, the Guarani grew a wide variety of vegetables and herbs, including mint, rosemary, chicory, endives, beets, apples, pears, peaches, lemons, wheat, corn, and sugar cane.[6] The reductions not only became quite successful farms, but also exported goods from their surplus. They raised sheep and chickens, and some reductions actually kept thousands of horses and cattle. The produce or income from the communal plots fed widows, orphans, and the sick—no poverty or homelessness existed in the reductions.

The Jesuits catechized the Guarani in the indigenous language. Those converts who acquired a good understanding of the faith were then assigned as catechists for other Indians. The missionaries observed that the Guarani were particularly impressed by the liturgy, processions, ritual, and music of the Church. Recognizing their love of music, the Fathers organized the Guarani into choirs and taught them to manufacture and play musical instruments such as the violin and the flute. However, though the Natives on the whole accepted the Jesuits, the missionaries did encounter opposition from the Guarani shamans—the religious leaders and healers in the indigenous community. The Jesuits believed the shamans were under the influence of the devil, and they tried to discredit them. In return, the shamans labeled the Europeans devils and denounced them for trying to limit the men, who were accustomed to having several wives, to only one wife.[7]

A much more dramatic conflict at the missions than the struggles between the Jesuits and the shamans was the slave raids. Even before the missions were established, large bands of armed slavers traveled throughout Paraguay capturing Guarani and other Native Americans for the slave markets of São Paulo and Asuncion. After the Guarani were concentrated in the reductions, Spanish and Portuguese settlers, beginning in 1611, raided the missions for slaves, killing many missionaries and Natives. The Jesuits estimated that 300,000 Guarani were lost in the raids; indeed, by 1628, only two of the eleven reductions were intact.[8]

One of the Fathers in the Paraguay missions, Antonio Ruiz de Montoya, was particularly prominent in opposing the incursions of the slavers, even traveling to Spain to agitate for the Guaranis' cause. Born in Lima, Peru in 1585, Ruiz de Montoya joined the Jesuits when he was 21. After working among the Guarani, he quickly mastered their language and wrote a Guarani grammar and dictionary.[9] During the time that Ruiz de Montoya worked among the Paraguayans, slave traders from São Paulo had raided several of the reductions, taking thousands of Guarani. To raise awareness of their plight, he wrote *The Spiritual Conquest* (1639) in which he described the citizens of São Paulo who carried out these raids:

> The inhabitants of the town are Castilians, Portuguese, Italians, and people of other nationalities gathered there by a desire to live as they like in freedom, without constraints of the law. Their way of life is the destruction of the human race: they kill all those who flee from them to escape the wretched slavery they inflict upon them. They go out for two or three years at a stretch hunting human beings like animals. . . . These people, worse than brigands, invaded our reductions; they seized captives, killed, and pillaged altars. . . . [The slave traders] entered the two reductions of San Antonio and San Miguel, striking down Indians with their cutlasses. The poor Indians took refuge in the church, where they were slain like cattle in a slaughterhouse.[10]

In 1631, while working at the missions of St. Ignacio Mini and Loreto, the Jesuits heard that Spanish and Portuguese slavers from São Paulo were approaching. The Jesuit missionaries and Guarani decided that they would make a dramatic escape. Led by Ruiz de Montoya, 12,000 Natives fled in a fleet of 700 canoes down the Paranapanema River. Before reaching a waterfall, they disembarked for a 75-mile trek into the forest to seek refuge.[11]

Six years later, Ruiz de Montoya traveled to Madrid to lobby for the Guarani. He argued that the slave trade should be stopped, and those already enslaved should be freed. He also asserted that the Guarani had a natural right to defend themselves against their attackers. This last point would be the most crucial and politically delicate; yet, Ruiz de Montoya succeeded in persuading King Philip IV to allow the Natives the use of firearms. Under the guidance of the Jesuits, the Guarani soon learned to use and manufacture firearms at the reductions. After constructing storehouses of arms and training with these arms, the Guarani so successfully defended their missions from attack that the raids stopped in 1642.[12]

The Jesuit protection of the Native peoples—and the inherent threat to the economic interests of many powerful Spanish and Portuguese settlers—brought false accusations and innuendos to the ears of the Iberian kings, and ultimately contributed to the suppression of the Jesuit order. Because the reductions were havens from slavery and because the commercial success of the reductions competed with the settlers' goods, the colonists became envious of the Jesuits. Using their political influence to neutralize the missionaries' pleas, many settlers and European opponents of the Jesuits accused the missionaries of ruling, in the jungles of Paraguay, an armed empire that was not obedient to the king.[13] These accusations, among others, damaged the reputation of the Order and contributed to its suppression, carried out in Spain by King Charles III in 1767. Colonial authorities then arrested the missionaries and imprisoned many of them. In 1767, 57 reductions held 100,000 Guarani; after the suppression, the reductions collapsed, and the settlers continued the slave trade virtually unopposed.[14]

The example of the reductions shows that the missionaries were not trying to justify the subjugation of the Guarani by claiming that they were non-Christian. Rather, the missionaries, for the most part, were directly opposed to the Spanish and Portuguese governments' policies concerning the treatment of indigenous peoples and even encouraged armed resistance to thwart the plans of the slavers.

The Missions of New France

In the seventeenth century, the Jesuits were active also in North America, where they evangelized several indigenous groups, including the Algonquin, Iroquois, Huron, Abenaki, Montagnais, Illinois, Potowatomi, Ojibwa, Ottawa, Sioux, and Miami. With no military force to support them, accompanied only by guides, the missionaries journeyed in small groups into the lands of the Native nations. Traveling to these communities was quite dangerous since wars between different Native bands were common. Even when the missionaries met the group which they desired to evangelize, they had no guarantee that the band would not reject them or even kill them. When the Native peoples did accept them, the missionaries had to adapt to a rigorous lifestyle. Therefore, the Jesuits primarily sent young men who were most likely to survive the hardships of traveling and enduring the cold winters. Missionaries traveled with nomadic bands, carried baggage, endured mosquitoes, paddled their canoes, slept in their dwellings, ate the same foods as the Native Americans, and shared the tasks at the camps they made. The Jesuits struggled to endure the rigors of Native American life cheerfully because they knew that if they became a burden, Native leaders might not have allowed them to continue traveling with them. Conforming themselves to the lifestyle of Native Americans, the Jesuits sought to convince them to accept Christianity.[15]

Much of the correspondence between the missionaries and their superiors from the seventeenth century has been preserved. As a result, historians have been able to grasp their opinions of Native American religion and culture. In many of their writings, the Jesuits showed that they believed that Native Americans had a knowledge of God through the natural law. According to Catholic doctrine, the natural law is God's law written on creation and on the consciences of all people. Even non-Christians, Catholics believed, could gain some knowledge of God through studying nature and through examining their own consciences. When the Jesuits came to the missions, they knew that Native Americans would have some kind of religion. They looked for evidence that the indigenous people perceived that a single creator existed and that they recognized the difference between good and evil. The missionaries did not see the Native peoples as godless and uncivilized, but rather believed that they had some idea of the true God through nature. They also saw that they had natural virtues such as patience, courage, perseverance, and charity. For example, in 1635, Jean de Brebeuf praised the Huron for their charity:

> We see among [the Huron] some rather noble moral virtues. You note, in the first place, a great love and union, which they are careful to cultivate by means of their marriages, of their presents, of their feasts, and of their frequent visits. On returning from their fishing, their hunting, and their trading, they exchange many gifts; if they have thus obtained something unusually good, even if they have bought it, or if it has been given to them, they make a feast to the whole village with it. Their hospitality towards all sorts of strangers is remarkable; they present to them, in their feasts, the best of what they have prepared, and as I have already said, I do not know if anything similar, in this regard is to be found anywhere. They never close the door upon a stranger, and, once having received him into their houses, they share with him the best they have.[16]

De Brebeuf and his brothers saw the Huron's charity, as well as their other virtues, as evidence of the Native Americans' perception of the truth through natural law.[17]

The Jesuits described the Huron and other peoples as intelligent and sincerely religious people. From living with them and observing their talents in hunting, woodworking, tracking, gathering medicinal plants, and surviving in the wilderness, the missionaries believed that Native peoples had a level of intelligence higher than that of European peasants.[18] The Jesuits also noted that the Native Americans were intellectually curious about Christianity; they asked the Jesuits many questions and made comments that indicated their interest in and understanding of theological matters. The Jesuits also found that when the Native Americans did convert, they were diligent in their prayers. Also, as in Paraguay, the Jesuits appointed Native Americans as catechists if they were zealous in their devotion to the Church so that others in their band might follow their example.[19]

The Jesuits faced several problems in their efforts to convert the Canadian tribes. They realized that smallpox and other diseases were ravaging these peoples, and recognized that the afflicted sometimes blamed Europeans for bringing the diseases. As with the South American reductions, the missionaries of New France had to convince Native men to give up polygyny, the practice of men marrying many wives. Similar, also, to the situation in Paraguay, the Jesuits waged an ongoing assault on the practice of consulting shamans when Native people fell ill; many Jesuits believed the shamans had dealings with the devil, and many rivalries broke out between the missionaries and the shamans. The Fathers tried to discredit the Native healers and also take over their role in the community. Since both Catholics and Native Americans believed that praying over a sick person might benefit that person, the missionaries prayed over the sick and substituted Catholic prayers for the prayers and rituals of the shamans. They also told the Native Americans to seek the intercession of Mary, the Mother of God, when they were ill. At times, Native Americans who were sick sought baptism, and if they recovered, they sometimes attributed their cure to the Catholic rite. Such events often enhanced the reputation of the priests.[20]

European and Native American religions shared several structural similarities that facilitated the indigenous peoples' acceptance of Catholicism. For example, Catholics and some Native peoples believed that the actions of the living benefitted the destiny of the dead. Furthermore, Native Americans had guardian spirits, and therefore their acceptance of the Catholic belief in guardian angels was consistent with their religious outlook.[21] Both peoples carried personal religious artifacts with them—usually amulets for the Native Americans, and crosses or medals for the Catholics.[22] The most significant of the similarities was their common emphasis on rituals. The Native Americans' traditional interest in ritual was one of the factors that drew them to the Catholic Church.[23]

The Jesuits tried to both adapt to Native American cultures and to change Native religions. They did not, however, attempt to change all their cultural practices, as previous historians have suggested. For example, the missionaries did not object to the Native practice of leaving the dead suspended in trees or on scaffolding rather then burying corpses. They also accepted their use of sacred pipes, even though the priests understood that the Native Americans believed the pipes were imbued with sacred power. The Jesuits did destroy many other forms of religious artifacts and even convinced some converts to destroy their own religious paraphernalia; yet, they did not see the pipe as a great obstacle.[24] Indeed, missionaries often made it a practice to carry a Native pipe and to display it as a sign of peace when they encountered unfamiliar bands. In some cases, the Jesuits' sacred pipes saved their lives, as bands which were hostile towards Europeans broke off their attacks when they saw the missionaries displaying the pipe.[25]

The Fathers adapted to Native American cultures also by retaining traditional forms of a practice and substituting Christian symbols or concepts in place of traditional beliefs. For example, rather than imposing the Latin or French language, the Jesuits taught through indigenous languages and used pictographs, a traditional Native American way of teaching, to help their listeners remember points of Christian doctrine.[26] Furthermore, when the priests held Mass, they frequently allowed communicants to interrupt the proceedings and ask for clarifications. After the Father had clarified an issue, Native interpreters would turn to the congregation to restate what he had said.[27] Even though this was not a tradition of European Christianity, the Jesuits felt it was an innocent custom that did not hurt and probably benefited the Native Americans' understanding of Catholic belief. In addition, some Native Americans of their own accord adapted Christianity to their culture. Sometimes, on their own initiative, the Native Americans substituted Christian prayers for their own at times during their feasts when they had prayed to a traditional deity. They retained the form of their ceremony, but changed the content of the prayers. The Jesuits often encouraged this practice of retaining some aspects, particularly the outward appearance of rituals, while at the same time changing the content. For example, in 1673 Father Louis Andre, a Jesuit missionary, noticed that the Menomini sought the aid of a "sun god" in fishing for sturgeon by placing an image of the sun on a pole and locating this device in the water. The ritual had been ineffective, however. Father Andre described his plan: "I asked them whether they would consent to my removing the picture of the sun, and replacing it by the image of Jesus Crucified . . . they consented . . . I put my crucifix in the place of the picture of the sun. On the following morning, sturgeon entered the river in great abundance."[28] Father Andre retained the form of the ritual, but changed the content, replacing a Menomini symbol with a Christian one. In sum, the Jesuits of New France believed that the lifestyle, political organization, dress, and other customs of Native Americans could be preserved. They sought to change only those customs that they believed were opposed to Catholic morals and teachings.[29]

Jesuit Contact with the Sioux

After the French government suppressed the Society of Jesus in 1763, their missions to Canada collapsed. However, in 1814 Pope Pius VII restored the Order, and the Jesuits once again sought to reestablish their contacts with the indigenous peoples there. One of the most prominent Catholic missionaries to the Native peoples during the nineteenth century was Pierre-Jean De Smet. A Belgian by birth, De Smet traveled to the Missouri River and established a mission to the Potowatomi in 1838. At the time, the Potowatomi and Yankton Sioux were feuding. De Smet arranged that they make peace by performing the traditional Native custom of exchanging gifts. During the next 40 years, he met with several different Native American groups—the Flathead, Kalispel, Blackfeet, Kickapoo, Omaha, Pawnee, Assiniboin, Mandan, Shoshone, Coeur d'Alene, Pend d'Oreille, and several others—and succeeded in establishing good relations with many of them. When he visited a village, he smoked the sacred pipe, attended their dances, ate at their feasts, and prayed with them to the Great Spirit. He believed that many Native American peoples had an idea of God through natural law, and when he prayed with them he used the term "Great Spirit" to acknowledge this perceived continuity. De Smet also accepted many of their rituals as morally good or neutral and participated in them. After witnessing traditional dances on one occasion, he declared that the dances were innocent. He also participated in an adoption ritual when Two Bears, a Sioux Chief, accepted the missionary as his brother.[30]

Because of De Smet's generally good relations with the tribes he encountered, U.S. Army officials requested that he travel with them and serve as a mediator between Army units and the Native Americans. In fact, De Smet also served as a mediator at several councils between government agents and tribal leaders. Sioux leaders even asked government agents and Army generals to send Catholic priests.[31] In an 1886 letter, Brigadier General and Special Indian Commissioner Alfred Sully advised De Smet of the Sioux request, noting,

Knowing the great interest you take in the welfare of the Indians, I write you in their behalf that you may interest yourself and such as may so be disposed to assist in the establishment of religious missions in the Indian Country. I would suggest as a commencement such institutions be established, one at the [?] village, Fort Berthold, another at the Yankton Agency, Dakota Territory. I would recommend the establishment of others as soon as the means could be procured. In making this request I am only asking what the Indians at these two above mentioned places have repeatedly requested me to do. Their predilections are decidedly in favor of the Catholic religion to the exclusion of any other. As I do not profess myself to be a Catholic, I can speak of the great good they have done towards civilizing the savage without fear of being accused of prejudice.[32]

In an interesting instance in 1868, when the Sioux were at war with the Army, Sitting Bull allowed De Smet to come to his camp and even sleep in his tent—at a time when the Sioux leader would have killed any other white man who tried to visit him. At this meeting, the missionary counseled the Sioux chiefs to meet with Army officials at Fort Rice to negotiate peace. As a mediator, he understood that white settlers were encroaching on Native lands, and he acknowledged that when conflicts broke out between whites and Native Americans, the Native peoples were usually the innocent party. He wrote,

> The grievances of the [Sioux] Indians against the whites are very numerous, and the vengeance which they on their side provoke are often most cruel and frightful. Never-theless, one is compelled to admit that they are less guilty than the whites. Nine times out of ten, the provocations come from the latter—that is to say, from the scum of civilization, who bring to them the lowest and grossest vices, and none of the virtues, of civilized men.[33]

De Smet believed that white frontier culture was fraught with many vices, including frequent divorce and drinking to excess, and he wanted to insulate the Native Americans from the evil influences of the settlers.

Grant's "Peace Policy"

During the 1870s, government officials pushed the Sioux onto reservations, ending their nomadic lifestyle of following the buffalo. By the 1880s, the buffalo population collapsed partly as a result of the U.S. Army's policy of overhunting the animals in order to destroy the Plains Indians' food supply. Settlers also hunted the buffalo for hides and tongues. The lives of many Plains Indians changed drastically at this time because they were unable to hunt buffalo and were forced to live on reservations. To encourage them to adapt to Western culture, President Ulysses S. Grant and Department of the Interior agents enacted in 1870 what was known as Grant's "Peace Policy:" a policy which advocated Christianizing the Native Americans as an integral step to "civilizing" and "pacifying" them.[34] To carry out his plan, Grant decided to assign one Christian denomination to each reservation. Once a denomination received an assignment, it had the exclusive right to evangelize the Native Americans on that reservation. Under this plan, a denomination could not evangelize any Native nation or band to which the government did not assign it. By prohibiting interdenominational competition, Grant attempted to insulate the Native Americans from the bitter tensions that existed between many religious denominations. He believed that such competition would hinder their acceptance of Christianity. Under the Peace Policy, the federal government also provided funding to run the schools that Protestant and Catholic missionaries established in their assigned areas.[35]

Aside from the infringement of religious liberty, one of the many problems with this system was the fact that the government did not consult with Native leaders adequately to determine which denomination they desired or, for that matter, if they desired any denomination at all. The government did not allow Catholic missionaries to evangelize the Lakota Sioux, who had been relocated to the Pine Ridge and Rosebud reservations in South Dakota in 1876. However, during a visit to Washington to attend a series of meetings with President Hayes beginning on 26 September 1877, Lakota chiefs Red Cloud and Little Wound both specifically requested Catholic priests for their bands. At these meetings, Red Cloud said:

> I would like to have stock of all kinds to work with, and live like white people; I also desire to have farming implements of all kinds. I also want schools to enable my children to read and write, so they will be as wise as the white man's children. . . . [On the second day of meetings he said] I want you to give me school teachers, so that we will have a good school house, and learn my children how to write and read. Catholic priests are good, and I want you to give me one of them also. . . . [On the third day he continued] We would like to have Catholic priests and nuns, so that they could teach our people how to read and write.[36]

Little Wound, too, stated:

> I wish to have all the provisions that a white man has—the animals that he has, so I can learn and bring my children up in the same way the whites do theirs. We want farming implements of all kinds to cultivate the soil. I also want a Catholic Priest.[37]

Moreover, on 15 July 1878, the *New York Times* reported that at a council in South Dakota with E. A. Hayt, Commissioner of Indian Affairs, Red Cloud repeated his request for a Catholic priest.[38]

The Permanent Mission to the Lakota Sioux

Ultimately, the government's policy to prohibit interdenominational competition fell under attack from both Protestants and Catholics. The combined lobbying efforts of both denominations forced the government to rescind the ban in 1881; consequently, all churches gained the legal right of access to all reservations.[39] As a result, the Jesuits were once again allowed to evangelize the Lakota Sioux, and Jesuit missionaries traveled to the Rosebud and Pine Ridge reservations in South Dakota in 1886 and 1887, respectively. On these reservations, they established boarding schools within a year of arriving. Beginning with basic English, math, science, and religion, the schools eventually added industrial education, including instruction for the boys in dairy farming, carpentry, poultry farming, cattle ranching, baking, electrical wiring, blacksmithing, and the farming of various agricultural products. The farms attached to the schools produced the bulk of the food used by the students. The girls of the schools learned, in addition to the standard academic subjects, canning, sewing, and embroidery, skills that would benefit them economically in their adult lives. Because the traditional Plains hunting economy had collapsed, the Jesuits taught skills that would allow them to survive in the changing economy of South Dakota. Boarding schools were necessary because the reservations were so spread out and had few paved roads before 1930. Thus, no way existed for the children to travel to the schools on a daily basis. Also, the Sioux were so poor that the children were often better fed and clothed in the mission schools than they would have been in their homes. The Sioux had the option to send their children to either the Jesuit schools or the public schools. Before children could attend the Jesuit schools, their parents had to sign a petition allowing them to attend. This method assured that the parents sent their children to the Catholic schools on a voluntary basis.[40]

When the Jesuits arrived on the Dakota reservations, many Sioux had already converted to Catholicism, including the Lakota Sioux leader Red Cloud and his family. Moreover, by this time many French and Mexican men, who were Catholic, had married Sioux women, and thus had brought Catholicism to the Sioux through marriage. Marriages between the Sioux and people of French and Mexican origin continued, and by the 1950s most of the people on the reservations were part French or Mexican. Thus, the practice of "traditional" religion had become a rather complex issue, given the fact that their heritage was mixed.

Despite the intermingling of these ethnic groups for hundreds of years, the tradition of celibacy still was foreign to Lakota culture; in fact, it was one reason for the lack of Native American vocations to the priesthood. Additionally, candidates to the priesthood had to study in seminaries that were far removed from their lands. Most Native Americans had no desire to leave their lands and people for long periods of time, and similarly most had no desire to learn Latin. The lack of Native American priests was a significant hinderance to the Catholic missions. Yet, the Jesuits did appoint many Native Americans as catechists. The Lakota catechists preached in the Lakota language at gatherings, led prayers, prayed with the sick, and performed funeral rites. They also traveled to other Native American nations as missionaries to spread the Catholic faith to them.

Although few Native Americans became priests, the Jesuits wanted the Lakotas to have Native role models and brought to their attention several Native Catholics whose profound holiness, they believed, should be imitated. In their sermons, the Jesuits spoke often of the Mohawk woman, Kateri Tekakwitha, as a way of illustrating the universality of the Catholic Church. Tekakwitha was born in New York in 1656 near a Jesuit mission. During her life the Jesuits recognized her as a model Catholic for enduring persecution from her fellow Mohawk on account of her faith. Desiring to pursue a religious vocation, she took a vow of chastity and made plans to found a convent. Even though she died at the age of 24, she acquired a reputation for her sanctity.[41] The Church declared Tekakwitha venerable in 1943 and beatified her in 1980. In their sermons, the Jesuits often spoke of Kateri Tekakwitha as a model for the Sioux to follow and used her as an example to show that the different peoples were equal in the eyes of God.[42] At the mission schools, the Sioux students, under the direction of the Jesuits, also performed several plays about the life of Tekakwitha to give Sioux children a strong Native American woman as a role model.[43]

The Jesuits on the Dakota reservations did not seek to eradicate Sioux culture completely; however, they did want to eradicate certain aspects of it. They certainly sought to rid the reservations of the influence of the shamans, since they thought the shamans were influenced by the devil.[44] The missionaries even engaged in seizing and destroying the shamans' paraphernalia. However, despite their opinion of the "medicine men," they did not believe that the entire Sioux religion was evil.

One aspect of Lakota culture about which the Jesuits had mixed feelings was the Lakota dance tradition, although the missionaries became increasingly tolerant of Lakota dances as the years progressed. Nevertheless, from the 1890s to the 1920s, many of the Jesuits tried to discourage Lakota Catholics from taking part in traditional dances or even ridiculed them for doing so.[45] They did not think the dances in themselves were evil, but rather believed that the dances led to illicit behavior at night.[46] Furthermore, the Lakotas would travel to dances that lasted several days, and the Jesuits maintained that this distraction caused them to leave their homes and neglect their domestic affairs. The Jesuits believed that the frequent absences from the house and farm because of dancing adversely affected the Lakotas' economic conditions.[47] Even so, the Jesuits became more tolerant of the Native American dances in the 1930s. Indeed, during the next two decades the Jesuits often attended Native dances, allowed Catholics to participate in them, and even praised them. By then, the Jesuits did not consider the dances a threat to Catholic discipline.[48]

One practice that the Jesuits believed adversely affected the Lakotas' economic conditions was a ceremony called the give-away. When a Lakota person died, his or her family traditionally gave away most of the family's possessions. The Lakotas also performed the give-away at dances, adoption ceremonies, coming-of-age ceremonies, or at other significant events. Despite the Jesuits' opposition, Lakota Catholics continued to perform the give-away. The continuation of this practice showed that Sioux Catholics on their own initiative preserved their traditional mourning customs.[49] In regard to other mourning rites, the Jesuits were more tolerant. Because some of the Lakotas wanted to continue the practice of burying their dead above ground on scaffolds or in trees, the Jesuits allowed this practice to continue.[50] In addition to their flexibility about modes of burial, the Jesuits accepted the Lakota custom of wailing over the graves of their dead.[51] For example, in 1910 after giving the rite of the anointing of the sick (extreme unction) to a dying Lakota man, one of the Jesuits in the Dakotas, Florentine Digmann, described a mourning ritual:

> At our arrival he was actually dying; gave him absolution, Extreme Unction and scapular. The house was full of Indians. During his agony I said all the prayers for the dying. They respectfully kept quiet. After I had finished one asked: "Are you through?" Upon my "Yes" the whole crowd began their mourning howl, in and outside of the tipi, nearly all night long.[52]

In their efforts to conform to Lakota culture, the missionaries participated in several Sioux customs. For example, the Sioux had a ritual in which they adopted people into their families as a sign of respect and friendship. The Sioux adopted several Jesuits, some of whom underwent elaborate adoption ceremonies.[53] The Lakotas also referred to the Jesuits with the Lakota names they gave to them. On some occasions, the Jesuits also smoked the pipe with the Lakotas.[54] In 1939, William Moore, a Jesuit missionary to the Sioux, explained the Jesuits' attitudes towards the Sioux: "The missionaries of St. Francis Mission on the Rosebud reservation, South Dakota, try to adapt their work to the Indian spirit. They are concerned about instilling the life of grace into the souls of their people, not about imposing alien customs upon a race which clings to its traditional ways."[55] Moore was saying that the Jesuits sought to offer the Sioux the Christian faith and not to give them a new culture.

The Jesuits also recognized that Lakota culture and religion possessed many natural virtues. They believed that long before they were Christianized, the Lakotas had the natural virtue of charity. In fact, some Jesuits said that the charity of the Sioux was greater than that of white people: For instance, in 1920 Charles Weisenhorn observed, "No people is more generous than the Indian and gladly does he put all he has at the disposal of his guest, no matter at what hour of the day or night the latter may show up."[56] Another Jesuit from the Dakotas, Placidus Sialm, noted in 1938: "It is an old Indian custom for the more prosperous to share with the needy. 'We Indians,' they say, 'are not like the white people. We feed our visitors when we have something to eat in our house.' Back of this I seem to hear One who says 'give and it shall be given to you.'"[57] The Jesuits desired to build on the natural virtues that the Sioux already possessed and, from their point of view, perfect these virtues with the Christian conception of love.[58] From the Jesuits' perspective, the Lakotas' generosity and charity were examples of their perception of the natural law. At the Dakota missions, the Jesuits advocated the preservation of Lakota art, medicine, food, games, and some of their traditional rituals and ethics. Furthermore, they believed that some continuity existed between traditional Lakota religion and Christianity. The Jesuits thought that some of the Lakotas' indigenous customs and religious beliefs contained rays of truth that could be built on and perfected by Christianity.[59]

An emphasis on ritual was common to both Catholicism and traditional Lakota religion, and the Jesuits in South Dakota certainly stressed ritual at the missions. The most popular procession at these missions, however, was the *Corpus Christi*, which the Jesuits and Lakotas performed each year from 1889 through the 1940s.[60] Celebrated in the Church since the thirteenth century, the solemnity of the *Corpus Christi* was the feast of the Blessed Sacrament, which usually occurred in June. During this celebration, which often took place outdoors, the priests carried the Eucharist in a monstrance accompanied by a procession of the laity and clergy. Often the laity carried banners in these processions and threw flowers in the path of the Eucharist. At St. Francis and Holy Rosary missions some *Corpus Christi* processions were small and just involved the people who went to a local chapel. But occasionally, the Jesuits and Lakotas organized large and elaborate processions, and sometimes over 1,000 Lakotas participated.[61] The *Corpus Christi* processions were actually similar in some ways to the Lakota dances. Many Lakota dances themselves were a kind of procession, a long line of dancers who danced behind one another as they moved forward. The *Corpus Christi* processions and Lakota dances were both elaborate outdoor celebrations that involved processions. Some elements of these two types of celebrations were similar, and the *Corpus Christi* processions were appealing to the Lakotas. One of the Jesuits at the Dakota missions, Joseph Zimmerman, S. J., believed that the Lakotas' traditional religious tendencies aided their transition to the Catholic Church: In 1933, he wrote, "The simplicity and reverence in worship is edifying. Age-old love of ceremony enables [the Lakotas] to fit into our Catholic practices."[62] Thus, the ritual life of the Catholic Church was one of the elements that attracted the Lakotas to the Church.[63]

The Jesuits conformed themselves to Native culture in several ways, and the most important of these was their use of the Lakota language. In fact, most of the Jesuits who came to the Sioux missions from 1886 to 1910 learned to speak Lakota.[64] Indeed many acquired it so quickly that they preached sermons in Lakota by 1887.[65] The government, however, prohibited the use of the Native language in the federally funded mission schools, and, therefore, the Jesuits complied and discouraged the use of Lakota in the schools.[66] Nevertheless, outside the mission schools, the Jesuits encouraged the use of Lakota in many ways. At the annual Catholic Sioux Congresses, which Sioux Catholics from both North and South Dakota attended, the participants primarily spoke either the Lakota or Dakota dialects of the Sioux language, and both the Jesuits and Sioux catechists preached in the Lakota or Dakota dialects.[67] The Jesuits also encouraged the Lakotas to write articles in the Lakota dialect to spread the faith. The Lakotas contributed these articles to a monthly periodical called the *Sina*

Sapa Wocekine Taeyanpaha, The Catholic Sioux Herald, which was published from 1893 to 1936, and was written primarily in the Lakota and Dakota dialects. Most of the authors of the articles were Sioux men or women who used this periodical to write of their experiences as Catholics and to keep each other informed about the Church's activities on the different Sioux reservations. Furthermore, in 1939, one of the Jesuits, Eugene Buechel, completed a book, *A Grammar of Lakota*, for the purpose of preserving the Lakota language.[68] Moreover, Buechel recorded, wholly in the Lakota language, 100 Lakota legends, which were published posthumously.[69] Even though these legends were an essential part of Lakota religion, Buechel wanted to preserve them and did not feel that they were a threat to the Catholic faith. Buechel also wrote a book of prayers and a Bible history, both in the Lakota language, to help the Lakotas understand the Catholic faith. In 1924, Buechel published *Wowapi Wakan: Bible History in the Language of the Teton Sioux Indians*, a work of over 300 pages, all in Lakota.[70] In 1925, Buechel had 3,500 copies of his *Bible History* produced, and he distributed them on Pine Ridge and Rosebud.[71] Buechel wrote *Lakota Wocekiye na Olowan Wowapi: Sioux Indian Prayer and Hymn Book*, which he published in 1927.[72] He distributed at least 5,000 of these prayer-books across the reservations.[73] Written mostly in Lakota, this 380-page book was a collection of Bible passages, hymns, and prayers. In sum, Buechel's books, the *Catholic Sioux Herald*, the Catholic Sioux Congresses, the Jesuits' willingness to study the Lakota language, and the Jesuits' and Lakota catechists' preaching in Lakota all created an atmosphere on the Pine Ridge and Rosebud reservations that fostered the use of the Lakota dialect during the period from 1886 to 1945.

One of the interesting aspects of the Jesuits' use of Lakota was that they translated the term "God" into the Native language as *Wakan Tanka*, the traditional Lakota term for God.[74] *Wakan Tanka* literally means the "Great Spirit" or the "Great Mystery." In their sermons and articles, the Jesuits at Holy Rosary and St. Francis used the term *Wakan Tanka* interchangeably with "God" to indicate to the Lakotas that continuity exists between their traditional religion and the Catholic faith. They believed that the Lakota were monotheists,[75] and because the Jesuits saw the Lakota religion as being relatively advanced,[76] they were able to use *Wakan Tanka* as a translation for "God." In an article he wrote in 1928, Leo Cunningham, a Jesuit of Holy Rosary mission on Pine Ridge Reservation, observed that at the Holy Rosary Mission boarding school "367 Sioux Indian boys and girls are being taught to know and love *Wakan Tanka*, the Great Spirit."[77] Similarly, another of the Jesuits in the Dakotas, John Scott, indicated that continuity existed between the two religions: "Thanks to the untiring efforts of the Blackrobe, the faith of the Sioux in *Wakan Tanka*, the Great Spirit, was not crushed under the wheels of invading *Waischu* [white people]."[78] Rather than trying to obliterate the Lakotas' faith, the Jesuits, in

Scott's opinion, preserved the Lakotas' faith in the Great Spirit. In addition, Jesuit Joseph Zimmerman of Holy Rosary commented that among the Lakotas "there is almost universal acceptance of the God of Christianity as the Great Spirit, *Wakan Tanka*, in whom the race has always believed."[79] Thus, in language and in ritual the Jesuits took significant steps to conform to Lakota culture.

Conversion and Coercion

In the history of the Catholic missions, the great majority of the Native Americans who converted to Catholicism did so of their own free will. However, in some cases, particularly in Mexico, a coercive atmosphere existed which pressured indigenous peoples to accept the missionaries. The example of the Yaqui of the Sonora desert (present-day Northern Mexico) shows that the circumstances of the Spanish conquest did put pressure on the Native Americans to allow the missionaries into their communities. The Yaqui, for example, had been fighting Spanish troops since 1609, but, in 1614, agreed to make peace and allow the Jesuits to establish a mission among them. They knew of the work of the Fathers through contact with groups such as the Mayo, among whom the Jesuits had already founded missions and established farming communities. The missionaries had successfully organized the Mayo communities' agricultural endeavors and had produced great surpluses of food. The mission not only protected the Mayo from most of the taxes that other Mexicans had to pay, but also gave them some protection from the Spanish who sought recruits for the gold and silver mines. Thus, the Yaqui realized that they had few options—to fight and be conquered by the Spanish, to submit to the rule of the Spanish, or to accept the establishment of a Jesuit mission. Yet, these forms of pressure were not present in Paraguay, New France, or the United States.[80]

For the most part, Native Americans converted not because missionaries forced them to, but rather because missionaries convinced them to do so. They converted because they were curious about Christianity, and when they learned more about it, they decided voluntarily to convert. Some people could argue that U.S. government officials used the missionaries to force the Native Americans to accept Christianity. However, applying pressure against a traditional religion does not necessarily make people convert. For example, the British government made the Catholic Mass illegal in Ireland and repressed the Church there, but the Irish did not abandon their faith; quite the contrary, the repression strengthened the Catholic Church in Ireland. Putting pressure on people to abandon their religious traditions does not force them away from their traditions. Native Americans could have ignored the missionaries, but they did not because they were attracted to the faith rather than coerced against their wills. Similarly, the missionaries did not force the Lakotas to attend Catholic schools. They had the choice of going to either public or religious schools and they chose the Catholic schools. Each year, Lakota parents had to sign petitions to send their children to Catholic schools; if they did not, the children would attend public schools.

If one examines the 400-year history of missionaries in the Americas, one will find some cases in which the missionaries were too harsh or used coercive measures to influence Native Americans. Harsh punishments and coercive measures, however, were rare in the missions because the missionaries did not want Christianity to be associated with punishment. Current historians often denounce the missionaries for striving to eradicate the cultures of the Native Americans, but this accusation is also misguided. The decimation of the buffalo changed the Native American culture of the plains and thus had a profound effect on Native American religion. Because Native religion was so closely linked to economic conditions and because many Native religious rituals were devoted to ensuring good buffalo hunts or providing for a good harvest, the Native Americans' attitudes toward their hunting or farming rituals changed when the buffalo were no longer present and when they were no longer dependent on farming for survival. The transition from traditional economies to modern ones changed the Plains peoples' dependence on religious rituals designed to secure food, either by hunting or agriculture. Native American rituals, then, would have disappeared even without the influence of the missionaries.

Throughout the history of the conquest and colonization of the Americas, Catholic missionaries defended Native Americans from exploitation and sought to insulate them from the vices that the colonists brought. In Mexico and South America, they endeavored to protect them from slavery. In New France, they tried to protect them from those who sold the Native Americans brandy and cheated them out of their lands. Because they did not believe that the lifestyle and values of the colonists on the frontier were ideal, the Jesuits did not want Native Americans to adopt the "culture" of the colonists. Rather, the missionaries adapted to the demands of the situation and conformed themselves to Native American cultures. Eradication of Native cultures was never a goal of the missionaries, and they realized that trying to do so would only make Native peoples resent them. Because the missionaries saw truth and virtues in Native customs, they often saw no need to change many of them, but rather wanted to preserve them. Often, they tried to take that which they saw as good in Native American religion and build on it with Christian teachings. In this way, they sought to perfect the truth and virtue that they believed was already present in Native religions and cultures.

Notes

1. Vine Deloria, Jr., *Custer Died for Your Sins* (New York: Avon, 1969).

2. Harvey Markowitz, "The Catholic Mission and the Sioux: A Crisis in the Early Paradigm," *Sioux Indian Religion* (Norman: University of Oklahoma Press, 1987), 113–37.

3. Bartolomé de Las Casas, *In Defence of the Indians*, trans. and ed. Stafford Poole, C. M. (DeKalb: Northern Illinois University Press, 1992), 26–27.

4. Ibid., 7–27, 175–81, 353–62; C. Lippy, R. Choquette, and S. Poole, *Christianity Comes to the Americas* (New York: Paragon, 1992), 81–90.

5. Philip Caraman, *The Lost Paradise: An Account of the Jesuits in Paraguay, 1607–1768* (London: Sidgwick & Jackson, 1975), 69–81, 99–169.

6. Ibid., 116–53.

7. Antonio Ruiz de Montoya, S. J., *The Spiritual Conquest* (1639; reprint St. Louis: The Institute of Jesuit Sources, 1993), 53.

8. William Bangert, S. J., *A History of the Society of Jesus* (St. Louis: Institute of Jesuit Sources, 1986), 256–60.

9. C. J. McNaspy, introduction to *The Spiritual Conquest* by Antonio Ruiz de Montoya, S. J., *The Spiritual Conquest* (1639; reprint, St. Louis: The Institute of Jesuit Sources), 11–24.

10. Ruiz de Montoya, 101.

11. Ibid., 15–16, 100–13.

12. Ibid., 18–19.

13. Bangert, 350–54.

14. Ibid., 256–60, 390; Caraman, 253–55, 272–80.

15. James Moore, *Indian and Jesuit* (Chicago: Loyola University Press, 1982), 73–76.

16. Edna Kenton, ed., *The Jesuit Relations* (New York: Vanguard Press, 1954), 113–14.

17. Ibid., 113–15; Moore, 41–58.

18. Moore, 43, 56.

19. Ibid., 41–58, 117, 131–33.

20. Ross Enochs, *The Jesuit Mission to the Lakota Sioux: Pastoral Theology and Ministry, 1886–1945* (Kansas City: Sheed & Ward, 1995), chapter 6.

21. Moore, 109–111.

22. Ibid., 118.

23. Ibid., 99–126.

24. Ibid., 131.

25. Enochs, chapter 1.

26. Moore, 132–33.

27. Ibid., 139–40.

28. Ibid., 146.

29. Ibid., 129–86.

30. Enochs, 5–19.

31. C. T. Campell to N. G. Taylor, Commissioner of Indian Affairs, Yankton, D. T., 13 June 1867, *Report on Indian Affairs by the Acting Commissioner for the Year 1867* (Washington, DC, 1868), 238; Enochs, 12–23.

32. Sully to De Smet, 28 Feb. 1866, in *The Jesuits of the Middle United States*, Gilbert Garraghan, S. J., ed. (New York: America Press, 1938), 2:481.

33. H. Chittenden and A. Richardson, *Life, Letters and Travels of Father Pierre-Jean De Smet, S. J.* (New York: Francis Harper, 1905), 3:856; De Smet to unknown priest, letter, Fort Benton, Montana, 10 June 1866.

34. E. S. Parker, "Report of the Commissioner of Indian Affairs," 31 Oct. 1870, in *Annual Report of the Commissioner of Indian Affairs*, Washington, DC, 1871), 10.

35. Peter Rahill, *The Catholic Indian Missions and Grant's Peace Policy: 1870–1884* (Washington, DC: Catholic University Press, 1953).

36. Transcript of meeting between Chiefs Red Cloud, Spotted Tail, and other Chiefs and President Hayes, Executive Mansion, 26 Sept. 1877, Council Proceedings 26 May 1875–19 April 1894, RG 75, Box 779, National Archives, Kansas City Branch, 201, 216, 226.

37. Ibid., 204–5.

38. "Red Cloud in an Ugly Temper," *New York Times*, 15 July 1878, 1; Enochs, 23.

39. Rahill, 305–7.

40. Enochs, chapter 2.

41. Ellen Walworth, "Our Little Sister Kateri Tekakwitha, the Lily of the Mohawks," *Indian Sentinel* (1908): 9.

42. Marquette University Archives, Saint Francis Mission Collection, series 7, box 3, folder 7; Eugene Buechel, S. J., "All Saints' Day: On Heaven," sermon, Holy Rosary Mission, 1 Nov. 1907.

43. Marquette University Archives, Holy Rosary Mission Collection, series 1/1, box 2, folder 1, Program, "The Princess of the Mohawks," Holy Rosary Mission, presented 19 and 20 May 1938.

44. Louis Goll, S. J., *Jesuit Missions Among the Sioux* (St. Francis: St. Francis Mission, 1940), 15.

45. Louis Goll, S. J., "Catholic and Protestant Missionaries Confer at Pierre," *Indian Sentinel* 3 (Jan. 1923): 13.

46. Marquette University Archives, Holy Rosary Mission Collection, series 7, box 14, folder 8, Florentine Digmann, S. J., diary, 21 Nov. 1889.

47. Marquette University Archives, Bureau of Catholic Indian Missions Collection, series 1, box 217, folder 2, Fr. Goll, 15 Dec. 1933, notes, 10 pages, p. 4.

48. John Scott, S. J., interview, Creighton University, Omaha, Oct. 1992. John Scott, S. J., "Sun Dance in Dakota," *Jesuit Missions* 15 (June 1941): 167.

49. Marquette University Archives, Holy Rosary Mission Collection series 7, box 17, folders (5–7), Fr. Placidus Sialm, S. J., *Camp Churches*, unpublished manuscript, p. 92.

50. Florentine Digmann, S. J., "I Want to See the Great Spirit," *Indian Sentinel* 4 (Jan. 1924): 26; Marquette University Archives, Holy Rosary Mission Collection series 7, box 14, folder 8, Digmann, diary, 1 Sept. 1887, p. 12.

51. Marquette University Archives, Holy Rosary Mission Collection, series 2/1, box 1, folder 6, "Chronicles of the Sisters of St. Francis," 1903 entry, p. 18.

52. Marquette University Archives, Holy Rosary Mission Collection series 7, box 14, folder 8, Digmann, diary, 27 Feb. 1910.

53. Fr. Albert Riester, S. J., "Sioux Trails all Lead to Big Road," *Indian Sentinel* 11 (winter 1930–31): 7; "Otto Moorman," *News-letter: Missouri Province, Society of Jesus Missouri Province Newsletter* 18 (March 1954): 70; Albert Muntsch, S. J., "White Eagle," *Indian Sentinel* 34 (Jan. 1954): 15–16; "Otto Moorman," *News-letter: Missouri Province, Society of Jesus Missouri Province Newsletter* 18 (March 1954): 70; Olivia and Hobert Pourier, interview, Sharps Corner, Pine Ridge Reservation, June and October, 1992; and *Tom Tom* 4 (June 1938): 3, Holy Rosary Collection 4–11, Missouri Province Archives of the Society of Jesus in St. Louis.

54. Marquette University Archives, Bureau of Catholic Indian Mission Collection, series 14/1, box 4, folder 2, Henry Westropp, S. J., "A Relic of Father DeSmet," *Calumet* (Dec. 1913).

55. William Moore, S. J., "With the Sioux in Camp," *Indian Sentinel* 19 (Oct. 1939): 118.

56. Charles Weisenhorn, S. J., "A Missionary Trip in South Dakota," *Woodstock Letters* 49 (1920): 157.

57. Placidus Sialm, S. J., "Dakota News," *Indian Sentinel* 18 (April 1938): 64.

58. Joseph Zimmerman, S. J., "Sioux Virtues," *Indian Sentinel* 20 (Jan. 1940): 11–12.

59. Enochs, *Jesuit Mission*, chapter 6.

60. Marquette University Archives, Holy Rosary Mission Collection, series 7, box 14, folder 8, Digmann, diary, 20 June 1889, p. 18.

61. "Corpus Christi Procession at Holy Rosary Mission," *Jesuit Bulletin* 3 (March 1924): 14.

62. Marquette University Archives, Bureau of Catholic Indian Missions Collection, series 1, box 217, folder 1, Joseph Zimmerman, S. J., to Mr. and Mrs. Poulter, 1 May 1933.

63. Enochs, chapter 6.

64. Placidus Sialm, S. J., "In Memory of Those Who Have Labored Among the Sioux," *Indian Sentinel* 1 (April 1919): 37–38; Marquette University Archives, St. Francis Mission

Collection series 7, box 5, folders 14–15, Emil Perrig, S. J., diary, 5 May 1889, 21 Sept. 1890; *Indian Sentinel* 3 (April 1923): 84; and Marquette University Archives, Bureau of Catholic Indian Missions, series 14/1, box 4, folder 2, *Calumet* (Oct. 1927).

65. Emil Perrig, S. J., St. Francis Mission, 15 Feb. 1887, *Woodstock Letters* 16 (1887) 173–75.

66. H. Price, Commissioner of Indian Affairs, "Report of the Commissioner of Indian Affairs," *Annual Report of the Commissioner of Indian Affairs to the Secretary of the Interior for the Year 1881*, p. xxxiv.

67. Marquette University Archives, St. Francis Mission Collection, series 7, boxes 2–3, Eugene Buechel, S. J., diary, 17 vols., 1893–1954.

68. Eugene Buechel, S. J., *A Grammar of Lakota* (Chicago: John Swift, 1939), iv.

69. Eugene Buechel, S. J., *Lakota Tales and Text* (St. Louis: John Swift, 1978).

70. Buechel, S. J., *Lakota Tales and Text*.

71. Marquette University Archives, Bureau of Catholic Indian Missions Collection, series 1, box 153, folder 1, Buechel to Lusk, 5 Feb. 1925, p. 2.

72. The Jesuit Fathers of St. Francis Mission (Eugene Buechel, S. J., was the primary author), *Lakota Wocekiye na Olowan Wowampi* (St. Louis: Central Verein of America, 1927).

73. Marquette University Archives, St. Francis Mission Collection, series 7, box 1, folder 4, Director of Central Verein to Buechel, 4 Feb. 1927.

74. Eugene Buechel, S. J., *Wowapi Wakan: Bible History in the Language of the Teton Sioux Indians* (Chicago: Benziger Brothers, 1924); The Jesuit Fathers of St. Francis Mission, Lakota Wocekiye na Olowan Wowampi.

75. Louis Goll, S. J., *Jesuit Missions and the Sioux*, 14.

76. Marquette University Archives, Holy Rosary Mission Collection, series 7, box 19, folder 10, Henry Westropp, S. J., "In the Land of the Wigwam," c. 1910, p. 2; *Indian Sentinel* 1 (April 1919): 36.

77. Marquette University Archives, Holy Rosary Mission Collection, series 7, box 19, folder 10, Henry Westropp, S. J., "In the Land of the Wigwam," c. 1910, p. 2; *Indian Sentinel* 1 (April 1919): 36.

78. Marquette University Archives, Holy Rosary Mission Collection, series 7, box 19, folder 10, Henry Westropp, S. J., "In the Land of the Wigwam," c. 1910, p. 2; *Indian Sentinel* 1 (April 1919): 36.

79. Marquette University Archives, Bureau of Catholic Indian Missions series 14/1, box 4, folder 4, Joseph Zimmerman, S. J., "The True Faith Versus Paganism," *Calumet* (May 1944): 16–17.

80. Evelyn Hu-DeHart, *Missionaries, Miners and Indians* (Tucson: University of Arizona Press, 1981); Edward Spicer, *Cycles of Conquest* (Tucson: University of Arizona Press, 1962).

11

Stolen Spirits:
An Illustrative Case of Indigenous
Survival Through Religious Freedom

Gabrielle A. Tayac

> In our ways, spiritual consciousness is the highest form of politics.
> —The Hau De No Sau Nee Message to the Western World, 1977
> (Akwesasne Notes, 1977, p. 71)

Religious Freedom and Cultural Genocide

The guarantee of religious freedom is an essential feature of the Constitution of the United States. It is a principle that is embedded throughout American law and moral precept. Full religious tolerance has not been extended to Native Americans, however. Not until 1978, when Congress passed the American Indian Religious Freedom Act (AIRFA), was religious freedom clearly established in the law of the republic for the indigenous peoples. Yet, even today, courts rarely uphold or enforce AIRFA (Vecsey, 1991). Congress has not yet passed legislation to adequately safeguard the free exercise of Native American religious traditions, particularly with regard to access to sacred sites (Peregoy, 1993). Native Americans, with their unique religious traditions that are inextricably intertwined with Mother Earth and her powers, are left unprotected in reality despite the promise of law.

The chasm between the ideology of the promised guarantee of religious freedom and the reality of the effective prohibition of religious practice is a problem of particular concern for students of sociology—especially when one is, like myself, Native American. In addressing this problem in my research, I have the opportunity to apply the insights of an academic discipline that I find fascinating to a social problem of deep, indeed personal, concern. There are hundreds of specific cases that clearly trace the lack of religious freedom for indigenous peoples. Behind these numbers are real people who experience continuous anguish, frustration, and anger because they cannot be themselves in their own homeland. They suffer the phenomenon known as "ethnostress." Ethnostress is, in our definition, the feel-ing "when the cultural beliefs or joyful identity of a people are disrupted"; it commonly occurs for individuals and communities whose spirituality is open to constant degradation (Antone, Miller, & Myers, 1986, p. 7). In response, throughout the history of our societies, indigenous peoples have organized effective resistance movements and strategies to counter the many effects of ethnostress and, its partner on a larger scale, "cultural genocide."

What is cultural genocide? Tinker (1993) defines it as "the effective destruction of a people by systematically or systemically (intentionally or unintentionally in order to achieve other goals) destroying, eroding, or undermining the integrity of the culture and system of values that defines a people and gives them life" (p. 6). Cultural genocide is carried out when vital traditions, such as religious belief and practice, are prohibited. The denial of religion by an invading power, either colonial or national, deeply and directly undercuts the sovereignty of indigenous nations. The mainte-nance and persistence of indigenous religious tradition, then, corresponds directly with the preservation of autonomy and self-determination for the entire indigenous society.

Religious tradition and spirituality are central to the shared identity of an ethnic group, as sociologists recognize. To appreciate the important role that religion plays in shaping a people's sense of themselves, consider another definition—that of ethnicity, offered by Orlando Patterson—"a form of commitment, an ideology, or more properly, a faith; one that is often secular, but is also frequently a secular faith layered on a more profound religious faith" (1977, p. 10). For indigenous peoples, religious and secular institutions are often integrated (Talamantez, 1991; Brown, 1991; Nelson, 1983; Martin, 1991). From this, we can see that religious faith and ethnic identity are not compartmentalized. Indeed, a body of traditional knowl-edge informed by sacred narratives of common origins, or creation myths, unifies people into a shared ethnicity (Anderson, 1991; Gellner, 1983). Fur-thermore, a people who commit themselves to the survival of their ethnic identity must protect their religious traditions. Conversely, the efforts of colonizing powers to undermine a group's ethnic identity are generally carried out through the destruction of those traditions.

In studying indigenous societies, such as Native Americans, we find that they tend to integrate ethnicity with nationhood. As Connor (1972, p. 248) concludes, "self-differentiating ethnic groups are in fact nations." Williams, as well, defines a nation as a "politically conscious ethny [ethnic group]" (1994, p. 53). Consistent with these concepts, then, we see further that indigenous societies fuse sovereign governmental powers with ethnicity through the practice of cultural traditions and collective actions. Acting as a sovereign nation, a traditional society maintains a government-to-govern-ment relationship with the dominant power, whether colonial or national.

Even the United States government recognizes Native American nations as holding quasi-sovereign status. Indigenous traditional governments, bounded by ethnic lines and pervaded by religious traditions, continue to operate either in their own homelands or, in effect, as governments-in-exile if they have been removed to other locations.

How can we understand how cultural genocide is carried out? One approach that sociologists take is to conduct analyses of many cases to see if there are common patterns. Through this kind of research, we can illuminate patterns of cultural genocide that such cases share in common. Yet, every act that prohibits the free exercise of religion is complex and unique within itself. By focusing on one case—a second research strategy—we can see more clearly why religious freedom is so central to identity maintenance and how its denial acts as a tool of assimilation. To this end, I have conducted fieldwork within the Piscataway Indian Nation from 1987 (Tayac, 1988) to the present. An examination of the Piscataway case lays bare the ways in which an invading society (first Britain and then the United States) attempts to assault indigenous identity, as well as how an indigenous society innovatively resists such attack. As it often happens in academic research, my study begins with a personal story.

The Meaning of Moyaone

Throughout an exceptionally warm November night one year, my relatives and I maintained the traditional annual vigil for the Feast of the Dead ceremony at the ancient Piscataway burial grounds called Moyaone, located in what is now called Maryland. Moyaone is also the site of the Piscataway Chiefdom's capital town, first reported by Captain John Smith in 1608 (Smith, 1984). Below us lay hundreds of ancestors whom their relatives had lovingly buried in ossuaries centuries ago. The calls of migrating Canada geese often overwhelmed our conversation. During this breezy night on the Potomac shore, we talked about how beautiful it must have been here before the consequences of English invasion forced the Piscataway to leave their stockaded village, fields, and ancestors. We could almost see it. Almost.

According to the traditional knowledge of the Piscataway people, the human remains interred at Moyaone make the site sacred. The ancestor's bones are all that is left of that person. Every smile, every sigh, every conversation, every thought that person expressed while he or she lived eventually is concentrated into all that remains of this ancestor after death—bones. These bones, in contact with Mother Earth, transport the dead on a journey to the spirit world. The ancestors act as intermediaries for the prayers of the living to the Creator. In that sense, a living person is never alone, but always has the company of ancestors in the spirit world to guide and to help him or her. The boundaries between the spirit world and the natural world are not concrete.

The Piscataway once practiced a treatment of the dead that was characteristic of the indigenous culture of the Eastern Woodlands—a ritual that endured from before the era of European contact until the early American National Period. When an individual died, he or she was raised on a scaffold. After a set period of time, a holy person known as the Vulture Man would strip the bodies of the dead and wrap them in deerskins. The body was then buried together with the remains of other deceased Piscataway in a mass grave or ossuary. A traditional ceremony—the Feast of the Dead— commemorated the burial. This practice has been described by European missionaries for many peoples of the Eastern Woodlands (Loskiel, 1794). For the Onondaga, a member nation of the Iroquois Confederacy, the term for warrior literally translates to "those who carry the bones of the ancestors upon their backs" (Lyons, 1990). The Feast of the Dead assured a final burial for the dead, who would then proceed on their journeys to the spirit world and help realize prayers of the living.

In contemporary times, Piscataway and other Native Americans have continued to draw upon the strengths of the ancestors. They have adapted the original Feast of the Dead ceremony to the constraints of the dominant Euro-American culture. While actual burials usually do not take place during the modern Feast of the Dead, the ancestors are honored and called upon to continue to guide the living in their daily lives. Although the method of burial has changed over the centuries and corresponds more in form to the norms of the dominant society, aboriginal customs and ceremonies persist. The meaning and sacredness of human remains have not changed.

The Problem at Moyaone

Over the past century, a series of archaeological excavations desecrated Moyaone (Ferguson & Ferguson, 1960; Stephenson, 1984). Archaeologists ripped hundreds of human remains from their final resting places, the ossuaries. Because these were non-Christian burials of non-white people, no law protecting cemeteries applied to Piscataway graves. The Piscataway themselves had no legal recourse to stop the excavations. Consistent with Piscataway traditions, it became the responsibility of the elders to provide an explanation that would give meaning to this unusual and despicable act. The kidnapped ancestors, as the Piscataway elders described, had been literally snatched from their journeys in the spirit world. These stolen spirits now existed in a type of "purgatory" (Slepicka, 1976). Without contact with Mother Earth, they could not carry out their divine instructions to fulfill the prayers of the living. Vast tracts of spiritually imbued land were left sterile. The Piscataway, both living and dead, had been assaulted.

By the 1970s, the Piscataway Indian Nation, or, more precisely, its incorporated tribal government, began a concerted effort to stop the continued desecration of their burial sites. In 1976, representatives of the Nation dismantled a cinder block structure, known as the "block house," that exhibited exposed Piscataway skeletons at Piscataway National Park. During the early 1980s, they achieved a moratorium on further excavations at Moyaone. In 1981, the International Indian Treaty Council, a non-governmental organization, selected the Moyaone case to exemplify desecration of indigenous sacred sites and burial grounds at the testimonials before the United Nations Working Group on Indigenous People in Geneva, Switzerland (Tayac, 1981). The excavated remains, however, linger in file cabinets in the Smithsonian Institution, the University of Michigan, and the Maryland Historical Trust. They are not alone. Thousands of disinterred indigenous remains from every region of the United States and the western hemisphere accompany them.

In other ways, we can document an ambiguous path toward resolution. Native Americans advocating for the repatriation of human remains and items of cultural patrimony, as well as future protection of graves, won a partial victory with the passage of the Native American Graves Protection and Repatriation Act of 1990 (NAGPRA). State governments, including Maryland, have also passed local versions of this federal legislation (Maryland Department of Housing and Community Development, 1994). The Smithsonian Institution, exempt from NAGPRA provisions, maintains its own guidelines for repatriation claims (Green & Mitchell, 1990; Killion, Bray, & Baugh, n.d.). These procedures maintain that tribes must prove that the human remains and objects that they claim are culturally affiliated to their modern populations. It is indigenous people, and not the desecrators, who must expend their limited resources in order to rectify past wrongs. Although some returns have been made to tribes under such legislation, most remains actually will stay in the custody of museums and government agencies because their cultural affiliation with existing peoples has not been documented by archaeologists and anthropologists. The Piscataway Indian Nation has filed claim for the Moyaone remains at the Smithsonian and at the Maryland Historical Trust, and currently awaits decisions from both agencies.

The Piscataway experience the problem as a restriction on their free exercise of religion. They see the constraints on their religious practices at Moyaone, as well, as a method of preventing the legitimation of their sovereignty, thus keeping them in a relatively powerless position. We can understand the dilemma, then, as a social conflict that arises out of differences in perceptions, socioeconomic resources, and political power between indigenous and immigrant groups. This is an important point for the sociologist. To understand how groups within a society interact, how they react to each other, and how they deal with their conflicts, both culture and social conditions must be analyzed.

The Death of Turkey Tayac

Moyaone today, located only fifteen miles south of Washington, DC, in Piscataway National Park, has survived intact partly because of a lucky historical accident. Moyaone at one time had been slated for development into a county sludge pit. Fortunately, Mount Vernon, the home of George Washington, lies directly in Moyaone's view. In 1961, as a National Park Service brochure states, Congress created Piscataway Park "to preserve for the benefit of present and future generations the historic and scenic values . . . of lands which provide the principal overview from the Mount Vernon estate" (National Park Service, 1990). A Piscataway chief also helped. Chief Turkey Tayac—named for the wild variety of a species the Piscataway consider holy, as other tribes think of the eagle—placed twenty acres of sacred land in the trust of the National Park Service for the creation of the park. Prior to the advent of the American Indian Movement during the 1960s, donations such as this were the sole means through which the Piscataway could protect Moyaone from industrial development. A verbal agreement between Chief Tayac and the Secretary of the Interior mandated that the Piscataway would always have free access to the site and that the Chief would be buried with his ancestors at Moyaone. Only through decades of constant political struggle would this promise be partially honored by the United States Government.

By the 1970s, the Piscataway sought to reclaim Moyaone. Turkey Tayac and others had come to believe that the National Park Service trust, instead of upholding their agreement to care for the land, actually contributed to its destruction. An additional shock to the Piscataway came soon after. In 1976, the chief grew ill—doctors diagnosed his condition as leukemia. Acknowledging his age and health, he decided to contact the Department of the Interior to make sure that his burial rights were in place. Astonishingly, Department officials told him that there was never such an agreement. In fact, they said, Secretary Stewart Udall, with whom the verbal deal was made, had never met him.

Chief Tayac died in 1978. However, in the two years before his death, the chief, along with other Piscataway and Native Americans of other nations who supported him, went to Congress to insist that the burial agreement be upheld. They produced photographs showing Secretary Udall and the chief embracing at the creation of Piscataway National Park (National Park Service, 1968). They emphasized the chief's respected standing as a traditional healer in the Native American community. And, they noted the honor that he achieved as a World War I veteran. Before this overwhelming evidence, Representative Gladys Noon Spellman introduced a bill into the

96th Congress to allow any chief of the Piscataway to be buried in Piscataway National Park. Yet, despite the outpouring of governmental, Native American, and public support, Congress failed to pass her measures. Finally, almost one year after his death, in November 1979, a bill introduced by Senator Paul Sarbanes did pass as federal legislation (Pub. L. 98–87, sec. 301, 1979). This law specifically permitted the Piscataway to bury Chief Tayac in the site which he had chosen during his lifetime. The General Assembly of Maryland unanimously passed a resolution to support the Act, "to honor Chief Turkey Tayac as Chief of the Piscataway Indian Nation" (General Assembly of Maryland, 1979).

The Piscataway Indian Nation chose to bury Chief Tayac where he had wished, in a site known to archaeologists as Ossuary 2, within the sacred twenty acres of Moyaone (Potter, 1980). There were two ways to reach Moyaone: a footpath through a swampy marsh or a dirt road with access to a paved road that ran through the Alice Ferguson Foundation. Because the road crossing through the Foundation provided the only vehicular access to Moyaone, the Piscataway arranged with the National Park Service that the hearse carrying Chief Tayac's body would enter Moyaone that way.

The sociologist can offer some insight into these events by pointing out the interests of the groups involved. The Alice Ferguson Foundation (AFF) had opposed the burial of the Piscataway chief at Moyaone. Composed of white land owners in the vicinity of Piscataway National Park, AFF feared any Piscataway land claims that might interfere with their own property claims. The sociologist can note a second significant observation, as well. Piscataway National Park is located in Prince George's County, which is characterized as Southern Maryland. A slave-owning area in the nineteenth century, Southern Maryland's residents sympathized heavily with the South during the American Civil War. Piscataways view the AFF's associates as members of the modern-day white gentry, which still holds racist notions about non-whites in the area.

The Alice Ferguson Foundation and the National Park Service (NPS) have a cooperative agreement (National Park Service, 1983). The Park Service freely utilizes the road for vehicular entry to that section of the park. The Foundation has open and unlimited access, both vehicular and pedestrian, to Moyaone. At Moyaone, directly beside and on top of the remaining ossuaries, the Foundation plows the earth to plant corn to feed their animals. The animals serve no economic purpose, but rather are displays for school children who visit the AFF demonstration farm. So, through agreements between the Foundation and the Park Service, the burial ground is zoned for agricultural purposes.

The day for Chief Turkey Tayac's burial finally came in November 1979, as torrents of freezing rain fell and cold winds whipped off of the Potomac River. Before the gate that would lead them through the Foundation to the Chief's ossuary, hundreds of mourners had gathered behind the hearse.

Surprisingly, AFF officials defied the procession—and the federal legislation. They refused to permit the hearse to pass their gate. Instead, pall bearers were forced to shoulder Chief Tayac's coffin and walk the mile down the muddy road. The elderly, the infirm, and the young also were forced to march in the bitter conditions. Meanwhile, Park Service personnel blankly stood by and, without interfering, watched events unfold.

Arriving at the site, the mourners continued the burial rites their people had followed for hundreds—perhaps thousands—of years. Billy Redwing Tayac, the Chief's son and successor, directed his father's body to be lifted out of its coffin and placed into the grave. Turkey's body now came into direct contact with Mother Earth, on a bed of tobacco and cedar. Mourners reminded each other what this meant. The elder chief's soul would remain at the site for four days and then begin his journey to the spirit world in accordance with his divine instructions. Today, a flourishing red cedar tree, planted by Chief Turkey Tayac in 1976 to mark the site of his own burial place, receives the prayers of the living. The ancestors and Chief Tayac nourish the tree, called the Tree of Life. And, so, they are not dead, in the world view of the Piscataway, who hold them to be part of a living thing. The grave, located on the western side of the tree, is protected by four spirit posts (one for each direction) that function to keep away evil. A sweatlodge sits near the grave. Piscataway and other Native Americans living in or visiting the area frequently practice their ceremonies beside the grave and surrounding ossuary.

The Problem Continues

Restrictions on the free exercise of Native American religious traditions still take place at Moyaone, both by the Alice Ferguson Foundation and by the National Park Service. For its part, the Foundation continues to reject the tribe's requests for free access to the road. Every year, the Piscataway hope to conduct a memorial procession that would re-enact Chief Turkey Tayac's burial for the annual Feast of the Dead. The procession would consist of about one hundred individuals walking down the road for fifteen minutes one time per year. The Foundation continues to reject this request. Curiously, before Chief Tayac died, the Piscataway enjoyed relatively easy access to Moyaone. They never applied for permits. Piscataways drove the AFF road at will for the annual ceremonies and other occasions. Their families camped together for days at Moyaone. In addition, because there is no longer a Piscataway reservation, and families live scattered around Southern Maryland and other parts of the country, the gatherings were crucial to maintaining community ties.

A change of administration in the AFF in 1979 brought locked gates and access restrictions. In October 1994, Foundation Director Kaye Powell stated the reason for rejection: "It would set a precedent for other groups" (personal communication, October 31, 1994). Yet, the Piscataway Indian Nation is the only group that has aboriginal ties to Moyaone; the only people tied to a person buried there, recognized by federal legislation. In meetings to try to negotiate a solution to the access problem, Foundation representatives claim other reasons: The presence of mourners would scare children visiting the farm; the Piscataway have no right to be on that land. However, the Piscataway observe bird-watching groups and girl scout troops easily obtain AFF permission to walk and ride on the road. In the meantime, indigenous people and their children stay locked out.

The nature of Piscataway ceremony clashes also with regular National Park Service protocol for Piscataway National Park. The four major annual Piscataway ceremonies require outdoor fires (maintained in a fire pit) and four-day vigils. Sweatlodge and tobacco burning ceremonies during the vigils take place after sundown. Most often, these events extend into the early hours of the morning. There is no fixed schedule for ending the event because time frames vary with the number of persons in attendance and their desire to remain engaged in prayer.

These forms of religious observation conflict with the norms of the federal bureaucracy. According to NPS regulations for Piscataway National Park, both fires and overnight vigils require a permit application. Each time the Piscataway have wanted to hold a religious event, they have had to apply for a permit. Although the permits have not been denied, each one is decided on a case-by-case basis. In addition, the restrictions vary over time. To help ease tensions, representatives of the Piscataway Indian Nation have repeatedly requested a cooperative agreement. They point to the special acknowledgment given to their relationship to Moyaone through the congressional act. And, they bring forward the point that the Park Service has granted such status to the Alice Ferguson Foundation for agricultural purposes. Although they have pursued this option since at least 1983 and Maryland federal legislators have encouraged the Park Service to accept this compromise, the NPS has continually ignored the request (International Indian Treaty Council Papers, n.d.). The one concession the Park Service has made was to construct a parking lot and boardwalk to alleviate the swampy footpath conditions.

By 1994, however, relations between the Piscataway and the Park Service were beginning to improve. National awareness of the need for respecting religious rights had finally made its way into various levels of government. Under a new superintendent, Gentry Davis, the NPS sought a more open stance with the Piscataway Indian Nation. Davis worked to develop a clean slate policy with them and other Native Americans in the area (Piscataway Indian Nation, n.d.). The NPS not only gave Piscataway officials a key to the parking lot gate, but also used its influence to try to convince the Alice

Ferguson Foundation to permit free vehicular access through their property. The Foundation refused to cooperate, however. Even today, Piscataway elderly and infirm still cannot easily enter their own sacred site.

The restrictions on vehicular access have created painful individual circumstances. In my research, this became a point of particular interest to me. Through my study of sociology, it has become clear that groups have a profound influence on the experience of the individual. By focusing on a single case, I was able to find important examples of the ways in which white groups act to disadvantage individual Native Americans. The problem is this: In addition to annual ceremonies, Native American people use Moyaone for specific concerns as others would use a church. The case of Jerry Goyette, a Seneca (Iroquois) who resided in Maryland, provides one illustrative example. Goyette, like many local Native Americans, frequented Moyaone for religious practice. His need for spiritual support intensified when he developed heart disease, as many people in such circumstances do. Goyette became ill to the point that he required bypass surgery. His feet had swollen, and he could barely walk. But, when he drove to the access road and asked the AFF staff to allow him to drive his car to the site, they refused. He explained his illness and physical inability to walk. The AFF staff again turned Goyette away and kept their gate locked (personal communication, David Goyette [Jerry Goyette's son], December 2, 1995). Jerry Goyette, unlike the vast majority of heart patients who seek spiritual counsel, had been effectively refused the right to pray in his "church." Thus, normal access to the free exercise of one's religion, an activity most Americans take for granted, was denied the Native American worshiper by the restrictive conditions set out by NPS policy and by AFF's exclusionary behaviors.

All these years of prohibitive access conditions since the burial of Turkey Tayac have taken a toll on Piscataway attendance and degree of community interaction. Many individuals, especially the elderly, have expressed fatigue with the harassment they feel. As one woman put it, "When will this end?" Despite permits and prior arrangements that allow NPS agents to open the AFF gates for vehicles, Piscataways often find themselves locked in or out of the site. Numerous times over the years, families with small children and elderly have been unable to leave the site (sometimes during winter or storm conditions) because NPS or AFF staff had padlocked the road gates and left the area.

At present, instead of attending the outdoor ceremony at Moyaone, a number of families choose to participate in the dinner and dance that follow in a nearby school. Because families can no longer bring campers or construct cook houses at Moyaone, only a few individuals can commit to maintaining the overnight vigils. So, through the years, the emotional connections galvanized by coming together have declined in rate and intensity. Piscataways continue to visit and to talk with one another on an informal basis. However, the character and intensity of interaction have necessarily changed, especially eroding the potential for bonding between children born after access to the site was restricted.

Shaping Piscataway Political Identity

A commitment to protecting Moyaone and to the free exercise of religious traditions largely informs the political activities that the Piscataway Indian Nation conducts today. Seeking out and networking with like-minded indigenous people to gain support has been a particularly salient feature of modern Piscataway politics. During the early 1970s, the Piscataway became deeply involved with the American Indian Movement (AIM). Birgil Kills Straight (1993), a Sioux AIM activist, describes the movement as "first, a spiritual movement, a religious re-birth, and then the re-birth of dignity and pride in a people" (p. 13). Kills Straight's observation is significant: The Piscataway were beginning to fuse traditional religious belief and practice to an emergent political identity. Piscataway AIM involvement resuscitated interest in their aboriginal culture. Prior to this, cultural traditions, particularly spiritual and herbal knowledge, had been left in the hands of Chief Turkey Tayac. After contact with AIM, young Piscataways and other area Native Americans flocked to the elders, asking for instruction and guidance.

AIM brought the Piscataway into regular contact with other indigenous peoples who faced similar struggles over the freedom to practice their religions in traditional ways. Always, sacred aboriginal grounds formed the central point of conflict between these peoples and non-indigenous society. Native Americans sought to have their rights of access and stewardship protected. For instance, in 1986 a group of Navajo journeyed to Washington in order to lobby Congress for a repeal of legislation (the Navajo-Hopi Land Settlement Act of 1974) that would forcibly relocate them from their homes (Parlow, 1988). Separation from their lands would inevitably remove the Navajo from their holy shrines, which exist within natural locations on the landscape. The purpose of removal is to further open the area, known as Big Mountain, for the economic development of natural resources such as coal and uranium mining (LaDuke & Churchill, 1992). Mining irrevocably destroys the land and renders its holiness desecrated. Final relocation, slated for June 1986, spurred widespread national protests. In Washington, the Piscataway and other Native Americans affiliated with them became central organizers of demonstrations against Big Mountain Navajo relocation. For the sociologist, this is a significant point on two counts: as an example of the growing political consciousness of the Piscataway during this period, and as a demonstration of the link they increasingly forged between political identity and religious practice. While in Washington, far away from their own homes, the activist Navajo went to Moyaone to pray and to collect their thoughts in preparation for political efforts. Similar to the Piscataway case, the Big Mountain Navajo view relocation from their sacred land as an assault on their identity and sovereignty.

Conclusion

The Piscataway case carries with it specifically applicable details, but the implications and outcomes of denial of free exercise of religion may be generally applied to other indigenous peoples. Several cases can be cited here. The Sioux struggle to win back the sacred Black Hills, or Paha Sapa, in South Dakota in order to continue their spiritual traditions and to protect the lands from mineral mining. The San Carlos Apache work against the Vatican-sponsored construction of a huge telescope on Mount Graham, where the Mountain Spirits reside. The Shoshone battle for an end to nuclear testing on their land. They reinforce their legal sovereignty by appealing for justice in international arenas, as well as in local courts. Significantly, however, all the peoples engaged in these collective efforts draw the strength to survive for coming generations from their ancestors. In other words, we can see the Piscataway as representative of an important trend in the ongoing struggle to protect their community against inroads by the dominant majority. And, we can see in this struggle the increasing integration of Native American political identity and religious practice.

References

Akwesasne Notes. (1977). *A basic call to consciousness.* Rooseveltown, NY: Akwesasne Notes Press.

American Indian Religious Freedom Act of 1978. Pub. L. 95–341, 92 Stat. 469.

Anderson, B. (1991). *Imagined communities: Reflections on the origin and spread of nationalism.* London: Verso.

Antone, R. A., Miller, D. L., & Myers, B. A. (1986). *The power within people: A community organizing perspective.* Deseronto, ONT: Peace Tree Technologies.

Brown, J. E. (1991). *The spiritual legacy of the American Indian.* New York: Crossroad.

Connor, W. (1972). Nation-building or nation-destroying? *World Politics, 24,* 319–355.

Ferguson, A., & Ferguson, H. G. (1960). *The Piscataway Indians of southern Maryland.* Accokeek, MD: Alice Ferguson Foundation.

Gellner, E. (1983). *Nations and nationalism.* Ithaca, NY: Cornell University Press.

General Assembly of Maryland. (1979). Joint House Resolution 32. Annapolis, MD.

Green, R., & Mitchell, N. M. (1990). *American Indian sacred objects, skeletal remains, repatriation, and reburial: A resource guide.* Washington, DC: Smithsonian Institution.

International Indian Treaty Council Papers. (n.d.). *Research and development. Piscataway Indian Nation.* Unpublished manuscript. International Indian Council Papers, San Francisco, CA.

Killion, T., Bray, T. L., & Baugh, T. G. (n.d.). *Repatriation at the Smithsonian.* Unpublished manuscript.

Kills Straight, B. (1993, October). What is the American Indian Movement? *News from Indian Country,* p. 13.

LaDuke, W., & Churchill, W. (1992). Native North America: The political economy of radioactive colonization. In M. A. Jaimes (Ed.), *The State of Native America* (pp. 241–266). Boston: South End Press.

Loskiel, G. H. (1794). *History of the mission of the United Brethren among the Indians in North America.* London: Brethren's Society for the Furtherance of the Gospel.

Lyons, O. (1990). Statement to Amnesty International Annual Conference. Syracuse, NY.

Martin, J. W. (1991). *Sacred revolt: The Muskogees' struggle for a new world.* Boston: Beacon Press.

Maryland, Department of Housing and Community Development. (1994, May 13). Transfer of human remains and associated funerary objects. *Maryland Register, 21* (10), 841–842.

National Park Service. (1968, February 22). Photo number 10071–G. Washington, DC: Author.

National Park Service. (1983). *General management plan.* Washington, DC: Author.

National Park Service. (1990). *Piscataway National Park.* Washington, DC: Author.

Native American Graves Protection and Repatriation Act of 1990. Pub. L. No. 101–601, 104 Stat. 3048.

Navajo-Hopi Land Settlement Act of 1974, Pub. L. No. 95–531, 93 Stat. 1712.

Nelson, R. K. (1983). *Make prayers to the raven: A Koyukon view of the northern forest.* Chicago: University of Chicago Press.

Parlow, A. (1988). *Cry, sacred ground: Big Mountain, USA.* Washington, DC: Christic Institute.

Patterson, O. (1977). *Ethnic chauvinism.* New York: Stein and Day.

Peregoy, R. M. (1993). *Briefing document: The need for specific Native American religious freedom legislation notwithstanding RFRA.* Unpublished manuscript.

Piscataway Indian Nation, Inc. (n.d.). *Papers.* Accokeek, MD.

Potter, S. R. (1980). *A review of the archeological resources in Piscataway Park, Maryland.* Washington, DC: National Park Service.

Pub. L. 98–87, sec. 301, 1979.

Slepicka, L. (1976, July 29). Piscataway Indians release souls of the dead. *Prince George's Journal,* p. B4.

Smith, J. (1984). Captain John Smith's description of Indians in area of present Maryland. In D. H. Kent (Ed.), *Maryland Treaties, 1632–1775* (pp. 4–5). Washington, DC: University Publications of America.

Stephenson, R. L. (1984). *The prehistoric people of Accokeek Creek.* Accokeek, MD: Alice Ferguson Foundation.

Talamantez, I. (1991, September-December). *Native American religious traditions.* Harvard University lecture series.

Tayac, G. (1988). So intermingled with the earth: A Piscataway oral history. *Northeast Indian Quarterly, 5* (4), 4–17.

Tayac, M. (1981). *Piscataway testimonial in Geneva, Switzerland.* International Indian Treaty Council Papers, San Francisco, CA.

Tinker, G. E. (1993). *Missionary conquest: The Gospel and Native American cultural genocide.* Minneapolis: Fortress Press.

Vecsey, C. (Ed.). (1991). *Handbook of American Indian religious freedom.* New York: Crossroad.

Williams, R. M. (1994). The sociology of ethnic conflicts: Comparative international perspectives. *Annual Review of Sociology, 20,* 49–79.

12

"The Supreme Law of the Land": Sources of Conflict between Native Americans and the Constitutional Order

Eric Mazur

> However extravagant the pretension of converting the discovery of an inhabited coun-
> try into conquest may appear; . . . if the property of the great mass of the community
> originates in it, it becomes the law of the land, and cannot be questioned. . . . However
> this restriction may be opposed to natural right, and to the usages of civilized nations,
> yet, if it be indispensable to that system under which the country has been settled, and
> be adapted to the actual condition of the two people, it may, perhaps, be supported by
> reason, and certainly cannot be rejected by Courts of justice.
>
> —Chief Justice John Marshall[1]

By December of 1992, Nathan Jim, Jr., an Oregon member of the Yakama Indian Nation, had already served a prison term for violating the *Eagle Protection Act* and the *Endangered Species Act*.[2] Yet, in that month, he was caught with the carcasses of several protected birds—including a bald eagle—in his truck. Though Jim argued that his actions were justified on religious grounds, in a plea bargain for probation in lieu of more prison time, he promised to stop killing the protected birds. "I will obey your law," he told the federal district court judge.[3]

The media reported the events involving Nathan Jim in simple terms—the conflict's potential to serve as an early test of the *Religious Freedom Restoration Act*.[4] Apparent in Jim's words, however, are deeper levels of meaning. His retort to the judge exposes a dilemma over authority in our society; the question Jim raises, and which our society must address, is this: How can different sources of authority be reconciled in a democracy which promises every citizen the right of religious free exercise? In a society in which different religious communities derive their understanding of the cosmos from the authority of their own particularistic theology, what is the price each community must pay to coexist with competing, contradicting authorities?

These are important questions which underlie basic issues of freedom in our society. In a culture such as ours, in which different groups must live together, the abstractions of pluralism and particularism become part of how we express ourselves. *Pluralism* is the idea that a society is composed of a unit made of different peoples and cultures, each of which is to be respected and represented in a democratic political system. *Particularism*, on the other hand, emphasizes the integrity of a distinct social group and calls for recognition of the particular elements of the group's culture which it needs to express, sometimes at the cost of interacting with other groups. Because the United States is composed of an array of groups to which individual citizens feel loyalty, how our culture balances pluralistic with particularistic tendencies provides a measure of how any one group can function in American society.

As Jim expressed it, there was no confusion or mingling of *his* sources of authority: "I will obey your law." Not *the* law, but *your* law. Jim did not accept the law as inherently applying to all, but admitted that, given his own legal situation, for the time being he would agree to abide by a law considered authoritative by others if not by him. Implied in his comment was an acknowledgment that the source of authority for his own actions was not co-opted by the legal authority threatening another prison term—he merely agreed not to act on beliefs he knew were justified. He promised that he would behave as the federal authorities demanded; but, by recognizing the difference between the two sources of authority, he implied he would not compromise his own system of beliefs.

Authority and the Constitutional Order

The authority commanded by the pluralistic American constitutional order is revealed in the power of the First Amendment. Although laws generally have an instrumental as well as symbolic power, the guarantee of religious free exercise contained in the First Amendment, and the subsequent jurisprudential history of its interpretation, lead unerringly to the conclusion that the U.S. Constitution is an ultimate authority in the American constitutional order. Not only does it command action based on the physical instrumentalities of the state, but also it coerces action based on its symbolic significance in the definition of what it means to be an American, even to the point of religious observance, and by implication, religious belief. In the context of the First Amendment, this ultimate authority to determine the symbolic meaning of American citizenship regularly confronts the theological authorities of minoritarian religious communities. In such a situation, the religious communities have three basic models they can follow to address this confrontation. They may:

1. Subordinate their particularistic theological authority in favor of the constitutional order;

2. Find a separate peace—a way of maintaining the integrity of their theological authority while living in harmony with the constitutional order, or

3. Face an inevitable conflict with the meaning of transcending authority in the constitutional order.

In other words, by agreeing even to have a governmental guarantee of religious freedom, religious communities in the United States implicitly agree to let the legal system, and ultimately the Supreme Court, arbitrate between individual religious communities and the government (which ostensibly represents the rest of the religious communities and also reserves the right to oversee the enforcement of constitutional rights). This means that rather than have an outcome determined by God, pluralistic religious communities seemingly agree to have an outcome determined by an interpretation of the Constitution. As Phillip Hammond writes, "In the face of expanding religious pluralism, we uphold religious liberty as a value taking precedence over any of our particularistic creeds."[5]

This precedence of pluralism has a profound effect on religious communities that are either unwilling or unable to choose pluralism over particularism and thus face a dilemma of conflicting theological authorities. While many religious communities in American history have made the transition from particularism to pluralism (such as the Catholic, Jewish, and Mormon communities), others have worked at maintaining their own theological justifications while accepting at least a minimum of behavioral harmony with the constitutional order (such as the Amish, Seventh-Day Adventists, ultra-Orthodox Jews, and Jehovah's Witnesses after 1962). Yet, there existed in American history, and remain in America today, religious communities whose understanding of their particular theological source of authority is such that even sacrifice on behalf of behavioral harmony with the constitutional order is unacceptable or impossible. These religious communities live in the most uncomfortable theological position, constantly in conflict with the dominant constitutional order over the value and meaning of authority and, ultimately, over what it means to be an American citizen.

Constitutional Order and the Conflict over Authority

Nathan Jim's comments regarding the two sources of legal authority express the dilemma faced by such communities which by choice or by circumstance may not be included in the pluralism envisioned by the Constitution. In 1852, the same sense of marginality and exclusion from the constitutional order was expressed by Frederick Douglass in his famous speech, "What to the Slave Is the Fourth of July?"[6] Noting that the Constitution—the foundation upon which any appeal to maintain the Union had to be built—

specifically gave less than full membership to the slaves, Douglass reached further back in history, to the ideals of the Declaration of Independence—of all men created equal—for greater inclusion within the framework of the American constitutional order. As Milner Ball notes, Douglass's conclusion that "[t]his Fourth [of] July is *yours*, not *mine*" was "a plea to make it his as well, a plea to render the story [of American origins] capable of embracing him."[7]

Rendering the story "capable of embracing" Native Americans has been a much greater challenge, making their inclusion within the constitutional order that much more difficult. Although the history of the Native American encounter with European Americans is in part analogous to that of African Americans, particularly in the arena of religion, structural differences have led to an apparently inherent conflict over authority between Native Americans and the constitutional order that were not present in the African encounter. African-American slaves, removed from the structures of their traditional religions throughout Africa, were compelled to adjust their religious beliefs to match their inherited religious behaviors by adopting slightly altered Christian meanings.[8] Native American communities were often placed in a similar situation, in the sense that the price of acceptance in American society often meant disregarding traditional indigenous religious behaviors in favor of Christianity.[9] As with the African Americans, Native American rights were not originally protected in the U.S. Constitution. Both communities experienced European culture through force and violence and found themselves in no position of advantage to negotiate an equilibrium. But, while Africans were forcibly and violently brought to this continent, Native Americans were here when the Europeans arrived and had developed intricate social structures and governed their own affairs free of European intrusion. They did not have their social structures destroyed by transplantation across an ocean; they had them destroyed by superior force. The introduction of a competing system of authority profoundly threatened the very structure of Native American society, and the integration of the two systems has continued to be a source of conflict.

For the Native Americans, the continuing dilemma over the authority of the American constitutional order can be linked to the depth of the systemic conflict of the competing authorities. In part, this is due to the manner in which interaction between Native Americans and the American constitutional order has unfolded historically. But, just as significantly, conflicts over the very notions of sovereignty and territoriality inevitably have led to continuing struggles over authority within the constitutional order. This struggle between Native American territorial claims and American political demands for sovereignty has been complicated by incongruous understandings of such categories expressed by Native Americans and the American legal system; the powerful meanings ascribed by Native Americans to the notions of tribal sovereignty or sacred land, for example, are virtually unrecognizable in the American constitutional order because of their use outside of the federalist context. This lack of recognition, combined with the evolving status of Native Americans in the United States, has put them in limbo with regard to American legal history. Subsequently, Native American communities have resisted accepting the demands of the constitutional order—and have been largely unable to live independently of them—because of the direct nature of the conflict over authority and the symbolic and tangible role of land in that conflict. Even the idealistic rhetoric found in the Declaration of Independence, the very embodiment of the competing authority to which Douglass was able to appeal, has not been sufficient to secure religious equality. Africans became African Americans through an appeal to universal equality, while the indigenous peoples of this continent have lost much of their collective identity through the forced application of the same principle by the federal government. Thus, because of the conflicts over group identities and the sources of authority for Native Americans and the constitutional order, the First Amendment guarantee of religious freedom continues to be a confounding ideal not yet fully realized by the Native American members of the American constitutional order.

A Brief History of Time

It is probably no understatement to suggest that the relationship between the federal government and the various Native American communities has been troubled from the very beginning of United States history. The predominantly British culture on the Atlantic seaboard, which developed in a world of competing colonial powers, treated the indigenous peoples they encountered on this continent with caution borne not out of respect for the sovereignty of tribal authority, but out of concern for the alliances these peoples would form with the other colonial powers. As Henry Bowden points out in his history of Native American missionary contact, although all of the colonial powers expressed a strong arrogance toward the indigenous peoples in the Americas, the English may have been the worst offenders and "the least concerned to preserve any aspect of native civilization."[10] Of more importance to the colonial powers (than the humanity of the indigenous peoples) were concerns with how the various tribes could be used as buffers against the competition. As R. Pierce Beaver notes, as far as religious motivation in the New World was concerned, "most of the settlers were more interested in extending the kingdom of God by the displacement or extermination of the Indians than by their conversion."[11]

Little was changed with the establishment of the United States as an independent nation. The federal government approached the indigenous peoples as instruments of foreign policy, and engagement with the tribes in the form of missionary work was promoted as an element of control in pacifying them, or in the more common parlance of the period, by "civilizing" them. "The new nation" notes Beaver, "inherited from the colonial era, and particularly from the New England colonies, a common assumption that the Indian missions were the proper concern of the state and were beneficial to the welfare of the state." With the missionaries working to contain the indigenous non-European peoples, the federal government could protect its citizenry from the threat of French, British, or Spanish expansionist policies. Indeed, concludes Beaver, because of their strategic significance to the new federal government, the role of the religious missions in controlling the Native Americans took on increased importance.[12]

This attitude would shift considerably once the European colonial powers were eliminated from competition. By the early nineteenth century, with competition from France and England effectively out of the way in the Midwest, the federal government was freed of its external national security concerns and could operate with greater self-confidence with regard to territorial expansion. The result was a shift in attitudes toward the Native American tribes, which were now removed as a factor in the equation of national security. "As long as the Indians were pawns in the larger chess game, they received a modicum of respect," notes Bowden, but once the threat of outside alliances disappeared, "they lost that small advantage and became simply obstacles in the path of American pioneers."[13] Native Americans as a group became less of an external threat and more of an internal nuisance. By the end of the War of 1812, interactions with the various tribes focused on public policy concerns and not international relations.

Needless to say, any public policy concerns addressed by the federal government did not have the interests of Native Americans in mind since, from the standpoint of the federal government, Native Americans were not considered part of the government's constituency. Article I of the new Constitution excluded "Indians not taxed" from the apportionment of representation, and empowered Congress to regulate commerce with the tribes in the same manner it would with foreign nations; by treaty signed by the President and ratified by the Senate.[14] Even when Article I was amended by the Fourteenth Amendment in 1868, Native Americans were still excluded from apportionment formulas.[15] In addition, even though the threat of collaboration with international forces was reduced significantly, oversight for matters concerning Native Americans was placed under the jurisdiction of the Secretary of War, who in 1824 created the Bureau of Indian Affairs. Only with the establishment of the Department of the Interior in 1849 did oversight of Native American issues transfer from the War Department.[16]

The tribes were not completely uninformed about their ambiguous standing in the new nation. On 4 July 1827, the Cherokee tribe in Georgia adopted a tribal constitution which itself was an adaptation of the federal Constitution. The state of Georgia, perceiving a threat to its state sovereignty, responded by extending state jurisdiction to the Cherokee territory and then incorporated the tribe's territory into the state. After being blocked by Georgia from suing in state court, the Cherokee tribe filed under the provisions of Article III, §2 of the United States Constitution, which permits foreign nations to bring legal actions to the Supreme Court. The resulting suit brought by the tribe was dismissed by the Court in 1831 on the grounds that, because the Cherokee tribe was not a foreign nation, the issue was not within the Court's jurisdiction.[17]

However, although the Court lacked jurisdiction, the Justices took the opportunity to discuss at some length the nature of the relationship of Native Americans within the constitutional order. "The relation of the Indians to the United States is marked by peculiar and cardinal distinctions which exist no where else," noted Chief Justice John Marshall, writing for the majority. Native Americans may be understood as "domestic dependent nations" he concluded, since "they occupy a territory to which we assert a title independent of their will. . . . Their relation to the United States resembles that of a ward to his guardian."[18] Justice Johnson, dissenting from the Court's decision, noted that the mere fact that the federal government interacted with the tribes through the mechanism of treaty indicated that they were considered foreign nations as understood by the Constitution. "And if, as here decided, a separate and distinct jurisdiction or government is the test by which to decide whether a nation be foreign or not, I am unable to perceive any sound and substantial reason why the Cherokee nation should not be so considered."[19]

The following year, the Supreme Court saw the logic of Justice Johnson's dissenting opinion in *Cherokee Nation v. Georgia* when it was again faced with a suit involving Native American standing in the constitutional order. This suit also involved the Cherokee tribe in Georgia, although this time the case was brought by a missionary who had defied a Georgia statute and entered the Cherokee territory without state authorization.[20] Justice Marshall, recognizing the futility of a land grant from a king in Europe over territory that was not his to give, as well as the constitutional reality of the treaty mechanism mentioned by Justice Johnson the previous year, nullified Georgia law over the Cherokee territory and identified the tribe as equal in status to any foreign nation. However, populist President Andrew Jackson, fearing that enforcing the Supreme Court's ruling would exacerbate separatist sentiment in the South, condemned the ruling, refused to enforce it, and suggested Justice Marshall enforce it himself,[21] while Christian missionaries chose to "sacrifice the Cherokees to save the Union," by counseling the tribe to settle the suit and relocate in the West.[22] The ruling left the status of Native American communities in an ambiguous position within the realm of political theory. Functionally, as Robert Michaelsen—a scholar of Native American constitutional issues—notes, the federal government assumed "broad or 'plenary' federal constitutional power" over issues involving Native Americans.[23]

Outside the Supreme Court, the country's territorial expansion continued to affect the status of Native Americans in the constitutional order. As Pierce Beaver notes, "As the Indians disappeared from the settled East, many churchmen found it easier to love them at a distance, and they began to feel a concern which had been absent from the thought of the early Puritans." These feelings of love at a distance translated into notions of remorse for their earlier behavior, and noting that "Americans had gravely wronged the Indians in killing them off, seizing their land, and breaking faith with them," they concluded that the only act of restitution available for them was to give the Native Americans that which was so valuable to the European Americans: the Gospel.[24] The government agreed with the "gift" to be given to the Native Americans, but not necessarily for the same reasons; the increased missionary zeal continued to serve public policy goals, and was therefore not only supported, but also was actively pursued.[25] Thus, for the better part of the nineteenth century, the federal government and the various churches worked in cooperation for the "elevation of the Indians."[26] In fact, by providing institutional and financial support, the federal government was able to make such missionary work more appealing to groups that might ordinarily have preferred more attractive assignments overseas.[27] Both the government and the missionary societies were able to benefit from the arrangement; the government secured political as well as military advantage by supporting the missionaries, and the missionary societies gained at least an imagined stake in the welfare of the nation.[28]

This mutual concern shared by the political authorities and the missionary societies did not specifically include respect for the personhood of the Native American or the dignity of Native American cultures. In fact, in a manner reminiscent of some of the political battles of the modern period, the availability of federal money encouraged competition for government financial support rather than enthusiasm for the stated goal of the funding. Notes Beaver, "Neither the Protestant nor the Roman Catholic missionaries and officials were really concerned about the Indian's right to maintain and defend his own religion, and they were fighting more for freedom of action by the missionary agencies."[29] In fact, the competition grew more fierce when, in an expression of virulent anti-Catholicism, the American Protective Association published a letter revealing the disproportionately high amount of money Catholic missionary societies were receiving from the federal government as part of President Grant's "Peace Policy."[30]

By the end of the nineteenth century, as Protestant social hegemony began to wane, the role of the missionary societies in negotiating the relationship between Native Americans and the federal government began to disappear.[31] Religion ceased to be a prime element in the relationship between the federal government and the Native Americans; as concern over Native Americans diminished, so did concern for their spiritual well-being. In 1871, in a rider to an appropriation bill, the House of Representatives effectively put an end to whatever "foreign" or independent position tribes might have had to that time by unilaterally ending the treaty process.[32] Although this unorthodox violation of constitutional protocol may have been an assertion of authority on the part of the House over the Senate, it is true also that this move represented the conclusion that Native Americans no longer posed even the slightest threat to American expansionist aims, and were completely a domestic rather than an international concern.[33] Coast to coast, Native Americans found themselves within American borders, and the frontier, declared closed by historian Frederick Jackson Turner only five years later, ceased to be either a place of refuge for Native Americans or the outer boundary of civilization for the expansionist Americans.

After Congress's recategorization of relations with Native Americans from an international to a domestic issue, the government was now in a position to make even greater (though possibly more subtle) demands for membership into the constitutional order. They insisted Native Americans had to be successfully integrated into the American constitutional order. To accomplish this goal, Native Americans had to be remade as recognizable constituents—individual citizens cognizant of the federal government's supreme position of authority. The government no longer would accept collective representation outside the framework of the federalist structure. Significantly, this meant that Native American participation in the constitutional order would have to be carried out by the individual—at the cost of tribal sovereignty. Now there was no place within the federal structure of authority for competing tribal authority.[34] In simpler terms, Native Americans would be encouraged to work the land, and even own it, but the federal government, through the theory of eminent domain, would possess the ultimate title, and no one else could lay any superior claim.

Actions symbolic of this altered stance toward Native American authority again came in the guise of good intentions. *The General Allotment Act of 1887* was intended to provide individual ownership of tribal land to the Native Americans who had lived on that land.[35] As Native American legal scholars Vine Deloria, Jr., and Clifford Lytle note, members of Congress, and American culture as a whole, seemed to believe that "[p]rivate property

... had mystical magical qualities about it that led people directly to a 'civilized state.'" (The program that emerged was disastrous, however, and led to an eventual diminution of Native American land holdings that was finally halted in 1934.)[36] American citizenship was awarded to Native American veterans of World War I in 1919, and to all Native Americans born within the United States in 1924.[37] In 1968, the *Indian Civil Rights Act* extended to Native Americans who lived on reservations under tribal jurisdiction most of the rights other Americans had secured nearly two hundred years earlier, including the First Amendment right to the free exercise of religion.[38] All of these programs of good intent for Native Americans came at great cost; individual property ownership removed the authority of the community from the land (and in many cases also removed the Native American from it, as well), and citizenship reinforced the individuality of identity and ignored or minimized the communal authority asserted by the tribe. Even the highly praised *Indian Civil Rights Act*, argues Milner Ball, "diminish[ed] the power of tribal government" and "threaten[ed] to remake tribal courts in the image of the federal judiciary."[39]

By the second half of this century, for well or ill, Native American status as defined by the federal government was more clearly established. In the 1955 case of *Tee-Hit-Ton Indians v. United States*, the Supreme Court voiced a position that represented the federal government's unilateral incorporation of Native American reservations, noting that "the savage tribes of this continent were deprived of their ancestral ranges by force and that, even when the Indians ceded millions of acres by treaty in return for blankets, food, and trinkets, it was not a sale but the conquerors' will that deprived them of their land."[40] The historic process of incorporation was symbolically concluded in 1978 when the Court, quoting from a nineteenth-century decision, noted in the case of *Oliphant v. Suquamish Indian Tribe*, "Indian reservations are 'a part of the territory of the United States. . . .' Indian tribes 'hold and occupy [the reservations] with the assent of the United States, and under their authority.'"[41] Although expressed as *dicta* (non-binding narrative that accompanies the Court's binding decision on the specific facts in a case) in both decisions, these comments clearly reflected the Court's evaluation of the relationship between Native Americans and the federal government; the federal government as possessor of ultimate authority clearly dominated the rhetoric. The emphasis in Justice Marshall's original phrase, "domestic dependent nations," was clearly placed on *domestic dependent* rather than *nation*.[42]

Thus, by the last quarter of the twentieth century, the Supreme Court unilaterally completed the goal of the Declaration of Independence by asserting that, indeed, all men were created equal. Any distinction to be found in Native American culture, however, was in jeopardy of eradication in the name of that equality. Although the U.S. Constitution of 1789 had distinguished between individual Native Americans and those who maintained their connection with their tribe ("Indians not taxed"), the Court now leveled the field by making tribal communities simply collections of individual Native Americans who merely happened to live on federal property. Members of Native American tribes, once feared for their ability to influence international relations, had now become ordinary citizens in the eyes of the law; they had been granted citizenship, they were taxed, they were given opportunities to own and farm land. Granted individual membership in the constitutional order without asking for it, Native Americans now could do virtually everything that all other citizens could, with one significant exception. They could not express themselves through their collective identity, in collective religious expressions of territorial sovereignty over land now controlled by the same Constitution that served them as individuals.[43]

Native American Religions Encounter the Constitutional Order

The precarious position of the Native American community within the constitutional order only exacerbated the position of Native American religious traditions within the framework of the First Amendment.[44] Because citizenship was not conferred upon Native Americans until recently in American history, the practitioners of various Native American religious traditions could not appeal for protection in the constitutional order.[45] Indeed, as we have seen, even when relief was sought through the court system, Christian (predominantly Protestant) presuppositions of the American legal system and its concomitant conceptualizations of authority and territoriality severely disadvantaged the Native Americans. Constitutional scholar Edward Gaffney points out that the legacy of biblical imagery is both a strong and necessary element in the construction of identity in the American constitutional order. As he observes, "Biblical traditions cannot be eliminated from the way that America tells her tale . . . without a significant loss of cultural identity and purpose."[46] This relationship has characterized American society since colonists first came ashore from Europe. As we have seen, the connection deeply affected how settlers interacted with the new peoples they encountered. Ventures such as John Eliot's "praying Indian" villages in seventeenth-century Massachusetts, organized on a model derived from Exodus 18:21, seemed perfectly logical to Europeans familiar with the passage. They were not, of course, a particularly familiar model for indigenous peoples on this continent.[47]

Often seen by European Americans as no religion at all, the various religious traditions of the Native Americans were easily overlooked. Indeed, because of the significant differences between European-American and Native American religious concepts, dialogue between the two worlds was virtually meaningless, and respect for Native American religious traditions on the part of the European settlers was virtually nonexistent. Native American human agency was generally ignored, notes historian Robert Berkhofer. European Americans merely assumed Native Americans to be a part of the Christian "cosmic drama," either a device used by God to aid them toward salvation or a device used by Satan to confound those efforts.[48] Referring to the contemporary period, but apparently true historically, Robert Michaelsen points out that "images of Indians in the Majority culture in this country generally mitigate against understanding of Indian life."[49]

Ironically, the same year that incorporation of tribal reservations was completed by unilateral Supreme Court fiat (1978), Congress passed the *American Indian Religious Freedom Act (AIRFA)*.[50] This non-binding resolution, which recognized the extension of the Free Exercise Clause to traditional Native American religions, urged federal agencies which interacted with Native Americans to be respectful of their religions.[51] However, the act was written without corresponding penalties, making it virtually meaningless. If *AIRFA* was to have any strength, its tenets would have to be tested in the courts. As Michaelsen has noted, "it is primarily through the law and the courts that Americans, including disadvantaged or excluded minorities, have become participants in the American covenant"[52] because one must establish that "'unorthodox' or 'different' religious beliefs and practices enjoy the protection of the Free Exercise Clause as much as common ones do."[53]

However, the few Native American claims for religious free exercise that have reached the Supreme Court have been singularly unsuccessful, leaving the practice of traditional Native American religions "more hampered and threatened than is the practice of any other traditional religion in this country."[54] As a result of the historical evolution of rights that we have traced above, combined with other First Amendment issues, by 1985 no Native American free exercise claim had been decided by the Supreme Court. In the lower federal courts, Native Americans had lost five of six cases. Not coincidentally, notes Michaelsen, "the most significant losses have occurred in connection with access to sacred site claims."[55]

The first Native American sacred site claim to reach the Supreme Court clearly demonstrates the disadvantageous position of traditional Native American religions in federal courts. The 1988 case, *Lyng v. Northwest Indian Cemetery Protective Association*, involved a proposal to build a logging road through parts of northern California. Several local tribes objected that construction would desecrate the sacred meaning of the region.[56] Prior to the *Lyng* decision (known informally as the "G-O Road" decision because the logging road would connect Gasquet and Orleans), the closest the Supreme Court had come to a sacred site dispute was the 1889 decision in *Late Corporation of the Church of Jesus Christ of Latter-Day Saints v. United States*.[57] It was hardly a model for optimism for Native Americans; it had resulted in the disenfranchisement of the Mormon state of Deseret and the wholesale dismantling of Church real estate holdings in the Utah territory (present-day Utah and its neighboring states). In *Lyng*, the Court followed the example established in this Mormon decision, but also relied heavily on the holding in *Bowen v. Roy*, which suggested that the federal government had the authority to determine its operational needs even at the cost of offending occasional religious sensibilities.[58] Overcoming objections on religious grounds raised by the Cemetery Protective Association, the Court determined there existed a "compelling interest" in building a road through lands deemed sacred by a number of tribes in northern California.[59]

The essential issue in the case was the nature of Native American religious activities. To win, the Native American plaintiffs had to prove to the Court that the very esthetic of the geography—their sense that the land is sacred—played a vital role in the case in question. The Justices, however, deemed that the plaintiffs had failed to prove that the land was "central" to their religious practices. Therefore, they were unable to overcome the seemingly feeble "compelling interest" of the government to facilitate the growth, harvesting, and removal of lumber.[60] As Michaelsen notes, "This [centrality doctrine] is a difficult standard for any free exercise litigant to meet; it is especially difficult for those who espouse and represent religions in which there are no clearly defined and agreed upon statements of orthodoxy and which rely heavily on oral tradition."[61] He concludes that

> Governmental interests have been generally well treated in Native American sacred site cases. Indeed, as the Circuit Court of the District of Columbia commented in one case, some courts have even implied that "The Free Exercise Clause can never supercede the government's ownership rights and duties of public management." On the contrary, that court continued in a statement that is both obvious and necessary: "The government must manage its lands in accordance with the Constitution. . . ."[62]

The Meaning of Land as an Uncommon Symbol

"The government must manage its lands in accordance with the Constitution. . . ."[63] This powerfully symbolic statement written in a circuit court opinion in 1981 makes painfully obvious the level of conflict over the meaning of land and its role in the power struggle between Native Americans and the American constitutional order. When the dispute over the authority of the Constitution involves religious issues, the conflict over simple land management and authority becomes a clash of cosmic proportions. It is in this area where the conflict between Native American religious traditions and the constitutional order meet; where the differences between what it means to be a practitioner of traditional Native American religions and what it means to be a citizen of the American constitutional order clash. While debate over the use of various sacraments or rituals may continue between the dominant religious community and various minority religious communities, it is the difference over the meaning of land that presents the most perplexing dilemmas between Native American religious communities and the dominant culture. Ultimately, what is at issue is authority over land. "There is a sizeable gulf," notes constitutional scholar Michaelsen, "between traditional Indian understanding of land and that typical of the majority of Americans."[64] Native American legal scholar, Vine Deloria, Jr., characterizes the "gulf" in terms of the difference in reference to space versus time:

> American Indians hold their lands—places—as having the highest possible meaning, and all their statements are made with this reference point in mind. Immigrants review the movement of their ancestors across the continent as a steady progression of basically good events and experiences, placing history—time—in the best possible light.[65]

In other words, because Christianity (the predominant religion of the European-American settlers) focuses on redemption through the grace of God, it describes this world as a temporary stage on which human actions are played out over time in preparation for elevation to another, higher stage. Traditional Native American religions, on the other hand, generally picture the land as an essential part of the cosmic world, in which "all aspects of life take on religious significance and religion and culture are intimately connected."[66] Christianity occupies space while it anticipates the passage of time; Native American religious traditions occupy time while orienting themselves to space.

This difference is most clearly manifest within the constitutional order in the reactions of the mainstream political religious community to the two most significant decisions handed down by the Supreme Court in cases involving Native American religious freedom. Following the *Lyng* decision, in which Native American sacred site land claims were rebuked for the construction of a logging road, there was hardly a reaction from the organized political religious community.[67] Conversely, there was an uproar after the Court upheld a state's prohibition of the ritual use of peyote in *Employment Division v. Smith*.[68] Scores of politically organized religious groups banded together (many for the first time) to ask for a rehearing from the Supreme Court;[69] failing that, they would seek legislative redress.[70] What accounted for these quite different responses? Significantly, many observers perceived that the Court's decision in *Smith* could mean sweeping changes in constitutional jurisprudence that potentially could affect the status of non-Native American religious communities. In other words, the non-Native American religious communities did not feel threatened by the Court's decision in a sacred land decision which was unlikely to affect them. They did, however, feel threatened by the Court's decision in a case involving ritual, a category more easily accessible to western religious traditions, and one that is used by them to mark the passage of time.

Western religions accept the assumption that land is a commodity that can be exchanged easily for another. This assumption stands in stark contrast to many traditional Native American religious beliefs which posit a custodial or partnership approach. Indeed, notes Ball quoting Standing Bear, the entire idea of wilderness—as in the European-American vision of it as wild and dangerous—is the creation of a society which has become alienated from nature. Conversely, Native American attitudes toward land were "characteristic of a gift economy";[71] these beliefs described the idea of land in terms of its interdependence with a community, and not as a commodity. Such attitudes toward land are virtually unrecognizable in European-American culture, except, as Michaelsen points out, in the case of the Mormons. In that community, however, the attachment is still based on a biblical construction of property, and not on the interrelationship between individual, land, and community. In contrast, many traditional Native American communities—the Cheyenne and Sioux (Black Hills) and the Taos Pueblo (Blue Lake and neighboring mountains), for example—recognize certain lands as sacred. Indeed, the Navajo believe that not only are the San Francisco Peaks the home of their gods, but also that the Peaks are a deity in the sacred cosmos.[72] As Ball concludes, this contrast in attitudes serves as the focus of the difference between the two cultures, and possibly the reason for the inability to reach a meaningful understanding about the religious significance of land.[73]

Such different levels of meaning have made cross-cultural dialogue difficult. Of greater significance, however, this conflict over meanings of space and time actually preserves the dispute over authority between Native Americans and the constitutional order. As missionary societies were attempting to convert the Native Americans to Christianity during the nineteenth and early twentieth centuries, the federal government was trying to make them into "good citizens." There can be no question that the former goal well served the latter, for several reasons. First, it is unlikely that the Framers of the Constitution wrote the First Amendment to include religious traditions that did not share a Protestant world view.[74] This assumption, articulated by early Supreme Court Justice Joseph Story in his multi-volume work *Commentaries on the Constitution of the United States*, suggests a close connection between the two categories of communion and citizenship, at least early in American history.[75] Second, although the preamble of the Constitution clearly rests its authority on a communal category ("We, the people . . ."), it actually expresses all rights in terms of the individual.[76] As we have seen, this individualistic understanding of rights proved to be a serious and continuing challenge to the structure and authority of Native American tribal communities. It ensured, as well, the dominance of the constitutional order in their stead. Third, the parallelism between the symbolic voice of authority for Protestant Christianity—"The

Word" (John 1:1) as represented by the Bible—and the symbolic voice of authority for the American constitutional order—the U.S. Constitution— masked the actual source of authority of the latter, namely territorial sovereignty. This masking obscured the full ramifications of the federal government's challenge to Native American land claims, even when they reached religious dimensions. As long as citizenship was symbolically defined by a written contract (in other words, the U.S. Constitution), the foundation of the federal government's authority over territory was not conflictual with underlying Protestant belief, but was actually a complementary element to the life of the citizen. But, because the source of authority rested on the federal government's ability to control territory (or to maintain sovereignty), Native American claims of sovereignty over land, whether religiously based or not, threatened the very foundation of the constitutional order's authority. The situation would be that much more significant if religious meaning and symbolism were located in the dispute.

From the earliest days of cultural interaction, the intellectual foundations through which European Americans could have understood Native American religious traditions were meager; the inclusion of Native Americans into the constitutional order probably never had much of a chance. As Michaelsen, the constitutional scholar, concludes, "While a superficial view might see all religions as being alike or even similar, history has shown that there is really not much common ground or common language between the major religious traditions of American culture and Indian traditions."[77] This lack of common ground has made dialogue extraordinarily difficult. More significantly, because it has masked the conflict over authority between the constitutional order and Native American religious traditions, the cultural vacuum has fostered an unresolved conflict of mythic proportions.

Early on, European Americans' appropriation of traditionally recognized title to land had little to do with the presence of Native Americans. In 1629, John Winthrop declared that possession of land in the Massachusetts Bay Colony would be determined by the doctrine of *vacuum domicilium*; ownership meant improvement (as in buildings or farming), not mere occupancy (as in transience or hunting patterns).[78] In the absence of such improvements, the entire colonial period was governed by the doctrine of discovery, in which any aboriginal claims to the land were virtually ignored.[79] Nearly one hundred and sixty years later, as Milner Ball points out, the Constitution would be "the supreme law of the land," thereby shifting authority from those political units which could voluntarily participate to a geographic region encompassing all, both willing and not.[80] For the federal government, and the dominant European heritage it represented, land was a possession, a tool in the business of this world, and had no greater significance than God's command to "have dominion over."[81] The federal government, as representative of the dominant culture and imbued with its own transcending authority, subsumed under its command the right to control all property for the benefit (salvation, even) of its citizenry. The doctrine of Manifest Destiny and its implicit theological presuppositions governed the attitude toward land expressed by the American constitutional order.[82]

Constitutional Order Meets Native American Religions

Because of the extraordinary differences between their cultures, as we have seen, Native American conceptualizations of religion and law were virtually unrecognizable to European settlers, colonists, and pioneers (and vice versa). Even when European Americans comprehended Native American religion and law, they did so in their own cultural terms, and so described Native American elements as inferior and uncivilized. Noted one Christian missionary, "The two great hindrances to progress were the Indian religion and the absence of law."[83]

Native Americans' religions and legal systems have functioned successfully in the frameworks of their various cultures for centuries, of course.[84] However, the tenuous position of Native American religious claims in American jurisprudence and the consequent need to combat the constitutional order's extension of its authority to Native American territorial claims have placed a heavy burden on traditional Native American religions. Writes Michaelsen, because of the negative, mythic image of "Indian" in American society, "If Indians do not conform to the majority image of them as a vanishing race which embraces a quaint but clearly other-worldly religion, then their keen interest in land must be understood in the earthbound terms of the majority view."[85]

Scholars have suggested several strategies for translating Native American religious concepts of land into the "earthbound terms of the majority view," thereby securing more reliable guarantees for religious free exercise. Such methods as the use of analogy or metaphor have been considered, with some degree of success.[86] Yet, the issue of reconciling Native American religious traditions with European-American constructs of law may not be as simple as explanation by analogy or narrative. Deep differences exist between the very communal structures of Native American religious traditions and the deeply individualistic pattern of rights recognized and celebrated in the American constitutional order. Indeed, the need to translate religious differences may have a profoundly adverse effect on traditional Native American patterns of religious authority by subordinating the particularistic religious authority to that of the Constitution and the pluralistic society which it represents.[87] But, if the root of the conflict itself is based in competing conceptualizations of authority, Native American religious expression may have little alternative than to face continuous struggle with the American constitutional order over land claims. Not simply a matter of rights or toleration, the heart of the matter rests on who has the right to define a particular space, and who has sovereignty over that space.

Ultimately, this problem of competing notions of authority underscores the dilemma of constitutional authority in the realm of religious free exercise. For traditional Native American religious expression, the conceptualization of authority rests within the very structure of the religious and social categories, and cannot be aligned with American constitutional authority merely by a slight adjustment. As Michaelsen explains, "Protection of the free exercise of religion for Native Americans requires, then, due attention to the distinctiveness of those religions and to the unique constitutional status of Native Americans."[88] Recent decisions suggest the courts have made the individual the overwhelming paradigm in the conferral of religious rights, as they have in other areas of rights. We must, however, recognize the danger that this trend poses. The threat is acute for Native American religions, especially as it is incorporated in the basic conflict over land. The power of European-American cultural dominance embraced in the definition of the No Establishment Clause of the Constitution may certainly decimate the ability of Native American religious communities to practice freely, simply because of the nature of the conflict over sovereignty.

The recognition of culture-based religious distinctions presents a challenge to American political rhetoric—although we say "all men are created equal," the rights of some are based on a collective identity, while the rights of others are founded on individual identities. In the past, the courts occasionally have conferred religious identity and rights on the basis of community designation. For instance, as recently as World War I, membership in specific "Peace Churches" served as sufficient reason for automatic dismissal from military service.[89] More recently, identification as a member of the Amish community permitted removal from public school before the state-mandated age.[90] Yet, these solutions were crafted for thoroughly European-American biblical traditions. It would seem that the very tangible foundation for constitutional authority, and thus the future of the legitimacy of the American constitutional order, rests on how well it integrates the religious expressions of traditional Native American religions.

Native religions are not merely a unique example from American history. Rather, they represent the challenge the American constitutional order will encounter as it faces the integration of larger non-Western communities which do not share the Framers' biblical presuppositions. Although the conflict over land may make the Native American struggle unique, it suggests that greater flexibility will be required if more diverse religious expressions are to be included in the constitutional order without sacrificing the authority of their theology. As Frederick Douglass proved in the 1850s, and as Milner Ball points out, the elements of this flexibility already exist in the nature of constitutional authority. On this point, Ball writes:

> The Declaration's second sentence tacitly recognizes that, in a democratic society, even self-evident truth requires mediation, dialogue, consent. Had the truths recited by Jefferson been self-evident in the sense that they were politically monologic, i.e., irresistibly compelling, he would simply have announced them rather than prefacing them with the formula "We hold." This introduction is a grammatical acknowledgement that truth, equality, and rights require agreement in the republic. They are matters of opinion exchanged and held.[91]

We might add also that notions of authority, sovereignty, and political participation are not necessarily constructed on a single intellectual foundation. In the case of Nathan Jim, our introduction to this wide-ranging conflict over authority, as well as in the broader historical development of the relationship of Native American religious traditions and the American constitutional order, there are clear differences over how authority is determined, and by whom and under what circumstances. Native traditions, centered (at least in part) on the cultural orientation toward land, cannot but conflict with the American constitutional order's orientation toward the same land. Not as easily integrated into American culture as Christianity's symbolic emphasis on "The Word" (and its parallel relationship to the Constitution as symbolic of the federal government's authority dependent on territoriality), Native American religious traditions expose the very real and tangible conflict that lies at the heart of the American constitutional order. The strengths behind the Constitution are grounded in the control of the land, and any challenge to that control can be met with subtle, but immeasurable resistance. Nathan Jim may not see the legal system of the American constitutional order as his law, but he has understood the power it holds over him, and has agreed to abide by it. So, too, in many ways, have Native American religious traditions agreed to abide by the American constitutional order. They may not accept the source of its authority, but in the face of overwhelming power, they may have had no other choice but to accept it.

Notes

A version of this paper was presented at the November 1995 American Academy of Religion Annual Meeting in Philadelphia, Pennsylvania. The author wishes to thank Heidi Burns, Robert Michaelsen, Dane Morrison, Inés Talamantez, and Gabrielle Tayac for their helpful contributions.

1. *Johnson v. McIntosh*, 21 U.S. (8 Wheat.) 543 (1823), 591–92.

2. *Eagle Protection Act, U.S. Code*, vol. 16, sec. 668 (1994); *Endangered Species Act, U.S. Code*, vol. 16, secs. 1531–43 (1994).

3. Marc Peyser, with Sonya Zalubowski, "Between a Wing and a Prayer," *Newsweek*, 19 September 1994, 58.

4. *The Religious Freedom Restoration Act, U.S. Code*, vol. 42, secs. 2000bb-2000bb4 (1994). See text accompanying note 70.

5. Phillip E. Hammond, *The Protestant Presence in Twentieth-Century America: Religion and Political Culture* (Albany: State University of New York Press, 1992), 18.

6. Frederick Douglass, "What to the Slave Is the Fourth of July? An Address Delivered in Rochester, New York, on 5 July 1852," in *The Frederick Douglass Papers, Series 1: Speeches, Debates, and Interviews*, John W. Blassingame, ed. (New Haven, CT: Yale University Press, 1982), 2: 359, quoted in Milner S. Ball, "Stories of Origin and Constitutional Possibilities," *Michigan Law Review* 87, no. 8 (August 1989): 2282–83.

7. Ball, "Stories of Origin," 2283. Emphasis in the original.

8. See Albert J. Raboteau, *Slave Religion: The "Invisible Institution" in the Antebellum South* (New York: Oxford University Press, 1978), especially 87–92.

9. See Joel Martin, *Sacred Revolt: The Muskogees' Struggle for a New World* (Boston: Beacon Press, 1991), especially 87–113.

10. Henry Warner Bowden, *American Indians and Christian Missions: Studies in Cultural Conflict* (Chicago: The University of Chicago Press, 1981), 113, 78.

11. R. Pierce Beaver, *Church, State and the American Indian: Two and a Half Centuries of Partnership in Missions between Protestant Churches and Government* (St. Louis: Concordia Publishing House, 1966), 25. See also R. Pierce Beaver, "Church, State, and the Indians: Indians Missions in the New Nation," *Journal of Church and State* 4, no. 1 (May 1962): 11–30.

12. Ibid., 53–54.

13. Bowden, *American Indians and Christian Missions*, 163.

14. U.S. Constitution, Article I, §§2, 8. Ratified 1787. However, in a structural ambiguity of federalism contained in section 8, the Constitution also provides for the same delega-

tion of authority to Congress when regulating commerce "among the several states." This inclusion confuses whatever parallelism might be asserted to exist between "foreign nations" and "Indian tribes." Chief Justice John Marshall addresses this issue in *Cherokee Nation v. Georgia*, 30 U.S. (5 Pet.) 1 (1831), 18–19. Taxed Indians generally were those who lived as individuals in urban settings, off reservations and outside of tribal territory.

15. U.S. Constitution, Amendment XIV, §2. Adopted 1868. Among other things, this amendment provided all former African-American slaves with full representation for the purposes of representation. Article I, §2, which this portion of the amendment replaced, had specified that slaves be counted as three-fifths of a person for the purposes of the apportionment of representation, a compromise which did not anticipate the independent status of Native Americans, but merely addressed the marginal status of African-American slaves and their role in preserving the Union, north and south.

16. Beaver, *Church, State, and the American Indian*, 63.

17. *Cherokee Nation v. Georgia*, 30 U.S. (5 Pet.) 1 (1831). For a history of the suit, see William G. McLoughlin, *Cherokee Renascence in the New Republic* (Princeton, NJ: Princeton University Press, 1986), 388–447. For an analysis of the resulting majority and dissenting opinions, see Vine Deloria, Jr., and Clifford M. Lytle, *American Indians, American Justice* (Austin: University of Texas Press, 1983), 29–32.

18. *Cherokee Nation v. Georgia*, 16–17.

19. *Cherokee Nation v. Georgia*, 57.

20. *Worcester v. Georgia*, 31 U.S. (6 Pet.) 515 (1832).

21. President Jackson allegedly exclaimed, "John Marshall has made his decision:—*now let him enforce it!*" Albert J. Beveridge, *The Life of John Marshall* (Boston: Houghton Mifflin Company, 1919), iv: 515 (emphasis in the original).

22. McLoughlin, *Cherokee Renascence*, 446.

23. Robert S. Michaelsen, "'We Also Have a Religion.' The Free Exercise of Religion Among Native Americans," *American Indian Quarterly* 7, no. 3 (summer 1983): 112.

24. Beaver, *Church, State, and the American Indian*, 62.

25. Ibid., 187.

26. Ibid., 68.

27. Ibid., 79.

28. Ibid., 85.

29. Ibid., 157. See also *Quick Bear v. Leupp*, 210 U.S. 50 (1908), in which the Supreme Court ruled that, among other things, the denial of a contract with the Catholic Church to provide education on the reservation would be a denial of the Native American community's First Amendment free exercise rights.

30. Ibid., 166–67. See also R. Pierce Beaver, "The Churches and President Grant's Peace Policy," *Journal of Church and State* 4, no. 2 (November 1962): 174–90.

31. For a general description of the shift in cultural hegemony experienced by Protestant missionary societies, see Robert T. Handy, *Undermined Establishment: Church-State Relations in America, 1880–1920* (Princeton, NJ: Princeton University Press, 1991).

32. *Indian Appropriation Act of 1871,* P. L. 120, 41st Cong., 2d sess. (3 March 1871), 566. The legislation honored the validity of those treaties already in existence. However, in 1903, the Supreme Court ruled that Congress could ignore provisions of treaties made with the various tribes. See *Lone Wolf v. Hitchcock,* 187 U.S. 553 (1903), in which the Court affirmed the government's motion to dismiss a suit over a treaty violation.

33. Under the structures of the Constitution and the doctrine of the separation of powers, the House of Representatives retains general primary responsibility over domestic affairs through its budgetary process, while the Senate retains primary responsibility for international affairs through the treaty process.

34. See Ralph Lerner, "Reds and Whites: Rights and Wrongs," in *The Supreme Court Review, 1971,* Philip B. Kurland, ed. (Chicago: The University of Chicago Press, 1971), 201–40. Lerner argues that the Native American political units may actually have been better treated than the Spanish and French political units the new American nation encountered as it expanded. There was never any question of incorporating the French or Spanish as separate political entities with equal rights in the American system, but an effort was attempted for the Native Americans, feeble though it might have been. See Lerner., 202–4.

35. *Indian General Allotment Act, U.S. Code,* vol. 25, secs. 331–58 (1994). The Act was also known as the *Dawes Act.*

36. Deloria and Lytle, *American Indians,* 9–14. The policy of allotment was overturned by the passage of the *Indian Reorganization Act, U.S. Code,* vol. 25, sec. 461 (1994) (also known as the *Wheeler-Howard Act*).

37. Ibid., 221. See also *Indian Citizenship Act of 1924,* P. L. 175, 68th Cong., 1st sess. (2 June 1924), 253 and *Elk v. Wilkins,* note 43.

38. *The Indian Civil Rights Act, U.S. Code,* vol. 25, secs. 1301–3 (1994). However, in recognition of the theocratic nature of some tribal governments, the *Indian Civil Rights Act* did not extend the prohibition against the establishment of religion to tribal authorities. See Michaelsen, "'We Also Have a Religion,'" 113–14. In addition, the act did not extend 15th Amendment rights, which guarantee voting rights regardless of race, for fear that this would limit the tribes' abilities to determine membership. See John R. Wunder, *"Retained by The People": A History of American Indians and the Bill of Rights* (New York: Oxford University Press, 1994), 138.

39. Ball, "Stories of Origin," 2308. The federal government's extension protected individual Native Americans from actions taken by their *tribal* authority, meaning that, similar to protection for citizens against state action (by the incorporation of the Bill of Rights through the Fourteenth Amendment), Native Americans could now initiate causes of action in federal courts against their own tribe for the denial of basic rights.

40. *Tee-Hit-Ton Indians v. United States,* 348 U.S. 272 (1955), 289–90. The Court denied compensation to a band of the Tlingit community in Alaska for the harvesting of lumber on property claimed by the Native Americans.

41. *Oliphant v. Suquamish Indian Tribe,* 435 U.S. 191 (1978), 208–9. The Court was quoting from *United States v. Rogers,* 45 U.S. (4 How.) 567 (1846), 571–72, in which the Court denied a European American who had been adopted by a Native American community immunity from federal jurisdiction over the murder on a reservation of another European American who had been adopted by a Native American community.

42. See note 18. See also Wunder, *"Retained by The People,"* 147–200.

43. This is not to suggest that the individuality of Native Americans is a new category of existence. Although it is recognized that not all Native Americans live in geographic proximity to their tribal affiliation, or even necessarily retain such affiliation with respect to religion, there can be no argument that the federal government, since its inception, has distinguished Native Americans in their tribal groupings from those who lived their lives seemingly independent of tribal authority (see note 15). In addition, because specific rights as well as potential financial settlements have rested on the very definition of who is or is not a member of a given Native American tribe, the very concept of affiliation has not escaped litigation. (See *Elk v. Wilkins*, 112 U.S. 94 [1884], in which the Court denied citizenship—in the form of voting rights—to a Native American who provided no evidence of having paid taxes, and thus still fell under the limitations of the Fourteenth Amendment; *Morton v. Mancari*, 417 U.S. 535 [1973], in which the Supreme Court ruled the BIA hiring preference for Native Americans was politically rather than racially based, and therefore not subject to employment restrictions; and *Santa Clara Pueblo v. Martinez*, 436 U.S. 49 [1978], in which the Supreme Court ruled that the *Indian Civil Rights Act* did not require federal jurisdiction over all internal Native American disputes, in this case a dispute over tribal membership standards.) It is also a category of obvious distinction in some contemporary Native American scholarship, which notes the tribal affiliations for Native Americans, but ignores parallel ethnic identifications for people of other non-Native American ethnicities. See Wunder, *"Retained by the People,"* 162.

44. For the purposes of this essay, I have conflated Native American and European-American religious traditions into general categories in much the same way, while recognizing their vast internal differences. With reference to the appropriateness of this convention for Native American religious traditions, Native American historian of religions Joel Martin notes that

> rather than focus upon their commonalities, pre-contact Native Americans must have been most conscious of the plethora of highly diverse religious, linguistic, political, social, and cultural forms that divided them into a great number of ethnic groups. . . . The situation changed dramatically when these diverse peoples were collectively misnamed 'Indians' and then reconstructed as colonized subjects within a world-system dominated by European nation-states. Though ethnic differences did not diminish, and intertribal conflicts did not cease, very deep and widespread cultural and religious commonalities could not help but become more apparent. . . . As they found their economies revolutionized, land bases threatened, and cosmologies challenged as a result of contact with the invaders, it was almost inevitable that a self-conscious pan-Native Americanism would emerge. Prophetic movements recognized this prospect most vigorously and dramatically. In these movements, prophets beckoned diverse peoples to put aside their differences and forge a new common identity.

Joel W. Martin, "Before and beyond the Sioux Ghost Dance: Native American Prophetic Movements and the Study of Religion," *Journal of the American Academy of Religion* 49, no. 4 (winter 1991): 691–92. See also Catherine L. Albanese, *America: Religions and Religion* (Belmont, CA: Wadsworth Publishing Company, 1981), 19–38.

45. For a brief discussion of limitations placed on Native American religions, see Lee Irwin, "Freedom, Law, and Native Religions: Sweating It Out with AIM, WARN, and SPIRIT"

(paper presented at the American Academy of Religion Annual Meeting, Philadelphia, PA, November 1995), 2–3.

46. Edward McGlynn Gaffney, Jr., "The Interaction of Biblical Religion and American Constitutional Law," in *The Bible in American Law, Politics, and Political Rhetoric*, James Turner Johnson, ed. (Philadelphia, PA: Fortress Press, 1985), 99.

47. Beaver, *Church, State, and the American Indian*, 34. The relevant portion of Exodus 18:21 reads: "Moreover thou shalt provide out of all the people able men, such as fear God, men of truth, hating unjust gain; and place such over them, to be rulers of thousands, rulers of hundreds, rulers of fifties, and rulers of tens; . . ." thus providing for a hierarchical social structure of governance. See also Dane Morrison, *A Praying People: Massachusett Acculturation and the Failure of the Puritan Mission, 1600–1690*, American Indian Studies, vol. 2 (New York: Peter Lang, 1995), especially 74–119.

48. Robert F. Berkhofer, Jr., *The White Man's Indian: Images of the American Indian from Columbus to the Present* (New York: Vintage Books, 1978), 81.

49. Robert S. Michaelsen, "American Indian Religious Freedom Litigation: Promise and Perils," *The Journal of Law and Religion* 3, no. 1 (1985): 63.

50. *American Indian Religious Freedom Act, U.S. Code*, vol. 42, sec. 1996 (1994).

51. Michaelsen, "'We Also Have a Religion,'" 114. The complete text of the Act is appended to Michaelsen's article.

52. Michaelsen, "American Indian Religious Freedom Litigation," 76.

53. Michaelsen, "'We Also Have a Religion,'" 135.

54. Michaelsen, "American Indian Religious Freedom Litigation," 50.

55. Ibid., 53. In its first Native American religious freedom decision (*Bowen v. Roy*, 476 U.S. 693 [1986]), the Supreme Court ruled that a parent's religious objections could not overrule the government's need to maintain its internal accounting procedures, in this case by providing a child with a Social Security number.

56. *Lyng v. Northwest Indian Cemetery Protective Association*, 485 U.S. 439 (1988).

57. *Late Corporation of the Church of Jesus Christ of Latter-Day Saints v. United States*, 136 U.S. 1 (1889).

58. See note 55.

59. For a detailed analysis of the decision, see Robert S. Michaelsen, "Is the Miner's Canary Silent? Implications of the Supreme Court's Denial of American Indian Free Exercise of Religion Claims," *The Journal of Law and Religion* 6, no. 1 (1988): 97–114. The Supreme Court handed down another Native American religious freedom decision (*Employment Division, Department of Human Resources of the State of Oregon v. Smith*, 485 U.S. 660 [1988]) in the same term as *Lyng*. However, in that decision the Court remanded the issue of a state's prohibition of sacramental peyote use for further consideration. This case returned to the Supreme Court two years later (*Employment Division, Department of Human Resources of Oregon et al. v. Smith et al.*, 494 U.S. 872 [1990]), and the state's prohibition was declared constitutional.

60. *Lyng v. Northwest Indian Cemetery Protective Association*, 447–53. (Justice O'Connor, writing for the Court). The Supreme Court overruled the lower court decisions which had

supported Native American objections to the road. See *Northwest Indian Cemetery Protective Association v. Peterson*, 565 F. Supp. 586 (1983); affirmed in part, 795 F. 2d 688 (1986).

61. Robert S. Michaelsen, "Sacred Land in America: What Is It? How Can It Be Protected?" *Religion* 16 (July 1986): 253.

62. Michaelsen, "'We Also Have a Religion,'" 132. (Professor Michaelsen's own citations and references have been omitted.)

63. Michaelsen, "'We Also Have a Religion,'" 132, quoting *Wilson v. Black; Hopi Indian Tribe v. Black; Navajo Medicinemen's Association v. Black*, D.D.C., Nos. 81–0558, 81–0481, 81–0493, 15 June, 1981, published in *Indian Law Reporter* (ILR) 8: 3073–79; 708 F.2d 735 (D.C. Cir. 1983).

64. Michaelsen, "American Indian Religious Freedom Litigation," 50.

65. Vine Deloria, Jr., *God Is Red: A Native View of Religion* (Golden, CO: Fulcrum Publishing, 1994), 62.

66. Michaelsen, "'We Also Have a Religion,'" 112. In another piece, Michaelsen suggests that the differences between traditional Native American religions and European-American religions could best be understood utilizing categories developed by Robert Bellah to describe the spectrum of religious behavior. See "Sacred Land," 249–68. Michaelsen is referring to Robert N. Bellah, "Religious Evolution," *American Sociological Review* 29, no. 3 (1964): 358–74.

67. No non-Native American organizations were represented as signatories in the amici filed in the *Lyng* case. See Brief for the Indian Respondents, *Richard E. Lyng, Secretary of Agriculture et al. v. Northwest Indian Cemetery Protective Association et al.* (No. 86–1013), signed by representatives from California Indian Legal Services; and Brief of Amici Curiae, *Richard E. Lyng, Secretary of Agriculture et al. v. Northwest Indian Cemetery Protective Association et al.* (No. 86–1013), which included representatives from eight Native American tribes or associations.

68. See note 59.

69. Petition for Rehearing for the Native American Program, Oregon Legal Services, *Employment Division, Department of Human Resources of Oregon et al. v. Smith et al.* (No. 88–1213). Representatives from 19 national political organizations and 48 faculty members of various law schools signed the petition. The petition was denied, 496 U.S. 913 (1990).

70. *Religious Freedom Restoration Act*, secs. 2000bb-2000bb4.

71. Milner S. Ball, *Lying Down Together: Law, Metaphor and Theology* (Madison: The University of Wisconsin Press, 1981), 7.

72. Michaelsen, "American Indian Religious Freedom Litigation," 60. For an interesting response to the magnified role of land within Native American scholarship, see Sam D. Gill, *Mother Earth: An American Story* (Chicago: The University of Chicago Press, 1987).

73. Ball, *Lying Down Together*, 13.

74. Michaelsen, "'We Also Have a Religion,'" 112.

75. For an early analysis of constitutional law, see Joseph Story, *Commentaries on the Constitution of the United States* (Cambridge, MA: Hilliard, Gray and Company, 1833; reprint, New York: Da Capo, 1970). See also Morton Borden, *Jews, Turks, and Infidels* (Chapel Hill: The University of North Carolina Press, 1984); H. Frank Way, "Death of the Christian Nation: The Judiciary and Church-State Relations," *Journal of Church and State* 29, no. 3 (autumn 1987): 509–29; and John K. Wilson, "Religion Under the State Constitutions, 1776–1800," *Journal of Church and State* 32, no. 4 (autumn 1990): 753–73.

76. Gaffney, "Interaction," 91.

77. Michaelsen, "American Indian Religious Freedom Litigation," 61.

78. Michaelsen, "Sacred Land," 256.

79. See *United States v. Kagama*, 118 U.S. 375 (1886), in which the Court ruled that the murder of a Native American by a Native American was under the jurisdiction of the federal courts, overturning its own ruling in *Ex parte Crow Dog*, 109 U.S. 556 (1883). Justice Miller provides an analysis of the doctrine of discovery and the U.S. attitude toward Native American protectorship, 381–85.

80. Ball, "Stories of Origin," 2305–6. Ball points out that an early draft of the Constitution's supremacy clause read that it would be "the supreme law of the several States." The change in wording indicated a radical shift in authority, since the first draft covered only those states participating in the Union, while the final version incorporated all land claimed by the Union—states, territories, possessions, and conquests. It also signified a shift in abstractions from authority over a polity to authority over space.

81. Genesis 1:26–30.

82. This same attitude toward discovery can be seen in events within the last thirty years, such as in the planting of an American flag on the surface of the Moon.

83. Beaver, *Church, State, and the American Indian*, 196.

84. See Deloria and Lytle, *American Indians, American Justice*, passim.

85. Michaelsen, "American Indian Religious Freedom Litigation," 64.

86. Michaelsen has suggested the use of analogy between Native American and European-American religious concepts, citing the Native American Church which chose to incorporate as a church in order to make its religious viability more readily understandable. See Michaelsen, "American Indian Religious Freedom Litigation," 50, 62. However, he and other scholars have noted limitations to this approach. See ibid., 68; Ball, *Lying Down Together*, 22. Ball has suggested the use of metaphors that are more inclusive, such as a creation narrative for Americans which stresses the successive arrivals of different peoples (including Native Americans, African Americans, and new immigrant communities, as well as the western European colonialists) rather than the conventional colonial narrative which privileges one culture. See Ball, "Stories of Origin," 2311.

87. Michaelsen, "American Indian Religious Freedom Litigation," 73–74. Michaelsen suggests a more specific erosion of authority, namely the need to meet legal standards to participate in the system.

88. Michaelsen, "We Also Have a Religion," 113.

89. *Selective Draft Law Cases*, 245 U.S. 366 (1918), 376. For an interesting discussion of the evolution of religion and the military draft, see *United States v. Seeger*, 380 U.S. 163 (1965).

90. *Wisconsin v. Yoder*, 406 U.S. 205 (1972).

91. Ball, "Stories of Origin," 2293.

PERCEPTIONS
AND
REPRESENTATIONS

V

Voices and Words

American Indian literature is the subject of Section V. The essays featured herein describe some of the Voices and Words through which writers of Native American heritage explore elements of their experience. As we see, the theme of alienation and recovery is prominent in these tales. In their fiction and poetry, writers such as Joseph Welch, Leslie Marmon Silko, Louise Erdrich, N. Scott Momaday, Joseph Bruchac, and Simon J. Ortiz portray both the alienation of the individual—from modernity, from mainstream white society, and from traditional Native societies—and the rediscovery of self through a connection to one's land and community.

The theme is explored in Robert M. Nelson's essay, "Place, Vision, and Identity in Native American Literatures." Nelson, who teaches English at the University of Richmond, makes a case for recognizing that what distinguishes contemporary Native American writing is its sense of place. He discusses Native American literatures as a distinct body of writing and traces the origins of Native ethnopoetics and the emergence of a "Native American Renaissance." As Nelson sees it, "The period since the 1970s has seen an exponential increase in literary texts written in English by Native Americans, thus augmenting the ongoing oral literatures of their respective cultural traditions." A significant theme in this body of literatures is the idea that "identity, like life itself, derives from the land. Whoever wishes either to recover or to sustain a healthy state of existence, then, must enter into some working identity not only with a cultural tradition, but also with a particular landscape." In the voices and words of Lipsha Morrissey, Ts'eh Mantano, and Sylvester Yellow Calf, Nelson demonstrates that identification with a specific environment is the means through which Native literary characters forge or recover a sense of self.

Irene Moser of The College of West Virginia develops other aspects of the theme of place in "Native American Imaginative Spaces." Much of Native American literature, she contends, "gets us to think about space . . . in a new way." She finds that a "manner of configuring spaces as processes, as circles, as centered points of access to creative and empowering forces, is common in contemporary writing by Native American authors." This creative and empowering centering also is typical of Native folktales, and, as in indigenous folktales, "extraordinary forces of the natural world"—

ancestral spirits, totems, natural features—make "expected appearances" in these works. Through this reorientation toward spaces in Native literature, Moser sees the "development of mutually reinforcing relationships between individuals and communities" which integrate the individual into the natural and spiritual worlds.

Tom Matchie, a professor of English at North Dakota State University, focuses on the work of a single Native American fiction writer in "Building on the Myth: Narration, Theme, and Style in Louise Erdrich's *The Bingo Palace*." In Erdrich's work, Matchie shows, the relationship between culture and written expression figures prominently in "the way in which she incorporates vital elements of Native culture—in both its traditional and alienated guises—and mainstream cultures to weave stories that challenge all of us to rethink the human experience." Here, too, a Native voice speaks of the importance of place for her people. Through the character of Lipsha Morrissey, recovery of one's sense of self is gained by coming home—to the earth and to the reservation—for moral sustenance and cultural healing. In *Bingo Palace* and throughout other examples of Erdrich's work, Matchie finds "an intriguing experiment with ways to bring the healing power of traditional Chippewa culture to bear on American Indians living in a fragmented contemporary world."

Finally, in her essay, "'What Does It Tell Us That We Are So Easily Deceived?' Impostor Indians," Laura Browder, a professor of English at Virginia Commonwealth University, takes a different approach to literary constructions of Native American identity. Browder tackles the phenomenon of non-Native people who faked their "Indianness." The issue exploded with the controversial unmasking of Forrest Carter, the author of *The Education of Little Tree*. Browder shows that impostor Indians have been around for some time; more unfortunate, still, she contends, through their charades those passing for Indian have only served to reinforce the facile, false stereotypes of Native people.

13

Place, Vision, and Identity in Native American Literatures

It is hard to imagine trying to understand any group of people without taking into account their own stories of who they are, where they came from, and what they stand for—their core literary traditions. Only recently, however, have Western-trained literary critics begun to study Native American texts in ways comparable to how they study, for instance, the collected works of Chaucer or Emily Dickinson or William Faulkner. One thing Western-trained critics like myself are learning is that we have a lot to *un*-learn about *how* literature means, or can mean. This essay highlights one of the recurring values that has begun to emerge from the methodical study of Native American literatures: the idea that the life of the land and human life at its best are inseparable.

Towards a Native American Literary Criticism

In order to distinguish between the kind of literary criticism that is practiced in most university English departments and the kind that has developed around the study of Native American texts, I want to call the latter "Native American literary criticism," even though that term can be easily misinterpreted as "literary criticism as practiced by Native Americans" rather than "critical approaches to Native American literatures."[1] In the sense I mean, Native American literary criticism has only very recently become thought of as appropriate to English or literature departments. As late as the first half of this century, Native American literatures were more likely to be studied by cultural anthropologists than by English majors. About that time, Franz Boas and his first generation of students began to develop the subdiscipline of cultural anthropology known as ethnography (the attempt to describe—and write out—the unique or characteristic ethos of any ethnic group). Arguably, Boas and his followers were the first academics to pay close, often quite respectful, attention to what Native Americans had to say about themselves, both as individuals and as members of non-Western cultures. Boas and his followers were also some of the first scholars to methodically transcribe Native American oral performances into written texts; later ethnographers, as well as literary critics, came to regard these written versions as examples of "authentic" Native American literature. Few of Boas's immediate followers, however, had any formal training in literary appreciation; as "scientists," they were prone to treat Native oral performances not as works of art, but rather as objects to be gathered, sorted, and preserved for later study.

The next step in the development of a Native American literary criticism was the development of *ethnopoetics*—literally, the study of the poetic sense of an ethnic group—as a site where the disciplines of ethnography and literary criticism intersect.[2] By the 1960s, such scholars as Karl Kroeber, Jarold Ramsey, Dell Hymes, and Dennis Tedlock, often working with earlier transcriptions of Native American oral performances collected by Boas and his followers, were learning how to look beyond the transcriptions to the *pre*-texts, the original-language oral performances themselves, in order to recover the art of these performances (such as rhythm and intonation, recurring phrase, and other verbal nuances) that so often had been lost in translation. Their pioneering work in ethnopoetics established some crucial principles of subsequent Native American literary criticism. They taught that an oral tradition is a species of literature. Like any other body of literature (including any print-text literature), Native American oral traditions have both culturally specific content or subject matter and culture-specific aesthetic criteria; these aesthetic norms regulate the composition of performances and these same criteria can be used to evaluate such performances. The ongoing attempt to identify and appreciate these distinctive values still drives much of Native American literary criticism.

In addition to the development of ethnopoetics around mid-century, a second historical phenomenon, which has been called the "Native American Renaissance" by literary critic and anthologist Kenneth Lincoln, has made the study of Native American literatures a viable discipline in its own right. The period since the 1970s has seen an exponential increase in literary texts written in English by Native Americans, thus augmenting the ongoing oral literatures of their respective cultural traditions. In their poems, short stories, novels, plays, memoirs and autobiographies, and essays of all sorts, many of these new writers have been working to find ways to adapt traditional Native American literary and cultural values to these Western performance modes—sometimes by revising the modes themselves to accommodate non-Western materials and values in exciting new ways. My comments in this essay are directed primarily toward this newer part of the ongoing Native American literary tradition, and even more particularly towards Native American poetry and fiction composed and published in the second half of the twentieth century.

Native American Identity and the Land

Understandably, one of the recurring themes of recent Native American literature[3] is the issue of Native American identity. What is sometimes hard to grasp is that "identity," correctly speaking, is not an attribute of either the individual or of the context—the environment, including cultural traditions—in which the individual is embedded. Rather, identity is an event that takes place in the creation of the *relationship* between individual and context. In recent Native American literature, as in many of the cultural traditions to which this body of literature refers and defers, identity, like life itself, derives from the land. Whoever wishes either to recover or to sustain a healthy state of existence, then, must enter into some working identity not only with a cultural tradition, but also with a particular landscape.

One of the clichés of New Age Nativism, American and European alike, is that Native spiritual vision is rooted in animal or "totem" identity. Nativists also tend to assume that the larger the animal one calls one's ally, the more powerful one's own vision must be—self-proclaimed New Age shamans seem more predisposed to adopt names like Black Bear or White Eagle than Pink Piglet or Gray Titmouse. Within the context of Western hierarchical traditions, as formulated perhaps most clearly and dramatically in the Renaissance concept of the Great Chain of Being, it makes more sense to think of oneself (at one's most "angelic" or most spiritually rarefied, at any rate) as being closer in nature to an animal than to a plant, and closer to a plant than to a mineral. In the universe as imagined by Western religious tradition, all life derives from God in such a way that one moves *away* from God in the direction of the earth and *towards* God in the direction of the sky. Accordingly, only the most degraded person would choose to identify with the worm rather than the eagle, let alone with the dirt the worm calls home.

But in the spiritual traditions of many Native American groups, the spirit and the life of the People derive from the land: life is a "property" of the land as well as of the creatures occupying it. In her ground-breaking collection of critical essays *The Sacred Hoop* (1986), one of the first large-scale attempts to apply Native American cultural (and literary) values to modern Native American writing, Paula Gunn Allen puts it this way:

> We are the land. To the best of my understanding, that is the fundamental idea embedded in Native American life and culture in the Southwest. . . . The land is not really the place (separate from ourselves) where we act out the drama of our isolate destinies. . . . It is rather a part of our being, dynamic, significant, real. It is ourself, in as real a sense as such notions as "ego," "libido" or social network. . . . Nor is this relationship one of mere "affinity" for the Earth. It is not a matter of being "close to nature." The relationship is more one of identity, in the mathematical sense, than of affinity. The Earth is, in

a very real sense, the same as ourself (or selves), and it is this primary point that is made in the fiction and poetry of the Native American writers of the Southwest. (191)

The notion that a human's relationship to the land can be more than an "affinity" or a matter of being "close to nature" probably does not come easily to most students of American literature. Yet, many Native Americans are born into family and cultural traditions that not only end with statements of this identity (as Protestant traditions do: "ashes to ashes . . ."), but also begin with this fundamental vision of identity. Within the context of such traditions, the most fundamental act of spiritual vision that one can experience is the act of seeing oneself as a living part of the living place where one's life *takes* place.

Emergence and Identity in Native American Poetry

This conviction about human identity with the land has shaped much of recent Native American poetry. A good illustration of both the conviction and of how it works to shape a writer's vision is "To Insure Survival," a short dramatic monologue written by Simon J. Ortiz, a native of the Pueblo of Acoma. The words of the text are being uttered by a father to his daughter as she is being born, and so the opening stanza of the poem is to be understood as the very first "story" this child ever hears about the nature of the world she is entering. In these first, consciousness-shaping words, the event of the child's delivery is identified with the event of a sunrise in the high country of New Mexico:

> You come forth
> the color of a stone cliff
> at dawn,
> changing colors,
> blue to red
> to all the colors of the earth.

This statement offers two bases of identification: the sequence of colors that both land and child undergo, and the unifying *vision* of both sunrise and birth as emergence events, as the "coming forth" of life from a relatively darker state into a relatively lighter, multichromatic one. It is important to notice here that the identification of the child with the land in this text depends upon an act of vision: it is an event that must be *seen* before it can be uttered, then heard.

Later in the poem, the child is told that later in her life, "In five more days, / they will come, / singing, dancing, / . . . / the stones with voices, / the plants with bells." Ortiz is alluding here to the *katsinas*. In Acoma spiritual tradition, as in the traditions of several other Southwestern Native peoples, the katsinas are the spirits of life who, on special ceremonial occasions, allow themselves to be seen in the form and motion of the masked katsina dancers. In Acoma tradition, if a newborn survives its first four full days of life, then the katsinas appear at the dawn of the fifth day to welcome this new human being to its extended family. In the traditions of this child's people, one's extended family includes spirit entities: Grandmother Spider (the Keresan creatrix figure who is weaving a life for the child to grow into in stanza two), as well as the "stones with voices" (the singing dancers representing the katsinas of the sacred mountains in all the directions) and the "plants with bells" (the dancing singers representing the katsinas of the corn and other nurture for human beings). The (re-)appearance of the katsinas is a promise of continued life to the People, just as the emergence of this child "insures" the physical survival of Acoma cultural identity for one more generation. The father's words can be read as both a prayer and a promise that the child will be there in five days to see and hear the katsinas dancing and singing in her honor. His words and the vision they encode also help to insure survival just the way oral tradition always has been helping the People, by articulating and passing along a vision of human identity with the land.

Not only in "To Insure Survival," but also throughout Native American cultural traditions, these two seemingly separate processes—the emergence of human life and the attainment of a vision of both individual and collective identity—often appear as aspects of a singular event. This unifying event is typically described in terms of a sunrise, birth, emergence, or other original moment, though usually (as in Ortiz's poem) as a combination of several such occasions. What distinguishes Native American origin stories from those of most other cultures is that these emergence events take particular and distinct place: emergence is an event that belongs to the land. Although individual human beings "emerge" from a biological mother's womb, the understanding at Acoma (as in many cultures' spiritual traditions, Indian and otherwise) is that each corporeal being houses spirits that emerge from other sources to abide in that body during its life, and that one of these sources of spirit is the land, the particular place where that being was born. This motif of human/land interconnectedness continues to influence Native American storytellers, including novelists, sometimes very overtly. In both Anna Lee Walters's *Ghost Singer* (1988) and Louis Owens's *The Sharpest Sight* (1992), for instance, plots hinge on the recurrent idea that human bones are invested with a quality of spirit that attaches to the bones even after the individual's death, and that this bone spirit is liable to wreak havoc until the bones themselves are returned to their place of origin.[4]

Just as the lives of individuals originate with the land, so does the life of the People, an ongoing collective human spirit that stretches from the beginning of human time through the present. Typically, the life of the People is connected to the land at the *sipapu,*[5] or "place of emergence." In many Native American origin stories, this is the place where the People first emerged into the Earth Surface world. Unlike the origin places of some other cultural traditions (Christianity's Eden, for instance), Native American sipapus are usually located, known sites. For instance, in the origin stories of the people of Laguna Pueblo, the setting of Leslie Silko's novel *Ceremony* (1977), sipapu is a small spring a little north of the village of Paguate.[6] In the Navajo chantway traditions, which, as Susan Scarberry-García has shown, are the pretext for much of Scott Momaday's Pulitzer Prize-winning *House Made of Dawn* (1968), the emerging place is at *tségihi*, literally "that canyon," possibly Cañon de Chelly.[7] For the people of Taos Pueblo, sipapu is the sacred Blue Lake, the subject of the protracted legal struggle between Taos and the U.S. Government earlier in this century that inspired Frank Waters's *The Man Who Killed the Deer* (1945).

In the origin stories of the Abenaki people, sipapu is located at a geyser in upstate New York—the setting, as well as the subject, of Joseph Bruchac's short poem "The Geyser." Like "To Insure Survival" a dramatic monologue, "The Geyser" opens with a statement of the relationship between human life, in this case the life of a group rather than of an individual, and the land from which it comes:

> There is a story
> some people tell
> of how they came
> from a world beneath
> this world through a hole in the Earth.

Like the origin story to which he alludes, Bruchac then invites us to acknowledge that at least two events are taking place at this sipapu: the ongoing life of the land ("feel the life that rises here . . .") and the ongoing life and vision of a people who have themselves learned how to see, "like people coming out of the darkness / of a world with no Sun / to this place of light," the intimate connection between their life and the land's. At the moment the narrator achieves that recognition, he, too, becomes one in his vision with the "we" who "on that first day . . . saw this place." He, too, becomes a part of the emergence story, still happening at his place, that "some people tell."

As we might expect, geographies as different as those of northcentral New Mexico and upstate New York give rise to different visions of life and how it is to be lived. Such differences of vision are the basis of differences in cultural identities, and such a difference underlies the dialog between the male and female voices in Joy Harjo's poem "The Last Song," about how life gets lived in northeast Oklahoma. From "the last song" of the man, we learn only that he is a native of New Mexico who feels out of place, a man who cannot "stand" the "hot oklahoma summers / where you were born / this humid thick air is choking me / and i want to go back / to new mexico." The identity of the female speaker, on the other hand, is one with this climate and milieu, and has been so from birth:

it is the only way
i know how to breathe
an ancient chant
that my mother knew
came out of a history
woven from wet tall grass
in her womb

Harjo's wording here reiterates the idea of human identity with the land that so strongly informs the works of Native American poets from other regions. She invites us to read "her"—the source of both the "ancient chant" and the very breath of the narrating "i" of these lines—as either the speaker's biological mother or the earth, whose womb holds a "history" that some humans cannot help but call their own. And, while the male presumably goes on to try to return to his natal New Mexico, the female already knows that "oklahoma will be the last song / i'll ever sing."

Landscape and Identity in Native American Novels

Ever since the writings of Aristotle were "re-discovered" during the English Renaissance, the British (and, later, American) narrative tradition has been shaped by Aristotelian theories of composition. One of the most common, and most powerful, of these Aristotelian critical tools is the idea that a work of fiction can be analyzed in terms of plot, character, setting, and theme. Within an Aristotelian context, then, we might expect a landscape to function as a "setting" for a narrative, while the issue of identity might be a part of "character" development or maybe even a "theme" of the work. However, in many recent Native American novels (as in the non-Aristotelian oral narrative traditions they grow out of), particular landscapes function not only as the "settings" of the narratives, but also as "characters." Further, the discovery or invention of the relationship between land and human beings (that is, the process of human identification) drives the "plot" and becomes the main "theme" in these works. Much of contemporary Native American poetry can be read as a celebration—or, sometimes, a cautionary reminder— of this individual or collective identity with the land. By the same token, many Native American novels can be read as more extended explorations of the *process* of discovering, or recovering, such an identity. Recent Native American fiction not only undercuts the principles of Aristotelian criticism, but, in its emphasis on the process of identity, also challenges some of the truisms about the nature of fiction itself which have come to hold sway over American literature in the twentieth century.

One of these truisms, almost everywhere apparent in mainstream American literature since World War II, is the existentialist doctrine that the "human condition" is one of utter estrangement, or *alienation*, from the world in which we find ourselves. This condition, and a human being's predictable first response to it, is neatly encapsulated by Kurt Vonnegut in the satirical rewriting of Genesis in one of his early novels, *Cat's Cradle* (1963):

> In the beginning, God created earth, and he looked upon it in His cosmic loneliness.
> And God said, "Let Us make living creatures out of mud, so the mud can see what We have done." And God created every living creature that now moveth, and one was man. Mud as man alone could speak. God leaned close as mud as man sat up, looked around, and spoke. Man blinked. "What is the *purpose* of all this?" he asked politely.
> "Everything must have a purpose?" asked God.
> "Certainly," said man.
> "Then I leave it to you to think of one for all this," said God.
> And He went away. (177)

As this little parable suggests, it is human nature to resist the "natural" condition of alienation; but any attempt to discover or invent any meaning, any attempt to overcome the condition of alienation through an act of identification with the world external to oneself, is doomed to failure. Accordingly, "character development" in many a mainstream American novel consists of the protagonist's coming to terms with the dis-easing realization of his or her alienated condition. In this paradigm of man's relationship to the universe, the only authentic act of identity is to *dis*-engage from the world.[8]

Many of recent Native American fictions' protagonists also suffer early on from the dis-easing effects of alienation. A typical case in this regard is the title character in James Welch's *The Death of Jim Loney* (1979). Loney seems to be experiencing that state of spiritual malaise that in existential thought goes by the name of *anomie*—the inability to identify with the surrounding cultural milieu. Loney is a "half-breed," culturally and biologically: his father is from Anglo-American stock, while his mother is equally fully Gros Ventre. Loney's girlfriend, Rhea, envies his half-bred condition, because she thinks it gives him a choice about which "half" he can identify with. But to Loney—who, unlike Rhea, has to *live* with this condition—identity is a matter not of choice but of circumstance, and Loney is by circumstance neither Anglo nor Gros Ventre: to both, he is Other, and he knows it. As Welch presents it, then, Loney's alienation is both broadly existential and more specifically cultural. The protagonists of some of the best-known Native American novels of this century, including D'Arcy McNickle's *The Surrounded*, Welch's *Winter in the Blood*, Leslie Marmon Silko's *Ceremony*, N. Scott Momaday's *House Made of Dawn*, Louise Erdrich's *Love Medicine*, and Louis Owens's *The Sharpest Sight*, are (like their authors) either half-breed or mixed-blood, but in either case born into a state of cultural alienation.

Unlike their twentieth-century literary counterparts, however, the protagonists of Native American novels typically overcome this alienation, along with the literal and figurative diseases from which they suffer (the most common ones being poor eyesight, indicative of the need for clear vision, and alcoholism, perhaps a metaphor for exposure to the sweet poison of genocidal U.S. social and political policies). By directly challenging the notion that alienation is the first, final, and necessary condition of human existence, these works and the cultural values informing them offer an alternative to the spiritual malaise and psychological anomie that so often accompany existential vision.

We can see this process of healing taking place in such exemplary Native American novels as Leslie Silko's *Ceremony*, N. Scott Momaday's *House Made of Dawn*, and James Welch's *The Death of Jim Loney*. In all three of these novels, the protagonists initially suffer alienation, including cultural estrangement. Like Loney, Tayo, in *Ceremony*, is a half-breed, child of a Laguna mother and an anonymous Anglo father, while Abel, in *House Made of Dawn*, is a mixed-blood, his mother a Towan from Jemez, but his father of some other tribe. As their respective stories open, all three feel separated from their surrounding communities, suffer from impaired vision (all three spend the early moments of their respective novels "blind drunk"), and seem strangely immobilized. Jim Loney spends much of the first half of the novel sitting at his kitchen table at night with a bottle of wine. The first time we encounter Abel, he is so drunk he cannot even stand up, and his grandfather must cart him home in the back of a wagon. In the opening moments of *Ceremony*, it is all Tayo can do to get out of bed, which he wants to do only because the morning light hurts his eyes, and he is physically too weak to keep his seat on the blind mule he is trying to ride a few hours later.

From such shaky beginnings as these, all three protagonists go on to overcome their alienation by shaping their vision and motion to a particular landscape (for Loney, the stretch of northern Montana between the town of Harlem and Mission Valley, about 50 miles to the south; for Abel, the place called *Walatowa*, the valley created by the Jemez River north and south of the village of Jemez Pueblo; for Tayo, the traditional Laguna lands in all directions from the present-day village of Old Laguna). Just as the voices in Ortiz's, Harjo's, and Bruchac's poems do, they recover their Native identities by becoming—and, just as importantly, by *seeing* themselves becoming—living extensions of the living landscapes of which they are part.[9] The cure for the disease of alienation in their cases depends on this willingness and ability to enter into identity with the landscape, the place where the event of their lives happens to have taken and to be taking place.

Personal Identity and Cultural Tradition

In the process of becoming identified with these landscapes, the protagonists of these and other Native American novels also move into identity with whatever tribal traditions—encoded in stories and ceremony—happen to have come about in these places. This should come as no surprise, because in these novels (as in the Native American oral-literary traditions from which they partially derive) the life of the People as a collective body, like the life of any individual who is a part of that body, is an extension of the life of the land. Or, to put it another way, the life story of an individual and the life story ("literary tradition") of a cultural group are but two expressions or articulations of a common pre-textual experience: the experience of acquiring a vision of the living landscape that they both occupy. For both individual protagonists and the cultural traditions they come to represent, the process is essentially the same. First, there is the land, made visible at sunrise, a beginning time. The human being is also there, to witness and, in so witnessing, to become a part of that landscape's (re-) animation. Only then is there the song, or the dance, or the story, or the ceremony that becomes the text of that vision, the *articulation* of that experience. The sum of these articulations *is* the literary tradition.

From the perspective of a developing Native American literary criticism, the key term here may be "articulation." We need to remember that from the time of earliest contact between the Europeans who came to this continent (as conquerors, missionaries, and finally settlers) and the indigenous peoples they encountered here, Native American literatures have been treated more as artifacts than as art: recall that even as recently as the turn of this century, virtually the only Westerners who were at all familiar with any Native American literatures were anthropologists, ethnographers, and museum curators, rather than English professors. Perhaps as a result of this legacy, critics and readers today may think that Native American novels are not as "accessible" as others. It is easy to assume that the only proper context or frame of reference for understanding these texts is whatever particularly Native cultural tradition their protagonists are taken to represent. From this perspective, *Ceremony*, for instance, becomes a novel about Tayo's recovery of an "authentic" Indian, specifically Keresan (Laguna), identity; the catch is that we cannot know whether he ever accomplishes this unless we already know which of the values or insights that Tayo acquires are specifically Laguna ones. In effect, this critical assumption assumes that the only authentic act of self-articulation is one that brings an individual into identity with some set of pre-existing cultural norms. Accordingly, we might be tempted to say that Ben Benally, the Navajo narrator of the third movement in Momaday's *House Made of Dawn*, is "really" Navajo while he is singing a passage from the Navajo Night Chant for Abel, but has an "inauthentic" identity when he talks about the assembly line he and Abel work on in Los Angeles.

It helps to remember, again, that cultural traditions, like individual identities, are expressions of the experience of coming to terms with the life of that culture's landscape: both arise out of, and may be understood as articulations in differing voices of, the same pre-verbal reality. But if cultural tradition is an articulation of a way of life, then the oral and written pretexts for these novels—be they literary, historical, or anthropological—are themselves "fictions" in the very same sense that a novel is a fiction. To evaluate one fiction in terms of another is to risk getting lost in the mirrors of contemporary critical reflexivity, in the process becoming as rootless and dislocated as Tayo, Abel, or Jim Loney at their most dis-eased. The point made over and over in these novels, as well as in the cultural traditions we tend to identify as their pretexts, is that tradition confirms but does not create identity. Articulation of identity must be preceded by an act of identity to articulate. In these novels, as in many other works of American Indian literature both traditional and recent, identity with a physical landscape precedes cultural re-entry.

I certainly do not mean to imply here that Native American literary traditions are irrelevant to an understanding of contemporary Native American fiction, any more than they are to an understanding of recent poetry. Indeed, knowing something about such traditions allows us to see more in these works than we might otherwise see, especially about the nurturing relationship between tradition and the individual.

Throughout the novel *Ceremony*, for instance, Silko strategically scatters a number of traditional Keresan stories and story fragments, cast to look like portions of poetry embedded in the larger, framing prose narrative. One of these is the nine-part story involving Pa'caya'nyi's introduction of Ck'o'yo medicine into the lives of the People and the subsequent effort by Hummingbird and Green Fly to return Our Mother Nau'ts'ityi to the Fifth World. The tale functions broadly as a template for Tayo's overall quest in the novel to reinvigorate the life of the land and the People, including his own. Another of these embedded pieces, the traditional Keresan story of Sun Man's quest to recover the stolen rain clouds from the Gambler Ka't'sina Kaup'a'ta, both previews and predicts the structure of Tayo's recovery of the speckled cattle in the Mount Taylor episode that immediately follows. Taken as pretexts, these stories certainly add an extra dimension to our understanding of Tayo's own motion. As texts, Silko's story of Tayo and these pre-existing Keresan stories interact to animate one another; they do not, however, animate landscape. Rather, the stories and the characters in them are animated by the landscapes through which they move. Silko makes this point by seeing to it that Tayo, despite repeated pleas from the elders of Laguna (36, 106, 218, 228), makes no attempt to *articulate* his experience until after he has revisited all of Laguna land and re-adjusted his vision to its life. He does this by moving into identity with the spirit of the land in all directions from the village of Old Laguna: with Mount Taylor to the northwest, with Patoch Butte to the southwest, and with the river-crossing to the southeast, but also with the dangerous Ck'o'yo element hovering about the recently savaged earth of the Jackpile Mine. Just as importantly, the oral text that Tayo finally articulates for the village

elders in the kiva at the end of the novel derives its ultimate authority not
from its analogy to previous oral texts, but rather from its structural geography, its grounding in particular, confirmable time and place: "they
stopped him frequently with questions about the location and the time of
day; they asked about the direction she had come . . ." (257).

Similarly, Momaday, in *House Made of Dawn*, provides, sometimes directly
and sometimes rather indirectly, "storysherds"[10] from at least three very
different Native American literary traditions—Towan (Jemez Pueblo),
Navajo, and Kiowa (the title of the novel is, in fact, taken from a relatively
well-known Navajo healing chantway). Still, throughout the novel a human
being's (re-)identification with an immediate landscape precedes cultural
re-entry. Abel, the principle protagonist of the novel, remains "inarticulate"
(58) until he utterly re-enters the motion of life at Walatowa (Jemez
Pueblo), his vision given over entirely to a vision of the land taking shape at
sunrise. Only at that moment does Ben Benally's Navajo song ("House
made of dawn, house made of pollen . . ."), which Ben sang to Abel at least
twice during their time together in Los Angeles, come to make sense as a
text congruent with the pretextual event of Abel's unqualified (re-)identifi-
cation with the land. But even as Abel recalls the words of the song, they
are not uttered; no sound, no text has more authority than the landscape
that such healing texts take as their final frame of reference. Momaday
makes the same point through Ben, whose Navajo identity is grounded in a
preverbal experience of identity with a particular landscape ("at first light
you went out and knew where you were. . . . And you were there where you
wanted to be, and alone. You didn't want to see anyone, or hear anyone
speak. There was nothing to say" [169–70]). He makes the point yet again
through Tosamah, a Kiowa "orator, physician, Priest of the Sun, [and] son
of Hummingbird," and the three religious ceremonies that he conducts
while Abel lies somewhere in the night, blinded and paralyzed, in Part 3 of
the novel. In the first ceremony, his Saturday sermon to his congregation of
the Relocated, Tosamah warns of the characteristically Euro-American
tendency to substitute worlds made of words for the world itself. Even more
telling is the structure of his Sunday sermon, the final words of that section
of the novel. The words of this sermon, which is also an example of
personal, self-defining oral narrative, fix all of Kiowa cultural history as
occurring between two moments of emergence: the first as the Kiowa
people emerge from their sipapu, a hollow log somewhere in the vicinity of
the Yellowstones, and the last as Tosamah, feeling terribly alone in the wake
of his grandmother's death, witnesses a sunrise at Rainy Mountain in
Oklahoma.

In these and other Native American novels, as in poetry such as Ortiz's
"To Insure Survival" and Bruchac's "The Geyser," the process of human
spiritual regeneration, of healing, depends most immediately not on articulation, but rather on conforming individual vision to the reality of a

physical landscape. Ontologically, a vision of the land, alive, empowers the protagonists of these novels and poems, much as some such vision empowers, characterizes, identifies, and authenticates the People and by extension their stories and traditions.

Conclusion

My claim that a powerful respect for place, in the sense of an actual and particular landscape, is characteristic of much of Native American poetry and fiction is not a new one. And yet, such claims about the shaping power of landscapes upon the literary imagination, made by writers and leading critics of American Indian literature alike, have rarely been demonstrated methodically in critical writings about that literature. Generally speaking, literary criticism resists the notion that the land has a life of its own. Western ideological tradition tends to hold that vitality is a quality that human imagination imposes on the land, not vice versa. This sort of pre-emption of significance, or privileging of human imagination, is one of the dangerous shortcomings of the Euro-American humanistic tradition in general, and of a conventional humanistic approach to this literature in particular. The tendency to presuppose, and then magnify, the shaping power of people in these stories limits our ability to recover the *pre*-human context of the human condition in these stories; busily admiring the human ability to see, we lose sight of what is there to see—the land, alive, waiting to hold and be held.

This is not to say that the humanistic impulse is not an integral element of American Indian fiction. Clearly it is. But, as I hope I have begun to suggest in this brief overview of some recent Native American texts, the test of humanity in these works is the land itself rather than any ideology. The protagonists of, and spokespersons in, these works prove their humanity not by conquering the land or by living in spite of it, but rather by finding ways—sometimes "traditional," sometimes "innovative," and sometimes a creative blend of the two—to live with the land, holding and being held by the life that precedes and survives the life of any individual, as well as the life of any culture.

Notes

1 I use the word "literatures" rather than the singular "literature" to draw attention to the fact that there is no singular, or even meaningfully representative, American Indian cultural tradition. Since any body of literature depends for much of its meaning on the language in which it is encoded, it is much more accurate to say that, since the time of European contact, there have been about 500 Native American literatures in the contiguous 48 United States alone. Because many of these distinct languages, along with the oral (and sometimes written) literary traditions encoded in them, are still in circulation, some works of Native American literature that are written in English are in fact translations of Native language texts into English.

2 For a quick summary of the development of ethnopoetics as a methodology, see (for instance) William Bright, *A Coyote Reader* (3).

3 I use this term to include works of prose and poetry written by Native Americans. But even this seemingly usable definition of the term "Native American literature" is problematic. For instance, most people would probably expect any work in this category also to be *about* Native American experience, as somehow distinct from other kinds of recognizably "non-Indian" experience. But, shall we then say that a novel like *Gorky Park* is not "Native American literature," even though its author, Martin Cruz Smith, is a Native American author? Or shall we say that Smith was writing "Native American literature" when he wrote *Nightwing* and *Stallion Gate*, but not when he was writing *Gorky Park* and *Red Square*? To add to the difficulty, there is the very troubling question of who qualifies as a "Native American." The U.S. government's longstanding use of "blood quantum" to make such determinations is at serious odds with many (if not most) Native groups' criteria, not to mention their best interests. For a somewhat one-sided, but nevertheless useful and eye-opening, discussion of this issue, see Ward Churchill's *Indians Are Us? Culture and Genocide in Native North America*.

4 This concept of bone-spirit helps to explain why some people so strongly support the recent NAGPRA (Native American Graves Protection and Repatriation Act) legislation, especially its provisions for museum repatriation efforts.

5 It is a little silly to talk about "standard" spelling of a language that never fixed itself in print the way most European languages have done: in such cases, there simply is no "authentic" orthography, only those that have been used by one translator or another. I nevertheless suspect that if this useful term ever finds its way into some future standard dictionary, this is how it will be spelled (both Leslie Silko and Paula Gunn Allen, two of the most prominent Laguna-born authors and critics, spell it this way). Some other spellings that I have seen include "ship-op" (John Gunn, in *Schat-Chen: History, Traditions and Narratives of the Queres Indians of Laguna and Acoma* [1917]), "cip'a·pu" (Boas, *Keresan Texts* [1925]), "shipapu" (Elsie Clews Parsons, *The Pueblo Indians of Jemez* [1925]), "sipápuni" (Frank Waters, *Book of the Hopi* [1963]), and "Sipofene" (Alfonso Ortiz, "The Tewa World View" [1966]).

6 See Leslie Silko, "Landscape, History, and the Pueblo Imagination" 91.

7 For one version of this emergence story, see Paul Zolbrod, *Diné bahane'* (35–78).

8   For a fuller treatment of this issue, see my "Introduction" in *Place and Vision*.

9   I analyze this process, in these three novels, at length in *Place and Vision*.

10 This useful term, which is a play on the term "potsherds," is Susan Scarberry-García's: see her *Landmarks of Healing*, especially 6, 118–19.

Works Cited

Allen, Paula Gunn. "Iyani: It Goes This Way." Hobson. 191–93. Rpt. *The Sacred Hoop: Recovering the Feminine in American Indian Traditions.* Boston: Beacon, 1986. 119.

Boas, Franz. *Keresan Texts.* Publications of the American Ethnological Society 8, Part 2. New York: American Ethnological Society, 1925.

Bright, William. *A Coyote Reader.* Berkeley: U of California P, 1993.

Bruchac, Joseph. "The Geyser." *Entering Onondaga.* Austin, TX: Cold Mountain, 1977. Rpt. Hobson. 35.

Churchill, Ward. *Indians Are Us? Culture and Genocide in Native North America.* Monroe, ME: Common Courage, 1994.

Erdrich, Louise. *Love Medicine.* New York: Bantam, 1984.

Gunn, John. *Schat-Chen: History, Traditions and Narratives of the Queres Indians of Laguna and Acoma.* Albuquerque: Albright & Anderson, 1917.

Harjo, Joy. "the last song." *The Last Song.* Las Cruces, NM: Puerto del Sol, 1975. Rpt. Hobson. 109–10.

Hobson, Geary, ed. *The Remembered Earth: An Anthology of Contemporary American Indian Literature.* Albuquerque: U of New Mexico P, 1980.

Hymes, Dell H. *"In Vain I Tried to Tell You": Essays in Native American Ethnopoetics.* Philadelphia: U of Pennsylvania P, 1981.

Kroeber, Karl, ed. *Traditional Literatures of the American Indian: Texts and Interpretations.* Lincoln: U of Nebraska P, 1981.

Lincoln, Kenneth. *Native American Renaissance.* Berkeley: U of California P, 1983.

McNickle, D'Arcy. *The Surrounded.* 1936. Albuquerque: U of New Mexico P, 1978.

Momaday, N. Scott. *House Made of Dawn.* New York: Harper, 1968.

Native American Graves Protection and Repatriation Act [NAGPRA]. Title 25 U.S.C. §3001 et seq. 1994.

Nelson, Robert M. *Place and Vision: The Function of Landscape in Native American Fiction.* American Indian Studies. 1. New York: Peter Lang, 1993.

Ortiz, Alfonso. "The Tewa World View." *Teachings from the American Earth: Indian Religion and Philosophy*. Ed. Dennis and Barbara Tedlock. New York: Liveright, 1975. 179–89.

Ortiz, Simon J. "To Insure Survival." Hobson. 271. Rpt. *Woven Stone*. Sun Tracks. 21. Tucson: U of Arizona P, 1992. 48–49.

Owens, Louis. *The Sharpest Sight*. Norman: U of Oklahoma P, 1992.

Parsons, Elsie Clews. *The Pueblo Indians of Jemez*. New Haven: Yale UP, 1925.

Ramsey, Jarold. *Reading the Fire: Essays in the Traditional Indian Literatures of the Far West*. Lincoln: U of Nebraska P, 1983.

Scarberry-García, Susan. *Landmarks of Healing: A Study of* House Made of Dawn. Albuquerque: U of New Mexico P, 1990.

Silko, Leslie. *Ceremony*. New York: Viking, 1977.

———. "Landscape, History, and the Pueblo Imagination." *Antaeus* 57 (Autumn 1986): 83–94.

Smith, Martin Cruz. *Gorky Park*. New York: Random, 1981.

———. *Nightwing*. New York: Norton, 1977.

———. *Red Square*. New York: Random, 1992.

———. *Stallion Gate*. New York: Random, 1986.

Tedlock, Dennis. *The Spoken Word and the Word of Interpretation*. Philadelphia: U of Pennsylvania P, 1983.

Vonnegut, Kurt. *Cat's Cradle*. 1963. New York: Dell Laurel, 1988.

Walters, Anna Lee. *Ghost Singer*. Flagstaff, AZ: Northland, 1988.

Waters, Frank. *The Book of the Hopi*. New York: Viking, 1963.

———. *The Man Who Killed the Deer*. Athens: Ohio UP, 1945.

Welch, James. *The Death of Jim Loney*. 1979. New York: Penguin, 1987.

———. *Winter in the Blood*. 1974. New York: Penguin, 1986.

Zolbrod, Paul G. *Diné bahane': The Navajo Creation Story*. Albuquerque: U of New Mexico P, 1984.

Some Native American Novels
(U.S. and Canadian) Published Since
House Made of Dawn and *Ceremony*

1995

Alexie, Sherman. *Reservation Blues*. New York: Atlantic Monthly.
Bruchac, Joseph. *Long River*. Golden, CO: Fulcrum.
Carr, A. A. *Eye Killers*. Norman: U of Oklahoma P.
Hogan, Linda. *Solar Storms*. New York: Scribner.
Louis, Adrian. *Skins*. New York: Crown.
Penn, W. S. *The Absence of Angels*. Norman: U of Oklahoma P.
Treuer, David. *Little*. Saint Paul, MN: Graywolf.

1994

Bell, Betty. *Faces in the Moon*. Norman: U of Oklahoma P.
Erdrich, Louise. *The Bingo Palace*. New York: HarperCollins.
Henry, Gordon. *The Light People*. Norman: U of Oklahoma P.
Owens, Louis. *Bone Game*. Norman: U of Oklahoma P.
Power, Susan. *The Grass Dancer*. New York: Putnam.
Sarris, Greg. *Grand Avenue*. New York: Hyperion.

1993

Barreiro, Jose. *The Indian Chronicles*. Houston: Arte Publico.
Bruchac, Joseph. *Dawn Land*. Golden, CO: Fulcrum.
King, Thomas. *Green Grass, Running Water*. Boston: Houghton Mifflin.
Maracle, Lee. *Sundogs*. Penticton, BC: Theytus.
Querry, Ron. *The Death of Bernadette Lefthand*. Santa Fe: Red Crane.

1992

Conley, Robert J. *Mountain Windsong*. Norman: U of Oklahoma P.
———. *Nickajack*. New York: Doubleday.
Owens, Louis. *The Sharpest Sight*. Norman: U of Oklahoma P.
Seals, David. *Sweet Medicine*. New York: Orion.
Vizenor, Gerald. *Dead Voices*. Norman: U of Oklahoma P.
Young Bear, Ray. *Black Eagle Child: The Facepaint Narratives*. Iowa City: U of Iowa P.

1991

Cook-Lynn, Elizabeth. *From the River's Edge*. New York: Arcade.
Dorris, Michael, and Louise Erdrich. *The Crown of Columbus*. New York: Harper
      Collins.
Owens, Louis. *Wolfsong*. Albuquerque: West End.
Silko, Leslie Marmon. *Almanac of the Dead*. New York: Simon & Schuster.

1990

Hogan, Linda. *Mean Spirit*. New York: Atheneum.
Vizenor, Gerald. *Bearheart: The Heirship Chronicles*. Minneapolis: U of Minnesota P.
———. *Griever: An American Monkey King in China*. Minneapolis: U of Minnesota P.
Welch, James. *The Indian Lawyer*. New York: Norton.

1989

King, Thomas. *Medicine River*. New York: Penguin.
Momaday, Scott. *The Ancient Child*. New York: Doubleday.

1988

Deloria, Ella. *Waterlily*. Lincoln: U of Nebraska P.
Erdrich, Louise. *Tracks*. New York: Henry Holt.
Walters, Anna Lee. *Ghost Singer*. Flagstaff, AZ: Northland.

1987

Hale, Janet Campbell. *The Jailing of Cecelia Capture*. Albuquerque: U of New Mexico P.
Dorris, Michael. *A Yellow Raft in Blue Water*. New York: Henry Holt.
Slipperjack, Ruby. *Honour the Sun*. Winnipeg: Pemmican Publications.

1986

Erdrich, Louise. *The Beet Queen*. New York: Henry Holt.
Smith, Martin Cruz. *Stallion Gate*. New York: Random.
Welch, James. *Fools Crow*. New York: Viking.

1984

Erdrich, Louise. *Love Medicine*. New York: Henry Holt.

1979

Seals, David. *The Powwow Highway*. New York: Plume-NAL.
Welch, James. *The Death of Jim Loney*. New York: Harper & Row.

1978

Vizenor, Gerald. *Wordarrows: Indians and Whites in the New Fur Trade*. Minneapolis: U of Minnesota P.

1977

Smith, Martin Cruz. *Nightwing*. New York: Norton.

14

Native American Imaginative Spaces

Irene Moser

The orange arc grew upon the land, curving out and downward to an impossible diameter. It must not go on, I thought, and I began to be afraid; then the air dissolved and
the sun backed away. But for a moment I had seen to the center of the world's being.
— Momaday, *House Made of Dawn* 125

This passage from N. Scott Momaday's first novel, a passage that also
appears in his historical work, *The Way to Rainy Mountain*, eloquently
celebrates dawn on the Oklahoma plains. But, it does even more. The
passage gets us to think about space—in this case, the Oklahoma plains and
Rainy Mountain—in a new way. Momaday's description of the rising sun
"eclipsed" by Rainy Mountain expresses a sense of space as a powerful
dynamic process, which the writer emphasizes by using terms such as
"curving" (a participle) and "being" (a gerund). Taking the form of a circle,
marked by its center and by the sun's expanding and receding arc, this
space also gives access to universal creativity—"for a moment I had seen to
the center of the world's being."

This manner of configuring spaces as processes, as circles, as centered
points of access to creative and empowering forces is common in contemporary writing by Native American authors. It is a way of seeing the world,
and of writing about what one sees and how one sees it, that depends upon
a special world view, what Christopher Vecsey and Robert Venables label
"Native American environmentalism." As a scholar of both folklore and
literature, I am especially interested in this way of integrating a people's
world view and their writing. And, in this essay, I introduce the reader to
the use of subjective and dynamic literary spaces that make the works of N.
Scott Momaday and other Native American writers so powerful.

In this special way of thinking about the relationship between the world
and one's own sense of self, physical, social, and cosmic spaces surround,
expand, and even fundamentally re-define the self. Such subjectively
defined and inherently dynamic spatial categories contrast with more
typical representations of space in American literature. Annette Kolodny
and Carl Bredahl, Jr., discuss this point in their studies of the American
frontier. They find in American literature that space is often presented as a
divisible object—a virgin frontier, hostile wilderness, or unexplored territory

to be possessed, mapped, and enclosed. Space as object, the social scientist Edward T. Hall notes, is "empty—one gets into it by intersecting it with lines" (159). Hall's description recalls the ancient Greek differentiation between "chaos"—unformed mass, infinite space, or any wide, empty space, and "metron"—space that is measured or measurable. For folklorists and literary scholars, this is an important distinction. By confining ourselves to a metronic perception of space, we neglect a fundamental aspect of the human condition. And, it is the human experience, of course, that is what writing is meant to express. Contemporary writers with Native American heritages offer readers compelling alternatives to that measurable emptiness.

Just as Native peoples differ from each other as social groups, as individuals, and as writers, so, also, their conceptions and representations of significant categories of space can differ. Nevertheless, some shared ways of thinking and expressing seem to influence the spatial designs of individuals with Native cultural backgrounds. In the current, growing Native literary movement, recurring narrative devices involving plot design, characterization, and imagery suggest shared ways of thinking about space. How these writers develop the construction of social spaces is especially significant. In the works of Momaday, Leslie Marmon Silko, Louise Erdrich, and others, these social spaces surround protagonists and interrelate individuals to each other, to history, and to the cosmos itself. These authors also often employ an imagery of space-as-process and an imagery of centering within a space that involve "directional referents" (a term literary scholars use for symbols of direction) and what William Bevis calls "the homing in" of protagonists.

Social Spaces

Folklorists generally recognize a fundamental assumption that is widespread in Native American philosophies. This assumption, an appreciation of the oneness and underlying unity of all life forms, not only constitutes an essential part of Native American world views, but also influences artistic design. For instance, many Native peoples traditionally have used the circle to represent the underlying unity of life and death and of the interrelatedness of the extraordinary forces that create life. Circular forms appear frequently as design motifs in architecture, jewelry, basketry, pottery, and other material culture items.

In contemporary Native American literature, one can see a unifying circularity emerging in the narrative structures and imageries of stories. A common plot design that Native writers follow is one that removes a physically or psychologically wounded or ill protagonist from home, then provides him or her an entry into extraordinary spaces and contact with extraordinary personae, and finally returns the individual—transformed in some significant psychological or perceptual sense—to the physical and social environment left at the work's beginning. Bevis identifies this recurring circular narrative movement as a "homing in" plot structure.

Often, in a work's opening and closing passages, you will see the author use circular imagery to reinforce the development of the protagonists' circular, "homing in" journey. Momaday's first novel, *House Made of Dawn*, begins and ends with the protagonist, Abel, ritually running in the dawn hour on the reservation. He leaves the reservation early in the novel and returns home after his murder trial and his relocation to Los Angeles. In analyzing Momaday's historical *The Way to Rainy Mountain*, literary scholar Helen Jaskoski identifies the images that bring the cultural traveler "from earth to sky and back to earth" (74). In fact, in Momaday's second novel, *The Ancient Child*, the epigraph from Jorge Luis Borges calls attention to the work's circularity of narrative form and style: "For myth is at the beginning of literature, and also at its end."

Like the journeys in Momaday's works, the plots of other works reveal circular physical movements, reinforced by opening and closing images. The ending of Leslie Marmon Silko's *Ceremony* returns the protagonist, Tayo, to the reservation, where his story began. The closing image cluster of storytelling, of illness, and of the life-renewing sunrise recalls the novel's opening images. Silko's construction of this work—you will not find chapter divisions in the novel—powerfully emphasizes the underlying unity of the text's disparate voices and stories. Circularity also shapes her second novel, *Almanac of the Dead*. Here, again, key characters and images introduced in the early chapters, notably the character of Sterling and the image of a giant stone snake of mythic and primordial origins, are returning home at the novel's close. Louise Erdrich's *Tracks*, the eloquent and powerful third novel in her four-volume set, opens with an address to the child Lulu, who is also its closing focus as she returns home from Indian boarding school. These are but a few of the many image patterns and plot developments that convey a sense of the traditional Native American sacred circle in works of fiction and poetry by contemporary Native writers. Like the circular form which has no beginning and no end, these circular narrative elements enclose and unify protagonists and their communities within ever-renewing life processes.

In addition to circularity in images and narrative movements, it is common for Native American writers to use the family members of protagonists as storytellers to unify the imaginative social spaces of their stories. Erdrich, for example, combines families of narrators with circular imageries and concluding scenes that focus on children who represent the future. The opening scene of *The Beet Queen* focuses on the separation of one family during a public celebration, the Orphans' Fair. In the novel's ironic closing, key members of this family are reunited at another celebration, the Beet Festival. The first-person narrators whose voices help to develop this circular narrative bear either an authentic kin relationship to each other, or behave as though they do (e.g., "Uncle" Wallace). In *Love Medicine*, also, the multiple voices of family members are integral to the creation of story and of community. Erdrich's sometimes antagonistic narrators are implicitly bonded through their shared goals of nurturing the young who represent the community's future. Michael Dorris, Erdrich's husband, also unites the mothers and daughters who narrate *A Yellow Raft in Blue Water* through bonds of storytelling and nurture. Such multiple storytelling voices are bonded by common goals and embedded in circular plots and image patterns. They give the reader a strong sense of the potential for unity within the rich diversity that characterizes these imagined social worlds.

If you compare works of Native fiction closely, you will see how diverse family voices that represent past and present communities are crucial even in works with more limited narrator viewpoints. The sole, unidentified protagonist who narrates James Welch's *Winter in the Blood* depends for his complete story, and thus for his personal healing, on the storytelling voices of other family members. He wanders in a seemingly aimless fashion throughout this work until the voices of his mother, his grandmother, and especially Yellow Calf, the old man who he learns is his grandfather, help him discover the coherence within his tribal and personal history. Kinship also links the two primary centers of consciousness in Momaday's *The Ancient Child*. In this work, the protagonist, Lock Setman, or Set ("bear" in Kiowa), and the medicine woman, Grey or Koi-ehm-toya, are cousins, and later also husband and wife. Protagonists in these novels often begin their transformative journeys in an alienated and chaotic social space, "I was as distant from myself as a hawk from the moon," says Welch's protagonist in *Winter* (2). Nevertheless, the circular narrative structures and imagery, along with the literal kinship and shared nurturing purpose of narrators and key centers of consciousness, suggest a strong impetus toward coherence and unity as underlying the design of social spaces that surround central characters.

Unity of the Past and the Present

It is fascinating to see in this body of literature how Native writers use these unifying, interrelated social spaces not only to unfold a story in the present, but also to encompass a community's earliest history and prehistory. The impulse that literary theorist Peter Brooks characterizes as "the aim of all narrative," that is, "the recovery of the past" (311), has strong thematic appeal for these writers. *The Way to Rainy Mountain* has been compared to the traditional pictographic hide or bark calendar used by the Kiowa and other Native peoples in their annual history-telling event, the Winter Count. Both the Winter Count and *Rainy Mountain* illustrate Brooks' desire to recover the past in a cultural sense. In the latter, Momaday combines the

Kiowa mythological history with Western documentary discourse and a personal lyrical voice. By so doing, he offers "a whole journey, intricate with motion and meaning" in order to recover "the whole memory, that experience of the mind which is legendary as well as historical, personal as well as cultural" (4).

Recovering personal and tribal memory is equally important in Erdrich's and Welch's novels. Erdrich's works create continua of past and present social spaces. In *Love Medicine*, for instance, notice how Lipsha Morrissey returns to the reservation following his successful search to answer questions about his personal origins. In Welch's works, this conceptual movement into history can be represented as a journey through physical space. Having turned down a political career, Sylvester Yellow Calf, the protagonist of Welch's recent novel, *The Indian Lawyer*, "dreams" his personal history as he commutes daily between Bismarck and the Standing Rock Reservation to work on an Indian water rights case. In Welch's historical novel about the Blackfeet, *Fools Crow*, the protagonist follows his power animal through a rock crevice to a meeting with the tribe's mythic mother. By showing Fools Crow a hide calendar that depicts the future, the mythic Feather Woman places his contemporary space within a continuum that begins with the distant, mythic past.

The Acoma poet Simon J. Ortiz reported that the elders among his Native Pueblo peoples "always tell a story from the beginning," that is, from the conceptual and physical point of the creation of the world; in this way, he concluded, "my people become part of this creation which is up to the present." Both traditional and contemporary works thus corroborate the conclusion of folklorist Barre Toelken that, for many Native peoples, "it is almost as if the individual is surrounded by the past" (274). The sacred circle of life, then, includes the immediate and mythic pasts.

We can understand these interrelated spaces that unite past and present social worlds more clearly in the context of traditional Native social behaviors. The ideal Native American social contract frequently depends upon the development of mutually reinforcing relationships between individuals and their communities. Both the individual and the community are necessary forces for maintaining life. This social ideal is evident in such widely dispersed creation stories as those of the ancient Maya, the Navajo, the Laguna, and the Cherokee. In these stories, several creator figures or a council of animals share responsibility for the creation of life as we know it.

The creative act of oral storytelling itself, as Momaday reminded me in a personal interview, can generate momentarily such a mutually reinforcing community focused on the storytelling performance: "I've been in situations," Momaday said, "in which . . . my father and an uncle, say, cousin, would begin to recall things, and then to tell stories. And, that was wonderful to listen to such rounds of stories." In contemporary writings, this traditional value of social reciprocity is implicit in family stories, in the kinship of multiple narrators who also nurture key individual characters, and in the importance assigned to relationships between the present and past. Reinforced by circular imagery and plot, these devices surround the individual with a far-reaching, yet nurturing, social space.

Extraordinary Dimensions of Social Space

In my research into Native American fiction, from the perspective of someone trained in both folklore and literature, I have found that these authors not only give physical form to the dialog with the past; they sometimes give characters access to extraordinary dimensions of experience. In Erdrich's *Tracks*, one of the two narrators, Nanapush, powerfully interrelates past and present social spaces. He is able to do so through his role as tribal historian and through his association with the Anishinabe (Chippewa) sacred trickster for whom he is named and whose mythic powers and foibles he shares. The presence of ancestral spirits, too, can give a literally interrelated form to the primordial, mythic social space of the past. Like Feather Woman in *Fools Crow*, ancestral spirits play active roles in Susan Power's *The Grass Dancer* and in Anna Lee Walters' *Ghost Singer*. Welch's Jim Loney catches glimpses of ancestral faces in the rock cliffs near his home. And in almost every work mentioned here, certain animal personae are critical to the process of transformation. Both the ancestral presences and powerful animal personae offer to the stories' characters thresholds into extraordinary dimensions of physical and psychological experience.

The Natural World

In the hands of the writers whose works I have analyzed, extraordinary forces of the natural world become compelling narrative elements. In these works, we can see present social worlds incorporating not only the two-legged peoples, but, like the creation stories mentioned above, the four-legged peoples, as well. Examples of extraordinary representatives of the natural world abound. In Silko's *Ceremony*, multiple animal and sacred natural forces work along with human beings to maintain the "fragile world" so that its inhabitants can "all go on" (96). One thinks of such crucial figures in the novel as Ts'eh Mantano, Ts'eh's hunter companion (who can shift his shape to that of a mountain lion), and the half-wild, mixed-breed cattle so important to the people's future. Grandmother Spider, who created the Laguna cosmos, becomes a powerful ally for Paula Gunn Allen's heroine in *The Woman Who Owned the Shadows*. Literary scholars have made much of the horse, Old Bird, and the deer that "can tell by the moon when the world is cockeyed" in Welch's *Winter* (68). In Welch's historical novel, Beaver Chief shares his medicine with the Blackfeet, Fools Crow communicates with Raven, and "Skunk Bear" (Wolverine) is Fools Crow's power animal. Bees and bats serve as allies and spiritual guides in Hogan's *Mean Spirit*, an extraordinarily sensitive dog appears in Power's *The Grass Dancer*, and the bear is a powerful medium of transformation in Momaday's *The Ancient Child*. Through such figures, these writers expand the social spaces that surround human characters into the natural world.

The Cosmic Design

Powerful animal allies, ancestral spirits, and figures which symbolize the powers of nature are expected appearances in the world views represented by much traditional Native American folklore. Such presences suggest an "other world" of experience, one which is accessible to human beings. This "other world," according to folklorists Dennis and Barbara Tedlock, "is above and below the horizontal plane of our everyday world, and it is reached through a vertical axis that passes through the seeker." The other world can also be encountered "at the periphery of the horizontal plane" (xiv). Differentiating themselves from authors of non-Native heritage, Native American writers frequently incorporate this defining trait of their cultures into their fiction.

When Welch's Fools Crow travels away from his familiar grounds, for instance, he comes to a distant rock crevice that takes him into the past and future as told by Feather Woman. Here, he enters into the extraordinary space of that other world at the periphery of human experience. Leslie Marmon Silko depicts her character, Tayo, momentarily gaining access to the other world in a ceremonial hogan in the mountains, where he is able to glimpse the entire cosmos within a sand painting (*Ceremony*). At the moment of Ephanie's attempted suicide, author Paula Gunn Allen has a spider emerge from a dark underground hole to remind Ephanie of her value within the circle of life (*The Woman*). In these moments of access to extraordinary spaces, protagonists gain crucial, life-preserving insights into a universal cosmic design and, in an integration of the natural and supernatural, into their own psyches.

Cosmic designs that incorporate extraordinary dimensions vary in form among Native peoples. The Swedish ethnographer Ake Hultkrantz identifies one such cosmic design that is widespread among Native agricultural peoples, such as the Pueblo and the Cherokee. Hultkrantz characterizes this cosmos as three-tiered with an upper or sky world, the surface world of ordinary space, and a world underneath. While variations exist among such cosmic representations—Pueblo peoples, for example, have multiple worlds beneath the surface—these cosmic designs share certain characteristics. All three cosmic dimensions incorporate forces and entities that contribute, however ambiguously at times, to the delicate balancing process necessary to maintain daily life within ordinary world space.

In other Native cultures, such as the Navajo, we find only two cosmic dimensions. The traditional Navajo house, the hogan, is built as a sacred space that replicates the universe; its smoke hole gives access to the sky world, its supporting beams are aligned with the cardinal and intercardinal compass points, its roof parallels the sky arch, and the light of creation enters its east-facing doorway each day with the sunrise. The circular hogan thus encloses its occupants within an intimate domestic space that extends into the outer cosmos. Furthermore, within this two-dimensional structure, the earthen floor connects the hogan, the arching sky above, and the hogan's human occupants with the earth surface and its underground inhabitants. Such traditional designs, symbolically interrelating sky worlds, underground worlds, and the space of ordinary experience, can guide readers in understanding the symbolic significance of extraordinary spatial categories in imaginative works.

You can see similar extraordinary dimensions of the cosmos in the Native American literature I research. When we compare the works of Welch, Allen, and others in this genre, we find a common pattern: These writers often associate extraordinary powers and experiences with high points in the landscape and their representative figures, as well as with places underground or leading into the earth, such as caves and water sources, and their representative figures. When characters enter into and pass through the dark physical and psychological shadows of the spaces underneath, they can gain a self-knowledge that frees and renews them as they return to the ordinary spaces of their lives. High points in the landscape that give access to the sky can engender significant moments of character insight, in a global or cosmic sense.

The underground dimensions of physical space in these works often become the physical symbols, or, in T. S. Eliot's terms, "objective correlatives," for psychic catharsis and rebirth. We see such catharses in *The Woman*, as Allen's Ephanie enters into the dark closet of her attempted suicide, in *Ceremony*, as Silko's Tayo revisits the arroyo of derelicts and of the homeless where he spent his childhood in Gallup, and in *House Made of Dawn*, as Momaday's Abel lies wounded by the Pacific Ocean. That the dark world underneath can empower individuals is evident in *Mean Spirit*, as well, as author Linda Hogan's medicine men consult the bats in their caves and Belle Graycloud returns renewed from meditating in the dark cellars of her house.

In *Mean Spirit*, the "river prophet," Lila Blanket, "was a listener to the voice of water, a woman who interpreted the river's story for her people" (5). The river could bring warnings as well as peace, for the lowest cosmic dimension can endanger as well as strengthen. One can become lost in the shadow spaces of the Spider Creatrix (Allen *Woman*). Author Erdrich especially acknowledges the danger and ambiguity inherent in the lower cosmic dimension. Her protagonist, Fleur, drowns three times in Lake Matchimanito. Although Fleur's rescue releases her as a powerful medium allied with the natural world, it has fatal consequences for her rescuers (*Tracks*). That ambiguous contact with the lower cosmic dimension associated with water also appears in Momaday's *The Way*, in which one of two brothers becomes a water beast. Likewise, Abel comes very close to death as he lies "in a shallow depression" beside the Pacific ocean (*House* 92); yet, like characters elsewhere in these works who return from their visits to the lower cosmic dimension, Abel gains perspective and insight that turn him toward the east and the life-giving dawn. As Abel lies in the shallow depression, he senses that

somewhere beyond the cold and the fog and the pain. . . . the fishes lay out in the black waters, holding still against all the force and motion of the sea; or . . . darting and rolling and spinning . . . they played. . . . and far away inland there were great gray migrant geese riding under the moon. (112)

The experience changes Abel's perception of his superficially human struggle and places it within a larger framework of cosmic dimensions. Similar phenomena occur at several points in *Ceremony*—at the medicine man Betonie's hogan overlooking Gallup, where his grandmother could "see the whole world"; at the ceremonial mountain hogan where Tayo sees the entire cosmos within a sand painting; and during Tayo's search for the half-wild spotted cattle high on Mt. Taylor. Momaday's image of the children who climb the "Rock Tree" (Devil's Tower) to become the stars—the Kiowa's "kinsmen in the night sky"—emphasizes the interrelatedness of the outer and personal cosmos (*Way* 8). Such moments place individuals at least momentarily within spaces and perspectives that include the entire cosmic design.

We can more clearly appreciate the significance of sky worlds as literary devices in these contemporary works by placing them in the context of the sophisticated knowledge of astronomy that anthropologists and archaeologists commonly find among traditional Native American peoples. In the recently developed interdisciplinary field of archaeoastronomy, scholars have identified a number of petroglyphs and architectural remains that they interpret to be solar or astronomical observation devices. These artifacts appear throughout the Americas, a few noted examples being at Machu Picchu, Chaco Canyon, Casa Grande, the Ohio serpent mound and Mound city, and various medicine wheels. The cosmic spaces of prehistoric Native American peoples extended deep into the earth and far out into the night sky. And, they continue to do so for contemporary writers who have inherited those ancient traditions of observation.

The Center of the Sacred Circle

The prehistoric inhabitants of the Americas, in archaeologists' interpretive reconstructions of the past, attempted to understand their place within the

vast space of land and cosmos by placing themselves ceremonially at "the
center" of things. This tradition continues today. Through ritual, the
grounding of self and community at the cosmic center occurs potentially
several times during a day as an individual acknowledges the powers of the
cardinal (or intercardinal) directions and the powers of "Grandfather Sky"
and "Grandmother Earth." This ceremonial centering within the cosmos,
widely documented through personal statement and ethnographic observation, has an ancient history. Such traditional stories of prehistoric travels as
the Lenape (Delaware) *Walam Olum*, the Zuni emergence myth, and some
versions of the Cherokee creation myth contain references not only to the
four directions, but also to the location of "the center" or "middle place"
toward which the primordial peoples traveled.

Writers today continue to celebrate these ancient directional motifs as a
means of "grounding" characters and of emphasizing the interrelatedness
of ordinary and extraordinary spaces. In *House Made of Dawn*, Momaday
names the cardinals as he describes the setting for the fateful feast of Santi-
ago that precedes Abel's killing of the albino (54). Erdrich, in *Tracks*,
describes a road leading west on which the Anishinabe follow their
deceased kin. As Ephanie, in Allen's *Woman*, journeys west toward the
Pacific coast, she struggles to "re-member" her divided self. Silko carefully
identifies the direction of characters' movements in both *Ceremony* and
Almanac of the Dead. Literature scholar Edith Swann has analyzed *Ceremony*,
and in an authoritative and insightful discussion of Silko's use of directional
referents, shows how the author draws on Laguna ceremonial tradition.
Swann concludes that the Night Swan and Ts'eh are traditional Laguna
summer and winter aspects of the South/North axis of Thought Woman's
mythic cosmos.

Swann argues that a critical aspect of Tayo's development into a culture
hero is his "internalization" of the powers of the cardinal compass points.
By learning to work with the forces of nature represented by animals and
by the directions, Tayo succeeds in his quest. In Welch's *Fools Crow*, prayers
to "the Above Ones, the Below Ones, the Underwater People" place the
speaker's activities within the vertical Blackfoot cosmic axis. Addresses to
the four directions complete the symbolic cosmic design in the horizontal
plane. Through such references protagonists and readers discover connectedness and pattern within an overtly chaotic world and gain access to the
"center" that defines self and cosmos.

Conclusion

The Native American literature we have examined in this essay is a genre
that has self-consciously drawn upon vital elements of Native cultures.
Within these cultures, individuals commonly make sense of the cosmos, and
their place within it, by orienting themselves in terms of directional refer-

ents. That orientation, they believe, gives them access to empowering physical, psychological, and cultural "center" points in space that recall
Momaday's eloquent evocation of "the center of the world's being." In
some of the best examples of this work, Native writers have exploited these
directional referents, one of a whole complex of narrative techniques that
create distinctive spatial categories. Drawing on traditional Native philosophies, these writers demonstrate certain common principles in their spatial
constructions. Those principles assume the unity and on-going renewal of
all life processes; the value of a reciprocal social contract; and the interrelatedness of all life forms and of cosmic and experiential dimensions. The
authors we have examined apply these principles to the development of
imagined social worlds, characters, and images. In so doing, they create
circular plots that return characters home; circular image patterns that
emphasize process; interrelated present and past social worlds; storytelling
voices linked by kinship and common goals of nurture; and personae representative of extraordinary natural and cosmic dimensions. As a result, these
writers symbolically surround and ground protagonists within a dynamic,
intimate personal space that is as immense as the cosmos itself.

Works Cited

Allen, Paula Gunn. *The Sacred Hoop: Recovering the Feminine in American Indian Traditions*. Boston: Beacon, 1986.

——. *The Woman Who Owned the Shadows*. San Francisco: Spinsters, Ink, 1983.

Bevis, William. "Native American Novels: Homing In." *Recovering the Word, Essays on Native American Literature*. Ed. Brian Swann and Arnold Krupat. Berkeley: U of California P, 1987. 580–620.

Bredahl, A. Carl, Jr. *New Ground: Western American Narrative and the Literary Canon*. Chapel Hill: U of North Carolina P, 1989.

Brooks, Peter. *Reading for the Plot, Design and Intention in Narrative*. 1984. New York: Vintage Books, 1985.

Dorris, Michael. *A Yellow Raft in Blue Water*. New York: Warner Books, 1987.

Erdrich, Louise. *The Beet Queen*. 1986. New York: Bantam Books, 1987.

——. *Love Medicine*. 1984. New York: Bantam Books, 1985.

——. *Tracks*. New York: Harper, 1988.

Hall, Edward T. *The Silent Language*. 1959. Greenwich: Fawcett, 1963.

Hogan, Linda. *Mean Spirit*. New York: Ivy Books, 1990.

Hultkrantz, Ake. *Belief and Worship in Native North America*. Syracuse: Syracuse UP, 1981.

Jaskoski, Helen. "Images and Silence." *Approaches to Teaching Momaday's* The Way to Rainy Mountain. Approaches to Teaching World Literature. 17. Ed. Kenneth Roemer. New York: MLA, 1988. 69–77.

Kolodny, Annette. *The Land before Her: Fantasy and Experience of the American Frontiers, 1630–1860*. Chapel Hill: U of North Carolina P, 1984.

Momaday, N. Scott. *The Ancient Child*. New York: Doubleday, 1989.

——. *House Made of Dawn*. 1968. New York: Signet, 1969.

——. Personal Interview. 26 March 1990.

——. *The Way to Rainy Mountain*. Albuquerque: U of New Mexico P, 1969.

Ortiz, Simon J. Lecture Series. Western Carolina University. Cullowhee and Cherokee. 26 and 28 Mar. 1992.

Pinxten, Rik, Ingrid van Dooren, and Frank Harvey. *The Anthropology of Space: Explorations into the Natural Philosophy and Semantics of the Navajo.* Philadelphia: U of Pennsylvania P, 1983.

Power, Susan. *The Grass Dancer.* New York: Berkley Books, 1994.

Silko, Leslie Marmon. *Ceremony.* New York: Viking P, 1977.

——. *Almanac of the Dead.* New York: Simon and Schuster, 1991.

Swann, Edith. "Laguna Symbolic Geography and Silko's Ceremony." *American Indian Quarterly* 12.3 (1988): 229–49.

Tedlock, Dennis, and Barbara Tedlock, eds. *Teachings from the American Earth: Indian Religion and Philosophy.* New York: Liveright, 1975.

Toelken, Barre. "Folklore, Worldview, and Communication." *Folklore, Performance and Communication.* Ed. Dan Ben-Amos and Kenneth S. Goldstein. Mouton: The Hague, 1975. 264–86.

Tuan, Yi-Fu. *Space and Place, the Perspective of Experience.* Minneapolis: U of Minnesota P, 1977.

Vecsey, Christopher, and Robert W. Venables, eds. *American Indian Environments: Ecological Issues in Native American History.* Syracuse: Syracuse UP, 1980.

"Walam Olum." *American Indian Literature: An Anthology.* Ed. Alan R. Velie. Rev. ed. Norman: U of Oklahoma P, 1991. 92–133.

Walters, Anna Lee. *Ghost Singer.* Flagstaff, AZ: Northland Publishing, 1988.

Welch, James. *The Death of Jim Loney.* New York: Harper, 1979.

——. *Fools Crow.* New York: Penguin, 1987.

——. *The Indian Lawyer.* New York: Penguin, 1990.

——. *Winter in the Blood.* 1974. New York: Penguin, 1986.

Williamson, Ray A., and Claire R. Farrer, eds. *Earth and Sky: Visions of the Cosmos in Native American Folklore.* Albuquerque: U of New Mexico P, 1992.

15

Building on the Myth:
Recovering Native American Culture in
Louise Erdrich's *The Bingo Palace*

Tom Matchie

Louise Erdrich has now published two novels in a series that has projected her into a leading role among writers of fiction in America. In *The Bingo Palace* (1994) and *Tales of Burning Love* (1996), she continues to develop a mythic world similar to that of Faulkner's Yoknapatawpha County in Mississippi. Her universe, however, centers around a Chippewa Indian Reservation in north central North Dakota, which she then expands to the whole state. Both of these novels sound out in profound and yet humorous ways her notions of personal and communal love. *Burning Love* is about the bizarre sensuous-sexual lives of several women, Native and white, mainly in Fargo and the Red River Valley. *Bingo Palace*, on the other hand, is set primarily on the reservation itself, where it addresses a pressing social problem—gambling. Although also rooted in love, it more directly deals with Native American thinking and its contribution to life in this century.

Why should any of this matter to a college student, even one who has an interest in Native American studies? For a professor of English, as I am, the answer is as clear as the question is valid. I believe that literature does something for us that few other disciplines can do. Literature opens to us worlds of ideas and experiences. Sometimes these worlds are filled with the novel and the unexpected; sometimes they confront us with strikingly, even painfully, familiar feelings. I have chosen to teach and write in this discipline because, for me, no other field captures the human experience more completely.

That is why, as well, that the works of a writer such as Erdrich are so important. Just as the pen of William Faulkner, seventy years ago, made it possible for readers to explore the human condition through his creation of the mythic world of Yoknapatawpha County—a world that drew from his own experiences and relationships—so, too, does Erdrich today enable us to explore the dimensions of who we are. What makes her work so powerful is the way in which she integrates her experience into well-crafted stories through which we can explore the human experience. She does this by breaking stereotypes. In her works, we explore the human condition in fresh ways that both incorporate and transcend elements of two cultures— that of alienated Native Americans and that of the dominant mainstream. For scholars of literature, this is exciting because it gives us a way to move beyond "the Canon"—Shakespeare, Milton, and others—in order to consider humanity in the twentieth century in fresh ways. For the college student, analyzing her work helps us to grasp ways of understanding and expressing experience. To do so, however, takes some understanding of how scholars of literature go about the task of analyzing fiction. In this essay, I hope to provide you, the student reader, with some of the tools that will help you to better appreciate the genre—the category of literature—of Native American writers, and to help you to better appreciate how this work enables you to understand your own experiences in new and, perhaps, more meaningful ways.

Pulling Together the Pieces in *Bingo Palace*

Erdrich began creating her mythic universe with *Love Medicine* (1984), then *Beet Queen* (1986) and *Tracks* (1988), before releasing *Bingo Palace* in the mid-1990s. Through the relationship between the hero throughout these works, Lipsha Morrissey, and a jingle dress dancer, Shawnee Ray Toose, *Bingo Palace* convincingly resolves a saga that began ten years earlier in *Love Medicine*. Reviews of the recent novel are mixed, however. Some critics see it as a profoundly moving love story couched in intensely poetic prose (Donahue 4D). Others find the love story and its ending all but aimless, with little connection between the main narrative and secondary stories, and claim that the characters, as well as the style, are artificial and strained (Thornton 7). Indeed, there may be some merit to these critiques—Erdrich confesses that in writing even the recently published *Tales of Burning Love* (1996), she begins writing short stories and then ties them together as a novel (Wood E2).

Yet, I see her works differently. My contention, one that resolves the controversy, is that *Bingo Palace* is a uniquely creative effort to bring together the best elements of her first three novels. To focus the narration, she returns to a device she developed in *Love Medicine*, the voice of Lipsha Morrissey, a modern version of Huckleberry Finn. For theme, she goes back to *Tracks*, in which she used the cutting of the trees at Turtle Mountain early in the century to make her strongest social statement; *Bingo Palace* updates it by dealing with the subject of Native gambling today. From *Beet Queen* she adapts some superlative elements of style, giving her new novel a magical flavor. Finally, there is the way in which she incorporates vital elements of Native culture—in both its traditional and alienated guises—and mainstream cultures to weave stories that challenge all of us to rethink the human experience at the close of the twentieth century. To smooth the transition across books, she prepared for *Bingo Palace* shortly before its publication by adding several chapters to a new version of *Love Medicine* (1993). *Bingo Palace* may have weaknesses, but an imaginative analysis of the full range of Erdrich's work shows it to be an intriguing experiment with ways to bring the healing power of traditional Chippewa culture to bear on American Indians living in a fragmented contemporary world—a world that includes the debilitating vice of gambling.

Lipsha Morrissey as a Native American Huck Finn

The first chapter of *Bingo Palace* is telltale. Lipsha Morrissey has "come home." Readers of *Love Medicine* might have thought that by the end of this novel he had come of age and could go on from there. Lipsha had discovered his identity, his roots—a major theme in Native American fiction. He had found his father, Gerry, in a card game and had brought "her (his mother June) home" across the water in a blue Firebird. Literary critics describe such a triumph, in which the boy becomes a "real person" with a "sense of belonging" as "internal" (Barry and Prescott 135). At the beginning of *Bingo Palace*, however, we discover that he has dissipated his life in Fargo. It is a sign of a skilled writer that she explores a coherent theme in great depth across several works; this Erdrich does through much of her fiction. In her works, the integrating theme is the "radical displacement" of the modern Indian as traditional culture is eroded (Owens 194), and here Lipsha joins that group. So, once again, not unlike Huck Finn searching for a father figure, Lipsha must come home to find his runagate father and again encounter his own abusive mother, although in *Bingo Palace* in a far more dramatic, comic, ghostly, even magical way.

Why does Erdrich rerun Lipsha's coming-of-age? A cynical reader might suggest that Erdrich decided she was successful in one place, so why not do it over again? The reader more widely read in Native American literature, however, would know that repetition serves an important purpose in this genre—as in oral traditions, the retelling of tales has a ritualistic effect. Even so, Erdrich does make changes in *Bingo Palace*, and here her changes are significant. In contrast to *Love Medicine*, in which Lipsha is one of several narrators, in *Bingo Palace* he narrates over one-third of the twenty-seven chapters (with no counter voice as we see in *Tracks*). Although some reviewers maintain the view that Lipsha is not a "palpable" character, that he does not really "come to life" (Rev. of *The Bingo Palace*, *Kirkus Reviews* 1410), my interpretation is that in Lipsha the author develops a voice akin to that of Twain's Huck Finn. Twain's linguistic skills must have intrigued Erdrich, for a large part of *Bingo Palace* depends on Lipsha's naive attitude and rich, memorable language.

To set up Lipsha's story, around which the subplots in *Bingo Palace* revolve, Erdrich borrows a device from Greek drama, introducing a chorus in the first chapter. Through this tribal "we," the Chippewa people voice their disappointment with him as they recount the history and status of the characters who populate the novel, much like Twain does through Huck himself in his novel. Even more important is the presence of Lulu Lemartine, who sends a letter and picture of her son, Gerry, to Lipsha in Fargo, telling him of Gerry's escape from prison. This message brings Lipsha home—the place where most of Erdrich's characters (and those of many other Native writers) come to discover themselves. Home—often the reservation in Native American literature—serves much like the river does for Huck Finn; as a literary device (if you do not have much background in literary analysis, think of a "literary device" as a tool that a writer uses to tell a story), its function is to regenerate.

Love Medicine Prepares for *Bingo Palace*

Now we must back up a moment to look at the author's strategy just prior to the publication of *Bingo Palace* (1994). In 1993, Erdrich added four more chapters to *Love Medicine*. One critic describes these pieces as "not equal to the best of the old" and finds the sequencing "hollow and a bit pointless" (Rev. of *Love Medicine, Kirkus Reviews* 1234), while another claims they "color and compliment" the original chapters (Love 87). In any case, think about the function of "home," again, as a literary device, which I believe Erdrich is using both to write as a Native American and to capture an essential twentieth-century Native American experience. Seeing the book in this way, we can appreciate that the real value of the new chapters in *Love Medicine* is to help the reader make an easier transition to the plot of *Bingo Palace*. In "The Island," Lulu visits her mother, Fleur, and sleeps with Moses Pillager; from this union comes Gerry, Lipsha's father. In "The Resurrection," Marie, after passing on Nector's pipe (an artifact important to *Bingo Palace*) to Lipsha, welcomes home the alcoholic Gordie, who imagines a night in a motel with June, Lipsha's mother. Thus, late in *Bingo Palace*, Lipsha integrates this event and Chippewa religious belief when he speaks of the Earthmaker myth, of going back to "primal clay" or the "big shell" to find one's self. These stories anticipate his own return to the reservation, and to the earth itself, for renewal (197).

Even more important to *Bingo Palace* are two additional chapters that Erdrich added to *Love Medicine*. In "The Tomahawk Factory," she describes how Lyman Lemartine, who is depressed over Henry, Jr.'s, death, recovers hope through a new enterprise—a bingo parlor. It is this "bingo palace" that becomes the orienting device for the 1994 book and which Lipsha, in his search to recover his own identity, later sees as "fake" (103). Established in the footsteps of his uncle Nector, the place "blows up" when Lulu and

Marie quarrel over Lipsha's origins. But, he does not give up on Nector's methods, and in the next story, "Lyman's Luck"—a title that anticipates ten chapter headings in *Bingo Palace*—he dreams of founding a bingo palace based on "greed and luck" (*Love Medicine* 328). Lyman, of course, is Erdrich's pejorative vehicle (a symbol for values the author sees as evil or immoral) for her discussion of the modern American Indian casino.

These four chapters prepare the reader for the essential dilemma of *Bingo Palace* and for what is an essential dilemma of the human condition in the twentieth century—the search for identity, which Erdrich represents through Lipsha's struggles, versus materialism and greed, or what her character Lyman calls reality, or "the sex of money" (101). Few authors change an earlier book to prepare for a new one. Indeed, few literary scholars can imagine a mainstream American author such as Twain altering *The Adventures of Huckleberry Finn* to prepare for "Huck Finn and Tom Sawyer Among the Indians." The rules of Native oral tradition, however, permit such changes, as stories are told and retold, and part of Erdrich's task is to make these traditions viable to a culture that she believes has long since rejected them. So, given this four-part introduction to the new novel in the old (changing) novel, and the fact that the new novel is a rerun of the old with some changes, we can now look more closely at Lipsha's voice which, crucial to the old novel, is also central to the new.

There are really four parts to Lipsha's story—first, his love for Shawnee Ray, whom he meets at the first powwow after his return home; second, his relationship to Lyman (his boss at the bingo palace and the father of Shawnee Ray's child, Redford); third, a comical vision quest he makes at the advice of Fleur to find a love potion to gain Shawnee Ray; and fourth, his final magical reunion with his parents. Like Huck Finn, Lipsha is naive in his relationships, innocent of worldly affairs, and quintessentially humble. Ultimately, he says, "I am weak and small" (117). In his business dealings he claims "I'm a fool, too simple for . . . complicated advice" (103). Comparable to Huck, his life touches on a larger world he does not understand—"a plan," he says, "greater than myself" (21). Still, for all his apparent ignorance, Lipsha has a remarkable perception of his own needs, as well as the needs of others, be it Zelda, Lyman, or Shawnee Ray.

Lipsha's Dilemma—Shawnee Ray or Lyman?

If Huck develops a love for his friend, Jim, the runaway slave, Lipsha falls immediately for Shawnee, a seamstress and fancy dancer interested in pursuing her own career as a woman, studying to be a professional designer. "I leak love" (104), he says, and like Huck he is willing to "live in hell" (161) rather than live without her. At least part of his infatuation is envy of her poised sense of self, as he describes her as an "I am" in contrast to himself as a "not yet" (33). He even envies her child, Redford, because he has a mother, and he, Lipsha, does not. Lipsha actually needs more than love; he wants Shawnee Ray "to mother me, heal me" (166), and this need will be a key factor in his later vision. To win Shawnee, he gives her the money he wins at bingo, though he thinks it is an "underhanded" (160) way to reach her. Then he goes too far, lecturing her on her own motives, saying she talks "about" Lyman, but "Your feelings don't mean shit" (112). Here, the young Chippewa shaman strikes at the heart of the matter, but Shawnee backs away, caught in her own dilemma.

Connected to the relationship Lipsha has with Shawnee Ray is the one he has with Lyman, whom Lipsha admires as "an island of have in a sea of have nots" (16). Yet, he also hates Lyman because of his own feelings for the woman, and even bargains away the sacred pipe he received from Nector through Marie to keep Lyman away from Shawnee. If we think of Huckleberry Finn as a product of a racist culture who ponders sending Jim back to his owner, then, in a parallel way, we can see how Lipsha, as a product of a fragmented culture, is manipulated by the materialistic Lyman. "Money helps" (97), he says to himself in resignation to the fact; "we all have holes in our lives" (96). On another level, however, Lipsha knows it is not all that "simple" (103), considering that "the good people" he knows are "cash poor" (102). Confused by the dizzying complexities of the modern world, and especially the difficulties of harmonizing traditional Native culture with modern values, Lipsha, the young medicine man, has begun to charge for his service, thus losing his "touch." Furthermore, in seeking to win a van in which he can court Shawnee, he knows he is "shaking hands with greed" (64). Finally, he buys into Lyman's talk of investing in land for a new bingo palace, which he knows is a "megalith of mediocrity" (198). Critics insist that *Tracks* is Erdrich's most "overtly political" novel (Owens 215), but the analysis above shows us that it is equally true of *Bingo Palace*, and in the latter work the writer may be even more political.

The novel is not without serious problems. One of the flaws that troubles me is the way Erdrich leaves the dilemma of "money versus love" for Lipsha to resolve in the third segment of his life, while Shawnee and Lyman remain undeveloped, both "disappearing" in the context of dancing. Yet, it is no secret that Erdrich has great empathy for her characters, even in their weaknesses (Flavin 64), and we can observe this trait in the way her words play out their lives. Lyman, for instance, takes a fruitless trip to Las Vegas where he uses Lipsha's sacred pipe for luck, only to lose all his money. Some critics complain that this chapter "leads nowhere at all" (Skow 71), but notice how sympathetically it does portray the fate of the hopeless gambler who contemplates suicide. Furthermore, in his dreams—and for Erdrich, as for many Native American writers, as well as embedded deeply within Native cultures—dreams are terribly powerful (Zaiser C8). Erdrich's characters somehow maintain "a tiny article of faith" (149) connected to the "grass dance" (160). In the chapter entitled "Lyman Dancing," he explores his relationship to Henry, Jr., begun in "Tomahawk Factory" in the reworked *Love Medicine,* and dramatized in *Bingo Palace* in a lyrical chapter, which describes a dance in which Lyman identifies ritualistically with his dead brother's spirit.

The same sympathetic treatment is given to Shawnee Ray, Erdrich's model of a strong woman who knows what she wants and will do what is necessary to get it. To some critics, she is simply "opportunistic" (Rev. of *The Bingo Palace, Publishers Weekly* 72); even Lipsha, however, describes her as the tribe's "hope of a future" (13)—a hope that demands more than love against the materialistic tide of mainstream American culture. Erdrich uses the illusive Albertine to support this view of Shawnee's role, telling Lipsha to "let Shawnee go" (229) for this reason. Shawnee Ray goes out with Lipsha, tells him, "I can't stop thinking of you, too" (67), and takes his money for her college education. Yet, when he presses her to marry him, she responds: "You got the medicine, Lipsha. But you ain't got the love" (112). Of course, Lipsha is driven by his love for her, but she will not give up her career to live on his bingo earnings. Instead, she stands up to Lyman, "the bingo brain" (188), and to everybody else, even walking out on her pushy foster mother, Zelda, and entrusting Redford to her alcoholic sisters, Tammy and Mary Fred. After Shawnee leaves for college, she dreams of a "kiss" (269) from Lipsha, an act which tells us where her heart lies, but the author places her real exit from the plot earlier, in a beautiful butterfly dance in which the character actually becomes what she imitates. In creating scenes such as this, Erdrich is at her lyrical best.

Fleur and the Vision Quest

When Lipsha realizes that Shawnee Ray is fed up with both Lyman and himself, that he is "losing ground" (111) after she tells him off, he goes to Fleur for a "love medicine" better than Lyman's (125). This chapter, entitled "Mindemoya" after Fleur's Chippewa name, is one of the most difficult to decipher. Through Lipsha, it represents a return to mother, and a going back to the Earth Mother—thus, a coming home in a larger sense. In the next chapter, "Fleur's Luck," she comes to town with a mysterious boy, a "young successor" (7), who undoubtedly represents the future. She has come to win a card game—a feat which again ties the book to Chippewa myth, for the author (in "Lyman's Luck" in *Love Medicine*) has already told us "Gambling fits into the old traditions" (326). But here, in the middle of *Bingo Palace,* in "Fleur's Luck," narrated by the tribe, it is significant that this eclectic integration of Native and mainstream cultures is acted out by the character Erdrich has made the moral center of the novel. Consistent with Native traditions, Erdrich depicts Fleur using the white man's games of chance to set Lipsha on different "tracks" (again, recall that "tracks" is both the title of one of Erdrich's works and one of the themes of her fiction) regarding his relationship to Lyman's modern casino.

This chapter provides a segue (a transition, or literary device which writers use to move a story from one phase to another) to the third part of Lipsha's journey, his vision quest. From this point, Erdrich's style resembles more closely the miraculous tone of *Beet Queen*, in which the adolescent, arrogant Dot literally takes to the air to make a dramatic statement. Here, Lyman and Lipsha journey to the sweat lodge in preparation for a possible spiritual awakening. Significantly, Lipsha is not given to visions, but, when he happens to sleep near a skunk, he imagines the creature to say, "This ain't real estate" (218). For some critics, this episode is part of Erdrich's lyrical "slap and slather" (Rev. of *The Bingo Palace, Kirkus Reviews* 1410), undermining the serious flow of the novel. They miss the point. The serious scholar of this genre appreciates the fact that vision quests are integral to Native cultures and a feature common to Native American literature. The reader who is enlightened to Native American Studies recognizes that in Native literature animals often act as "tricksters"; in Native myth, they may take on the character of humans to undercut the established order in contexts that may be humorous, absurd, even immoral (Velie 122). Erdrich's change of style here may bother uninformed critics, but it is consistent with important elements of her culture and her genre.

The incident, of course, is not only humorous; it precludes sentimentality (Ott 723). Indeed, the scholar of Native American writing recognizes that Lipsha's sudden, startling awareness—what we call an epiphany—is every bit as important as Huck's awakening when he decides not to turn in the slave, Jim, to the authorities. Whether Lipsha's radical change is convincing to a reader, however, is questionable. Lipsha now gives up bingo, for which he sees he has been "too eager," claiming with the skunk, "Our reservation is not real estate, luck fades when sold" (221). For some critics, this is downright "sermonizing" (Rev. of *The Bingo Palace, Kirkus Reviews* 1410). In Native cultures, however, this is what tricksters are about, and Lipsha responds accordingly. Though hopelessly hooked on Shawnee, who now has enrolled in the university, he says that his love is "larger than myself," larger than when it was "blasted by fire" (229). It does not matter to the plot, of course, for Lyman and Shawnee Ray have "danced" out of Lipsha's life, making room for Lipsha's return (once again) to his family roots and to the Native Chippewa tiyospaye, or extended family.

Automobiles and Recovering the Spirit of the Family

In Erdrich's fiction, cars and specific places (such as noted establishments in Fargo) tie the action to the modern world, just as movement in the spirit world keeps the reader anchored in traditional Chippewa values, like the importance of the family. Early in *Bingo Palace*, June appears to Lipsha working in Lyman's bingo bar, and takes two actions that will be significant to the development of Erdrich's plot—she gives him winning bingo tickets (one of which gets him a van) and she takes his Firebird. The meaning of the latter action only becomes clear to the reader when she returns in it in part four of her son's drama. June's first appearance is part of the magical realism Erdrich injects into *Bingo Palace*. Some scholars equate this technique with the "slickly entertaining" style of Dorris and Erdrich's *Crown of Columbus* (Kakutani C20). Again, they miss the ease with which Erdrich incorporates Native culture into a characteristic Native literature, in this case moving her characters into the realm of spirits (Zaiser C1). The van, therefore, only brings Lipsha bad luck: he is captured and his van wrecked by a gang of boys who tie him up while the irritated Russell—who believes that Lipsha failed to cure him because the shaman was now "charging for services" (64)—tattoos a star on Lipsha's arm. Neither the van nor the artificial star "turns on" Shawnee Ray, who is more interested in his proposed investment in real estate. "Where's the land for the bingo palace? What Lake?" (109) she asks, while the reader wonders if this is all part of June's mystical plan.

Later, following the vision quest, Lipsha receives a call that alerts him to his father's presence in Fargo. The young medicine man goes to search, imagining Gerry jumping out of a garbage can, "like a spring-loaded child's toy" (239). Erdrich now changes styles, mixing humorous mythic images with realistic places, such as the Sons of Norway, old King Leo's Drive In, and Fargo's downtown Metro Drug. From the drug store, Lipsha steals a bird before joining Gerry in a stolen white sedan with a baby in an eggshell case in the back seat. At the same time, their flight takes on a spiritual dimension as June joins them in her blue Firebird. This escape reminds us of Dot's airplane ride in *Beet Queen*, though the flight in *Bingo Palace* is again magical, an aspect some see as "contrived" and "artificial" (Thornton 7). To appreciate her style here, however, the reader must realize that it is only in Erdrich's spiritual realm that "luck, love, desire, risk-taking, and chance" all begin to make sense (Donahue 4D).

Actually, the meeting in various automobiles of mother, father, son, and the mysterious baby is apocalyptic—an event paralleling the Book of Revelation in the New Testament—and represents the timeless climax of Erdrich's main narrative. At the same time, it is filled with Chippewa mythology, including the garbage can, reflecting an old creation story, and the eggshell, suggesting a Chippewa story of rebirth. This detail, along with the blazing snow, connect the action to the opening scene in *Love Medicine* where June rejects her lover (who as we now know from *Tales of Burning Love* is her second husband), is dumped from his truck onto the Dakota prairie, and dies in the snow on her way home to Turtle Mountain. A similar scene is repeated in "June's Luck" earlier in *Bingo Palace*, but in this novel she finally returns in ghostly fashion in the full context of the family, baby and all.

Lipsha throws the bird into the windshield of the police car—an action which not only reminds us of Gerry's spread eagle position in prison (he escapes after a plane crash in "Gerry's Luck"), but which also signifies the white man's ignorance of the spiritual importance of this car chase. The baby points to the future, as does the boy who accompanied the timeless Fleur in her white Pace Arrow in "Fleur's Luck." The text here is rich with meaning as Erdrich recreates Lipsha's coming of age in a highly dramatic way. This time it is different from *Love Medicine*, however, as Erdrich roots her apocalypse in cyclic or (for the Chippewa) ceremonial, rather than linear, time (cf. Rainwater 416).

Affirming Secondary Characters

A main criticism of *Bingo Palace* is that the parts fail to cohere (Rev. of *The Bingo Palace, Publishers Weekly* 72). In her first three works, Erdrich focuses on many people's stories rather than a single narrative; in this novel, she highlights Lipsha's love story. Nevertheless, she always tends to balance main characters with those of lesser importance (Rainwater 406). Although some think Erdrich loses interest in Lyman and Shawnee Ray (Skow 71), we leave both in contexts of compassion; Lyman dancing in Henry's grass suit and Shawnee dreaming of Lipsha's kiss. Gerry may have arrived too late to be convincing (Thornton 7), but his "surge" of "feelings" (258) for June ties him to the main narrative. If Erdrich's other novels are characterized by water, earth, and sky (Owens 197), it is the "fire" of love itself which holds this book together, as it looks forward to variations on this motif in *Tales of Burning Love*.

Another problem is that Erdrich may have created what some call "a cruel hothouse of human weaknesses" (Skow 71). It is true Erdrich is well aware of "the holes" in her characters' lives. Witness Lipsha's dissipated life in Fargo, Lyman's interest in luck and greed, Zelda's manipulative approach to her relatives, Shawnee Ray's preoccupation with her success, and Shawnee Ray's two alcoholic sisters, one of whom is knocked unconscious by Pukwan, the policeman, when Zelda brings him to rescue Redford from the sisters' grasp. What is more telling, however, is that Erdrich does not demean her characters because of their weaknesses (Flavin 64). All of them "come home," even Mary Fred; for, as Redford is taken away by Zelda and the social worker, he imagines seeing his aunt in a fetal position on the floor, "running full tilt into the ground, as though she were trying to bury herself" (178). It is an image of death, coupled with a longing for rebirth. In this way, Erdrich recognizes the dangers of alcohol, while emphasizing everyone's need for affirmation, love, and understanding, rather than simply moralistic judgments from the likes of Zelda.

Perhaps the best example of a secondary, negative character is Zelda herself. She "comes home" in a love story that also reflects the main narrative. The equivalent of Twain's Miss Watson, whose religious ideas Huck flees, Zelda is described by Lipsha as a "household saint" whose "goodness" he dreads (13). Lipsha knows she is in Lyman's corner and works for his marriage to Shawnee, even "making novenas for unwed mothers" (17). She leads the policeman to rescue Redford from Shawnee Ray's drunken sisters, the boy only imagining himself hooked "by barbs and chains" (178). Ironically, however, it is Lipsha in "Zelda's Luck" who listens to her longing for her first love, Xavier Toose. She thinks she is dying and confesses that she is "most sorry for what she has not done" (242). This admission to the medicine man, together with some tough talk about love from Albertine, stirs her to go to Xavier where she becomes "like a naked child" (249), an image not unconnected to the eggshell and baby in the back seat of Gerry's car where Lipsha himself is reborn.

Only Albertine remains on the outside of the action, except to challenge Lipsha and Zelda. Lipsha is convinced that the latter looks at him as a "catalyst" for Lyman and Shawnee Ray's love, but the reader senses that Albertine is the most influential character in the novel. As in *Love Medicine*, she advises Lipsha, but here she suggests he let the dancer go to college, which he does. In "Albertine's Luck," she challenges Zelda to consider the fact that Shawnee Ray might love Lipsha rather than Lyman. This insight stirs Zelda to her own roots regarding the meaning of love, and she moves in "Zelda's Luck" to her own "tale of burning love." One critic of Erdrich's first three novels asks that the writer give us far more on Lipsha and Albertine (Portales 7). Lipsha does reappear in *Bingo Palace*. Perhaps Albertine will blossom in another "tale of burning love" (46), or like Erdrich herself, she may simply keep her distance, much as Twain does in *Huckleberry Finn*.

Conclusion—People's Lives and the Cycles of Nature

The endings of many great novels, such as *Huckleberry Finn* where Huck decides not to return home, are often clouded in ambiguity. Some think the conclusion of *Bingo Palace* "makes no sense" (Skow 71). In "Pillager Bones," the old bear Fleur coughs, and we are left wondering what this all means. Some critics say it begs another novel (Donahue 4D), but that is not necessary here. The ending, again narrated by the tribal "we," is vague, but it is no mystery—or it is part of the mystery—that if the novel is about "coming home," Fleur (and remember it is she to whom Lipsha goes for advice, or love medicine) is the earth to which all Erdrich's characters must return for moral and spiritual sustenance. Time for Erdrich is both linear—moving forward through the real world of the 1990s—and cyclic, but here the perennial cycle of nature predominates and brackets the novel as a whole. This Chippewa emphasis on one season following another, continually renewing the earth, reminds us of Huck Finn going into the territory, not sure whether the same situation will begin all over again.

Bingo Palace is an experiment and a tribute to Erdrich's creativity. She attempts so much that it is hard to believe she pulls it all together—themes, styles, characters. It is a love story that fails, but only in the short run. It is a search for identity that succeeds on a magical level, but demands a combination of styles to accomplish. It is a discussion of a modern issue, gambling on and off the reservation—a subject that receives little encouragement from the author. It is a mosaic of stories about the fragmentation of many lives that need healing. It is about people who need to "come home" if they are to be spiritually recreated, if they are to become whole in a modern materialistic world that harbors so many destructive forces symbolized by such a seemingly harmless thing as a bingo palace.

Works Cited

Barry, Nora, and Mary Prescott. "The Triumph of the Brave: *Love Medicine's* Holistic Vision." *Critique* 4.2 (1989): 123–38.

Rev. of *The Bingo Palace*, by Louise Erdrich. *Kirkus Reviews* 15 Nov. 1993: 1410.

Rev. of *The Bingo Palace*, by Louise Erdrich. *Publishers Weekly* 15 Nov. 1993: 72.

Donahue, Deirdre. "Louise Erdrich: A Heritage That Invites Literary Dualities." *USA Today* 20 Jan. 1994: 4D.

Dorris, Michael, and Louise Erdrich. *The Crown of Columbus.* New York: HarperCollins, 1991.

Erdrich, Louise. *Beet Queen.* New York: Holt, Rinehart & Winston, 1986.

——. *The Bingo Palace.* New York: HarperCollins, 1994.

——. *Love Medicine.* New York: Holt, Rinehart & Winston, 1984.

——. *Love Medicine.* 1984. Rev. and exp. ed. New York: HarperCollins, 1993.

——. *Tales of Burning Love.* New York: HarperCollins, 1996.

——. *Tracks.* New York: Harper & Row, 1988.

Flavin, Louise. "Louise Erdrich's *Love Medicine:* Loving over Time and Distance." *Critique* 2.2 (1989): 55–65.

Kakutani, Michiko. "Reinvention of a Past Rich with Tribal Magic." Rev. of *The Bingo Palace*, by Louise Erdrich. *New York Times* 18 Jan. 1994: C20.

Love, Barbara. Rev. of *Love Medicine*, by Louise Erdrich. *Library Journal* 15 Oct. 1993: 87.

Rev. of *Love Medicine*, by Louise Erdrich. *Kirkus Reviews* 1 Oct. 1993: 1234.

The New American Bible. New York: Catholic Books, 1970.

Ott, Bill. Rev. of *The Bingo Palace*, by Louise Erdrich. *Booklist* 15 Dec. 1993: 723.

Owens, Louis. *Other Destinies: Understanding the American Indian Novel.* Norman: U of Oklahoma P, 1992.

Portales, Marco. "People with Holes in Their Lives." Rev. of *Love Medicine*, by Louise Erdrich. *New York Times Book Review* 23 Dec. 1984: 6–7.

Rainwater, Catherine. "Reading between Worlds: Narrativity in the Fiction of Louise Erdrich." *American Literature* 2.2 (1990): 405–22.

Skow, John. "An Old Bear Laughing." Rev. of *The Bingo Palace*, by Louise Erdrich. *Time* 15 Feb. 1994: 71.

Thornton, Lawrence. "Gambling with Their Heritage." Rev. of *The Bingo Palace*, by Louise Erdrich. *New York Times Book Review* 16 Jan. 1994: 7.

Twain, Mark. *The Adventures of Huckleberry Finn*. 1885. New York: Holt, Rinehart & Winston, 1948.

——. "Huck Finn and Tom Sawyer among the Indians." *Hannibal, Huck & Tom*. Ed. Walter Blair. Berkeley: U of California P, 1969. 92–140.

Velie, Alan. "The Trickster Novel." *Narrative Chance*. Ed. Gerald Vizenor. Norman: U of Oklahoma P, 1993. 121–39.

Wood, Dave. "The Book Queen." *Minneapolis Star Tribune* 15 April 1996: E1–2.

Zaiser, Catherine. "Erdrich's *The Bingo Palace* Is Adeptly Woven Together." Rev. of *The Bingo Palace*, by Louise Erdrich. *The Forum* 6 Feb. 1994: C1, C8.

16

"What Does It Tell Us That We Are So Easily Deceived?" Impostor Indians

Laura Browder

In October of 1991, *The Education of Little Tree*, Forrest Carter's memoir of his Cherokee boyhood, was the book of the moment. It had sold more than half a million copies since its first publication in 1976 and was then number one on the *New York Times* best-seller list. It had won the first Abby Award from the American Booksellers Association "as the title Booksellers enjoyed selling most" (Reid 16). There was a strong basis for their enjoyment, for sales of the book seemed effortless. Treated in the industry as a publishing phenomenon, *Little Tree* was a true word-of-mouth success. First published by Delacorte Press, it took fifteen years and a reprinting by the University of New Mexico Press in 1986 for the book to become a best-seller. Groups of school children had formed "*Little Tree*" fan clubs, and there was talk that Hollywood was planning to bring Carter's gentle, New Age-tinged message of multiculturalism and environmentalism to the big screen (Reid 16). For thousands of *New York Times* readers, then, 4 October 1991 must have brought an unpleasant surprise (D. Carter).

According to an op-ed piece written by Dan T. Carter, a history professor at Emory University (and possibly a distant relation of the author of *Little Tree*, who had died in 1979), the critically acclaimed Cherokee memoir was a fake. Not only was its author, Forrest Carter, a.k.a. Asa Carter, not the full-blooded Native American he claimed to be (he is thought to have had one Cherokee grandparent), but, as Dan T. Carter wrote, "Between 1946 and 1973, the Alabama native carved out a violent career in Southern politics as a Ku Klux Klan terrorist, right-wing radio announcer, home-grown American Fascist and anti-Semite, rabble-rousing demagogue, and secret author of the famous 1963 speech by Gov. George Wallace of Alabama: 'Segregation now ... Segregation tomorrow ... Segregation forever.'" Even his new first name, Carter revealed, had been taken from Nathan Bedford Forrest, founder of the original Ku Klux Klan in 1866. Articles on the hoax appeared in *People*, *Newsweek*, and *Publishers Weekly*, among others.

For editorialists across the country, the exposure of Forrest Carter was an occasion for soul-searching. "What does it tell us that we are so easily deceived?" Professor Carter had asked—a question echoed not only by pundits, but by the film studio heads who had been involved in a bidding war over movie rights until that point. Readers swamped his office with heartbroken calls. Equally taken aback were friends of Forrest's in his later years, for whom he would, after a couple of drinks, perform "Indian war dances" and chant in what he said was the Cherokee language (Rubin). Eleanor Friede, his former agent, did not acknowledge his true identity for a long time. However, Calvin Reid states in his *Publishers Weekly* article that Friede admitted that Forrest Carter was indeed Asa Carter, after Friede had spoken with India Carter, Forrest Carter's widow (Reid 16). Nobody seemed able to come up with an explanation for Carter's ethnic imposture: The story seemed so bizarre as to be anomalous. And yet, Carter was only working in what might be reviewed as a long, if not always honorable, tradition of Native American impostors.

For nearly as long as the United States has been in existence, there have been fake Indians. First as embodiments of threat and then as living legacies of conquest, the image of the Indian has provided non-Native Americans with a focal point for a range of cultural anxieties. The successful Native impostor offers perhaps the purest expression of American fantasies about those whose near extermination provided a basis for our nation's existence. Created to fulfill the needs both of impostor and culture, the success of the ersatz Indian rests on his or her ability to embody the cultural fantasies of an age. The book sales, cinematic appearances, published interviews, and other hallmarks of impostor success are the tangible evidence of the love affair between invented Indian and audience. Just as infatuated lovers may be blind to the flaws of their beloved, so audiences will ignore the most glaring evidence that an Indian spokesman may not be quite what he or she appears. Thus, readers of the 1920s failed to remark that Chief Buffalo Child Long Lance's account of his youth described roaming the plains with his Blackfoot tribe and participating in the great buffalo hunts of the mid-1890s—a time when the buffalo had long been reduced to heaps of bleached bones and the Blackfoot had been settled onto reservations for fifteen years. Lovers may turn a blind eye to evidence of duplicity. Thus, the publication of Wayne Greenhaw's 1976 article exposing the imposture of *Little Tree* went generally unremarked: Fifteen years and six hundred thousand copies later, the news came as a fresh shock to the public. Furthermore, just as an affair may, in retrospect, take on an entirely new meaning, so an impostor, reviled at one time for his or her deception, may be embraced by a subsequent generation for reasons that would seem baffling to us today.

Although there are many impostors on whose lives it would be tempting to dwell, three of them—Forrest Carter, James P. Beckwourth, and Chief

Buffalo Child Long Lance—seem as emblematic of the complex dance of successful imposture as they once seemed representative of an authentic voice. James P. Beckwourth, whose autobiography was published in the 1850s, provides an ironic exemplar of how one generation's imposture may be seen as another's multiculturalism. Long Lance offers us a look at the first imposture to take place in the age of mass media. It is possible that, seen in the context of the ersatz Indians who preceded him, the story of *Little Tree* will seem all too understandable.

A Double Passage: The Curious Case of James P. Beckwourth

The autobiography of James P. Beckwourth was published by Harper & Brothers in 1856, when Beckwourth was fifty-six, or perhaps fifty-eight years old. Dictated by Beckwourth to T. D. Bonner, a con man, temperance advocate, and drunk, *The Life and Adventures of James P. Beckwourth, Mountaineer, Scout and Pioneer, and Chief of the Crow Nation of Indians* fulfills all the expectations its title suggests. Beckwourth's life seems exemplary of Western adventure, beginning with his first stint as a fur trapper, work he took on after getting into a fight with the St. Louis blacksmith to whom he was apprenticed as a teenager. Beckwourth's colleagues at the trapping company included William Sublette, who would discover the geysers at Yellowstone; Jim Bridger, the future discoverer of the Great Salt Lake, and Jedediah Smith, supposed by many to be the greatest mountain man of all time. Most of Beckwourth's narrative is centered on the thirteen years he spent as a war chief with the Crow Indians, but his book also includes accounts of his dozen or so marriages, his later work with trapping companies, his employment as a soldier on the U.S. government side of the Seminole wars of 1837, the restless wanderings which took him through Taos and Denver to California, where he blazed the Beckwourth Trail, which became the most commonly used route for pioneers coming from the Great Basin of Nevada to California, and his retirement as an innkeeper at Beckwourth Ranch, along the trail. The autobiography, with its tales of exotic adventure and bloody heroism, was an immediate best-seller and an immediate source of controversy.

In fact, Beckwourth was not white, as he represented himself in his memoir, but had started out as a slave, the son of his master. Although he speaks of his childhood relocation to St. Louis, to which "my father removed . . . taking with him all his family and twenty-two negroes," he was not among the "family" that he described (Beckwourth 14). Thus, the autobiography entails what might be called a double passage, for in it Beckwourth, a black man, passes as a white man who is himself passing as Indian. It was not just the nature of Beckwourth's racial identity that was challenged by his contemporaries. Even the ownership of Beckwourth's memories of his Crow life was thrown into question: Upon the publication

of his autobiography, Beckwourth was angrily denounced by a fellow trapper from Kentucky, Robert Meldrum. Meldrum attacked him for the usual
racial reasons, on the grounds that his mother had been a Negress and that
he was therefore a mulatto. More than a desire to debunk, however, was a
competitor's jealousy. According to the journals of Lieutenant James H.
Bradley, Meldrum

> upon quitting his service, enamoured of the savage life he had tasted for three years,
> [he] remained upon the plains making his home among the Crow Indians. Adopting
> their dress, gluing long hair to his own to make it conform to the savage fashion,
> having his squaw and lodge, and living in all respects the life of an Indian, he was
> quickly enabled by a superior intelligence and courage to acquire great influence with
> his savage associates. . . . He was a man of many adventures, and was accustomed to
> complain bitterly that Beckwourth in the autobiography published by Harper Brothers,
> had arrogated to himself many of his own experiences. (Bradley 255)

However, Meldrum refused to be mollified by Harper Brothers' offer to
publish his more authentic memories. As Bradley recalls, "he proudly
rejected all overtures" (Bradley 255).

Life and Adventures is far from being a tale of the solidarity of people of
color. It is, instead, an apologia for white racism. Rather than demonstrating empathy for the Crow, among whom he lived for so long, Beckwourth
describes them as "savages" and as "wily Indians." His chosen stance is as
interpreter to white America of Crow and other Native cultures, "a subject
which at the present day is but imperfectly understood by the general
reader" (Beckwourth 26). Significantly, then, his autobiography points up
both the fluidity of racial and ethnic identity in the nineteenth century, and
the dangers of trying to simplify the narrative of race and ethnicity.

After all, Beckwourth's book appeared just a year before the 1857
Oregon state constitution, which mandated the exclusion from the state of
free Blacks. This provision was popular among voters. As Oregon's delegate
to Congress explained in 1850, the issue of admitting free blacks to the
state

> is a question of life and death to us in Oregon. . . . The negroes associate with the
> Indians and intermarry, and, if their free ingress is encouraged or allowed, there would
> a relationship spring up between them and the different tribes, and a mixed race would
> ensue inimical to the whites; and the Indians being led on by the negro who is better
> acquainted with the customs, language, and manners of the whites, than the Indians,
> these savages would become much more formidable than they otherwise would, and
> long and bloody wars would be the fruits of the commingling of the races. (Qtd. in
> McGlagan 30–31)

Within the context of this legally encoded fear of racial alliances, Beckwourth's positioning of himself as a white writer makes sense. Mid-nineteenth century literacy rates among Indians and African Americans ensure
that he was, after all, addressing a primarily white audience. However, the

ambivalence of such a strategy shines through on the page—in his comparison of his presumably white self to a slave, and in his pride at the success of his racial imposture. Adding another layer of complexity to the story is the fact that Beckwourth, as an African American, had an advantage in trading with Indians, who were more inclined to trust him than his white counterparts. As Colonel James Stevenson of the Bureau of American Ethnology, who had spent thirty years working with and studying Native Americans, wrote in 1888, "the old fur trappers always got a Negro if possible to negotiate for them with the Indians, because of their 'pacifying effect.' They could manage them better than the white men, and with less friction" (qtd. in Katz 115). With his dark skin a commodity whose value was heavily situational, Beckwourth was able to use, deny, and change his racial identity as he saw fit.

While taking care to distinguish his own work from that of other travelers, whose "tales that were related as actual experience now mislead the speaker and the audience" (Beckwourth 51), Beckwourth relates in detail the way he himself has created a life out of such stories. His life as a Crow Indian begins when one of his fellow trappers "invented a fiction, which greatly amused me for its ingenuity" (Beckwourth 140). This fiction—that Beckwourth as a Crow child had been kidnapped by Cheyenne raiders and sold to the whites—was apparently accepted by the Crow. Taking the slavery metaphor further, Beckwourth, who has become a restored, favorite son, one redeemed from captivity, finds himself captured by Crow, who, anxious to verify his false biography, form an examining committee. "I believe," Beckwourth writes, "never was mortal gazed at with such intense and sustained interest as I was on that occasion." In a scene highly reminiscent of a slave market, "Arms and legs were critically scrutinized. My face next passed the ordeal; then my neck, back, breast, and all parts of my body, even down to my feet" (Beckwourth 146).

However, this is a story in which the black man whose body was being so minutely examined ends up triumphant. When one of the old women discovers a resemblance in him to her lost son, Beckwourth accepts her interpretation without commentary, other than to marvel that "it is but nature, either in the savage breast or civilized, that hails such a return with overwhelming joy" (Beckwourth 146).

His imposture is successful not only with the Crow, but also with white settlers. After only a brief interval, Beckwourth accompanies the Indians to Fort Clarke to trade pelts, and goes unremarked upon by the white trappers. "Speaking nothing but Crow language, dressed like a Crow, my hair long as a Crow's, and myself black as a Crow," Beckwourth tells us, "No one at the post doubted my being a Crow" (Beckwourth 177).

However proud he might be of his ability to "pass" as a Crow, Beckwourth is anxious to reassure white readers where his primary loyalties lie. He may claim to have lived as a Crow, taking eight Indian wives. Most pages of his narrative may be replete with accounts of the warfare in which he engaged and the enemy scalps he took, leading historian Bernard De Voto to assert that Beckwourth "gave our literature our goriest lies" and that in no other book are as many Indians killed (De Voto 63). Yet, Beckwourth is careful to distance himself from the violence he examines at such loving length. After describing, in graphic detail, a battle in which he killed eleven men, he extends a caveat:

> I trust that the reader does not suppose that I walked through these scenes of carnage and desolation without some serious reflections on the matter. Disgusted at the repeated acts of cruelty I witnessed, I often resolved to leave these wild children of the forest and return to civilized life; but before I could act upon my decision, another scene of strife would occur, and the Enemy of Horses was always the first sought for by the tribe. (Beckwourth 198)

His tribe needed him, as he justifies his actions; as the Crows' best warrior, he could not let them down. Even so, in another logical flip-flop, Beckwourth claims that he is acting in the best interests of white Americans:

> But, in justification, it may be urged that the Crows had never shed the blood of the white man during my stay in their camp, and I did not intend they ever should, if I could raise a voice to prevent it. They were constantly at war with tribes who coveted the scalps of the white man, but the Crows were uniformly faithful in their obligations to my race, and would rather serve than injure their white brethren without any consideration of profit. (Beckwourth 198)

Beckwourth describes the "natural ferocity of the savage, who thirsts for the blood of the white man for no other purpose than to gratify the vindictive spirit that animates him. . . . Such is Indian nature" (Beckwourth 233). Yet, he follows up the assertion by noting, "When I fought with the Crow nation, I fought in their behalf against the most relentless enemies of the white man. If I chose to become an Indian while living among them, it concerned no person but myself; and by doing so, I saved more life and property for the white man than a whole regiment of United States regulars could have done in the same time" (Beckwourth 233). Beckwourth's use of "white man," rather than "American" is hardly accidental. He constantly draws racial and ethnic distinctions in which others come out unfavorably. On one occasion, for instance, he notes that "quelling the Indian problem" will be impossible "as long as our government continues to enlist the offscouring of European cities into our army." In contrast, "with five hundred men of my selection I could exterminate any tribe in North America in a very few months" (Beckwourth 233). He not only compares himself to European offscourings, but to other African Americans. When he hears that a mulatto has joined with a number of "my Indians" (Beckwourth 249) and a group of white men in robbing a trader, he confronts the man. Indeed, he assigns primary responsibility for the crime to the mulatto, asking him, "What are you doing here, you black velvet-headed scoundrel?

. . . I will have your scalp torn off, you consummate villain" (Beckwourth 250). On another occasion, he compares an escaping Indian to "a negro with an alligator at his heels" (Beckwourth 339).

James Beckwourth passed away in 1866 from an undiagnosed illness while visiting the Crow. Yet, a persistent rumor would have it that the Crow, delighted to have Beckwourth back among them, asked him to be their chief again, an honor which he graciously refused, on the grounds that he was too old. At the feast to celebrate Beckwourth's return, the story goes, he was fed poisoned dog because even in death he would be "good medicine" (Wilson 183). The annals of nineteenth-century disease and medicine being what they are, it is impossible to say what finally killed James Beckwourth. However, it seems only fitting that his death was as ambiguous as his life.

As the conquest of the West continued and Native Americans were forced onto steadily shrinking reservations, popular and official attitudes toward the "vanishing American" began to change. By 1890, the U.S. Census declared the frontier officially closed. The western tribes' refusal to be quietly relocated to reservations had resulted in a series of "Indian Wars" that swept the prairies and mountains, but which left the tribes devastated and nearly powerless. The "savages" whom Beckwourth had joined were no longer the threat they had once seemed. After the Civil War, Christian evangelical concern for the defeated Indians gained momentum. A group that called themselves "the friends of the Indian" began to dominate the debate over the direction of government policy. This direction was one of "Americanization" and Christianization. As reformer Carl Schurz rhetorically asked in calling for the establishment of Indian boarding schools like Carlisle, "Can Indians be civilized?" (Prucha 14). His answer was a resounding "yes." As Schurz and other reformers, now in charge of many Indian agencies, diligently worked to assimilate the defeated tribes into white America, a new kind of Indian autobiography began to emerge. Perhaps the most noteworthy of these early twentieth-century works was that of Chief Buffalo Child Long Lance. His autobiography stressed both his American success and his connection to a tragically vanished past; it was an exemplar of the cult of personality which began to emerge in the 1920s.

Chief Buffalo Child Long Lance: Romantic Racialism and Native American Autobiography

In his foreword to *Long Lance*, the 1928 autobiography of Chief Buffalo Child Long Lance, humorist Irvin S. Cobb wrote admiringly of his friend's many accomplishments, not included in this childhood memoir: his mastery of half a dozen tribal languages besides his own, his presidential award of appointment to West Point, his bravery in World War I, from which he came out "as a captain of infantry, his body covered with wounds and his breast glittering with medals bestowed for high conduct and gallantry," his distinction as a writer for magazines (Cobb vii).

Indeed, by the time Long Lance's autobiography appeared, he was well on his way to becoming a celebrity. The international press showered praise on his autobiography. *The Silent Enemy*, an ethnographic film about Indian life in Northern Canada in which Long Lance starred the following year, was dubbed by Paramount into German, Swedish, Dutch, Polish, French, Spanish, Italian, and Portuguese. Authenticated at the time by Madison Grant, one of America's leading naturalists, it is a movie still acclaimed by film historians. Long Lance became a cultural icon. He appeared in comic strips, attended glittering cocktail parties with movie stars and aristocrats, lived at the famed Explorers Club in New York, whose members included Fritjof Nansen, Theodore Roosevelt, and Ernest Thomas Seton. He authored a best-selling book on Indian sign language and even had his own line of B. F. Goodrich running shoes, endorsed by none other than the great athlete Jim Thorpe.

However, Long Lance was a fake. Born in North Carolina in 1890 as Sylvester Long, the son of former slaves who claimed white and Indian, rather than African-American, forebears, Long Lance was classified according to the racial laws of the age as colored. His family was part of the African-American community in Winston-Salem, where Sylvester Long, as he was then known, worked as a janitor, one of the few jobs open to him. His first act of self-fashioning occurred when he lied about his ancestry on his application to the Carlisle Indian Residential School in Pennsylvania. At Carlisle, he was shunned by other students who suspected him of being black. As his Indian classmates shed their pasts as part of the assimilationist policies mandated by the school, Sylvester Long took on their stories as his own. By the time he left the school, he had become Sylvester Long Lance, half-white and half-Cherokee (D. B. Smith 20). In 1913, as Sylvester Long Lance continued his education at St. John's, a prestigious military school, President Wilson was pushing for increased formal and official segregation. While Long Lance was enlisting in the Canadian army and working his way up as a journalist, Wilson was arranging for the segregation and systematic firing of African-American federal employees. Ten years later, realizing that Cherokees were not sufficiently iconographically Indian to the general public, Sylvester Long Lance, who by this time was working as a journalist in Alberta, had evolved into Chief Buffalo Child Long Lance, a Blackfoot Indian (D. B. Smith 100).

The story of Long Lance offers useful lessons about the slippery nature of racial and ethnic identity in America. By taking on an Indian identity, Sylvester Long managed to escape the limitations of his "colored" status. As an articulate, handsome international spokesman for Native Americans, he proved appealing to Europeans and Americans alike, furnishing them with a focus for their primitivist fantasies. Long Lance took what could have been disabilities, e.g., his dark skin, and used them to transform himself into a consumable icon, becoming in Europe the symbol of Native Americanness. He took on an identity from the past and racially cross-dressed, making his color performative. Having a racial identity that was indeterminate, and at present tragic, he inserted himself into one that, fifty years previously, would have been immensely problematic. Because the battles were long over, this reconfigured identity became nostalgic rather than fraught. Classified as colored, he took his color and packaged it. By dressing in "tribal" costume one night and a tuxedo the next, he assumed a variety of postures that called into question the categories under discussion. His politics, likewise, seem slippery. Although he began by criticizing the Bureau of Indian Affairs, he ended by consorting with aristocratic Nazi sympathizers in Europe. Thus, a study of Long Lance points up the provisional nature not only of race and class, but of nationality and the self.

Irvin S. Cobb's foreword to Long Lance's autobiography served as an endorsement not only of the book's literary quality, but also of its authenticity: "I claim there is authentic history in these pages and verity and most of all a power to describe in English words the thoughts, the instincts, the events which originally were framed in a native language" (Cobb viii). These words are clearly similar to those of the abolitionists who authenticated slave narratives; no slave narrative would appear without an endorsement by a white sponsor. However, although most of the authenticators of slave narratives pledged themselves to racial justice, or, at the very least, the end of slavery, as the son of a Confederate army veteran, Cobb was a humorist whose living depended on his vast store of "darkie" jokes. Likewise, Madison Grant, the naturalist who authenticated *The Silent Enemy*, was the author of *The Passing of a Great Race* (1916), in which he alerted Americans to the danger of its superior races, the Nordics, being submerged by inferior immigrants. In his 1933 work, *The Conquest of a Continent*, he warned of the dangers of racial miscegenation, advocating not only laws banning intermarriage, but also the constant vigilance that Nordics must maintain to unmask mulattos passing for white (Grant, *Continent* 288).

It was no accident that both Long Lance's autobiography and his film were authenticated by men dedicated to racist theories. By the turn of the century Native American autobiography held a special place in an American culture which was concerned both with mourning a people that could never return and with using Indian narratives to maintain racial theories of the time. Indeed, a prominent Native American autobiography published in 1931, *We Indians: The Passing of a Great Race*, the autobiography of White Horse Eagle, an Osage, was elicited and edited by Edgar von Schmidt-Pauli, a German academic whose chief scholarly interest lay in demonstrating the inevitability of the rise of the German race in general, and of Adolf Hitler in particular. According to Schmidt-Pauli, White Horse Eagle was, because of his race, capable of a number of remarkable feats, among them the ability to sense the presence of gold, silver, or water in the earth beneath his feet, and the ability to read Egyptian hieroglyphics. As H. David Brumble points out, to Schmidt-Pauli, "White Horse Eagle and the Indians in general [were] living—or rather dying—evidence of inborn racial characteristic" (Brumble 152). According to some reports, "White Horse Eagle found it profitable to travel Europe in the 1920s and 1930s, adopting unsuspecting museum directors and chairmen of anthropology departments into his tribe. Photographs show him sporting a feather bonnet, Navajo silver jewelry, and a button reading 'Lions Club Pasadena.' A Viennese museum director found him particularly convincing, because the Big Chief had made it a matter of principle "not to shake hands with Jews" (Feest 323).

Long Lance's autobiography occupied a curious place within this nexus of Social Darwinist or romantic racialist thought. It appeared just four years after the Indian Citizenship Act of 1924, which made every Native American an American citizen, and 15 years after the publication of Joseph K. Dixon's 1913 volume of photographs and text, *The Vanishing Race*, a book which had come out of what might be termed the Bureau of Indian Affairs' official farewell to the disappearing Indians. With Dixon as prime mover, the Bureau had arranged the Last Council, a meeting of chiefs and aging warriors from several of the Western tribes. The achievement of Long Lance was to negotiate the territory between the tragic nostalgia emblematized by Dixon's work and the assimilationist claims of the Citizenship Act.

Long Lance, in his autobiography, was able both to present a vanished way of life—he even included a chapter on hunting the Buffalo, which in any event had vanished long before his childhood—and to present himself as an example of one who, as witnessed by the title of his 1926 *Cosmopolitan* article, "My Trail Upward," had managed to effect a Booker T. Washington style transformation. Writing that "I'm proud to be as much like a white man as I am—and I'm proud, too, of every drop of Indian blood that runs through my veins," he built a reassuring bridge between the white and Indian worlds. As he concluded,

> I have reached no dizzying heights of material success, but I have succeeded in pulling myself up by my boot straps from a primitive and backward life into this great new world of white civilization. Anyone with determination and will can do as much. (Long Lance, "Trail" 38)

Thus, Long Lance both maintained an affectionate distance from his "roots" and from the reservation he claimed to visit a few times a year, while asserting the superiority of a white way of life. Most importantly, he offered a reassuring message to those who might have qualms about the laws, dating back from the Indian Removal Act of 1830, which mandated the forced migration of the eastern tribes to locations west of the Mississippi and had effectively destroyed the possibility of Native Americans living their traditional lives. It was all right, Long Lance seemed to say. Although the end of this way of life may be sad, it was not tragic because any Indian with determination could succeed in the white world—and, as Irvin Cobb writes of Long Lance in his foreword, not only to survive, but also to conspicuously flourish. In fact, he dedicated his autobiography to "The two White Men who have guided and encouraged me most since I have taken a place in civilization." While acknowledging that his grandfather's dire predictions of the end of the traditional Indian way of life have come true, Long Lance ends his autobiography by claiming that these changes are, in fact, not only inevitable but ordained by the deity: "But the new day is here: it is here to stay. And now we must leave it for our old people to sit stolidly and dream of the glories of our past. Our job is to try to fit ourselves into the new scheme of life which the Great Spirit has decreed for North America" (Long Lance, *Long Lance* 278).

In an autobiography full of stirring scenes of warfare fit for an audience which craved boys' adventure stories, Long Lance perfectly fulfilled the needs of an audience perhaps not fully comfortable with the conditions that had made Indian autobiography possible. Indian autobiography is a postcontact literary form predicated on defeat and disappearance. Native American memoirs did not exist before the passage of the Indian Removal Act of 1830. The first Indian autobiography, the *Life of Ma-Ka-tai-me-she-kia-kiak or Black Hawk*, by the Sauk leader, appeared in 1833, after his defeat by Federal troops in the campaign known as the Black Hawk War. Native American autobiography has always been a solicited form, traditionally elicited and edited by a white, though narrated by its subject, for, as Arnold Krupat points out, "the production of an Indian's own statement of his inevitable disappearance required that the Indian be represented as speaking in his own voice" (Krupat 34). Although nineteenth-century Native American autobiographies were the stories of defeated leaders, of heroes in the mold of Kit Carson or Sam Houston, twentieth-century Indian autobiographies began to represent the process of Americanization. Many of these works, like Long Lance's, stress not only the assimilation, but also the Americanness of their tellers. The title of Charles Eastman's 1916 memoir, *From the Deep Woods to Civilization*, for example, emphasized the same kind of progress as did Long Lance's.

Long Lance's self-fashioning to fit the needs of his audience was particularly successful, as evidenced by a 1930 *Herald Tribune* article about him, entitled "One Hundred Percent American." It begins with the claim that "There is romance always in the man who can play the game and live the life of another race" (B. Smith). Rather than questioning Long Lance's identity, though, Beverly Smith, the article's author, attributes the American success of Long Lance, "a splendid specimen of the American Indian," to his Indian background. It was his very foreignness, his exotic qualities, which made his heroism in the service of the nation possible, she asserted. For instance, his acts of bravery in World War I, for which he claimed to have been decorated by three governments, came about because "there was war in Europe, and it called to the warrior blood in Long Lance" (B. Smith).

Although in his *Cosmopolitan* article Long Lance emphasized individual accomplishment, his fake autobiography, ironically enough, exemplified many of the traditions of Indian autobiography as enumerated by Hertha Wong in its "lack of rigid chronology, incorporation of multiple voices that emphasize tribal identity" (Wong 142). Long Lance's chronology, including such iconographic, yet historically impossible, scenes as hunting buffalo, can hardly be called rigid. Because Long Lance incorporated stories from his Blackfoot friends like Mike Eagle Speaker, as well as those that he had heard from his classmates at the Carlisle Indian School, into his narrative, he was in a sense creating a new tribal identity; it just was not his own. In addition, the fact that his autobiography had been elicited and edited by Ray Long, the editor-in-chief of *Cosmopolitan*, simply placed him in a long tradition of other Native speakers.

If, as Arnold Krupat writes, "victory is the ennobling condition of western autobiography, [but] defeat is the ennobling condition of Indian autobiography" (48), Long Lance managed to have his cake and eat it, too, by recording both the tribal defeat and his individual triumph. Thus, Long Lance was drawing from two distinct traditions of American autobiography: that of ethnic autobiography, understood by both teller and audience to be the story of a group as much as of an individual, and that of self-construction, the triumphant individual struggle upward of Benjamin Franklin or Booker T. Washington.

Long Lance's masquerade entailed not only an act of literary imposture, but also demanded a facade which encompassed his every waking moment. His life was a stage he could never leave, whether inventing Indian sign language at a cocktail party or politely listening to Irvin Cobb's seemingly endless, and oft-repeated, store of "darkie" jokes. This charade meant that he could never go home to see his parents or siblings, who were firmly ensconced in the African-American community of Winston-Salem. Although his stories, which became increasingly grandiose, were generally believed, there were dangerous moments, questions put to him that forced him to improvise a past quickly. Interestingly enough, one man who had his suspicions about Long Lance and might have been expected to voice them—Chauncey Yellow Robe, the great-nephew of Sitting Bull and Long Lance's co-star in *The Silent Enemy*, remained silent. Yellow Robe was made suspicious by Long Lance's demeanor on the set—his punctuality, his boisterousness, his small talk with strangers. This was behavior which, though it may have fulfilled white expectations, certainly did not meet those of Yellow Robe, who made discreet inquiries while in New York on a lecture tour following the production of the movie. Although he eventually had his suspicions confirmed by the Bureau of Indian Affairs, and went so far as to contact the movie's legal counsel, he eventually came to Long Lance's defense. Perhaps his own difficulties with the color bar led him to respect Long Lance's decision to transform himself.

At best, Long Lance's was an ambiguous accomplishment. Although in the early years of his journalistic career he had rethought the assimilationist goals of the Carlisle Indian School, and was using his position to forcefully criticize positions taken by the Canadian Department of Indian Affairs, such as the government decree to ban potlatch ceremonies, he eventually retreated from this confrontational stance. When members of the Blood Indian tribe expressed dismay that Long Lance was using his ceremonial adoption by them for his own ends, he grew resentful that they were not sufficiently grateful. One sign of his movement away from activism was the dedication of his autobiography to Duncan Campbell Scott, the Deputy Superintendent of Indian Affairs in Ottawa, a powerful government official who had questioned the sense of expending money and social services on a "dying people" and had lobbied for Indians to conform to what he called "that worldwide tendency towards universal standardization which would appear to be the essential underlying purport of all modern social evolution" (D. B. Smith 95).

Unfortunately, Long Lance was finally unable to inhabit the narrative he had written for himself. He committed suicide at the age of 42, in the home of Anita Baldwin, one of his wealthy patrons. He left no note, so one can only guess that the strain of living a lie for over twenty years had finally become unbearable. Back in Winston-Salem, where Long Lance had not visited in twenty years, his brother, Abe Long, whom Long Lance had written to request that "If there is anything in the papers, Abe, you will be careful about names, won't you" (D. B. Smith 210), spent the thirties and forties directing the flow of traffic up the steps to the colored gallery of the Carolina Theater. In a diary he kept all his life, he commented on progress in civil rights. He opened one such entry by writing, "We the better thinking negroes . . ."

Long Lance's autobiography continued to be reprinted for decades.

The Education of Little Tree Reconsidered

A little more than forty years after Long Lance's death, Forrest Carter was "born," with the publication of his first novel, *Gone to Texas* (1973), which became the source for the Clint Eastwood film, *The Outlaw Josey Wales*. The publication of *The Education of Little Tree* followed three years later. Some Alabamans, acquainted with Asa, recognized him in Forrest Carter's 1975 interview with Barbara Walters on the *Today* show (Leland with Peyser), and one, journalist Wayne Greenhaw, went so far as to publicize the fact in a brief *New York Times* article in August 1976. News of the imposture seemed not to have registered in the public consciousness, however.

What was it about the book that seemed to resonate so with the readers? *Little Tree* sold much better than any other Native American autobiography published at the same time. In fact, it found adherents in the Washington State court system, where it was used to rehabilitate youthful offenders, and among the cast of the Broadway musical, *The Will Rogers Follies*, who received copies from their director, Tommy Tune (McWhorter 120).

Asa Carter's past, grinding out impassioned speeches in a basement office of George Wallace's state house, seems to have served him well in writing *The Education of Little Tree*. The book is, in fact, a hack's dream, a slender volume (216 pages) in which every rhetorical trick known to the speechwriter is used to full advantage. Carter manages to appeal effectively to a number of different constituencies in telling the story of Little Tree's life with the grandparents who have adopted him after the death of his parents.

Environmentally-oriented audiences can warm to Little Tree's descriptions of "Mon-o-lah, the earth mother, [who] came to me through my moccasins. I could feel her push and swell here . . . and the life of the water-blood, deep inside her" (7). Nature is not only a mother, but one whose creatures, especially the hunting dogs belonging to Little Tree and his grandparents, seem incessantly to perform cute, Disneyfied antics. Living in harmony with Mother Earth is a theme endlessly repeated throughout the text—as the narrator notes, "Granpa lived with game not at it" (23).

Little Tree may be only the latest iteration of what the English impostor, Archie Belaney—who became Grey Owl, an Apache half-breed—expressed when he declared, "The Indians were always conservationists. Indians are in tune with their surroundings" (qtd. in Hayman 43). Grey Owl's "authenticity" as a spokesperson enabled him to lecture so effectively throughout North America and Britain on the subject of conservation, to broadcast his appeals, and to publish a number of books on the subject of conservation, specifically on beavers, which he referred to as "little Indians." Whatever his other motivations, Grey Owl used his identity to present his environmental message in the most dramatic way he knew. By the time of his death in 1938, he had used his position as "caretaker of animals" for the Canadian Park Service as a platform to advance his environmental cause across the world. Advising his publicity agent that he wished to be packaged as a "modern Hiawatha," Grey Owl posed in his version of full Native Dress when on tour (during his first British tour, in 1935, he addressed more than fifty thousand people), while giving a Royal Performance in 1937 for the King and Queen of England, or while starring in the movies produced by the Canadian Park Service. Although Grey Owl may have anthropomorphized the beavers whose preservation he advocated, he seems to have used his Native persona primarily for political purposes. His version of Indianness involved a somewhat romantic, but relatively uncomplicated vision of nature. For Little Tree, nature is a much more directive force.

Knowledge of Mother Earth, is, of course, integral to understanding The Way, for in *The Education of Little Tree* nature is not just a mother who must be respected, but a guide to wisdom. Little Tree's grandparents teach him the secret of living in harmony with nature. Interestingly, Granpa also preaches a kind of Social Darwinism of the forest, telling Little Tree not to be distressed at the sight of a hawk eating a quail, for "it is The Way. Talcon caught the slow and so the slow will raise no children who are also slow" (9). In one of the poems that stud the text, Little Tree advises readers to "learn the wisdom of the Man-oh-lah," his (invented) term for the earth in order to "know The Way of all the Cherokee" (12).

In this mystical amalgam, spiritual knowledge is tied to the Cherokee Way, which is itself tied to a knowledge of nature. The idea that Native Americans have a primordial wisdom is one to which many Americans have responded, especially since the 1960s. *Little Tree* enhances this notion one better and mixes such New Age concerns as reincarnation into the spiritual stew.

Furthermore, *The Education of Little Tree* plays into the idea that "authenticity" is to be found through a return to cultural primitivism and, not incidentally, anti-intellectualism. Thus, the boy tells us that "Granma began to hum a tune behind me and I knew it was Indian, . . ." (4). And Granpa, who is by turns mystically attuned to the earth and homespun, tells Little Tree that the "meddlesome son of a bitch that invented the dictionary ought to be taken out and shot" (90). The primal wisdom of the Native Americans occurs in a universe outside of time, outside politics. Thus, when Granpa hears the news of the ravages of the Depression, epitomized by large numbers of suicides, he explains to Little Tree that "New York was crowded all up with people who didn't have enough land to live on, and likely half of them was run crazy from living that-a-way, which accounted for the shootin's and the winder jumping" (91).

The Education of Little Tree is not only a fantasy about Native American primal spirituality, it is also a fantasy perfectly attuned to an American public well versed in the rhetoric of the recovery movement. If previous impostors have given us Indians as noble savages, as romantic racialists, as spiritual guides, as the original environmentalists, *Little Tree* offers us a new vision of Native American identity for the 1970s and beyond— what I call the inner child Indian. We look to our image of the Indian for what we think we have lost. If Long Lance and Grey Owl presented themselves in the 1920s and 1930s as Indians whose virility was unquestioned and whose masculinity in fact rested on their Native identities, *Little Tree* offers us a world in which sex is not even an issue. In the era of AIDS, this idealized world of childhood appealed to many readers.

In a time of rising divorce rates and fractured families, *Little Tree* provides a vision of an idyllic family unit. In a period when pop psychology writers like Jon Bradshaw have brought discussions of the inner child or of toxic families to talk shows seen by millions, and when such works as M. Scott Peck's *The Road Less Traveled* remained firmly ensconced on the *New York Times* best-seller list, *Little Tree* offered readers a vision of a family which healed, rather than inflicted, pain. And, in his portrait of his grandparents, especially his grandfather, whose father had survived the Trail of Tears, Little Tree offered a model of successful recovery from trauma.

When we first meet Little Tree, it is on the occasion of his mother's death, when he is five, a year after the loss of his father. The bond between the child and his newly discovered grandfather is instantaneous and instinctive. While a crowd of relatives argue over Little Tree's future (1), Granpa stays aloof from the fray, uninterested in material possessions and in treating the child as a thing to be disposed of. He is every child's fantasy, the chosen parent. Little Tree literally picks him from the crowd, holds on to his leg, and will not let go—and so the matter is decided. Granma lulls the boy to sleep with an Indian song in which the forest, wind, and various animals welcome him, promising that "Little Tree will never be alone" and "I was happy that they loved me and wanted me" (5).

Little Tree grows up in a near-Rousseauistic idyll. Granma does not restrain Little Tree. No matter how dirty or wet he gets while playing, his grandmother doesn't mind, for "Cherokees never scolded their children for having anything to do with the woods" (57). Instead, she encourages every aspect of his growth. Not once in the book does Little Tree feel anger at either grandparent, nor does either grandparent behave, at any point, in a less than loving way. The world of the family is safe, free from conflict, a nurturing cocoon.

Tellingly, family happiness is dependent on isolation from the mainstream of American life, in which dysfunction is rampant. Little Tree must venture into the wider world to find brutality (a sharecropper whipping his daughter), dishonesty, and sanctimony (he is sold a dying calf by a man claiming to be Christian), exploitation (big-city bootleggers trying to muscle their way into Granpa's moonshining business), and racism. Whereas James P. Beckwourth claimed to have become an Indian only in order to aid the American government, and while Long Lance prides himself on his "trail upward" from the enclosed world of his tribe and his family into American "civilization," Little Tree can only attain maturity within the sheltered context of his family. Exposure to the outside world is scarring both literally and figuratively. Furthermore, whereas citizenship and its responsibility are eagerly embraced by Beckwourth and Long Lance, it is only the folly of government intervention which can endanger Little Tree's idyll.

Government intervention takes many forms, such as Granpa's imprisonment for bootlegging, but attains its worst horrors when the state takes
Little Tree from his grandparents and places him in an orphanage of Dick-
ensian horrors. Within the orphanage can be found childhood in its most
dysfunctional form, civilization at it most discontented. The Reverend who
runs the orphanage brands Little Tree a bastard, and tells him that as such,
he cannot be saved. According to the Reverend, "Granpa was not fittin' to
raise a young'un, and that I more than likely had not ever had any discipline," which—to Little Tree and his readers—is the beauty of the arrangement (184). Discipline, in the Reverend's terms, includes a beating severe
enough that he breaks a stout stick across Little Tree's back and fills his
shoes with blood. The reason for this punishment is the boy's innocent
reference, in class, to mating deer, which causes his teacher to lose control
"filth . . . filth . . . would come out of you . . . you . . . little *bastard*" (191).
The orphanage is a world in which the disabled, as represented by Little
Tree's roommate and only friend, are humiliated. It is a world of disconnec-
tion from nature, of sexual repression, of Christian pieties and manufactured sentiment. Politicians visit at Christmas, as do drunken country club
members, who distribute broken gifts to the children; to mark the occasion,
a dying pine tree has been placed in the hall (194). It is only through talking
to an oak tree and communicating with his grandparents by watching Dog
Star at night—so that they can "sen[d] me remembrance" (189)—that Little
Tree can finally tell them that he wants to return home. As conditions in
the orphanage worsen, Little Tree relies more and more heavily on Indian
ways to survive—whether he is letting his "body mind" sleep in order to
endure the pain of the reverend's physical abuse or whether he is listening
to the oak tree (193).

Little Tree has no doubts that his grandparents will rescue him, and
indeed, Granpa shows up on Christmas Day to reclaim Little Tree and to
return him to the world of the mountain. Here, he can live happily, listening to his grandparents' message of harmony with nature, freedom from
government intervention, distrust of language, love and respect of one
another, and condemnation of racial and ethnic prejudice. Jews, for
instance, are personified by the kind old peddler, Mr. Wine. At one point,
Little Tree overhears a slur, and asks in response "Granpa, what is a damn
Jew?" The answer is slow in coming, concluding in a comparison to Native
Americans "Like the Indian . . . I hear tell they ain't got no nation, neither"
(177). Granma and Granpa preach tolerance, and they remain dignified in
the face of prejudice. Little Tree is full of touching stories of people reaching out across seemingly unsurmountable cultural and ideological chasms to
help one another—a fragile peace which is, as not, shattered by government
intervention. Two Union soldiers help former Confederates and their still
loyal former slave (this episode recounts one of Granpa's experiences

when he was nine years old in 1867; to Little Tree's surprise, Granpa, too, was once a boy [114]); Granpa and Mr. Wine find common cause; brotherhood seems not only possible but the only real choice, if one is to follow The Way.

The story of Little Tree, unfortunately, does not square with its author's own past. Having been hired as a spokesman by the anti-integration American States Rights Association, Asa Carter was fired for his on-air diatribes against National Brotherhood Week, sponsored by the National Conference of Christians and Jews. Caught up in the movement to halt civil rights progress, he ran into trouble with other Alabama citizens council leaders because he would not allow Jews into his white supremacist organization. As late as 1978, one year before his death, in his guise as Forrest Carter, he delivered a drunken speech to the Wellesley College Club in Dallas, in which he talked, a la *Little Tree*, about the need for people to love one another. Yet, as reporter Dana Rubin writes,

> In an expansive moment, Carter pointed across the podium at his fellow speaker historian Barbara Tuchman. "Now, she's a good ol' Jew girl," Carter said. Then he swung his arm toward Stanley Marcus, who was in the audience. "Now, Stanley," he went on, "there's a good ol' Jew boy." (Rubin)

As far as is known, however, Carter confined his anti-Semitism to verbal abuse. This was not true of his feelings towards African Americans. In the mid-1950s, he was among the men who incorporated a shadowy paramilitary organization called the Original Ku Klux Klan of the Confederacy—a group later accused of gruesome acts against African Americans. In speeches, Asa Carter vowed to put his "blood on the ground" to halt integration. By the time George Wallace hired him as a speechwriter in 1958, after his own trouncing by a Klan-backed candidate in his quest for the lieutenant governorship, Carter's reputation as an extremist was such that Wallace's men, nervous about having him linked to their candidate, paid him through back channels. After Wallace's victory, he gained a rear office in the capitol. Over time, he became disillusioned with Wallace, whom he saw as caving in to integrationist forces (Leland with Peyser). He came in fifth in a field of five in his protest bid against Wallace for the 1970 governor's race. The statewide paramilitary force he set up in 1971 failed, as had his venture the previous year to set up a string of all-white private schools. The following year, Carter was arrested three times on alcohol-related charges. The year after that, he and his wife sold their house, bought their sons a home in Abilene, Texas, and moved to Florida. That year, Forrest Carter, who sold his first book, a Confederate adventure novel, *Gone to Texas*, was born.

Little Tree was very much an Indian for the 1990s. As the waif look became fashionable in the late 1980s, as lifestyle pages reported that "cocooning" had become a new trend, as Earth Day was resurrected in

1990, and New Age and spiritual volumes filled the shelves of bookstores, *The Education of Little Tree* gave Americans the Native American they wanted. Ironically, while James P. Beckwourth and Sylvester Long escaped the historical trap of their racial identities by becoming Indian, Asa Carter took on a Native self as, among other things, a way of leaving his racist reputation behind him. After the exposure, pundits wondered how so many could have been so easily fooled. The real question, perhaps, is who the next successful invented Indian will be—and what he or she will be able to tell us about the needs of our culture.

Works Cited

Primary Sources

Beckwourth, James P. *The Life and Adventures of James P. Beckwourth, Mountaineer, Scout, and Pioneer, and Chief of the Crow Indians.* Written from his own dictation by T. D. Bonner. 1856. New York: Alfred A. Knopf, 1931.

Carter, Forrest. *The Education of Little Tree.* 1976. 15th ed. Albuquerque: U of New Mexico P, 1993.

Long Lance, Chief Buffalo Child. *Long Lance.* New York: Cosmopolitan Book Corporation, 1928.

———. "My Trail Upward." *Cosmopolitan* June 1926: 72+.

Secondary Sources

Black Hawk. *Life of Ma-Ka-tai-me-she-kia-kiak or Black Hawk.* Cincinnati, 1833.

Bradley, James H. "Affairs at Fort Benton from 1831 to 1869." *Contributions to the Historical Society of Montana.* Vol. 3. Helena: Historical Society of Montana, 1900. 201–87.

Brumble, H. David, III. *American Indian Autobiography.* Berkeley: U of California P, 1988.

Carter, Dan T. "The Transformation of a Klansman." *New York Times* 4 Oct. 1991: A 31.

Carter, Forrest. *Gone to Texas.* Gantt, AL: Whipporwill Publisher, 1973.

———. Interview with Barbara Walters. *Today Show.* NBC. New York. July 1975.

Cobb, Irvin. Foreword. *Long Lance.* By Chief Buffalo Child Long Lance. New York: Cosmopolitan Book Corporation, 1928. vii–viii.

De Voto, Bernard. *The Year of Decision.* 1846. Boston: Houghton Mifflin Co., 1943.

Dixon, Joseph. *The Vanishing Race.* Garden City, NY: Doubleday, 1913.

Eastman, Charles A. *From the Deep Woods to Civilization.* Boston: Little, Brown, 1916.

Feest, Christian F. "Europe's Indians." *The Invented Indian: Cultural Fictions and Government Policies.* Ed. James Clifton. New Brunswick, NJ: Transaction Publishers, 1990. 313–32.

Grant, Madison. *The Conquest of a Continent.* New York: Charles Scribner, 1933.

——. *The Passing of a Great Race.* New York: Charles Scribner, 1916.

Greenhaw, Wayne. "Is Forrest Carter Really Asa Carter? Only Josey Wales May Know for Sure." *New York Times* 26 Aug. 1976: 45.

Hayman, John. "Grey Owl's Wild Goose Chase." *History Today* Jan. 1994: 42–48.

Indian Citizenship Act of 1924. 2 June 1924. c. 233. Stat. 43.253.

Indian Removal Act of 1830. 28 May 1830, c. 148. Stat. 4.412.

Katz, William Loren. *Black Indians: A Hidden Heritage.* New York: Atheneum, 1986.

Krupat, Arnold. *For Those Who Come After: A Study of Native American Autobiography.* Berkeley: U of California P, 1985.

Leland, John, with Marc Peyser. "New Age Fable from an Old School Bigot?" *Newsweek* 14 Oct. 1991: 62.

McGlagan, Elizabeth. *A Peculiar Paradise: A History of Blacks in Oregon, 1788–1944.* Portland, OR: Gregorian Press, 1980.

McWhorter, Diane. "Little Tree, Big Lies." *People* 28 Oct. 1991: 119.

The Outlaw Josey Wales. Dir. Clint Eastwood. Perf. Clint Eastwood, Chief Dan George, Sondra Locke. Warner Brothers, 1976.

Peck, M. Scott. *The Road Less Traveled: A New Psychology of Love, Traditional Values, and Spiritual Growth.* New York: Simon and Schuster, 1978.

Prucha, Francis Paul, ed. *Americanizing the American Indians: Writings by the "Friends of the Indian," 1880–1900.* Cambridge: Harvard UP, 1973.

Reid, Calvin. "Widow of 'Little Tree' Author Admits He Changed Identity." *Publishers Weekly* 25 Oct. 1991: 16, 18.

Rubin, Dana. "The Real Education of Little Tree." *Texas Monthly* Feb. 1992: 79+.

The Silent Enemy. Dir. Douglas Burden. Perf. Chief Buffalo Child Long Lance, Chauncey Yellow Robe, Molly Spotted Elk. Paramount, 1930.

Smith, Beverly. "One Hundred Percent American." *Herald Tribune* 19 Jan. 1930: 17.

Smith, Donald B. *Long Lance: The True Story of an Impostor.* Lincoln: U of Nebraska P, 1982.

White Horse Eagle. *We Indians: The Passing of a Great Race.* New York: E. P. Dutton, 1931.

Wilson, Elinor. *Jim Beckwourth: Black Mountain Man and War Chief of the Crows.* Norman: U of Oklahoma P, 1972.

Wong, Hertha. *Sending My Heart Back across the Years: Tradition and Innovation in Native American Autobiography.* New York: Oxford UP, 1992.

VI

Images and Icons

Section VI explores the Images and Icons through which American popular culture—television, film, radio, popular magazines, and similar forms of expression in everyday life—represents Native Americans. In film studies, for instance, analysis of plot, character, and theme is complemented by an examination of camera angle, color or black-and-white film, acting, and a host of related issues.

On this topic, we find the essay, "Tomahawkin' the Redskins: 'Indian' Images in Sports and Commerce," by Jane Frazier of East Georgia College. Frazier contends that the use of "Indian" images—as distinct from authentic representations of Native American people—in sports and business shapes our views of Native Americans. She argues that how we use these images focuses our attention on a select set of characteristics which we then associate with Native Americans. In so doing, she maintains, we reduce Native Americans to the status of mascots and shills to sell our products. "What these stereotypes do, finally," Frazier concludes, "is to lull us into believing that they truly depict the Native American." Thus, the "tomahawk chop" and war dances at sporting events and the use of Native names and icons may look innocent enough, but the rituals perpetuate simplistic "cowboys and Indians" images of Native Americans.

The image of the Indian in Hollywood film is the focus of the next two contributions. In "Reframing the Hollywood Indian: A Feminist Re-reading of *Powwow Highway* and *Thunderheart*," Ellen L. Arnold of Emory University analyzes two recent examples of Hollywood Westerns. Arnold argues that the Western is "a flawed genre . . . because its treatment of Native Americans as stereotyped 'Indians' has perpetuated long-held misconceptions and prejudices in American culture." Indeed, Arnold contends, Hollywood has given us an ethnic and gender "tradition of stereotypes" and, especially, "glorification of male roles" over female leads. In examining one film from 1988 and one from 1992, she asks us to consider what, if anything, has changed: Do we see new directions or do we uncover instead the old stereotypes of Hollywood's Native Americans?

"Native Americans have never ceased to fascinate, frighten, and attract other Americans," observes English Professor Mary Alice Money of Gordon College (Georgia) in her contribution, "Images of Native Americans in the

Popular Western." Like Arnold, Money shows how scholars analyze the symbolism developed in the film genre of the Hollywood Western. Using an analytical framework—Seven Stages in Images of Native Americans—she dissects representations of the "Indian" in the novels of James Fenimore Cooper and Owen Wister, in television series such as *The Lone Ranger, Gunsmoke,* and *Have Gun, Will Travel,* in films such as *Broken Arrow* and *Little Big Man,* and in paperback books. She sees a "seismic shift" in images of Native Americans in popular culture with the 1990 release of *Dances with Wolves,* in which Indians were presented as people who exhibited a full range of human traits, and a greater number of Native American roles were played by Native actors. In an interpretation that diverges from those of Frazier and Arnold, Money concludes that, although the earliest films, books, and television series consistently and powerfully reinforced the familiar, tired stereotypes that have dogged Native peoples for centuries, "popular Westerns in the multicultural 1990s are depicting more realistic, individual humans instead of conventionally racist fearsome 'wild savages'. . . ."

17

Tomahawkin' the Redskins: "Indian" Images in Sports and Commerce

Jane Frazier

The Problem of Indian Images

Americans—those of a non-Native background, at least—have long accepted and even enjoyed applying Native American images and names to many of our consumer products and athletic teams. The practice recently has opened up questions, however. The general public, mainstream media, and, especially, Native American activists have begun to question the appropriateness of such symbols. Most of the attention has been paid to sports mascots, but consumer goods and services which carry these labels also are under increased scrutiny. At its core the issue is: Is there any harm in a title such as the Washington "Redskins," or, does it matter that we drive automobiles called "Pontiacs"? Native American activists have protested these images at least since the 1960s; yet, not until the 1991 World Series (with "Braves" on the field) did the issue become broadly publicized and a topic of national debate.

The number of Native American names and terms which have been appropriated as Indian logos among our businesses is almost staggering. We are surrounded by an ocean of products such as "Cherokee" Jeeps and "Cheyenne" trucks, "Thunderbird" and "Pontiac" automobiles, "Mohawk" carpets, "Pequot" sheets, "Oneida" tableware, "Big Chief" writing tablets, "Red Man" chewing tobacco, "Land O' Lakes" Butter (with its Indian princess on the label), "Eskimo" Pies, Piper "Cherokee" and "Navaho" airplanes, and "Winnebago" motor homes. Perhaps the most ironic and tragic label is that of the state-of-the-art helicopters used by the U.S. military, the "Apache" and "Comanche." The labels are ironic and tragic because it was the United States Army that finally defeated these peoples after a series of battles during the 1880s and then confined them to the restraints and poverty of reservation life, a life far different from their customary semi-nomadic hunting-and-gathering patterns.

The examples above are, indeed, a small sample of Native American references that commercial advertisers have appropriated. Local companies as well as national ones share in the practice. It is not uncommon to see signs for businesses such as Sioux Sporting Goods, Osage Hardware, or Chickasaw Moving Company wherever one travels across the country. Furthermore, this practice exists on top of the historic appropriation of tribal names for state, county, and town labels, as well as geographic sites. Among the best known are Massachusetts, Kansas, Florida, Arkansas, Illinois, Iowa, and North and South Dakota, as well as Narragansett, Ottawa, Piscataway, Pontiac, Sioux City, Roanoke, and Arapaho.

The Indian as Mascot

Sports teams, particularly, have latched onto popular images of the Indian. In fact, it seems that athletic teams have the greatest affinity for such labels. The Kansas City "Chiefs," Washington "Redskins," Atlanta "Braves," and Cleveland "Indians" are professional examples, while college teams such as the Florida State "Seminoles" or the Illinois "Fighting Illini" have reinforced the tradition. An extraordinary public exposure of such names came when the Cleveland Indians and Atlanta Braves played for baseball's 1995 World Series title. Atlanta, owing in large part to owner Ted Turner's national cable network, is famous for its fans' "tomahawk chop" and their pseudo-Indian chanting. Bumper stickers proclaim the phrase, "tomahawkin'." Fans often dress in Indian-like attire or "warpaint," and some perform mock-Indian dances.

What is the problem with this? Why do so many Native Americans object to such displays? Just as "Indian" images and names on products relegate their referents to an imaginary past, so, too, do "Indian" mascots. Mascots confine Indians into a history—in much the same way that they have been confined to reservations—and the history itself has been incorrect. Yet, activists against these stereotypes believe that their voice may help to correct the record. A social science researcher recently found that Native American activists who oppose such usages object to the misrepresentation and trivialization of important parts of their culture. One activist who was interviewed by the researcher explained the conflict by noting,

> I compose memorial songs, I compose burial songs for my grandmothers and my grandfathers, my family. And, when people [imitate] that at an athletic event, like at a baseball game, it hurts me, to see that people are making a mockery of me. We don't do that, what they're doing, this chanting. (Davis 13)

Sports fans, most people probably will agree, intend no malice toward modern-day Native Americans, nor do they see any insult in their antics. To many fans, it is all a part of the sport, all a part of the role-playing that helps them emotionally "get into the game." Even so, to many Native Americans this is game-playing with their very image and with those traditions which they hold most sacred. Dance, song, costume, and symbolic paint remain elements of deeply valued ceremonial traditions. From prayers for the sick to offerings of tokens to the earth in recognition of its gifts to humankind, they often are imbued with religious meaning.

Some commentators have asserted that Native Americans are not insulted by these usages and that some even feel honored by them. Yet, one only has to enquire casually among Native American spokespeople to learn that far too many feel dishonored. Many feel that their only place in society is as abstract images, as essentially fictional characters for the Euro-American advertising industry or athletic world. Football teams, in particular, seem to choose mascots which convey aggressive, fierce, and even belligerent meanings. Who would name a football team "the kittens," "the deer," or "the rabbits?" Aggressive or combative names pervade in the sport, sometimes borrowing from the traditions of masculine work culture: for instance, the Green Bay Packers, the Pittsburgh Steelers, the Dallas Cowboys, the San Francisco Forty-Niners. Some clearly identify their franchises with mythical warriors or heroic traditions, as with the Los Angeles Raiders, the Tampa Bay Buccaneers, and the New England Patriots. Occasional examples of more peaceful associations exist—the New Orleans Saints and the Miami Dolphins play on their cities' connections to a local tourist industry. However, most football franchises attempt to connote the concept of power in their labels. In this line of thought, the use of "Indian" terms—interpreted through the lens of popular culture—follows. American popular culture has stereotyped Native Americans as fierce, often brutal warriors. Teams which appropriate "Indian" names obviously wish the connection to this traditional image. In addition, the relationship carries over into discussion of sports events. Sports broadcasters, for instance, commonly speak of competitions between sports teams through "Indian" references—a solid defeat may be styled a "massacre" or a "scalping," while a team on a winning streak may be "on the warpath."

In their defense, supporters of Indian mascots point to the fact that sports teams exploit other ethnic group names, as well. Although it is true that the Minnesota professional football team is the Vikings and that this group is perceived as having been fierce warriors, "Vikings" no longer exist. Notre Dame may have its Fighting Irish and Boston its basketball Celtics, but these names were chosen by people of Irish descent, a choice Native Americans have not had. Also, with Notre Dame's "Irish," some obviously thought it necessary for the adjective "fighting" to be applied. No adjectives need to be applied to Indians, Chiefs, or Braves. The words carry with them their own heavy weight of ferocity.

In response, a few newspapers have attempted to treat Native American concerns with greater sensitivity. Some have dropped the use of team names which Native Americans have labeled offensive. For example, Portland's *Oregonian* and Minneapolis-St. Paul's *Star Tribune* refer to groups such as the Redskins, for instance, as "the Washington team." Paul DeMain, a former president of the Native American Journalists' Association and a member of the Lac Coute Oreille band of Ojibwa, took another tack—he began his own publication in the late 1980s. Indeed, there should be ample readership for such newspapers, as the Phoenix-based *American Indian Digest* has reported that there are approximately two million self-declared Native Americans affiliated within 318 tribes in the United States (Sunoo 108).

Native-run newspapers and those few which are beginning to omit "Indian" team names have made a start at ending the practice. Even so, they have far to go. Opposition to losing the labels is strongly expressed by many fans. When Native American protestors were removed from the University of Minnesota basketball court, spectators cheered. A United States senator from Illinois was so flooded with telephone calls against his opposition to the Chief Illiniwek mascot used by the University of Illinois that his office workers were unable to handle other duties (Davis 12). It appears that fans have not only accepted such images through their familiarity, but also have come to cherish their association with favorite teams.

The Indian as Shill

Corporate marketers long have understood the psychological power of the "lifestyle" advertisement. When they create an ad, they incorporate into it subtle messages which appeal to the emotional needs and psychological drives that motivate our behavior. In Madison Avenue adspeak, they "push our hot buttons." Advertisers, as well, have found that popular stereotypes of the Native American experience have particular appeal in lifestyle ads that feature "Indian" themes. For instance, a common message which underlies automobile ads appeals to our psychological need for independence, power, individualism, and the lost notion that there are frontiers waiting to be conquered. Thus, so many of our cars and trucks carry Indian names—the "Pontiac" or the Jeep "Cherokee," for instance—in order to create an association with an "Indian" lifestyle. We use our cars to obtain a sense of freedom, to get away, and especially in the case of trucks and jeeps, to explore the "wilderness." What better way than in an "Indian" vehicle? Similarly, the outdoor sporting goods industry also has participated in this advertising opportunity. One can find Modoc and Arapaho backpacks, Aymara boots, Mohawk canoes, and Cayuga and Iroquois sleeping bags, to name just a few. Some gear is even named after Native American personages: Red Cloud backpacks and Black Hawk and Sitting Bull sleeping bags. The problem with such images lies in the way they reinforce our popular stereotypes of the Indian. Such icons actually interfere with a more important message that Native Americans have been trying to present for decades—that the reality of the Native American experience is quite different from the Indian icons that Hollywood and Madison Avenue have, with their corporate dollars and media domination, more successfully foisted onto the public.

The use of "Indian" terms and images on products, businesses, or sports teams creates another kind of problem for Native Americans, as well. This obstacle stems from the way in which Indian icons "historicize" Native peoples. To choose perhaps the most innocuous example, a Big Chief Writing tablet may instill in the child inscribing within its pages a certain sense of awe toward the bonneted chief on the cover, but it also tends to perpetuate a sense of Native Americans as belonging to an earlier era and having no place in contemporary society. He remains forever to the child (who later becomes an adult) the wild man of the past. Current issues, such as fishing rights, rampant reservation poverty and unemployment, or alcoholism, are obscured. Because the Indian image resonates more powerfully with the public than American Indian realities, they are easily ignored or dismissed in political discourse. As one Native American activist leader commented, "Respect the living Indian, you know. Don't memorialize us. . . . [The mascots are] almost like a monument to the vanished American Indian." According to some of the activists, recognizing and understanding the lives of present-day Native Americans both challenges the stereotypes, and in some ways provides evidence of past oppression. As an interviewed leader explained, "The Indian is evidence of the crime. . . . When the real live Indian stands up, they're reminded of the fact that we're still here. . . . It shatters the myth. It shatters the myth of history" (Davis 13).

The Hollywood Indian

The myth of the Indian—the popular belief that Native Americans were wild and violent, strangely admirable for their fighting spirit and exotic nature, yet at the same time justifiably exterminable for the threat they posed to the expanding American enterprise—has been reinforced nowhere more powerfully than in Hollywood films. Classics such as *They Died with Their Boots On* (1941), *Fort Apache* (1948), and *She Wore a Yellow Ribbon* (1949), for instance, presented Native Americans as Indian savages, symbolizing a challenge to be conquered, like the frontier itself. Although the white cowboy could at times observe and respect the stoic and brave qualities of the Indian, more than likely he was placed into conflict with him, and the Indian was killed out of "necessity."

Moreover, the movie industry of the middle of the twentieth century reflects the double-edged feelings that mainstream America historically has

had about the Indian. Native Americans have been simultaneously perceived throughout our history as wild, stoic, courageous, and bloodthirsty.
Especially since the closing of the West in the late nineteenth century have
Indian images been able to take on more "positive" attributes, as fits the
"noble" stereotype. Yet, this nobility still does not make of the Native American a human being; it still does not present him beyond the level of image,
and it still does not diminish his "wildness." Even cinematic efforts to
present the Native American experience in a more favorable light, as in
Soldier Blue (1970) or *Dances with Wolves* (1990), continue the emphasis
on "Indians" as merely the passive victims of white "civilization" and
"progress."

Tomahawkin' Reconsidered

Roy Harvey Pearce's *Savagism and Civilization: A Study of the Indian and the
American Mind* points out that by the end of the first quarter of the nineteenth century, the two popular images of the Indian—noble and ignoble—
had been combined into one impression in America's literature, and that
was one of savagism. "Indian" vices and virtues both were admitted, but,
generally, "Indian" life was viewed as morally lacking, an inferiority based
upon the Native American's absence of historical progression. In short, the
Indian was out of contact with civilization (199–200). The icon provided
writers with a conventional "story of the tension between savagism and
civilization," a conflict which would finally end with the affirmation that the
conquest of "the Indian" and westward expansion were divinely sanctioned
(232).

   Now, we are left in the twentieth century with the luxury of looking back
with pleasure upon the "Indian's" "savageness" and his "nobility." To us, the
Native American is reduced to the image of a warrior of the past whom we
may use to denote the qualities of bravery and wildness that we admire and
that we may adopt when advantageous. Since it was Native Americans who
first introduced European settlers to tobacco, marketers saw them as a
logical image for "Red Man" Chewing Tobacco, a product which has been
around for many years. The bonneted Sioux Indian on the package, which
looks much like the Chief of the "Big Chief" Writing Tablet, conveys the
sense that the product is of a world of the past and the masculine. Another
tobacco product, "Natural American Spirit," an additive-free cigarette made
by the Santa Fe Natural Tobacco Company and launched in 1985, pictures
an Indian smoking a peace pipe. The background colors of either turquoise
or sand and the thunderbird icon consciously utilize images from the
cultures of Southwestern Indians (Chun 31). No longer having anything to
fear from Indians, and harboring our own regrets at living a modern-day
life with little adventure, we relish imposing our ideas of what "the Indian"
was upon our goods that seem to match the image.

Although some companies which display these logos sell products or services that apparently have nothing to do with what is historical or masculine, they still, I propose, rely upon the connotations of the Indian icon. Mutual of Omaha Insurance (with another bonneted Indian logo) and "Mohawk" Carpets are not engaged in enterprises which suggest anything of the past or of the wilderness. Yet, although the product does not outwardly relate to the stereotype, they seek to derive what are perceived by the average American customer as the "positive" associations of the stereotype. Any products bearing an Indian's face on their ads or employing an Indian name must somehow be tied with our romantic American wilderness in which the stoic and fierce Indian lived.

It is both true and important to know that Native Americans lived in the wilderness and did exist on a daily basis in intimate connection with the natural world. Of perhaps greater significance, however, is the fact that commercialization of the Indian icon trivializes or even discounts the central fact of Native American history—the white man's settling of the continent brought great tragedy to the lives of these peoples. The "lost" Indian is also "lost" because his numbers since the Europeans' coming have dropped by untold millions. War-bonneted logos are certainly not attempting to call up massacres of Native Americans, such as those that occurred at Wounded Knee or Sand Creek. Furthermore, as one Native American critic of commercialization has observed, the logos imply nothing of present-day Indians; it is as if the connection between the two is nonexistent (Davis 13). The Native American has become a myth, and the realities of history may be ignored as they have been over the centuries.

We can recognize the consequences of the commercialization of "the Indian" through analysis of a telling example. A 1994 article in the *ABA Banking Journal* glibly carried the title, "Watch Those Stereotypes, Kemosabe." The article described the opposing arguments that the Native American Council at Dartmouth College had made against the placement of the "Indian" logo of Shawmut National Corporation, of Hartford, Connecticut, on a bank they had acquired in New Hampshire. The article implicitly argued that since researchers agree that no Shawmut tribe ever existed, the logo of the institution should not offend anyone. Supporting arguments were drawn from Indian name usages by sports teams and an Arizona bank which used a drawing of a kachina doll as its logo before having been bought out by another company. Support also was drawn from the fact that the executive director of the Massachusetts Bureau of Indian Affairs, himself a Wampanoag and Mashpee, was not offended by the bank's logo (Lunt 88). Although a Shawmut tribe may have never existed, the bank's name and logo clearly brought the "Indian" image into play. In addition, although indigenous names and images do not bother many Native Americans, the issue is not so simple as proponents of this advertising and mascot habit would have it. That there are many Native Americans who are deeply offended by them is enough to raise serious questions about their propriety. Three thousand people are reported to have protested at the 1992 Super Bowl in Minneapolis-St. Paul, Minnesota, when the Washington Redskins played there, a figure which activists felt was probably half as large as the number actually present (Davis 11). Many Native Americans would like to see these labels stopped, and since they are the subjects of them, they deserve, at least, to be listened to.

Ward Churchill, a Creek-Cherokee who has published numerous books on American Indian issues, contends that the position of team fans and owners that no harm is being done is completely wrongheaded. As evidence of the fervor of supporters of Indian mascots, Churchill cites the fact that some proponents are angered at critics who want to get in the way of "good, clean fun," and that some have even gone so far as to suggest that the Native American opposition creates barriers to communication in our multicultural society (36). In his essay, "Crimes against Humanity," he satirically suggests that if Indian mascots are acceptable, we should allow, as well, mascots bearing names from all ethnic groups, including the derogatory names that have been applied to those groups (36–37). Although it is debatable that "Chiefs," as Churchill suggests, carries the same inflammatory charge as "Kikes," "Dagos," or "Spics," nevertheless, his assertion that the long heritage of Indian stereotyping has supported a program of exile and extermination is legitimate (37–39).

An interesting example of the subtle complexity which inheres in the issue of Indian icons and mascots is Ted Turner. Pioneer of the innovative Cable News Network (CNN), husband of the erstwhile Hollywood radical Jane Fonda, and owner of the Braves (whose fans, we recall, perform the "tomahawk chop"), Turner has produced numerous films offering the Native American viewpoint to a history long seen through Euro-American eyes. Moreover, Turner's films are so out of the ordinary that some critics have faulted them for overemphasizing the Native side of things, thus distorting history, and for romanticizing the societies that mainstream America has long believed to be fundamentally savage. Turner has created several television movies which run on his cable channels—among them, *Geronimo* (1993) and *The Broken Chain* (1993). His series, *The Native Americans* (1994), beautifully documents the history and the culture of American Indians from all regions of the United States. The narration, by Native Americans singly and in small groups, expresses a distinctly Native perspective. The aim of the speakers in *The Native Americans* clearly is to present to the rest of America (in the best way possible in one-hour programs) how they have seen their past and why the elements and ceremonies of their cultures carry for them the significance of their very lives. Curiously, then, even to Turner, ostensibly a supporter of the Native American perspective, the title, "Braves," and the resulting mimicking by fans does not appear derogatory. Again, this viewpoint, held by so many Americans, originates from the long-held dual image we have assigned to

Native peoples. Indians may be "reverentially" looked upon as stoic, brave, and embodying a fighting spirit. To name a team after them is to "honor" their courageous battles against an overwhelming migration of newcomers. Yet, the problem remains—"brave" or "bloodthirsty"—Indians still are perceived as a fighting people, not peaceful or peaceable by their nature.

What these stereotypes do, finally, is to lull us into believing that they truly depict the Native American. If we have an image before us of Native Americans that is identical to our past conceptions absorbed from a host of product images, popular opinion, literature, and the film industry, then we believe that the image must be correct. We have little reason to try to learn of the profound meaning to Native Americans of a ceremony celebrating the return of spring, the interconnection felt between them and other living things, or the symbolism permeating the hoop dance. Only by stepping back from these commercial images and reflecting upon them, can we see the sharp distinction that separates the two perspectives in comparing the subtle beauty which characterizes Native American concepts of totemism with the obvious shallowness of the commercial world's use of mascots.

In a legend of the Jicarrilla Apache, a raven delivers meat to four hungry children whose parents are out searching for food during the time when "the world was new" ("Secret World" 75). One of the children, a boy, experiences being changed into a puppy and the magical appearance of buffalo after he and his village journey to the mountainous home of the ravens. Once a boy again, his descent from there into a lush land filled with buffalo leads to the arrival of herds in the "Land of People" and, subsequently, ample food for humankind ("Secret World" 79). The legend contains elements sacred to these people and to other Native Americans: the white buffalo, the eagle feather, the four directions, the ceremonial pipe, the earth, the sky, and all creatures. Sacrifice—and thankfulness—are key to the tale, and through its telling we humans will not forget what we owe to the earth and to its creatures who feed us.

Such legend is typical of American Indians. Their stories reveal a people cognizant of the interconnectedness of life, the value of community, and the results of folly. So, apart from the negative connotations and historicizing of Native Americans, stereotyping leaves us ignorant of their culture and even unaware that we are so ignorant. As with our own Euro-American history (and past culture), we can only hope to know part, but our indifference to Native American reality and our virtual exclusion of the truth about it through history is shameful. Indian mascots and Indian labels on products or companies do not help us to understand one another, but quite the opposite. If we wish to include Native Americans in our society and our history, we should dispense with the easy picture. We should make the effort to understand the needs of the modern-day Native Americans among us, as we also try to understand a world view far richer and far more complex than we ever have been able to admit.

Works Cited

The Broken Chain. Dir. Lamont Johnson. Turner Pictures, 1993.

Chun, Rene. "New Cigarette, but Same Old Problem." *New York Times* 3 July 1994, late ed., sec. 1: 31.

Churchill, Ward. "Crimes against Humanity." *Cultural Survival Quarterly* 17.4 (1994): 36–9.

Dances with Wolves. Dir. Kevin Costner. Perf. Kevin Costner, Mary McDonnell, and Graham Greene. Orion, 1990.

Davis, Laurel R. "Protest against the Use of Native American Mascots: A Challenge to Traditional American Identity." *Journal of Sport & Social Issues* 17.1 (1993): 9–22.

Fort Apache. Dir. John Ford. Perf. John Wayne, Henry Fonda, and Shirley Temple. RKO, 1948.

Geronimo. Dir. Roger Young. Turner Pictures, 1993.

Lunt, Penny. "Watch Those Stereotypes, Kemosabe." *ABA Banking Journal* Oct. 1994: 88.

The Native Americans. TBS Productions, 1994.

Pearce, Roy Harvey. *Savagism and Civilization: A Study of the Indian and the American Mind*. Berkeley: U of California P, 1988.

"The Secret World of the Ravens." *Earth Magic, Sky Magic: North American Indian Tales*. Ed. Rosalind Kerven. Cambridge: Cambridge UP, 1991. 75–79.

She Wore a Yellow Ribbon. Dir. John Ford. Perf. John Wayne and Joanne Dru. RKO, 1949.

Soldier Blue. Dir. Ralph Nelson. Perf. Candice Bergen and Peter Strauss. Embassy, 1970.

Sunoo, Brenda Paik. "Native American Journalists Oppose Media Stereotypes." *Personnel Journal* Nov. 1994: 108.

They Died with Their Boots On. Dir. Raoul Walsh. Perf. Errol Flynn and Olivia de Haviland. Warner, 1941.

18

Reframing the Hollywood Indian: A Feminist Re-reading of *Powwow Highway* and *Thunderheart*

Ellen L. Arnold

The Hollywood Western: A Tradition of Stereotypes

The "Indian" has been a staple of the Western movie since its inception with the silent newsreels of Buffalo Bill's Wild West Show in 1898. The Hollywood Western has been a flawed genre, however, largely because its treatment of Native Americans as stereotyped "Indians" has perpetuated long-held misconceptions and prejudices in American culture. Historian Robert Berkhofer describes these cultural stereotypes in his excellent study, *The White Man's Indian* (1978). Berkhofer observes that since Europeans first arrived in the "New World," two contradictory images have predominated in mainstream thought: on the one hand, the bloodthirsty savage, vengeful and sadistic, an obstacle to civilization and progress; on the other, the noble savage, an Edenic innocent and friend to White settlers. The history of the representation of Indians in the popular imagination is an interplay of these two stereotypes. However, the image of the bloodthirsty savage predominated until the end of the nineteenth century, primarily as justification for Euro-American expansion in the name of Manifest Destiny—the belief in the divine right of the "civilized" to tame the wilderness and subdue or destroy its "primitive" inhabitants. Gretchen Bataille and Charles Silet underscore this public use of a stereotyped Indian in the introduction to their 1985 bibliography of Native Americans in film, observing, "The very experience of the westward movement, the very rationale for the subjugation of the continent depended on [the] adversary relationship between whites and Indians" (xxii). Ironically, only when Whites assumed that Indians were thoroughly defeated and assimilating to mainstream America (hence the term "vanishing American" or "vanishing Indian") did they deem Native Americans worthy of preservation and closer attention.[1]

It was not until the 1950s that some Westerns, such as Delmer Daves's *Broken Arrow* (1950) or Robert Aldrich's *Apache* (1954), began to portray

Indians sympathetically, as individuals with specific tribal affiliations, rather than as generic "Red men."[2] To a large extent, Hollywood responded to the dramatic events of the 1950s and 1960s, when the Black civil rights movement and its offshoots, the Women's Liberation and Red Power movements, influenced changes in social attitudes toward minorities. Only then did the "good Indian" prevail and the noble savage, often in his new guise as a wise environmentalist, come into his own. However, even these portrayals played on traditional stereotypes. Berkhofer makes the point that the image of the Indian has been used always as a foil against which Euro-American culture could be defined, justified, or critiqued. Thus, he maintains, this new "countercultural" use of the Indian to reflect the fragmentation, alienation, and destructiveness of modern industrial society does "not equal a realistic portrayal but merely a reversal of judgment upon the standard stereotype" (Berkhofer 104). Such a "countercultural" use can be illustrated by John Ford's *The Searchers*. Released in 1956, in the wake of the *Brown v. Board of Education* decision to desegregate public schools, *The Searchers* displaced conflicts between Blacks and Whites in the 1950s onto conflicts with Indians in the late 1800s in order to comment on contemporary issues of racism and miscegenation (see, e.g., Henderson). This trend continued into the 1970s, when a number of "pro-Indian" films appeared. *Soldier Blue* (1970), *Little Big Man* (1970), and *Ulzana's Raid* (1972) reflected the "national soul searching" occasioned by the Vietnam War (Bataille and Silet, *Image* xxv; *Pretend* passim).

The wave of revisionist Indian films released in the early 1990s, including *Dances with Wolves* (1990), *Black Robe* (1991), and *Geronimo* (1993), has been widely praised for historical accuracy and "authenticity." Although these films portray Indians as individuals with feelings and motives within the contexts of their specific tribal cultures, they are not about Native Americans. They center on White men, in what Native American Ward Churchill describes as the "Great White Hunter theme" (*Fantasies* 245). Referring to *Dances with Wolves* as "Lawrence of South Dakota," Churchill points out that while Native American culture is presented respectfully in this film (like that of the Bedouins in *Lawrence of Arabia*), it still provides the backdrop for the development of the White hero, and is (like Bedouin culture) portrayed tragically as beautiful, but vanishing. Such films not only continue to define Native Americans in terms of interactions with Euro-Americans and Euro-American values, but also by relegating those interactions to the past (as most Westerns do), they also imply that "real" Indians are extinct (Churchill, *Fantasies* 232–39).

Maryann Oshana points to another kind of problem with these films. "The emphasis in Westerns," she writes, "has been on the glorification of male roles—both white and Native; the Native American woman has remained almost invisible" (50). Trapped in what Rayna Green terms the

"Pocahontas Perplex,"[3] she has been limited to the roles of the "noble Princess"—exotic and beautiful friend to the White man—or "savage squaw" —drudge or beast of burden, often "motivated by lust" (702–703). Oshana surveys Westerns through 1981 to demonstrate that, in spite of the more sympathetic portrayals accorded Native men since the 1950s, "the woman's image has remained consistently backward and static. . . . Women are most often portrayed as victims, convenient objects for men to rape, murder, avenge or ridicule" (48). More recent films offer little improvement: *Dances with Wolves* features a White woman captive, with Native American women as background; *Geronimo* has no female roles at all; *Black Robe* provides the epitome of the "savage squaw"—a young Indian woman who appears in four graphic sex scenes with a young White translator who instructs her in the "missionary position" as a substitute for the "dog style" she practices (see Churchill's analysis, *Indians* 115–38). Such images misrepresent the powerful social roles that Native American women historically played in their cultures. Not only were Native American cultures frequently matrilineal and matrilocal,[4] but women in these cultures often served as warriors, political and religious leaders, healers and shamans. These stereotypes, by influencing public perceptions, also interfere with the recognition of contemporary Native American women's vital roles as cultural mediators, political activists, and leaders of resistance (see Jaimes and Halsey). Even *Black Robe*, praised for its exceptional historicism, depicts captives brutally slaughtered by young Mohawk males, in a culture in which elder women traditionally decided the fate of captives, who were most often adopted (Churchill, *Indians* 126).

Powwow Highway and *Thunderheart*: New Directions or Familiar Stereotypes?

In the context of this long history of inaccurate and superficial stereotyping, the release of two mainstream movies offers hope of a breakthrough in the representation of Native Americans in film. Jonathan Wacks's *Powwow Highway* (1988) and Michael Apted's *Thunderheart* (1992) focus on Native American characters in contemporary contexts and include significant roles for women. On the surface, the two movies have much in common. Both are set during the unrest of the 1970s. *Thunderheart* is based on events following the historical 1975 "firefight" on the Oglala Sioux Reservation of Pine Ridge, South Dakota, in which two FBI agents and one Native American were killed. *Powwow Highway*, centered on the nearby Northern Cheyenne Dull Knife Reservation in Montana, takes place shortly after these events, and makes reference to them and to the 1973 occupation of Wounded Knee by American Indian Movement (AIM) activists that preceded them.[5] Both films make genuine attempts to raise the consciousness of mainstream audiences about historical and contemporary issues affecting Native Americans. They are filmed partly on location and pan ramshackle reservation housing, rusting hulks of old cars and trucks, dirty children and limping dogs, and general devastating poverty. Both films make the political point of referring to the reservations as "Third World."

In addition, *Powwow Highway* and *Thunderheart* both are framed by issues of land use and resource appropriation by the federal government and corporate interests. They highlight difficult internal political issues, as well— splits between Native "progressives," who wish to cooperate with and bene- fit from White bureaucracy and capitalism, and "traditionals," who wish to preserve a distinctively Native American way of life and some independence. Both films are highly sympathetic to the activism of AIM. Yet, both films self-consciously place themselves within the context of the conventional Hollywood Western, utilizing the techniques and narrative formats typical of the genre. They feature panoramic shots of magnificent desolate landscapes reminiscent of classics such as Ford's *The Searchers* (though they include eagle cries on the soundtrack to signify the Indian point-of-view). They are structured by the traditional hero-villain format and action/ adventure dynamics of the Western, complete with dramatic chase scenes— embodying what Andre Bazin calls the Western's characteristic theme, the "knight errant in search of his grail" (153). Each also contains a variant of the revenge motif that Alan Lovell pronounces elemental to classical Western form: *Powwow Highway's* twinned heroes take direct revenge on the White man, while in *Thunderheart* "the desire for revenge is translated into . . . the attempt to establish law and order" (Lovell 169). Ultimately, this traditional male quest story line obscures the political and social issues raised by the two films, undermining their subversive potential. Subscription to the Hollywood formula undercuts their more realistic view of the Native American experience and reaffirms the status quo of the dominant culture, a status quo which includes the treatment of women as objects of exchange or as obstacles to masculine bonding, adventure, and power.

The screenplay for *Powwow Highway* was adapted with reasonable faithfulness from former AIM member David Seals's 1979 novel, *The Powwow Highway*. In the film, hot-headed radical Buddy Red Bow (played by non-Native actor A Martinez) and Philbert Bono, a gentle, naive bear of a man in search of medicine power and a traditional identity (played with great charm by Native American Gary Farmer), join forces to rescue Buddy's sister, Bonnie, from the Santa Fe city jail. Bonnie has been imprisoned through the collusion of government agents, corporate mining interests, and "apple" Indians (Red on the outside, White on the inside) in order to lure Buddy away from the reservation during a crucial tribal vote on mining rights. Buddy opposes the "progressive" faction that wishes to cooperate with the government-backed Overdyne Corporation's exploitation of reservation resources. In Philbert's "war pony," a rattletrap Buick named Protector, the two men make a journey that roughly covers the traditional homeland of the Cheyenne (Toman and Gerster 37). In the process Philbert acquires courage, visions, medicine tokens, and the new name that make him a warrior. Meanwhile, Buddy's rage becomes tempered with a new sensitivity and a growing respect for the traditional ways of his people. Toman and Gerster observe that "the film dismisses stereotypes, retells the cowboy-Indian conflict from a Native American perspective, and demonstrates the dual importance of reclaiming a traditional tribal identity and continuing the political struggle for justice" (30). Furthermore, it does so with great good humor and a cheer-inspiring ending, as the heroes escape to the safety of a local reservation after a dramatic jail-break and police chase. Not only have they rescued Bonnie and her children, but also they have acquired a White "captive"—Bonnie's friend, Rabbit—in another small act of revenge against the White man. In addition, Philbert manages to steal enough money from the police station vault to replace the tribal funds Buddy "borrowed" to make Bonnie's bail (but spent on sound equipment) and the money Rabbit actually put up for bail. Thus, the film evokes what Langen and Shanley term a divided reaction: "enjoying the film and disapproving of it" (23).

On one level, *Powwow Highway* can be read as an appropriation of the typical Western format to serve Indian purposes. In fact, Toman and Gerster point out, the film is a reversal of *The Searchers* (1956), in which the "red men" are the heroes and use the White man's methods and machines to rescue the captured "red princess"—a feat accomplished when Philbert and Protector pull the bars out of the jail wall after Philbert observes a similar escape in a TV Western. Thus, the heroes "escape one specific instance of the political imprisonment, the forced removal from one part of the country to another, and the economic hardship that reflects the historical Native American experience" (Toman and Gerster 36). Like Debbie in *The Searchers*, Bonnie has also "gone over" to the enemy, having left the reservation ten years earlier to live in the White world. Her children by a White father know almost nothing about their Native heritage. Bonnie—paired with Philbert—is returned to "her people," defying the forced assimilation of Native people historically.

In their essay discussing the uses of *Powwow Highway* in a course on ethnic film and literature, Toman and Gerster point out that the film revises standard stereotypes of the hostile savage (Buddy) and the noble savage (Philbert). They show that the film interprets Buddy's "hostility" as the result of mistreatment by the White world. I would add that the film further alters these conventions by blending the characteristics of the two stereotypes together as Buddy and Philbert develop and bond. However, Toman and Gerster fail to elaborate the parallel role reversal of Bonnie and Rabbit, and the subversion of the stereotypes of the "virginal White woman" and her counterpart, the "lusty squaw," conventional to many Westerns. Their essay follows the film in focusing solely on the development of the male characters, supporting the film's use of women as "props" by failing to note it.

Toman and Gerster provide an important ethnic critique of *Powwow Highway*, but like many scholars who have made similar analyses of the misrepresentation of Native Americans in film, they fall short of a full appraisal of the Native American experience by neglecting issues of gender. A more balanced critique of the film, integrating the complex issues of ethnicity and gender, has been offered by Rodney Simard, who objects to the film's "anti-feminism" and "anti-Indian portrayal of women" (21). Simard comments on Native American Joanelle Nadine Romero's portrayal of Bonnie as "madonna-like" (20). She is shown consistently either in the company of her two children, Jane and Sky, or completely passive, behind bars or with her rescuers. The close-ups of her face, framed in long black braids and a halo of light, as she visits with her children and Rabbit in the jail, emphasize her quiet innocence and maternal qualities. The contrast with the bleached-blonde Texas bombshell, introduced to the viewer in a classic "butt shot" as she wiggles up the jail steps in tight jeans, completes the "red virgin"/"white whore" reversal. However, both women remain defined totally in terms of their relationships with men.

The other women in *Powwow Highway* also fail to escape male-defined stereotypes. In case the viewer missed the "rescue of the princess" motif, it is stated overtly as Bonnie's daughter, Jane, leads her brother in a gutsy escape from the social services center where they are held. As they climb out of the window, other children watch a television cartoon from which a female voice calls "Save me!" and a male voice responds, "Take it easy honey, you're okay. We'll protect you. Take care of the girl, Rick, while we hold him off." This brief moment of potential subversion, as Jane defies this message, never bears fruit. Nor does the hopeful declaration by a confident Rabbit to the incarcerated Bonnie, "Don't worry, I'll think of something!" Almost immediately, she succumbs to Buddy's macho display in his bar scene attack on Sandy Youngblood, the "apple" Indian who works for the mining company. "I know what I want," she says passionately to Buddy, and signs on as his dutiful helpmate. In addition, all the women in the film—from Buddy's Aunt Harriett, who cracks bitter jokes about Philbert's quest, to Jane, who criticizes all that "warrior stuff" and informs Philbert his "pony's a nag," to the vicious White prison guard who keeps the rescuers from Bonnie on Christmas Eve—are obstacles to male dreams and adventures. Nor is there any indication that Bonnie or Jane is recovering any kind of Native identity, as are Buddy, Philbert, and Sky. By implication, "real Indians" are male and warriors. The only exception is the brief appearance of the traditional Indian matriarch in Santa Fe Plaza who gives

Jane and Sky money for a phone call and admonishes them to "know their ancestors."

Powwow Highway ends with an exciting and funny chase scene and the triumphant escape of the heroes and their newly acquired families. The score has been evened, and the viewer is left with a feeling of satisfaction and closure. In the meantime, however, all the real issues the film raises have been dropped. What happened to the mining deal at Lame Deer and the water poisoned by uranium mining at Pine Ridge? What happened to the violent regime of Bull Miller (the real Dick Wilson) and his GOON Squad at Pine Ridge, from whom Buddy's friends, Wolf Tooth and Imogene, were fleeing when they joined the heroes on their journey? What about all that poverty and bitterness, expressed so disquietingly by Buddy's desire for consumer goods and his destruction of the Radio Shack store following the racial slurs of employees and his perception of having been "ripped off"? The very charm and good humor that make this movie so much fun to watch are potentially its most dangerous elements. Viewers from the dominant majority can feel uplifted by their new awareness of Indian issues and exonerated of their guilt through the "success" of the heroes, who, not incidentally, must now "vanish" back to the reservation, never to leave again on pain of arrest. For Native American audiences, the film carries the disturbing message that political activism and resistance are less effective (and certainly less fun) than lawless revenge. And finally, by enfolding the Indian quest within familiar Euro-American narratives— cowboys versus Indians, knights to the rescue of the captured princess— *Powwow Highway* implies that Indians pose no threat to Euro-American safety, resources, or self-images; after all, they're "just like us"—cowboys, consumers, and patriarchal sexists at heart.

Thunderheart makes a more self-consciously serious attempt than *Powwow Highway* to foreground political issues. In an unusual move, director Michael Apted released at the same time as the mainstream film a companion documentary, *Incident at Oglala*, funded and narrated by activist actor Robert Redford. The two films were frequently reviewed together, stimulating a dialogue between and around them, and creating a wider audience for both. *Thunderheart* imaginatively adapts events surrounding the 1975 "firefight" incident at Pine Ridge, following which AIM leader Leonard Peltier ("Jimmy Looks Twice" in the movie) was arrested for the murder of two FBI agents (see note 5). AIM (renamed ARM—the Aboriginal Rights Movement—in the film) had been invited to the reservation by traditional Sioux to protest the "reign of terror" of tribal president Dick Wilson ("Dick Milton" in the fictional version) and his GOON Squad. While the documentary presents the various versions of events straightforwardly in a series of interviews, the popular film imbeds the events in the mythic male quest/ adventure narrative formula of the conventional Hollywood Western. To solve one of the GOON Squad murders, mixed-blood FBI agent Ray Levoi (Val Kilmer, who is of Native descent) is sent to Pine Ridge on the assumption that, as an "Indian," he will fare better with the locals. The veteran agent with whom he is assigned to work, Frank Coutelle (played by Sam Shepherd), turns out to be in cahoots with the bad guys, who hope to convict ARM leader "Looks Twice" for murder. By breaking up the ARM organization, they intend to clear the way to exploit uranium stores secretly discovered on the reservation. In the process of solving the crime, Levoi comes to terms with his resentment of his deceased, alcoholic half-Sioux father, embraces his Indian heritage, and saves "his people."

Like Martin in *The Searchers*, Levoi is a mixed-blood who has assimilated to White culture, and he assumes the role of both White and Native, depending on the situation. Partner Coutelle tells him he looks like Sal Mineo, another non-Indian actor favored for Indian roles in decades past, emphasizing the fact that a White man is playing at being Native, both in the movie and within the story itself. The film's opening scenes highlight Levoi's "foreignness," contrasting his drive through busy Washington, DC, in his red convertible, dressed impeccably in starched shirt and Raybans, with his introduction to the "Third World" of the Reservation. As he learns more about the situation there and about "his people," he gradually sheds the trappings of "civilization," losing his Raybans and Rolex to the crafty medicine man, Sam Reaches (played memorably by Native American Ted Thin Elk). He replaces his suit and Italian shoes with jeans and boots, and his company car first with an old pickup and finally with a rattletrap Buick, complete with three-legged dog. (Clearly, as both *Powwow Highway* and *Thunderheart* demonstrate, jeans and boots, rattletraps, and scruffy dogs are signs of Indianness.)

In fact, Levoi, who is one-quarter Sioux, all too easily becomes Indian. It is revealed to him in visions and Grandpa Reaches's prophecies that the blood of a powerful warrior named Thunderheart, slaughtered in the original 1890 Wounded Knee massacre, runs in his veins. Thus, it is "blood" (not community membership and life experience) that provides his Native identity, a problematically racial definition of Indianness. Yet, it is Levoi's Whiteness, his experience and role in the outside world, that enables him to save the day for the traditionals. As Ward Churchill puts it, this "cross between Mike Hammer and Tonto . . . jumps in to save his backwards reservation brethren" (Fantasies 247). To complete the image, after befriending doomed activist Maggie Eagle Bear (Sheila Tousey), bonding with tribal officer Walter Crow Horse (Graham Greene), evading the bad guys in another dramatic car chase, and receiving the sacred medicine pipe of his people, Levoi rides away "into the sunset."

It is a major problem of the film that Levoi assumes an essential Native identity with so little effort. It is difficult to resist comparing the movie's events to a "Men's Movement Weekend," like those Ward Churchill satirizes in *Indians Are Us?* Levoi comes to the reservation for a few days, has some visions, acquires a totem animal/spirit guide (the three-legged dog that accompanies him when he leaves), becomes a pipe-carrier for his tribe, and having discovered the "wild man within," returns to civilization. However, he leaves behind the same set of troubling questions that *Powwow Highway* left unanswered: What happened to Looks Twice/Peltier? To Dick Milton/Wilson? What about the uranium deal? The radiation-contaminated water?

Within this narrative there does occur an event probably unique in film history: a portrait of a Native American woman, played by a Native American actress, who is knowledgeable, intelligent, confident, assertive, and powerful, and who, at least for a moment, gives voice to the many Native American women who act as tribal leaders and mediators. When Levoi, seeking information about the shooting that occurred nearby, first approaches Maggie Eagle Bear outside her home, he is aggressive and superior. Unimpressed, Maggie informs him of her work with the media regarding tribal burial rights, her educational background, and, in no uncertain terms, her legal rights. She steps inside her house and shuts the door in Levoi's face, an act that produced audience cheers in the theater in which I first saw the film. Unfortunately, this small breakthrough is soon undermined, contained by and subjected to the demands of the male quest story line. Levoi returns, having removed his coat and tie and adopted a more ingratiating attitude. In a highly symbolic move, he gains entry to Maggie's house and penetrates her privacy—and ultimately her autonomy.

Using information he has acquired from FBI records, Levoi retells Maggie's own life story to her, adding to it the gratuitous mention of her rape. In doing so, he appropriates her story and disempowers her; her vulnerability is written on her face in this moment, and is actualized immediately. Milton's GOONs attack, Maggie's son is shot, and hysterical and helpless, she begs for Levoi's help to get the boy to the hospital. After this point, the story takes a Pocahontas twist; Maggie befriends the still-White Levoi, instructs him in Indian ways, and helps him to heal the wounds of his memory of his drunken father and the rift in his own identity. She also provides, against the will of her people, the final clue that allows Levoi, in his role as FBI agent, to solve the crime.

Maggie's identity is stereotyped in another way—through her association with nature. Her first scenes of exchange with Levoi, while she is still self-defining and independent, are in close-up, against the background of her own house. In the scene following the drive-by shooting, Maggie meets Levoi by the river, dwarfed against its wide sweep. In her efforts to save the river from contamination, she acts as its guardian, and she speaks to Levoi of the "power of the river, the power of rain." She departs this scene for "The Source," a tribal sacred place which also proves to be the site of the future uranium mine. In her death (presumably she is killed by Milton's men for this discovery), she literally "returns to the source," to the earth. Levoi and Crow Horse find her body face down, covered with dirt. The peculiar blue light in which this moonlit scene is filmed blends her even more strikingly into her surroundings. As Levoi turns her over, her open eyes reflect the light of the moon, and she disappears into the landscape as he closes her eyes and the camera moves up and away, leaving the two men alone in the scene. As Rayna Green points out in her analysis of Pocahontas narratives, often the "good Indian woman" must "suffer death" (704) as a sacrifice to the White man and to the advance of civilization. Not incidentally, Maggie's death, precluding the possibility of a romance with Levoi, also removes her as an obstacle to the bonding of the two lawmen. From the beginning, Levoi's relationship to the witty and handsome tribal policeman has been laden with tension. Gradually, as Levoi's visions and experiences begin to frighten him and alter his attitude, Crow Horse becomes his confidant and guide, and together they confront the evildoers in a climactic show of bravado. The movie's final scene is their touching farewell. Once again, woman has played the foil to male development.

Viewing *Thunderheart* against *Incident at Oglala* is absolutely chilling, as the stories unfold of the real women on whom Maggie's character is based. In the documentary, Deborah White Plume calmly describes the drive-by shooting in which her son was shot, as well as her mother and herself; several other women repeat similar stories. AIM member John Trudell (who played Jimmy Looks Twice in *Thunderheart*, and whose wife, three children, and mother-in-law were killed in a house fire after Trudell made an anti-FBI speech), introduces the story of Anna Mae Aquash, the AIM activist on whom Maggie is also modeled. An FBI spokesman matter-of-factly reports how, after Aquash's body was found in 1976, shot in the head, and dumped in a ravine, the FBI cut off her hands and sent them to Washington for identification. Later in the documentary, Myrtle Poor Bear recounts how she was threatened by the FBI with Aquash's story and pictures of her hands, to induce her to make a false affidavit against Leonard Peltier. Disturbingly, the documentary parallels *Thunderheart* in its use of women; they are portrayed solely as victims or in relationship to male AIM members. No context is provided even for Aquash's murder, no history of her life or her resistance activities; her dead body and her severed hands become mere icons of martyrdom. But at least *Incident at Oglala* presents different viewpoints and draws no hard and fast conclusions; it leaves viewers frustrated and confused, desiring to know more, as opposed to the sense of triumph and artificial closure that allow us to walk away from *Thunderheart* feeling satisfied that the "good guys" won.

Both *Powwow Highway* and *Thunderheart* can be interpreted as attempts to reassert masculine values and power in the face of social and political challenges, much as Susan Jeffords's book, *The Remasculinization of America*, interprets the wave of *Rambo*-style movies that followed the failure of the

Vietnam War. This reassertion of masculinity requires the reinscription of women as objects—as either passive and ineffectual, or subject to punishment for the transgressions of self-definition and rebellion. These two movies reflect also what literary critic bell hooks identifies as "imperialist nostalgia"—defined by anthropologist Renato Rosaldo as a "yearning for what one has destroyed" (hooks 25)—by projecting this effort onto the "Indian Other." Often taking the form of commodification, this desire for and consumption of the Other as an image or product assuages both "the guilt of the past" (25) and feelings of loss, at the same time that it reaffirms the power and privilege of the dominant culture. In the case of Native America, this reaffirmation is also colonialist, since, as Ward Churchill, Jimmie Durham, and many other Indian spokespersons have pointed out, Native Americans are still quite literally colonized within their own country. Thus, even sincere attempts to challenge racism and oppression are swallowed up by the process of commodification, in this case the demands of the entertainment industry to appeal to large audiences for profit. As Jimmie Durham puts it, "'Indian suffering' is part of the entertainment" (435). By eliciting viewers' sympathy and outrage over the plight of the Indian and then allowing their catharsis, these movies could be said to enable the continuation of the very oppressions they attempt to expose and oppose.[6]

Notes

1 There is great variation in the usage of the terms "Indian" and "Native American." For the purpose of this essay, I have attempted as much as possible to follow Berkhofer's example, using Indian to refer to the representation or general construct, and Native American to refer to real persons. Like Berkhofer, I have chosen to capitalize the term White; I have done so to call attention to the fact (which Berkhofer does not) that the category "White" is also an artificial construction.

2 There were some earlier exceptions; Larry Langman, in *The Guide to Silent Westerns*, maintains that some early Westerns painted sympathetic portraits of the Indian, citing the short film, *The Justice of the Redskin* (1908) and D. W. Griffith's *The Indian Runner's Romance* (1909). Such exceptions carried at least into Maurice Tourneur's *The Last of the Mohicans* (1920), yet these portrayals remained stylized.

   The Western's stereotypical "Red man" tended to be a warrior of the high Plains, an expert horseman and buffalo hunter whose speech, dress, and traditions represented an amalgam of various tribal cultures and outright invention (see, for example, Churchill, "Categories of Stereotyping of American Indians in Film," in *Fantasies of the Master Race*). This invented Indian obscures the vast diversity of pre-contact Native America, which numbered some 2,000 separate cultural groups speaking 500 mutually unintelligible languages. There remain approximately 500 federally recognized tribes in the U.S. and 200 spoken languages (see essays in Jaimes for more details).

3 The story of Pocahontas, daughter of the powerful chief Powhatan—who saved Englishman John Smith from execution by her father, mediated between her tribe and the English colonists, and later married another Englishman—has been variously interpreted in literature, drama, song, and historical account from both of these perspectives. The continuing power of this story is illustrated by the release of a widely popular animated version, *Pocahontas*, by Walt Disney Studios in 1995.

4 In the majority of pre-contact tribes, descent was traced through the mother (matrilineality) and the man joined the family of the woman he married (matrilocality). Property and children were also often controlled by women (see Green, "Review"; Jaimes and Halsey).

5 AIM, the American Indian Movement, is an Indian rights group formed in 1968 to pursue treaty rights, land recovery, and national sovereignty. AIM's intervention helped achieve justice for Raymond Yellow Thunder, killed by two White men in Nebraska in 1972, and AIM was called in to protest the corrupt Pine Ridge Tribal Government under the control of Dick Wilson. Wilson, with the backing of the federal government, armed his supporters (the GOON Squad—Guardians of the Oglala Nation) and harassed (and allegedly killed many) AIM leaders and supporters. Also at issue was a large tract of uranium-rich sacred reservation land that the U.S. Government was in the process of annexing. These events led to the 1972 AIM occupation of Wounded Knee, the site of the 1890 massacre of 350 unarmed Sioux men, women, and children by the U.S. Army.

   The siege of Wounded Knee II by federal armed forces and GOON Squad members lasted 71 days, and has been described as "the largest armed conflict in the U.S. since the Civil War" (Toman and Gerster 30). After AIM's surrender, no action was taken against Wilson, and more than 60 people were murdered at Pine Ridge over the next three years. (Most of these murders remain unsolved.) In 1975, Leonard Peltier led a group of AIM members back to Pine Ridge to try to protect their supporters. In a "firefight" with this group, thought to have been a botched attempt by the government to wipe out AIM, two FBI agents and one Native American were killed. Peltier was convicted of the murders of the FBI agents and remains in prison, in spite of numerous appeals and mounting evidence that he could not be guilty. Afterwards, Wilson was defeated for re-election, AIM activity died down, and in 1976 the piece of land in question (one-eighth of the Pine Ridge Reservation) was transferred to the Department of the Interior.

For a more detailed history of AIM activism and the Wounded Knee occupation and its aftermath, see, for example: Churchill, *Indians* (173–85, 197-205); Jaimes (87–122, 139–88, 291–310); and Matthiessen's massively detailed account, *In the Spirit of Crazy Horse*.

6 I would like to express my gratitude to friend and colleague Janet McAdams for the many hours of discussion that contributed to the ideas in this essay.

Works Cited

Apache. Dir. Robert Aldrich. Perf. Burt Lancaster, Jean Peters, and Charles Bronson. United Artists, 1954.

Bataille, Gretchen M., and Charles L. P. Silet. *Images of American Indians on Film: An Annotated Bibliography*. New York: Garland, 1985.

——. *The Pretend Indians: Images of Native Americans in the Movies*. Ames: Iowa State UP, 1980.

Bazin, Andre. "The Evolution of the Western." *Movies and Methods*. Ed. Bill Nichols. Vol. 2. Berkeley: U of California P, 1985. 150–57. 2 vols.

Berkhofer, Robert F., Jr. *The White Man's Indian: Images of the American Indian from Columbus to the Present*. New York: Knopf, 1978.

Black Robe. Dir. Bruce Beresford. Perf. Lothaire Bluteau, Aden Young, and Sandrine Holt. Alliance, 1991.

Broken Arrow. Dir. Delmer Daves. Perf. James Stewart, Jeff Chandler, and Debra Paget. Fox, 1950.

Brown v. Board of Ed. 75 SCt 753. US Sup. Ct. 1954.

Churchill, Ward. *Fantasies of the Master Race: Literature, Cinema and the Colonization of American Indians*. Monroe, ME: Common Courage, 1992.

——. *Indians Are Us? Culture and Genocide in Native North America*. Monroe, ME: Common Courage, 1994.

——. *Struggle for the Land: Indigenous Resistance to Genocide, Ecocide and Expropriation in Contemporary North America*. Monroe, ME: Common Courage, 1993.

Dances with Wolves. Dir. Kevin Costner. Perf. Kevin Costner, Mary McDonnell, and Graham Greene. Orion, 1990.

Durham, Jimmie. "Cowboys and . . . Notes on Art, Literature, and American Indians in the Modern American Mind." *The State of Native America: Genocide, Colonization, and Resistance*. Ed. M. Annette Jaimes. Boston: South End, 1992. 423–38.

Geronimo: An American Legend. Dir. Walter Hill. Perf. Jason Patric, Robert Duvall, Gene Hackman, and Wes Studi. Columbia, 1993.

Green, Rayna. "The Pocahontas Perplex: The Image of Indian Women in American Cultures." *Massachusetts Review* 16.4 (1975): 698–714.

————. "Review Essay: Native American Women." *Signs* 6.2 (1980): 248–67.

Henderson, Brian. "The Searchers: An American Dilemma." *Movies and Methods*. Ed. Bill Nichols. Vol. 2. Berkeley: U of California P, 1985. 429–49. 2 vols.

hooks, bell. *Black Looks: Race and Representation*. Boston: South End, 1992.

Incident at Oglala. Dir. Michael Apted. Narr. Robert Redford. Perf. Leonard Peltier and John Trudell. Miramax, 1992.

The Indian Runner's Romance. Dir. D. W. Griffith. 1909.

Jaimes, M. Annette, ed. *The State of Native America: Genocide, Colonization, and Resistance*. Boston: South End, 1992.

————, and Theresa Halsey. "American Indian Women: At the Center of Indigenous Resistance in Contemporary North America." *The State of Native America: Genocide, Colonization, and Resistance*. Ed. M. Annette Jaimes. Boston: South End, 1992. 311–44.

Jeffords, Susan. *The Remasculinization of America: Gender and the Vietnam War*. Bloomington: Indiana UP, 1989.

The Justice of the Redskin. Pathé Frères. 1908.

Langen, Toby, and Kathryn Shanley. "Culture Isn't Buckskin Shoes: A Conversation around *Powwow Highway*." *Studies in American Indian Literatures* 3.3 (Fall 1991): 23–29.

Langman, Larry. *A Guide to Silent Westerns*. Westport, CT: Greenwood, 1992.

The Last of the Mohicans. Dir. Maurice Tourneur. Perf. Theodore Lorch and Harry Lorrain. 1920.

Lawrence of Arabia. Dir. David Lean. Perf. Alec Guiness, Anthony Quinn, and Peter O'Toole. Columbia, 1963.

Little Big Man. Dir. Arthur Penn. Perf. Dustin Hoffman, Faye Dunaway, Martin Balsam, and Chief Dan George. National General, 1970.

Lovell, Alan. "The Western." *Movies and Methods*. Ed. Bill Nichols. Vol. 2. Berkeley: U of California P, 1985. 164–75. 2 vols.

Matthiessen, Peter. *In the Spirit of Crazy Horse*. New York: Penguin, 1991.

Oshana, Maryann. "Native American Women in Westerns: Reality and Myth." *Frontiers* 6.3 (1982): 46–50.

Pocahontas. Art Dir. Michael Giaimo. Voices Irene Bedard and Mel Gibson. Disney, 1995.

Powwow Highway. Dir. Jonathan Wacks. Perf. A Martinez and Gary Farmer. Hand-Made Films, 1988.

Seals, David. *The Powwow Highway*. 1979. New York: Plume, 1990.

The Searchers. Dir. John Ford. Perf. John Wayne, Jeffrey Hunter, and Vera Miles. Warner Brothers, 1956.

Simard, Rodney. "Easin' on Down the Powwow Highway(s)." *Studies in American Indian Literatures* 3.3 (Fall 1991): 29–38.

Soldier Blue. Dir. Ralph Nelson. Perf. Candice Bergen and Peter Strauss. Embassy, 1970.

Toman, Marshall, and Carole Gerster. "*Powwow Highway* in an Ethnic Film and Literature Course." *Studies in American Indian Literatures* 3.3 (Fall 1991): 29–38.

Thunderheart. Dir. Michael Apted. Perf. Val Kilmer, Sam Shepard, Graham Greene, and Sheila Tousey. TriStar, 1992.

Ulzana's Raid. Dir. Robert Aldrich. Perf. Burt Lancaster and Bruce Davison. Universal, 1972.

19

Broken Arrows: Images of Native Americans in the Popular Western

Mary Alice Money

An image can be seen as a reflection, a refraction, an illusion. It may or may not be an accurate depiction of whatever it pictures. If the image is a reflection in a mirror, it reveals whoever looks into it—reversed in a mirror image, of course. If the image is a refraction, it still reveals something of whoever looks at it, but in a bent, distorted manner. If the image is an illusion, it reveals perhaps something deep within whoever creates the illusion. Whether it reflects, refracts, or creates, an image is not reality; it cannot exist without someone to see or imagine it. When many imaginers commit their images to paper or film or videotape, over and over, year after year, those distorted images take on a semblance of reality that can convince readers or viewers that the image is truth. It is not.

From the earliest days of American narrative, Native Americans have appeared as images of Nature's noblemen or of faceless evils in diaries, histories, and captivity narratives. From the earliest days of American film, as well, similar images of Native Americans look back at us—in the form of Plains Indians in warbonnets performing in Buffalo Bill Cody's Wild West Show, first filmed in 1894.[1] And, from the earliest days of television, images of Native Americans have continued to provide shadows of warpainted evil to threaten countless white (seldom black, until the 1960s!) settlers and soldiers. Every year, every week, more Native Americans appear in movies and television and novels, from Kevin Costner's *Dances with Wolves* to Richard S. Wheeler's Mister Skye series of paperback Westerns.

From the outpouring of images of the Indian that literature, film, and television have delivered, it would seem to follow that popular culture must have taught non-Indian Americans a great deal about Native Americans. On the contrary, I suspect that we other Americans—black, white, brown, yellow, and various combinations thereof—know little more than we did when we started.

What images do I see? What images do most Americans see? What images have most Americans seen for the last century? Those images have been fairly—and unfairly—consistent in portraying Native Americans as cruel savages, noble savages, "good Indians" (sometimes "apples"—red on the outside, white on the inside), mystics, even exotic pets—but seldom as individual people.[2] I see these images through different lenses, from various points of view that sometimes conflict and sometimes overlap. As a reader and viewer who first enjoyed Westerns as a child in the 1940s, I remember the thrill of seeing the cavalry come over the hill just in time to rescue yet another wagon train from yet another generic tribe of hostile Indians; but I also remember my fascination with the Native American lore—from beading buckskin to tracking game to constructing teepees—in the back pages of every issue of the Lone Ranger comic books. I remember my outrage at corrupt Indian agents cheating every tribe just as vividly as I remember my horror at corrupt whites selling guns to the Indians.

Even as a child exposed to the standard images of Native Americans as savages and as victims, I could never quite forget that they were here first and that they had just as legitimate and valuable cultures as those of the immigrants who were invading their lands. Today, as a professor of English, I cannot keep from applying the same techniques of analysis that I apply to other works of literature: here I identify an archetypal trickster, there a trace of chivalric romance; first I spot a stereotype, then a *deus ex machina*; and everywhere I sense that Westerns seldom develop Native American characters as much more than flat, two-dimensional images. I certainly see that *Gunsmoke* and *Dances with Wolves* are not Shakespeare; but teaching and loving great literature does not stop me from valuing and loving popular culture. As a student of popular culture, I feel compelled to trace the American society's changing evaluations of different cultures as reflected in popular Westerns—and speculate upon the ways the Western mythos has shaped and misshaped the ideals of that society. The images I see are ones that both reveal and influence the society's collective evaluation of Native Americans, no matter how false, demeaning, and racist those images are. Finally, as a person who grew up in a working-class neighborhood in Knoxville, Tennessee, and taught college English in Knoxville, Austin, Texas, and Barnesville, Georgia, I have little personal knowledge of Native Americans to contradict the images shown me by fiction, films, and television. What I do have is enough common sense to understand that Native Americans are people, and people of any cultural background are much more complex and varied than they are portrayed in popular culture. What I also have is decades of reading and studying literature that allow me to recognize a literary convention or cliché for the image it is, and not reality. I believe that any scholar must reconcile the elements of such multiple visions in studying popular culture.

Generations of people have gained a warped knowledge of Native Americans from popular Westerns. Since the nineteenth century, the Western has been one of the most popular genres of American popular culture in fiction and later in film and television. Traditionally, the Western is a story of adventures set west of the Mississippi in the last half of the nineteenth century, but most commonly between the end of the Civil War in 1865 and the official closing of the frontier in 1890. Although the form is descended from medieval tales of knighthood, Westerns before the 1950s were generally considered to be unsophisticated genre fiction. Most Westerns were filled with exciting elements: gunslingers and lawmen, rustlers and wild Indians, cattle drives and wagon trains, schoolma'ams and saloon "hostesses," hairsbreadth escapes and showdown gunfights, bravery and endurance. Exacting conventions dictated the heroes' actions until the Code of the West became as strict a system of honor as that of medieval chivalry. Nearly always, the settling of the frontier was seen as the Manifest Destiny of the United States, the bringing of order out of chaos rather than the invasion of the homelands of 500 Native American tribal cultures.

However, some continental shifts have occurred in the Western. During the 1950s, a new sensibility began to emerge with the release of Delmer Daves's film, *Broken Arrow* (1950). After decades of cheaply made "B" Westerns that used hordes of "wild Indians" as forces of alien menace, popular depictions shifted towards more sympathetic portrayals of Native Americans. The shift gained strength from the 1960s–1970s multicultural renaissance; between 1969 and 1971 two movies (*Little Big Man* and *A Man Called Horse*) and two Native American accounts of history (Dee Brown's *Bury My Heart at Wounded Knee* and Vine Deloria's *Custer Died for Your Sins*) reawakened interest in tribal cultures. With the release of *Dances With Wolves* in 1990, popular literature again discovered "red America." In the 1990s, perhaps for the first time in the history of American popular culture, images of Native Americans seem to be more varied and, perhaps, closer to reality than ever before.

Yet, beneath the apparent variety of Indian images depicted through the decades, popular culture scholars have discovered a consistent series of images. In my own research into Indian images in literature, film, and television, I have found that popular Westerns of whichever medium reveal:

Seven Stages in Images of Native Americans

[with position relative to reader/viewer]:

1. The "other"/The faceless, alien, bloodthirsty savage/The enemy
   [seeing outside]
2. The "respected enemy"
   [outside]
3. Exotic object of anthropological study/Alien passion
   [outside]
4. The pitiable victim/The doomed victim/"Lo, the poor savage"
   [seeing below]

5. The mascot/The pet/The subservient inferior/The "good Indian"
   [below]
6. The noble savage/The mystic/The wise old chief
   [seeing above and outside]
7. A human being/Us/The same
   [seeing beside]

These stages do not necessarily succeed one another. Indeed, we find several or all of the images coexisting in the imaginary worlds of fiction, film, and television, especially in the last decade. Sometimes the viewer's image of the characters progresses or regresses along stages/images within the same work. The research and analysis of the popular culture scholar make it possible to trace some of these images through one of the most important mediums of our culture—the imaginary worlds of representative twentieth-century Western films.

The Indians of Cooper, Hunt, Wister, and Ford

First, a brief side trip through the nineteenth and early twentieth centuries might be useful. In the "Leatherstocking Tales" (1823–41), especially *The Last of the Mohicans* (1826), James Fenimore Cooper created or popularized some of the images of "the Indian" that had begun to collect in the American consciousness. We can see Chingachgook as the "good Indian," loyal friend to whites (Hawkeye, in particular) who is doomed to be the last of his people. As many critics comment, the typical Western depicts "good Indians" as those who cooperate with the invading whites. Yet, the two peoples were expected to remain separate. Thus, when the "good Indian" Uncas dares to feel love for a white woman, he dooms both himself and Alice. In contrast, Cooper sets off the Huron to represent the "bad" or wild, alien, evil Indians; only Magua becomes more than a faceless menace. Helen Hunt Jackson further developed the tradition with her publication of *Ramona* in 1884, a sentimental, romantic novel that celebrated the "noble savage" who was soon transformed into the "doomed savage," victimized and destroyed by white society despite the love of an unprejudiced white woman.

By this time in popular literature, dime novels of the West had taken possession of the Indian. The most common image used by such hacks as Ned Buntline became the faceless evil of hordes of alien savages as their conventional *deus ex machina*. Since the times of the classical Greek dramatists, writers have used the device of the *deus ex machina* ("the god from the machine"). In *A Handbook to Literature*, Holman and Harmon define the term as:

The employment of some unexpected and improbable incident in a story or play to make things turn out right . . . [or] the abrupt but timely appearance of a god. . . , used to extricate mortal characters from a situation so perplexing that the solution seems beyond mortal powers. . . . The term now characterizes any device whereby an author solves a difficult situation by a forced invention. (138)

While the dime novelists certainly relied on many a *deus ex machina* to save Buffalo Bill or any other hero, they also depended on the "bloodthirsty savages" as demons *ex machina*. That is, whenever the dime novel hero had done nothing heroic for a paragraph or two, readers could expect the absurd appearance of an entire tribe of warpainted Indians (perhaps Apaches in Kansas or Sioux in New Mexico) to provide a pretext for the white hero to demonstrate his skills with a six-shooter (which always held at least thirty-six bullets) or his ability to rescue a kidnapped white virgin. By century's end, Buffalo Bill Cody, himself, renowned scout and slaughterer of buffalo, had induced Geronimo, Sitting Bull, Gall, and Yellow Hand to appear with his Wild West Show, sometimes re-enacting (or creating) mounted battles and hand-to-hand fights for the entertainment of audiences from the American masses to Queen Victoria.[3]

Just past the turn of the century, in 1902, Owen Wister invented the Western as we knew it before 1950 in his best-seller, *The Virginian*. Later the source of five Hollywood films and the first ninety-minute weekly series on television, *The Virginian* represented Native Americans only as a faceless menace—"bloodthirsty savages" who conveniently ambush the hero so that he can be cared for by the heroine. Surprisingly, a significant number of early silent films avoided the stereotype of the "bloodthirsty Indian." In a recent issue of *Cineaste*, Angela Aleiss documents "the use of Native Americans to play themselves, the employment of Native Americans behind the camera, and the fashioning of positive images and storylines . . . in the silent era" (1). However, in the "B" Western talkies, Indians soon came to be used mainly as the epitome of alien evil. In the tradition of Manifest Destiny, the Indian quickly became a symbol of the forces of chaos that must be destroyed by the white forces of progress, civilization, and order.

Michael Hilger is a good example of a scholar who helps us to understand the hidden meanings inherent within American popular culture. Hilger's study, *From Savage to Noble Man* (1995), admirably delineates the dichotomy of Indian images which literature, film, and television have created. What he finds is that nineteenth- and early twentieth-century popular literature engrave warring images on the consciousness of Americans: Indian as force of alien evil/Indian as noble savage. So trapped in this simplistic framework have Americans become that, even when some writers and filmmakers have attempted to recognize Native Americans as worthy human beings, as they have from the beginning, these attempts often have been embarrassing failures.[4] Furthermore, this schizophrenic view of Indians as noble/evil has persisted until the politically correct 1990s outlawed the latter view.

In *West of Everything*, Jane Tompkins comments with chagrin on another problem with the way popular culture treats Native Americans—the "absence of Indians in Western movies, . . . the lack of their serious presence as individuals. . . ." (10); instead, she says, they are memorable only in disconnected images, "most vividly, a line of warriors—war paint, feathers, spotted horses—appearing suddenly on a ridge" (9). John Ford's 1939 masterpiece *Stagecoach* is a good example. The viewer first endures the menace; "the time to worry about Apaches is when you don't see 'em," as countless cowboys have informed moviegoers. Then: the first arrow pins the whiskey drummer to the seat, hordes of faceless Indians chase the stagecoach, the driver is shot, John Wayne recovers the trailing reins by leaping from team to team, two Indians fall every time a white man shoots, the gambler starts to use his last bullet on the innocent young wife to save her from a fate worse than death, but the *deus ex machina* cavalry comes over the hill with bugles and flags—the essence of the Western. Too bad about all those "bloodthirsty savages," but few people are politically correct enough to resist the drama of that chase scene. Yet, since this was the film in which John Ford "discovered" Monument Valley and first used many local Navajo actors (Ford 7) to play those faceless, menacing savages, perhaps this is one attack scene that should be forgiven.

Conversely, the popular culture scholar must ask, what of Native American viewers? Can they see such scenes as harmless? Even if so, such "harmless" scenes influence American consciousness, reinforcing stereotyped images of Native Americans. The issue is one of balance. If other films had routinely shown individualized, admirable Native American characters portrayed by dashing Native American actors, viewers of whichever culture would have had choices. Then, those anonymous, befeathered savages would have been merely the villains of one movie, no different from WASP villains. On other Saturday nights, fans could have cheered for a Native American John Wayne/Davy Crockett in one movie and idolized a Native American Gregory Peck/Atticus Finch in another; they could have been charmed by a Native American Cary Grant, danced along with a Native American Fred Astaire, and fallen in love with a Native American Sidney Poitier. (On second thought, neither Sidney Poitier nor any other African-American cinematic hero was then available; African-American characters and actors were even more stereotyped than Native Americans. In addition, all of these icons are male; women were present in front of the camera, but in most movies they, too, were offensively stereotyped. How did Americans get away with such racist, sexist portrayals for so many years? Why did Americans even want to? As scholar and as American, I have no answer.) Without these choices, twentieth-century moviegoers were still seeing nineteenth-century images of Native Americans. Yet, popular culture's monochromatic depiction of heroism and nobility was about to change.

Broken Arrow: Breaking the Mold

Western fans as well as critics generally recognize Delmer Daves's 1950 film, *Broken Arrow*, as the work that transformed the depiction of Native Americans and resulted in a new cycle of "Indian Westerns." Before this time, John A. Price points out, while white villains were required to have some semblance of motive, Indians automatically could be villains just because they were Indians; viewers generally had expected no other motive for their depredations in the older, blatantly racist Westerns (83). After *Broken Arrow*, Native Americans were likely to be heroes or, at least, admirable characters defending their homelands against invaders. In the course of that noble defense, Native Americans still were shown most often as "noble savages" doomed to choose between extinction or assimilation. However, the greater emphasis was now on positive images.

Broken Arrow* was much admired then—and is respected among critics, still—as an anti-racist Western. On that count, the film remains worthy of admiration. The 1950 film is adapted from Elliott Arnold's fact-based novel, *Blood Brother*. The hero, Tom Jeffords (James Stewart), openly defends Cochise's reasons for attacking white settlers in Arizona, bravely acts on his ideals by riding into Cochise's stronghold to talk peace, and shows open respect for and interest in the tribe's culture (and thus introduces viewers to Apache daily life). Soon, Jeffords courts and marries Cochise's young ward, the beautiful Sonseeahray, played by Debra Paget, the one obviously white actress among the obviously red extras in each scene. After ending the raids by Geronimo, the movie's embodiment of the old "bloodthirsty savage" image, Cochise (Jeff Chandler) and Jeffords cobble together a peace agreement. Then, local white racists murder Sonseeahray and wound Jeffords. Cochise and other warriors kill the white villains, and Jeffords and Cochise avert any further violence. As soon as the other settlers hear of the shameful murder, they develop a collective conscience and stop killing Indians. The sacrifice of Sonseeahray has led to peace on the frontier!

The film raised the consciousness of a generation of moviegoers and inspired a cycle of films sympathetic to Native Americans. Some scenes are genuinely affecting; one could hardly fail to be moved by James Stewart's performance of anguish at Paget's cinematic death. Both Stewart and Jeff Chandler (white though he is) are impressive. The occasional views of Apache customs—though presented in what Phil Hardy characterizes as a patronizing fashion (188)—are admirable for the times, and a few scenes even show the Apache's sense of humor.

Yet, despite all these qualities, seeing *Broken Arrow* disappoints contemporary scholars. Today's cynical, post-Vietnam viewer is unlikely to believe a word of the scene declaring an easy end to a complex war. A feminist viewer might remark that once more the woman is a convenient token used to reveal the male hero's nobility and then exchanged for a phony happy ending. A racially sensitive viewer might note that another white hero is ever so conveniently saved from further miscegenation and the parenting of an inconvenient little "half-breed." Any historian might snort in derision at whites making peace over the death of one "squaw." Yes, the end of the film is incredible nonsense; but, for those who study popular culture, the important point is in the underlying meaning that, in 1950, *Broken Arrow's* indictment of racism, violence, and war made a deep impression on Americans' consciousness and conscience.

Hollywood did not alter its image of "the Indian" completely, however. Michael Hilger also points out that other films of the era continued the concurrent use of the image of the "bloodthirsty savage," worthy only of being reviled and killed by the white hero. He rightly condemns the John Ford-John Wayne classic, *The Searchers* (1956), for its racist view of Native Americans (108). Despite the movie's qualities of greatness, today's viewer finds it difficult to ignore the hero's obsessive hatred. In contrast, one of the most cinematically effective portrayals of faceless evil occurs in *The Stalking Moon* (1968). The Apache antagonist stalking the white hero (Gregory Peck) is actually named Salvaje ("savage") and until the final scene is never clearly seen by the hero or the viewer. The film goes beyond mere stereotype to involve the characters and viewers in pure terror.

These stock celluloid images were still present, but the peaceful coexistence idealized in *Broken Arrow* emerged as the most influential pattern for two decades of Westerns. Other films, television series, and paperback Westerns followed the themes of martyred Native American wives/lovers of tolerant white heroes, white bigots and red hostiles (with historical accuracy) threatening the peace of noble chiefs, and white heroes validating their liberal credentials by befriending assorted "noble savages." Hilger traces the subsequent development of the Cochise figure into a stock Western character: "a peace-loving friend to a white man . . . [and] a new version of the Noble Red Man, a historical chief as a central positive character. . . ." (98). Films such as *The Battle at Apache Pass* (1951), *Seminole* (1953), *Taza, Son of Cochise* (1954), *Sitting Bull* (1954), and *Chief Crazy Horse* (1955) often transferred the cinematic characteristics of Cochise to other historical tribal leaders (Hilger 98–108). To the popular culture scholar, this image is obviously preferable to earlier ones, even if it does sometimes degrade into the "wise old chief" stereotype that Vine Deloria, Jr., mocks in his essay on "American Fantasy" (xii-xiv).

Unfortunately, the positive version of that image is often linked with *Broken Arrow's* unrealistically easy peace in such later movies as *Seminole*

(Hilger 106). Hilger concludes that the "noble savages" of these 1950s Indian Westerns are "too good to be believed and too divorced from history to be taken seriously" (111). Of course, such a grafted-on movie peace was not originated by *Broken Arrow*. In *Past Imperfect: History According to the Movies*, Alvin M. Josephy, Jr., exposes the total inaccuracy of the 1941 Custer movie, *They Died with Their Boots On*, which makes a hero of Custer and ends with General Phil Sheridan awarding peace to the Sioux after the battle at the Little Big Horn—in the name of Custer, "friend to the Indian" (146–49). In *Sitting Bull*, as well, an improbable (and historically absurd) peace succeeds the Custer fiasco, although here Yellowhair is depicted as an arrogant, incompetent glory-hunter. As Josephy explains, the vengeful campaign following Custer's defeat actually culminated in the destruction of the Sioux nation's power and the confiscation of the Black Hills (149).

There are many reasons for such silver screen lies. Hollywood is notorious for tacking on improbable happy endings to let the audience go home with a warm fuzzy feeling—and return to the movies next week.[5] Admitting genocide would not be good "box office." Perhaps a deeper reason is the desire to avoid confronting the sins of the past. Douglas Brode's 1972 article tracing the *Broken Arrow* cycle suggests that blaming (or mythologizing) Custer for all white extremism allows us to overlook the historical fact that the United States government and army were sincerely, straightforwardly dedicated to "a program of Indian extermination" for much of the nineteenth century (45). Even John Ford's impressive *Cheyenne Autumn* (1964) is marred by the dramatic but incredible last-minute personal intervention of Secretary of the Interior Carl Schurz to save the Cheyenne from imminent massacre by the U.S. Cavalry. With a promise to "tell the people" about the "noble red man's" plight, he persuades the tribe to "take a gamble" on peace and reservation life. (Today's viewer knows they lost.) Max Westbrook, in his 1993 essay, "The Night John Wayne Danced with Shirley Temple," calls the scene a "*deus ex* bureaucracy" finale intended to affirm the goodness of the system (71). Thus, moviegoers can continue to ignore the nineteenth-century genocide if they are told that it was an isolated incident practiced by a few bigots and madmen; that the System or the Government really had good intentions; or that a few people (whether Sonseeahray or the 7th Cavalry) had to be sacrificed for the greater good in bringing peace to the frontier and fair treatment to the quaint "noble savages" who did not need all that land anyway.

Television's Indian

Film was not the only medium in the 1950s and 1960s to re-evaluate images of Native Americans; television soon became a powerful format, as well. Some of the series with major Indian characters were juvenile Westerns. Tonto was still "the faithful Indian companion" on *The Lone Ranger*, broadcast from 1949 to 1957 (MacDonald 356–57); the hero of *Brave Eagle* (1955–56) was a young peace-making Cherokee chief in the tradition of film depictions of Cochise (MacDonald 84); and Chingachgook continued as sidekick to the sharpshooter in *Hawkeye and the Last of the Mohicans* in 1957 (MacDonald 35). Even more influential were TV's adult Westerns, which began in 1955 when *Gunsmoke* arrived, accompanied by *The Life and Legend of Wyatt Earp* and *Cheyenne*.[6] Soon, adult Westerns proliferated.[7] J. Fred MacDonald, in *Who Shot the Sheriff? The Rise and Fall of the Television Western*, tabulates six shows beginning in 1956, 16 in 1957, 24 in 1958, 28 in 1959, 22 in 1960, and 10–13 in six of the next eight seasons, 1961–68 (58). With so many Westerns competing for ratings, each new series attempted to develop some unusual hero or other gimmick that would set it above the others. According to MacDonald, adult Western heroes included not only the usual peace officers and gunslingers, but also mercenaries, bounty hunters, ranchers, cowboys, cavalry officers, Indian scouts, newspaper editors, cattle drovers, gamblers, railroaders, secret service agents, doctors, lawyers—but few Indian chiefs (59–60).

Three of the most influential adult Westerns were *Broken Arrow* (1956–60), *Law of the Plainsman* (1959–62), and *The High Chaparral* (1967–71). The most complete study of the adult Westerns—and, indeed, of all TV Westerns—is Gary A. Yoggy's 1995 book, *Riding the Video Range: The Rise and Fall of the Western on Television*. Yoggy discusses these three shows and many others, emphasizing the changing images of Native Americans.[8] *The High Chaparral* was the most polished of the three series and often depicted Apaches as complex individuals. At least the Apache characters were played by Native Americans; indeed, the role of Cochise was played by one of the historical chief's descendants. Still, none of its Native Americans had major continuing roles. *Broken Arrow* (1956–60) was, of course, based on the 1950 movie, with John Lupton and Lebanese-American Michael Ansara assuming the roles of James Stewart and Jeff Chandler. The series was fairly conventional and not as psychologically complex as, for instance, *Gunsmoke*; however, it treated the Chiricahua at least as fairly as did the original movie and actually became more effective in some respects. The weekly series could reveal the fragility of the film's easily achieved peace as the heroes continually faced prejudice, hostile outbreaks, encroaching whites, and bureaucrats who seldom understood even the need for honesty in an Indian agent. Given thirty minutes each week, writers could smoothly fit in the depiction of tribal daily life and customs such as boys' training and initiation. The inclusion of many Indian characters—many still played by non-Native Americans!—made it possible to present varied personalities. Of course, the Apache as a group remained stereotyped "noble savages" and generally depicted only Hollywood's ideas of Native American cultures. In contemporary interviews, Michael Ansara lamented the fact that he was allowed only two expressions: noble with arms folded and noble with arms at sides.[9] In *The Only Good Indian*, Friar and Friar make much of the clichéd depiction of movie Indians with folded arms and beaded headbands, surmising that early filmmakers invented the ahistorical headband to anchor the wigs of white actors portraying Native Americans (95).

Ansara also starred in *The Law of the Plainsman*, this time as the Harvard-educated Apache and Deputy U.S. Marshal, Sam Buckhart. MacDonald notes that the character first appeared in two 1959 episodes of the adult Western series, *The Rifleman* (1958–63), the latter pitting enlightened white ranchers and the assimilated "noble savage" Buckhart against stereotyped, faceless, "bloodthirsty savages" (Apache) who have kidnapped the hero's son (113–14). While Marshal Buckhart is clearly another "noble savage," the character does mark a revision of the old image. For the first time, a full-blooded Indian is shown as a typical Western hero with six-guns and badge, working on the side of law and order and speaking standard English. Even more surprising, he has a white adoptive daughter whom he had rescued after her parents were killed. The one problem with this new image is that Sam Buckhart now is hardly Apache at all; almost the only time his true identity is significant occurs when white criminals and bigoted strangers object to a "redskin" having authority over whites. Even so, this image of the assimilated "noble savage" influenced popular attitudes and soon became fairly common in the paperback Westerns of the 1960s and 1970s.

Once television Westerns discovered multiculturalism, many individual episodes included characters and actors who were African-American, Asian, Hispanic, or Native American. People of various tribes appear on different series, sometimes as faceless "bloodthirsty savages" or "noble savages," but often as "doomed noble savages." From 1962 until 1966 on *Gunsmoke* (1955–75), Burt Reynolds appeared in a recurring role as Quint Asper, a mixed-blood blacksmith in Dodge City. The character inspired several episodes condemning racism, but sometimes was treated as simply another featured character without regard to race (Peel 88–108). In one episode of the 1960 series *Tate*, the gunslinger hero is hired to buy back a white woman from the now-starving Paiute tribe that had captured her years before. Upon her return, her white husband condemns her for bearing a child by her Paiute husband, whom she still loves. When he attempts to beat and rape her, the hero intervenes, kills the husband, and returns her and her child to her Paiute husband. The story is based on the same Jack Schaefer story, "Sergeant Houck," that later was a partial source for *The Stalking Moon* (1965).

Perhaps the epiphany for the Indians of adult Westerns occurs in an episode of *Have Gun, Will Travel* (1957–63) that featured an educated Indian (played by a white actor, as usual) who was a war hero and Medal of Honor winner.[10] The episode echoes the 1950 movie *The Devil's Doorway*, in which a Shoshone Medal of Honor winner is destroyed by his bigoted neighbors when he tries to hold his land (Hilger 109–10). In the *Have Gun, Will Travel* episode, when the Indian attempts to homestead, local bigots beat him and burn his small house.[11] Paladin, the mercenary series hero, rescues him and later tries to encourage him by saying that he is the equal of any of the white townspeople. The outraged Indian remarks, "Has it ever occurred to you that I might be a little better than some of them?" For the first time in a television Western, a media Indian demands not just "tolerance," but the recognition of his superiority as a human being instead of a noble symbol. Of course, the townspeople do finally accept him, although some bitterness and unease linger on each side. In the midst of all these positive images, the old image of Indian as "respected enemy" still flourishes, as evidenced by Louis L'Amour's *Hondo* (1953) and the movie based on this novel.

Media interest in Native Americans again increased with a cluster of works between 1969 and 1971. The Red Power movement had begun in the early 1960s, but it took the publication of two books to raise the consciousness of Americans of all cultures: Vine Deloria's first book, *Custer Died for Your Sins: An Indian Manifesto* (1969), and Dee Brown's *Bury My Heart at Wounded Knee: An Indian History of the American West* (1971). During the same period appeared two films, each about a white man living with a nineteenth-century tribe: *A Man Called Horse* and *Little Big Man* (both 1970). At the time, *A Man Called Horse* impressed many viewers with its inside look at life among the Dakotas, climaxing with an enactment of the Sun ceremony. Yet, the film remains a trite representation of "noble savages," with the white captive soon proving his superiority. Any authenticity lent by the Dakota dialogue is damaged by such flaws as the casting of Dame Judith Anderson as a Dakota matriarch; once more, Native Americans were not trusted to portray Indians. In addition, Dan Georgakas, in a contemporary review, explains that the "authenticity" is false: The film misrepresents and trivializes the Sun Dance, most sacred rite of the Dakotas (135–36).

Little Big Man, a fine adaptation of Thomas Berger's brilliant 1964 novel, is much more successful. Even as it parodies Westerns and satirizes white society, the film manages to reveal Cheyenne culture and expose the Washita massacre of a village and a credible version of Custer's Last Stand. Surprisingly enough, Chief Dan George portrays Old Lodge Skins, the first time since silent days that a Native American starred as an Indian in a big-budget film. Berger's novel, perhaps even more than the film, respectfully presents Cheyenne philosophy and culture as a reasonable alternative to its European-American counterparts.[12] Six years later, in Clint Eastwood's 1976 Western, *The Outlaw Josey Wales*, Chief Dan George again plays a major role with humor and dignity. The film portrays several Indian characters as individuals of integrity and wit, including a chief who goes into the cattle business with the white hero.

Paperback Indians

Indian heroes also began to appear in popular paperback Westerns during the 1960s and 1970s. In most instances, the hero was a "half-breed" (i.e., one parent is Native American, the other of a different race) who took on the usual characteristics of a white or black Western hero, with the addition of some inner conflict as he came to terms with white racism or his own ambivalent feelings about his heritage. Among the best of this cycle of Westerns are Ann Aylswede's archetypal revenge quest novel, *Hunting Wolf* (1960), and Wade Everett's *The Whiskey Traders* (1968), a historically accurate novel in which the hero destroys a whiskey fort on the Montana-Canadian border. In some fiction, the hero could just as easily be white; Luke Short's Pawnee hero in *The Some-Day Country* (1963) is an example. Only occasionally does a popular Western use a full-blooded Native American as a hero in a tribal setting. Finally, Chad Oliver's novel *The Wolf Is My Brother* (1967) parallels the lives of a young Comanche and a young white cavalry officer in an unusual double initiation story.

The most remarkable of the Native heroes is Jim Sundance, hero of a series of ten paperbacks by "John Benteen" (most written by Ben Haas), published between 1972 and 1973. The series cleverly adapts images and conventions of white Western heroes to develop a new kind of Indian hero. The series begins as an obvious attempt to exploit not only the contemporary pro-Native American trend, but also the popularity of the amoral, ultraviolent "spaghetti Westerns" originated by Sergio Leone and Clint Eastwood. The hero is the mixed-blood son of an Englishman who was the first white man to undergo the Sun Dance ritual, a transparent attempt to link the series to *A Man Called Horse*. The first novel begins with the hero's successful quest for revenge on the six renegades (three white and three Indian—equality in villainy) who murdered his parents. After serving in the Civil War, he becomes a mercenary gunfighter in imitation of many other heroes of adult Westerns.

So far, the hero could pass for white, but then the series takes some unconventional turns. First, Sundance becomes a high-priced (sometimes $10,000 for a difficult assignment) mercenary and uses half of each fee to support a Washington lobbyist for Native American rights in the West. The image of a gunslinging activist who uses white money against the white power structure is completely outside contemporary images of Native Americans. Second, many of the conventions of traditional and ultraviolent Westerns are cleverly adapted to the Indian hero. His war horse is neither pure black nor pure white, but a fine Appaloosa stallion, the only appropriate horse for a militant Indian, since the breed was developed by the Nez Percé tribe rather than any white men. The hero's weapons also reflect his heritage: the Navy Colt, Henry rifle, and Bowie knife; and the Cheyenne bow, hand-chipped arrowheads, throwing axe, and buffalo-hide shield—with six scalps attached. Most effectively, conventional plots are also revised to suit the hero. Instead of being on the scene of the events important to white Westerners (such as the building of the trans-continental railroad, the Johnson County and Lincoln County range wars, and the gunfight at the O. K. Corral), Sundance is involved with each of the famous Native American leaders: Cochise and Geronimo of the Apache; Gall, Sitting Bull, Roman Nose, and Crazy Horse of the northern plains tribes; Captain Jack of the Modoc; the Dakotas at the Little Big Horn; and the Ghost Dancers at Wounded Knee.

Third, and most unconventional of all, the hero changes and matures; in the final novel of John Benteen's original series, *The Ghost Dancers* (1973), Sundance has aged the twenty-three years that have supposedly passed since the first of the series, *Overkill*. He has long ceased to believe, as he naively did in the earlier novels, that mere abstract precepts of law and justice will protect the Western tribes when gold or some other precious substance is discovered on Native American lands. After years of crossing back and forth from white to Native American and considering himself master of both ways of life, he finally realizes that he is more white than Native American. He does not dream visions or believe in the invulnerability of the Ghost Shirts; he is basically a civilized, materialistic, calculating white man. But, when he sees that the two races are drifting into battle one morning at Wounded Knee, he discards his white weapons, dons a Ghost Shirt, and fights alongside the Dakotas. Benteen uses all the traditional motifs and scenes of death in his recreation of the Massacre at Wounded Knee: the inexperienced and naive white officer screaming for both sides to stop when he sees the horror he has wrought, the Indian woman and baby killed by the same bullet,[13] the hero and a cavalryman friend of twenty years meeting and recognizing each other in the thick of battle and shooting at each other anyway, the hero in barbaric splendor charging the chief villain, and all the rest. The hero does survive the battle, but not to fight again another day; he and the Dakotas realize that Wounded Knee was the last battle.

Hollywood *ex machina*

In 1990 came the latest seismic shift in popular culture's depiction of Native Americans—Kevin Costner's *Dances with Wolves*. Costner's effort is one of the few Hollywood Westerns to depict Native Americans as individuals. For a popular culture scholar like myself, it is also one of the few to approach that last stage of images I developed in my research, the "Seven Stages in Images of Native Americans." Although the white characters are portrayed by white performers, Native Americans play Native Americans in major as well as minor roles: Graham Greene, Rodney A. Grant, Floyd Red Crow

Westerman, and Tantoo Cardinal are all featured players. Subtitles give English translations for those of us who cannot read Lakota. The filmmakers took the trouble to teach the non-Dakota actors the Lakota dialect, rather than assuming, as had some directors in other Westerns, that the audience would never notice the difference if each Native actor used his own language (Costner, Blake, and Wilson 53). The hero, Dunbar, learns Lakota with many comic interpretations. The subtitles give the viewers access to a certain dramatic irony by allowing them to read what the Lakotas are saying, even though Dunbar cannot understand the language. Thus, when Dunbar tries to learn the Lakota word for buffalo by imitating a buffalo, Wind-in-His-Face politely comments, "He must be mad. Let's go." Tribes are seen as distinct nations, not just generic Indians. James Fenimore Cooper distinguished the "noble" Mohican from the "evil" Huron in the 1820s; here, the noble, independent Lakotas are differentiated from the Pawnee, who had sold out to the whites. More importantly, the Lakotas are shown as people who laugh, tell jokes, misunderstand each other, and have petty and mean moments. Indeed, they even change expression; Michael Ansara would be delighted. It would be difficult to find in earlier Westerns any parallels with the scenes in which Dunbar and Wind-in-His-Face first meet and frighten each other into panic flight and dead faint, respectively. Seldom since *Little Big Man* have Indians been so much like "people," however noble.

The Lakotas also possess the admirable quality of being able and willing to distinguish among members of a different people. At the beginning of the film, they suspect that they should see Dunbar as "other" and alien (what I identify as the first stage of images of a different race), but they are unprejudiced enough to make his acquaintance before deciding. For a while, Dunbar remains their tame white man, a pet (the image in Stage 5), while he still sees them as something close to Stage 3, anthropological subjects; but eventually both races see each other as humans and individuals (Stage 7). Granted, the movie exaggerates the nobility of the Lakotas and the depravity of the whites. Granted, the movie sometimes manipulates the viewer in obvious ways. Granted, the white hero is the main focal point, and he does become a leader among his new friends—but he does not instantly become chief because of his white "superiority." Despite flaws, *Dances with Wolves* still has much for an audience to enjoy and for a popular culture scholar to praise.

During the 1990s, since *Dances with Wolves*, more Native Americans have appeared in increasingly sympathetic and, sometimes, realistic roles instead of mere false images. Television Western series have almost disappeared, but in the underrated 1988–91 series, *Paradise* (later *Guns of Paradise*), one of the major characters, John Taylor (portrayed effectively by Dehl Berti), was a sort of Indian philosopher in the tradition of the "wise old chief" (Stage 6). However, while he was intended to present a positive image of an educated Native American, his advice and philosophical parables were embarrassingly sententious more often than they were effective.[14] In *Maverick*, the 1994 film based on the television series, one of the major characters and the hero's occasional partner is an educated Indian trickster played by Graham Greene at his most engaging.[15] The character satirically exploits the "bloodthirsty savage" image to help Maverick con several other characters, and then out-cons even the trickster Maverick himself.

Recent fiction and television have further expanded Native American roles. In today's paperback Westerns, the best portraits of Native American characters are in the novels of Richard S. Wheeler. In *Santa Fe*, the 1995 installment of his "Skye's West" series, the main characters are as always complex individuals—Mr. Skye, the mountain man, and his two wives, one Shoshone and one Crow. Indians appear in many other roles, ranging from heroes to villains. Wheeler's 1992 novel, *Badlands*, shows the Dakotas' very civilized reactions to a nineteenth-century fossil-hunting expedition, surely one of the few Westerns to deal with the issue of scientific grave robbing of Native artifacts. Thus, Wheeler straightforwardly shows his white British and American characters regarding the Dakotas as subjects of anthropological and scientific study, exemplifying the image I identify as Stage 3. Each white character reveals his or her (one amateur investigator is a woman) own worth in the manner of studying the Dakotas: the heroine and other admirable whites treat the Native Americans as individual human beings and as representatives of a valuable culture; the villains see the Indians as near-animals to be robbed. The Dakota characters are drawn too realistically to be mere "noble savages," and the novel continually surprises and delights the reader. One episode of the TV series *The Lazarus Man* (1996) also depicts white scientists studying and stealing Anasazi artifacts. Here, the image transforms into Stage 6, the Indian as "mystic," when some of the thieves are mysteriously slain by an Indian shape-shifter dedicated to protecting his tribal heritage.[16] The delightful Canadian series, *Due South*, is set on the mean streets of contemporary Chicago, but it consistently uses, parodies, and glorifies elements of the traditional Western heroes and plots. One episode manages to combine several of the images in use today in the story of an Tsimshiam trickster hero (played by Rodney A. Grant) stealing back his tribe's sacred transformation masks from a Chicago museum. The trickster (who may or may not be a shape-shifter) finally tricks even the show's straight-arrow hero, Constable Benton Fraser, R. C. M. P., into letting the tribe keep the genuine masks and return counterfeits to the museum. Thus, the single episode combines today's images of the Native American as spiritual custodian of heritage, as mystic shape-shifter, and as trickster, all the while taking sly potshots at white misunderstanding of Native cultures and underestimation of Native people.[17] At the least, the different media of popular culture are varying the images in the 1990s and even adding the trickster figure.

What do all of these Westerns in films, television, and novels reveal? Native Americans have never ceased to fascinate, frighten, and attract other Americans. The images of Indians still include most of the same images developed during the nineteenth century, but popular Westerns in the multicultural 1990s are depicting more realistic, individual humans instead of conventionally racist, fearsome "wild savages," "doomed savages," and "noble savages." However, perhaps another stage of images needs to be added to the original seven, an X Stage. At this level, it seems to this student of American popular culture that we have always looked into the mirror and seen not "red people," but all Americans. When peaceful coexistence was a necessity during the Cold War, a popular image of Native Americans was the peace-making chief. As the Civil Rights movement gained strength, the plea of many Westerns was for red (read black?) and white to become friends. When half of America shuddered at the thought of U.S. soldiers murdering Vietnamese villagers at My Lai, Westerns abhorred the U.S. Cavalry murdering Native Americans at Washita, Sand Creek, and Wounded Knee. Today, America is no longer united against an "evil empire," but there is no easy way to achieve internal peace and plenty. Perhaps now, we need to look into the mirror of art and see ourselves as complex, real individuals instead of shadows of the past.

Notes

1 Kevin Brownlow, in *The War, the West, and the Wilderness* (224) states that Buffalo Bill's Wild West Show was "photographed for the Edison Kinetoscope, a peepshow machine" in 1894. A 1968 *Blackhawk Films Bulletin* lists for sale a two-reel film entitled *Buffalo Bill's Wild West Show*: The first portion of this film is devoted to the showing of Wild West Show parades, the first photographed by Edison cameramen in 1898, the second by a Biograph cameraman in 1902. Following this is the kind of action for which the Wild West Show was famous—Indians, scouts, cavalrymen, fast riding and re-enactments of typical frontier events (5).

There is some debate over the use of the terms, "Indian," "American Indian," and "Native American." Some Native leaders complain that the term "Indian" is a Western construct, or intellectual category, imposed on the indigenous peoples of North America. In order to help readers differentiate characters featured in movies and TV series from the actors and actresses who depict them, in this essay I use the term "Indian" to denote characters and "Native American" to depict actors and actresses.

2 Perhaps one of the inherent flaws of humanity is the difficulty in recognizing as individuals and as humans those people who are different from whatever one perceives as one's own cultural-racial-religious group. In many cases, a cultural group's term for itself translates as "the people" (such as *Diné* or *Navajo*) or "the human beings" (*Cheyenne*). Before the Civil Rights Movement in the 1960s, southern white-controlled newspapers referred to whites only by name (whites equaled people, the standard model); but African Americans were generally labeled as Negro (a variation from the white norm). Long ago, Shakespeare stated the siblinghood of all humanity most effectively in the Jewish Shylock's soliloquy—"If you prick me, do I not bleed?"—from *The Merchant of Venice*. In a 1959 episode of the TV Western, *The Rifleman*, Apache lawman Sam Buckhart echoes Shakespeare when he answers an attack by a white racist: "Has not an Indian eyes, hands, organs, senses, affections, fed with the same food, hurt with the same weapons, warmed and cooled by the same winter and summer as a white man? If you prick him, does he not bleed? If you tickle him, does he not laugh? And if you wrong him will he not revenge?" (Qtd. in Yoggy 357).

3 Cody vividly describes his experiences performing for Europeans, both royal and common, in *An Autobiography of Buffalo Bill* (319–26). In *West of Everything*, Jane Tompkins also discusses royal reactions to the Wild West Show (200–201). Cody figures in another strange footnote to the study of popular Westerns. Kevin Brownlow explains in *The War, the West, and the Wilderness* that Cody made a 1913 movie about the "Battle" at Wounded Knee, South Dakota, with the cooperation of the Sioux nation and the federal government, and with General Nelson Miles as technical advisor. Cody directed several hundred Native Americans and three troops of U.S. Cavalry (but not the 7th, the unit originally involved!) in what was supposed to be a historically accurate re-enactment; this scene was filmed at the Pine Ridge Agency over the actual battleground graves of the men, women, and children massacred there in 1890. The film was shown to the Secretary of the Interior and others in President Wilson's administration and to a few public audiences, but only part of one reel has survived; Brownlow includes

photographs made during the filming. According to Brownlow, some people at the time believed that the government had suppressed the film (224–45).

4 One example is *White Feather*, a 1955 film that *The Overlook Film Encyclopedia: The Western* labels "an intelligent, well-meaning Indian Western severely marred by . . . nondescript direction" despite a screenplay by Delmer Daves, of *Broken Arrow* fame (244). However conscientiously the film tries to be sympathetic to Native Americans, it patronizes the characters and has no connection with the historical or psychological reality of red or white cultures.

5 Hollywood's grafted-on happy endings continue to proliferate. In *Past Imperfect*, Richard White points out the outrageous historical inaccuracies of the 1992 Daniel Day-Lewis version of Cooper's *Last of the Mohicans*. More stunning for anyone who ever read the novel are the movie's invention of and shifts in romantic attachments. As White states: "Duncan no longer loves Alice; he proposes to Cora. Cora falls in love with Nathaniel. Uncas seems to be interested in Alice. Colonel Munro quite literally loses his heart to Magua. Magua hates everyone" (84). One can only wonder what Cooper would have thought of Natty and Cora living happily ever after. However, one hesitates even to speculate about the reaction of Nathaniel Hawthorne to the 1995 Demi Moore version of *The Scarlet Letter*, complete with a *deus ex machina* Indian attack that saves Hester and Dimmesdale from hanging and allows them to ride happily off into the sunset—together.

6 Unless otherwise noted, dates of television series are from Brooks and Marsh's *Complete Directory to Prime Time Network TV Shows 1946-Present* [1978].

7 The term *adult Western* was used to distinguish the mid-1950s Westerns from *juvenile Westerns*, the older, traditional Westerns—ranging from Roy Rogers movies to the radio and television *Lone Ranger* shows—which supposedly appealed mainly to juvenile viewers of whatever age. The films generally credited with starting the adult Western cycle are *Broken Arrow* (1950), *The Gunfighter* (1950), *Shane* (1953), and, perhaps most influential, *High Noon* (1952). Radio contributed the original *Gunsmoke*, with William Conrad creating the role of Marshall Matt Dillon. *Gunsmoke*, starring James Arness, Dennis Weaver, and Amanda Blake, moved to television in 1955 and maintained a high degree of popularity as well as dramatic integrity for its record-breaking run of twenty years. Other notable adult Westerns on television include *Maverick* (1957–62), *Have Gun, Will Travel* (1957–63), *Wanted: Dead or Alive* (1958–61), *Rawhide* (1959–66), and *The Westerner* (1960). Heroes could still be brave lawmen or cowboys, but now they could also be mercenary gunfighters, tough bounty hunters, cautious if not cowardly gamblers, or educated sophisticates. Adult Westerns quickly developed their own conventions and clichés, and some shows (such as *Cheyenne*, 1955–63) seemed much more "adult" at the time than they do in retrospect. Yet the television adult Westerns revolutionized every element of the traditional genre. Plots often dealt with such controversial issues as racism, religious intolerance, child abuse, rape, prostitution, drug addiction, the disastrous consequences of casual violence, and the exploitation of the environment; these issues seldom had easy solutions and often were left unresolved when the last commercial was played. Many shows demanded greater historical accuracy than had the older Westerns, and writers seemed to relish overturning conventions and kicking sacred cows. Most of the adult Westerns made a point of showing respect for cultural and religious minorities and even for women characters. Most revolutionary was the portrayal of psychologically complex characters: introspective heroes who displayed and recognized their own fallibility; villains who sometimes had a defensible code, and heroines who occasionally were more than mere prizes to be rescued by and awarded to heroes

in white hats. All in all, since the first episode of *Gunsmoke*, in which hero Matt Dillon lost a gunfight to the villain, the Old West has never been the same.

8   In one chapter, "Meanwhile Back on the Reservation" (345–94), and many other passages, Yoggy perceptively analyzes Native American characters and performers in continuing roles as well as in individual episodes of various series, in made-for-television movies, and in Westerns with twentieth-century settings.

9   "Michael Ansara—Perennial Indian," *TV Guide* 30 Apr. 1960: 29. In the 1992 collection *The TV Guide TV Book*, Ed Weiner quotes the passage (113). Also, various contemporary writers about Westerns referred to Ansara's quip.

10 Yoggy (254) also mentions this episode. ·

11 Yoggy (254) briefly uses this episode to exemplify Paladin's ethics.

12 See Landon (30–46) for a perceptive analysis of the white hero's intellectual and emotional difficulties in committing himself to either culture.

13 This image, which is used in other Westerns, is a reflection of the actual massacre scene, as narrated by American Horse, a witness. Josephy, *500 Nations* (441), quotes American Horse from a contemporary source: James Mooney, "The Ghost Dance Religion," *14th Annual Report of the Bureau of Ethnology* (Washington, DC: GPO, 1896), 885–86.

14 Yoggy praises the character, but he concludes that "while Paradise presents a multidimensional portrait of the Native American in the person of John Taylor, he is still stereotypically wise, brave and weak" (367).

15 *The Merriam Webster Encyclopedia of Literature* defines the trickster as "a mischievous supernatural being much given to capricious acts of sly deception, found in the folklore of various preliterate peoples, often functioning as a culture hero, or one that symbolizes the ideal of a people. . . . A trickster-hero . . . within a single society may be regarded as both creator god and innocent fool, evil destroyer and childlike prankster" (1130). This archetypal figure is personified by Coyote in many Native American stories, by Hermes in Classical mythology, and by Loki in Nordic myths. However, tricksters are by no means limited to preliterate cultures; Americans seem particularly enamored of the archetype, as evidenced by movies ranging from *The Sting* to *Powwow Highway*.

16 Teleplay by Vera Appleyard and Alex Metcalf, *The Lazarus Man* 21 Apr. 1996. Perhaps a trend is developing here. *The X-Files* used a very similar plot in which scientists removing South American artifacts were killed by a shape-shifter or an ancient Native American spirit embodied in feline forms: John Shiban, "Teso Dos Bichos," 8 Mar. 1996. In addition, the three-part cliffhanger ending the second season and beginning the third season utilized Floyd Red Crow Westerman as a Navajo shaman (and former World War II code talker—one of the few instances of popular culture mentioning the Navajo contribution) singing a Blessing Way to bring the hero, Mulder, back from a near-fatal encounter with the usual villains. All three *X-Files* teleplays were written by Chris Carter, the show's creator: "Anazasi," 19 May 1995; "The Blessing Way," 22 Sept. 1995; and "Paper Clip," 29 Sept. 1995. As popular culture discards the Stage 1 "bloodthirsty savage" image and becomes too sophisticated to believe the Stage 6 "noble savage" image, the collective unconscious is experimenting with the Stage 3 "anthropological study" and Stage 6 "mystic" images.

17 Teleplay by Jeff King, *Due South* 19 Jan. 1996.

Works Cited

Ahlswede, Ann. *Hunting Wolf.* New York: Ballantine, 1960.

Aleiss, Angela. "Race in Contemporary American Cinema: Part 4—Native Americans: The Surprising Silents." *Cineaste* 2.3 (1995): 34–35. *Periodical Abstracts Research.* Online. Galileo. 15 Dec. 1995.

Arnold, Elliott. *Blood Brother.* New York: Duall, Sloan, and Pearce, 1947.

Bataille, Gretchen M., and Charles L. P. Silet, eds. *The Pretend Indians: Images of Native Americans in the Movies.* Ames: Iowa State UP, 1980.

The Battle at Apache Pass. Screenplay by Gerald Drayson Adams. Dir. George Sherman. Perf. John Lund, Jeff Chandler, Jay Silverheels. Universal-International, 1951.

Benteen, John [Ben Haas?]. *Sundance #1: Overkill.* New York: Leisure Books, 1972.

——. *Sundance #10: The Ghost Dancers.* New York: Leisure Books, 1973.

Berger, Thomas. *Little Big Man.* New York: Dial, 1964.

Blackhawk Films Bulletin [sales catalogue] no. 184 (Feb.-Mar. 1968).

Brave Eagle. CBS, 1955–56.

Brode, Douglas. "The Image of the Indian on Film." *Show* Feb. 1972: 44–48.

Broken Arrow. Screenplay by Michael Blankfort. Based on *Blood Brother* by Elliott Arnold. Dir. Delmer Daves. Perf. James Stewart, Jeff Chandler, Debra Paget. Fox, 1950.

Broken Arrow. ABC, 1956–60.

Brooks, Tim, and Earle Marsh. *The Complete Directory to Prime Time Network TV Shows 1946–Present* [1978]. New York: Ballantine, 1978.

Brown, Dee. *Bury My Heart at Wounded Knee: An Indian History of the American West.* 1971. New York: Bantam, 1972.

Brownlow, Kevin. *The War, the West, and the Wilderness.* New York: Knopf, 1979.

Carnes, Mark C., ed. *Past Imperfect: History According to the Movies.* New York: Holt, 1995.

Cheyenne [*Warner Brothers Present: Cheyenne* 1955–56]. ABC, 1955–63.

Cheyenne Autumn. Screenplay by James R. Webb. Based on *Cheyenne Autumn* by Mari Sandoz. Dir. John Ford. Perf. Richard Widmark, Carroll Baker. Warner, 1964.

Chief Crazy Horse. Screenplay by Gerald Drayson Adams and Franklin Coen. Dir. George Sherman. Perf. Victor Mature. Universal, 1955.

Cody, William Frederick. *An Autobiography of Buffalo Bill (Colonel W. F. Cody).* New York: Farrar and Rinehart, 1920.

Cooper, James Fenimore. *The Last of the Mohicans. The Complete Works of James Fenimore Cooper.* 33 vols. New York: Putman, 1895–1900.

Costner, Kevin, Michael Blake, and Jim Wilson. Dances with Wolves: *The Illustrated Story of the Epic Film.* New York: Newmarket, 1990.

Dances with Wolves. Screenplay by Michael Blake. Dir. Kevin Costner. Perf. Kevin Costner, Mary McDonnell, Graham Greene. Tig Productions, 1990.

Dawson, Peter [Jonathan Glidden]. *The Half-Breed.* New York: Bantam, 1962.

Deloria, Vine. *Custer Died for Your Sins.* New York: Macmillan, 1969.

——. "Foreword / American Fantasy." Bataille and Silet ix-xvi.

Devil's Doorway. Screenplay by Guy Trosper. Dir. Anthony Mann. Perf. Robert Taylor. MGM, 1950.

Due South. CBS, 1995–96.

Everett, Wade [Giles A. Lutz]. *The Whiskey Traders.* New York: Ballantine, 1968.

Ford, John. "John Ford on *Stagecoach*." *Action Magazine* n.d. N. pag. Rpt. John Ford's *Stagecoach* Starring John Wayne. 6–7.

Friar, Ralph, and Natasha Friar. *The Only Good Indian . . .: The Hollywood Gospel.* New York: Drama Book Specialists, 1972.

Georgakas, Dan. "They Have Not Spoken: American Indians in Film." *Film Quarterly* 25.2 (1972): 26-32. Bataille and Silet 134–42.

The Gunfighter. Screenplay by William Bowers and William Sellers. Dir. Henry King. Perf. Gregory Peck. Fox, 1950.

Gunsmoke. CBS, 1955–75.

Gunsmoke. CBS radio, 1952–61.

Hardy, Phil, ed. *The Overlook Film Encyclopedia of the Western.* 2nd ed. Woodstock, NY: Overlook, 1994.

Have Gun, Will Travel. CBS, 1957–63.

Hawkeye and the Last of the Mohicans. CBS, 1957.

Hawthorne, Nathaniel. *The Scarlet Letter*. 1850.

The High Chaparral. NBC, 1967–71.

High Noon. Screenplay by Carl Foreman. Dir. Fred Zinnemann. Perf. Gary Cooper. United Artists, 1952.

Hilger, Michael. *From Savage to Nobleman: Images of Native Americans in Film*. Lanham, MD: Scarecrow, 1995.

Holman, C. Hugh, and William Harmon. *A Handbook to Literature*. 5th ed. New York: Macmillan, 1986.

Hondo. Screenplay by James Edward Grant. Based on *Hondo* by Louis L'Amour. Dir. John Farrow. Perf. John Wayne, Geraldine Page. Wayne-Fellows. 1953.

Jackson, Helen Hunt. *Ramona*. 1884.

John Ford's Stagecoach *Starring John Wayne*. Ed. Richard J. Anobile. Film Classics Library. New York: Flare-Avon, 1975.

Josephy, Alvin M., Jr. *500 Nations: An Illustrated History of North American Indians*. Based on a documentary filmscript by Jack Leustag, et al. New York: Knopf, 1994.

——. "They Died with Their Boots On." *Carnes* 146–49.

L'Amour, Louis. *Hondo*. New York: Gold Medal, 1953.

Landon, Brooks. *Thomas Berger*. TUSAS Ser. 550. Boston: Twayne, 1989.

The Last of the Mohicans. Screenplay by Michael Mann, Christopher Howe, and Phillip Dunne. Based on *The Last of the Mohicans* by James Fenimore Cooper. Dir. Michael Mann. Perf. Daniel Day-Lewis, Madeline Stowe, Russell Means, Eric Schweig. Twentieth Century Fox, 1992.

Lazarus Man. TNT, 1996.

Law of the Plainsman. NBC, 1959–60; ABC, 1962.

The Life and Legend of Wyatt Earp. ABC, 1955–61.

Little Big Man. Screenplay by Calder Willingham. Based on *Little Big Man* by Thomas Berger. Dir. Arthur Penn. Perf. Dustin Hoffman, Chief Dan George. Cinema Center Films, 1970.

The Lone Ranger. ABC, 1949–57.

MacDonald, J. Fred. *Who Shot the Sheriff? The Rise and Fall of the Television Western*. Media and Society Series. New York: Praeger, 1987.

A Man Called Horse. Screenplay by Jack DeWitt. Dir. Eliot Silverstein. Perf. Richard Harris, Judith Anderson. Fox, 1970.

Maverick. ABC, 1957–62.

Maverick. Screenplay by William Goldman. Based on *Maverick* by Roy Huggins. Dir. Richard Donner. Perf. Mel Gibson, Jodie Foster, James Garner, Graham Greene. Warner Brothers, 1994.

Merriam-Webster's Encyclopedia of Literature. Springfield, MA: Merriam-Webster, 1995.

"Michael Ansara—Perennial Indian." *TV Guide* 30 Apr. 1960: 28–29.

Mooney, James. "The Ghost Dance Religion." *14th Annual Report of the Bureau of Ethnology*. Washington, DC: GPO, 1896.

Oliver, Chad. *The Wolf Is My Brother*. New York: Signet, 1967.

The Outlaw Josey Wales. Screenplay by Phil Kaufman and Sonia Chernus. Based on *Gone to Texas* by Forrest Carter. Dir. Clint Eastwood. Perf. Clint Eastwood, Chief Dan George. Malpaso, 1976.

Paradise / Guns of Paradise. ABC, 1988–89.

Peel, John. *The Gunsmoke Years*. Ed. Hal Schuster. Las Vegas: Pioneer, 1989.

Powwow Highway. Screenplay by Janet Heany and Jean Stawarz. Based on *Powwow Highway* by David Seals. Dir. Jonathan Wacks. Perf. A Martinez, Gary Farmer. Warner Brothers, 1988.

Price, John A. "The Stereotyping of North American Indians in Motion Pictures." *Ethnohistory* 20 (Spring 1973): 153–71. Bataille and Silet 75–91.

Rawhide. CBS, 1959–66.

The Rifleman. ABC, 1958–63.

The Scarlet Letter. Screenplay by Douglas Day Stewart. Based on *The Scarlet Letter* by Nathaniel Hawthorne. Dir. Roland Joffe. Perf. Demi Moore. Cinergi, 1995.

Schaefer, Jack. "Sergeant Houck." *The Collected Stories of Jack Schaefer*. Boston: Houghton, 1966.

The Searchers. Screenplay by Frank S. Nugent. Based on *The Searchers* by Alan LeMay. Dir. John Ford. Perf. John Wayne. Warner, 1956.

Seminole. Screenplay by Charles K. Peck, Jr. Dir. Budd Boetticher. Perf. Rock Hudson. Universal, 1953.

Shakespeare, William. *The Merchant of Venice.* 1598.

Shane. Screenplay by A. B. Guthrie, Jr. Based on *Shane* by Jack Schaefer. Dir. George Stevens. Perf. Alan Ladd. Paramount, 1953.

Short, Luke [Frederick D. Glidden]. *The Some-Day Country.* New York: Bantam, 1964.

Sitting Bull. Screenplay by Jack DeWitt. Dir. Sidney Salkow. Perf. Dale Robertson, J. Carrol Naish, Iron Eyes Cody. United Artists, 1954.

Stagecoach. Screenplay by Dudley Nichols. Based on "Stage to Lordsburg" by Ernest Haycox. Dir. John Ford. Perf. John Wayne. United Artists. 1939.

The Stalking Moon. Screenplay by Alvin Sargent. Based on *The Stalking Moon* by T. V. Olsen. Dir. Robert Mulligan. Perf. Gregory Peck. National General, 1968.

The Sting. Dir. George Roy Hill. Perf. Paul Newman, Robert Redford. Universal Pictures, 1973.

Tate. NBC, 1960.

Taza, Son of Cochise. Screenplay by George Zuckerman. Dir. Douglas Sirk. Perf. Rock Hudson. Universal, 1954.

They Died with Their Boots On. Screenplay by Wally Kline and Aeneas MacKenzie. Dir. Raoul Walsh. Perf. Errol Flynn. Warner. 1941.

Tompkins, Jane. *West of Everything: The Inner Life of Westerns.* New York: Oxford UP: 1992.

"Trickster." *Merriam-Webster Encyclopedia of Literature.*

The Virginian. NBC, 1962–71.

Wanted: Dead or Alive. CBS, 1958–61.

Weiner, Ed, and the Editors of *TV Guide. The TV Guide TV Book.* New York: HarperCollins, 1992.

Westbrook, Max. "The Night John Wayne Danced with Shirley Temple." *Old West–New West: Centennial Essays.* Ed. Barbara Howard Meldrum. Moscow: U of Idaho P, 1993. 60–73.

The Westerner. NBC, 1960.

Wheeler, Richard S. *Badlands.* New York: Tor, 1992.

——. *Santa Fe.* Skye's West. New York: Forge, 1995.

White, Richard. "The Last of the Mohicans." *Carnes* 82–85.

White Feather. Screenplay by Leo Townsend and Delmer Daves. Dir. Robert Webb. Perf. Robert Wagner, John Lund, Debra Paget, Jeffrey Hunter. Fox, 1955.

Wister, Owen. *The Virginian*. New York: Macmillan, 1902.

The X-Files. Fox, 1994– .

Yoggy, Gary A. *Riding the Video Range: The Rise and Fall of the Western on Television*. Jefferson, NC: McFarland, 1995.

VII

"A Usable Indian": The Current Controversy in Museums

Our last group of essays, in Section VII, "'A Usable Indian': The Current Controversy in Museums," also deals with perceptions and representations. For the museum studies professional, the problem of finding ways to depict Native culture to the general public is an ongoing challenge. Combining education and entertainment, the museum curator must break layers of misconception, myth, and outright distortion through strategies that keep the public both interested and informed. Due to the expertise museum curators develop, they frequently have a broader public policy role, as well. Entering the public interest arena, they are called upon to inform politicians about crucial policy matters. The details of such work are sketched out in the pieces by Dan L. Monroe of the Peabody Essex Museum of Salem, Massachusetts in "The Politics of Repatriation" and Karen Coody Cooper of the Smithsonian Institution in "Museums and American Indians: Ambivalent Partners."

Monroe provides the context for the *Native American Graves Protection and Repatriation Act (NAGPRA)* of 1990. His essay describes the history of museum acquisition of Native artifacts and grave site items, the organized opposition to the practice which emerged during the 1960s, and the movement to sponsor a federal law that would protect Native American burial sites. As one who played a key role in framing *NAGPRA* and in securing its passage, and as one who is currently a member of the Federal Repatriation Review Committee, Monroe offers a well-informed perspective on the issue of repatriation. He concludes that, through the cooperative efforts of Native American, museum, and scientific representatives, a number of museums have begun the difficult process of returning, or "repatriating," sacred objects and burial remains.

Cooper, a member of the Cherokee Nation of Oklahoma, describes the development and current status of some of the nearly 200 tribal museums in North America today. Cooper explains how museums have frequently reinforced stereotypes or even presented exhibits that have "relegated American Indians to the status of flora and fauna of the 'New World.'" Indeed, in her interpretation, museums stand as institutions that represent mainstream values and "serve to spread the dogma of a nation." Under pressure from Native activists, however, Cooper believes that "American Indians [can] look forward to the innovative exhibitions" at sites such as the planned National Museum of the American Indian.

20

The Politics of Repatriation

Dan L. Monroe

Setting the Stage

The first Americans had occupied the North American continent for more than 12,000 years before the arrival of Europeans, who came seeking land for permanent settlements. Since Native people were seldom willing to sell their land, it was most often simply taken through a variety of means. The newcomers sought to eliminate the threat of retaliation by killing Native people and/or moving them to distant locales. These actions, repeated again and again over several hundred years, required justification because most of the arrivals from Europe considered themselves religious people. Killing Native people and stealing their lands were not morally acceptable without some rationale that relieved national and individual consciences. The rationalizations were many, but all demeaned the humanity and culture of Native peoples, living and dead, and all found ultimate vindication in the will of God or, later, in the laws of nature. The attitudes born of colonization and conquest, and their attendant justifications, resulted in a long and painful history of violating the basic human rights of American Indians—not only the living, but also the dead.

The Vanishing Red Man

By the early nineteenth century, many of those in closest contact with the "Indian problem" held that Native Americans were faced with extinction. Some, like Thomas Jefferson, thought it might be possible to create an "Indian country" west of the Mississippi. Others felt like Speaker of the House Henry Clay, who stated in 1818 that ". . . the poor children of the forest have been driven by the great wave which has flowed in from the Atlantic ocean to almost the base of the Rocky Mountains, and overwhelming them in its terrible progress, has left no other remains of hundreds of tribes, now extinct, than those which indicate the remote existence of their former companion, the mammoth of New York."[1] By mid-century, many Americans held that annihilation of the American Indian was inevitable.

". . . the stern, proud Indian cannot be enslaved," observed *De Bow's Review*. "The type of savage beasts among whom he lives, like them he will disappear before the new tide of human life now rolling from the East, and with the buffalo, will have vanished the red man of America."[2]

This expectation of extinction was not without cause. Earliest estimates of the indigenous population of the Americas in 1492 ranged between 6 and 12 million. These numbers were absurdly low, used perhaps to support the myth that America was largely an unoccupied wilderness. More recent estimates range up to 50–80 million in all of the Americas.[3] Whatever the number, many scholars today believe that as many as 90 percent of all Native peoples in the Americas were dead within 150 years of the arrival of Columbus, killed by European diseases to which they had no immunity.[4] These numbers explain why the Separatist settlers of Plymouth Colony—the people we know as the Pilgrims—and other early colonists found so many empty villages and cleared fields when they reached New England. A massive wave of death had preceded their arrival.

Subsequent losses to the Native American population—which virtually extinguished many tribes—were brought about by warfare, repeated epidemics, forced removal from homelands, and alcohol. Although the survivors fought long and hard, the last armed White and Indian "conflict" of the nineteenth century occurred in 1890 when units of the Seventh Cavalry, reformed after its annihilation at the Little Bighorn in 1876, massacred more than 150 Sioux men, women, and children at Wounded Knee, South Dakota. This shameful and tragic event seemed to support the already widely held assumption that Native Americans would soon disappear. Within this context, it is not surprising that White treatment of Native American dead violated basic human rights extended to other Americans.[5]

The practice of collecting Native American dead began in the middle of the nineteenth century. Samuel Morton, sometimes called the "father of physical anthropology," recruited people to obtain Native American human remains for his studies. His collectors did not ask permission of heirs or tribes to remove remains from graves. They simply looted burials and took what they wanted. Several of these men recorded that robbing Native American graves was a risky business, since Native people often closely guarded their burial sites. One of his field workers noted in a letter to Morton that an epidemic was raging among a tribe from whom he was collecting, and so many were dying that soon there would be no one left to interfere with his collecting activities.[6]

Morton was an advocate of the popular nineteenth-century pseudoscience of phrenology. Deeply interested in the racial differences among humans, he collected and studied the shapes and volumes of human skulls in the belief that such attributes could determine individual and racial characteristics. Morton concluded that Native Americans had smaller brains than Caucasians, or even than other groups associated with the "Mongol race." He reasoned, erroneously, that Native people must therefore be less intelligent than other races and thus have less aptitude for civilization. Morton claimed that Indians had an "eccentric" and "peculiar" moral constitution in which "wildness" was an indelible trait.

Although it is difficult for us today to accept Morton's assumptions or his conclusions, this "science" was well-received in his day. For one thing, it had great political value as a defense of the American government's policy of dispossessing Native peoples of their lands; it lent an air of scientific objectivity to the long-held view that Native Americans were destined to extinction as an inferior race. Taking lands from an inferior race seemed far more acceptable—perhaps it was even, as often claimed, "God's will."

After Morton died in the early 1850s, other scientists took up the work he had begun. However, they needed skulls to study. In 1859, the Surgeon General asked the United States Army to collect Native American human remains from battlefields. The corpses of hundreds of men, women, and children were decapitated; their remains were "treated" to remove tissues, and the skulls were sent to the Army Medical Museum in Washington, DC. Some years later these remains were transferred to the Smithsonian Institution. So began the systematic "collecting" of Native American people for the purpose of scientific study.

Language has unlimited power to describe actions in positive, negative, or neutral ways. In the last quarter of the nineteenth century and well into the twentieth, the "collecting" of American Indian remains was perceived as legitimate, or quasi-legitimate; yet, robbing the graves of other Americans was against the law. Ironically, scientists supported federal legislation that would prosecute "looting" (by non-scientists) of Native American graves and legitimize "collecting" (by scientists). The beliefs and desires of Native people were not consulted in either case. Even today, some scientists look upon earlier practices of "collecting" as essentially acceptable. One must ask, however, from the standpoint of human rights what is the difference between scientists excavating graves and non-scientists doing the same?

Starting in the 1880s, museums and universities, perceiving that Native Americans were rapidly disappearing, began a massive effort to collect all things Indian. Competition for collections, including human remains, became intense. Even Franz Boas, still considered among the most respected early anthropologists, and a strong advocate for Native peoples and cultures, commissioned and engaged in grave robbing to build collections. Museums and universities most often purchased unburied objects from Indian people while taking grave goods and human remains without permission.

It was widely understood among scientists and field workers that tribes generally had strong feelings against grave robbing. But because most

Indian people were locked in a fierce struggle to remain among the ranks of the living, and because Indians seldom had access to courts, there was little they could do to stop the activity. If collectors and institutions had any moral qualms about their acquisition practices, these were put aside in the drive to procure yet more objects and more knowledge.

In 1906, in the conservationist climate generated by President Theodore Roosevelt, Congress passed the *Antiquities Act*,[7] intended to provide greater protection to archaeological sites. The new law made it illegal to excavate Native grave sites located on public lands without a permit. However, the remains of Native Americans, unlike those of other Americans, were categorized as "natural resources." Museums, universities, and federal agencies "acquired" tens of thousands of human remains under the provisions of the 1906 Act and subsequent historic preservation legislation. None of these laws required consulting Native people or obtaining their approval before removing the remains of their ancestors.

Notwithstanding laws against non-scientific grave robbing, the art market provided tremendous motivation for private collectors to steal from Indian graves. After being classified as "curios" and a form of natural history specimens throughout the eighteenth and nineteenth centuries, Native American art began to achieve recognition as "art" in the 1930s and 1940s.[8] This recognition, in turn, helped create a new art market. To supply this market, which focused almost solely on so-called traditional art, dealers and pot-hunters plundered and often destroyed thousands of graves in search of objects that had become extremely valuable.

Neither scientists nor pot-hunters gave much consideration to the effect of their activities on the living. While scientific literature is rife with negative comments about pot-hunters who ruin archaeological sites, there is no debate about what, if any, rights Native Americans may have with respect to control over the graves of their ancestors. This lack of sensitivity manifested itself in many ways. Many museums publicly displayed the remains of Native people. Information gained from scientific studies of human remains and archaeological sites was seldom shared with Native people. The despoiling of graves and the taking of human remains was extremely painful to many Native individuals and tribes. Few among us would like our grandparents dug up and their remains transported to distant, often unknown, locations and sometimes put on public display.

As prescribed by the world views of many Native American tribes, the remains of the ancestors must be returned to the earth to assure the passage of their spirits into other worlds and to safeguard the well-being of the tribe. Failure to treat the dead in accordance with traditional beliefs is believed to put the living in jeopardy. Thus, to many Native people today, violation of the graves of their ancestors is a deeply painful reminder of a vast catalog of injustices.

Challenge

In conjunction with growing political activism in the 1960s and 1970s, some Native Americans began to seek return of their dead from museums, universities, and federal agencies. These people generally were not well-received by institutions. Requests for repatriation were usually ignored, and those who made the requests were often perceived as trouble-making radicals. Unconscious ethnocentrism on the part of institutions and individual archaeologists, anthropologists, and historians caused many of them to consider the remains of Native people their domain, if not their property. Several centuries of cultural conflict and almost absolute political power over Native people had infected the minds and hearts of the dominant society, including many who represented themselves as the best friends of Native people. By the mid-1980s, Native people had grown stronger, and they resolved to return the remains of their ancestors by legislation if no other means worked. A repatriation law was drafted with the support of several key members of the House and Senate and introduced to Congress. The museum and scientific communities immediately responded by wholeheartedly and vigorously opposing the legislation.

Museum officials and scientists marshaled a host of arguments against any repatriation legislation. First and foremost, they argued that extremely valuable scientific information had been and would continue to be gleaned from the study of Native American human remains. To return these remains for reburial would rob science and the world of vitally important knowledge.

Native people responded by pointing out that there had been gross inequality under the law with respect to the treatment of Native American dead: The dead of all other Americans were protected by legislation that prevented grave robbing. Native people also pointed out that human remains cannot be considered as property. They recounted the pain and suffering caused by disregard of their basic human rights. In addition, their testimony generally made it clear that Native American religious beliefs often conflicted with scientific accounts of Native American history and origins. For the vast majority of tribes, the value of their religion far outweighed the value of future scientific discoveries.

Some museum workers and scientists argued that a repatriation law would result in the gutting of museum collections and loss of the ability to interpret Native American art and culture to millions of people. Native people generally responded by pointing out that they wanted the remains of their ancestors returned—remains that had been disinterred without their permission—along with funerary objects, sacred objects, and objects of cultural patrimony. They further argued that many sacred objects were needed to practice traditional Native American religions. Thus, the highest and best use of these objects was for religious purposes, not for the education of White people. Finally, objects of cultural patrimony were collectively owned. They could never have been legally sold or given away to institutions or individuals by a single person. Thus, institutions which had such objects did not have a legal right to them, in accordance with long-established principles of common law.

Congress, sensitized to repatriation issues by the nation's efforts to recover missing war dead from Vietnam, responded most strongly to the Native American arguments. Although repatriation legislation failed to pass in several sessions of Congress, by early 1990 it had become increasingly clear that the arguments of the museum and scientific communities would not prevail.

The Creation of the *Native American Graves Protection and Repatriation Act of 1990*

During the long debate over repatriation, increasing numbers of museum professionals and scientists recognized that many of the actions taken by their institutions in the past were morally untenable. A year-long dialogue between Native American representatives and several museum officials, while difficult, helped shift the ground in the debate. Congressional leaders showed renewed commitment to passing some kind of repatriation legislation. During the fall of 1990, a handful of representatives from the Native American, museum, and scientific communities met to craft compromise legislation.

The process was not easy, but through good will and hard negotiations, a revised repatriation bill was drafted with the support of a majority of tribes and institutions. Native people, museums, and the scientific community worked together to guide the bill through Congress, and it was signed into law by President George Bush in November of 1990.[9] The *Native American Graves Protection and Repatriation Act* (*NAGPRA*) marked a watershed in the relationship among museums, federal agencies, universities, American Indians, and Native Hawaiians.

The Act applies to all agencies that receive federal funds. The main provisions of the Act provide mechanisms for the return of Native American human remains and funerary objects associated with these remains. The law also establishes procedures, if specific conditions are met, for return of certain cultural items, including funerary objects not associated with human remains, sacred objects, and objects of cultural patrimony. New legal protections also are given to Native American graves located on federal lands. Finally, the Act prohibits the sale or trade of Native American human remains or most objects containing Native American human remains.

All agencies that receive federal funds and possess Native American collections must provide summaries of their collections to relevant tribes.

They also must provide inventories of any Native American human remains in their care to appropriate tribes. Summaries were to be filed by November of 1992, while inventories were due in November of 1995. Tribes that are "culturally affiliated" with remains or cultural items are eligible to file claims for their repatriation.

The repatriation process for human remains is comparatively simple and straightforward. If tribes that are culturally affiliated to these remains and associated funerary objects request their return, then agencies must expeditiously return the items. The process for repatriation of cultural items is more complicated. Individual heirs or culturally affiliated tribes may request return of unassociated funerary objects, i.e., burial objects not associated with a specific set of human remains. Sacred objects, defined as "specific ceremonial objects which are needed by traditional Native American religious leaders for the practice of traditional Native American religions by their present day adherents" may be identified and requested only by traditional Native American religious leaders acting on behalf of tribes. The return of an object of cultural patrimony, defined as "an object having ongoing historical, traditional, or cultural importance central to the Native American group or culture itself, rather than property owned by an individual Native or group" may only be requested by culturally affiliated tribes.

Repatriation claims must be substantiated by concrete evidence. Individuals or tribes requesting the return of cultural items must demonstrate their legal standing, and they must show that the object they seek fulfills the definitions of the Act. Finally, they must present a case for right of possession, which, if standing alone, would demonstrate that right of possession. Museums, in response, must decide whether or not their claims to possession supersede those of the Native claimants. If they do not, then the items in question must be returned expeditiously.

If, on the other hand, an agency or museum decides that it has a greater right of possession than the Native American claimants, or if it otherwise disqualifies the repatriation claim, then the matter may be decided by referral to a special Review Committee appointed by the Secretary of the Interior or by taking the matter to court. The *NAGPRA* Review Committee consists of seven members, four selected from among museum and scientific communities, and three selected from among Native American communities. One of the Native American representatives must be a traditional religious leader. The Review Committee may make "findings" in disputed cases. These findings are not judicially binding, though they will carry substantial weight in a court of law.

Implementation of *NAGPRA*

The *Native American Graves Protection and Repatriation Act of 1990* (*NAGPRA*) fundamentally changed the relationship between Native Americans and mainstream museums and academic institutions in the United States. The law explicitly recognized the view that rights of scientific inquiry do not supersede basic human rights with respect to the dead. This is a tremendously important decision. Until the passage of *NAGPRA*, Native Americans had little control over their cemeteries and burial grounds.

Boundaries have always been placed on scientific inquiry. Because something may be learned by a certain kind of research does not automatically convey the right to carry out such research. For example, professional ethics and laws limit the kinds of medical or biological research considered acceptable. *NAGPRA* placed distinct limits on the scientific study of Native American human remains when those remains are clearly affiliated with a specific tribe or with lineal descendants.

NAGPRA also established the stipulation that Native peoples have a right to regain cultural items that were not, or could not have been, legally acquired by agencies that receive federal funds. Wampum belts, for example, were never owned by individuals, but rather by tribes. It is unlikely, then, that museums or other agencies ever legally acquired such objects of cultural patrimony. Under *NAGPRA*, institutions holding objects of cultural patrimony are held to the common law principle that whoever transfers title to property must have the authority to effect the transfer.

Sacred objects present a more difficult problem because of the diversity of Native American religions. Although they broadly share some common ideas—that people are a part of the land and the world, not separate from it—Native American religions often differ sharply in many ways. *NAGPRA* recognizes the idea that certain objects are central to the continuation of some Native American religions. The law implicitly states that religious use of such objects takes precedence over their use for scientific study or aesthetic appreciation. The determination of what is sacred and what is not is made by traditional Native American religious leaders, acting on behalf of their tribes. Many agencies already have been surprised to learn that objects they considered sacred may not be, and what they did not consider sacred may be. Perhaps more than any other part of the Act, the provisions regarding repatriation of sacred objects rest on Native American good faith and serious intent.

In carrying out the Act, agencies and tribes must engage in dialogue. In the end, the dialogue process may prove at least as important as the outcomes of specific repatriation requests. Scientists, museum officials, and Indians must deal with each other directly, often for the first time. The dialogue process frequently has been difficult for all involved. A legacy of generations of mistrust, misunderstanding, and bad faith must be overcome. Also, a vast gulf often separates the world views of museum and scientific representatives and those of Native people. The values of both parties are often at odds, and each side may have only a slight grasp of the other's beliefs. Nonetheless, these dialogues often produce increased understanding and appreciation of the diverse views that implementation of the Act involves. This, in turn, sometimes leads to new collaborations between tribes and agencies.

Change is not easy. Without doubt, the vast majority of museums, federal agencies, and universities subject to *NAGPRA* have implemented the Act in good faith, regardless of any doubts or misgivings they may have. It is equally true that old attitudes linger among these groups as they attempt to reconcile past actions of their professions with current values and to grapple with new realities that can affect the future of their careers or their institutions.

Native people have been inundated with information. Many tribes struggle to meet the basic requirements of survival for their members: jobs, good health, and good education. Tribes are not monolithic structures comprising people who share uniform beliefs and outlooks. Tribal politics are often complex and fierce. *NAGPRA* issues have the potential to raise a host of old problems that may divide tribes rather than bring them together.

Already, though, it is clear that new approaches to the interpretation of Native American art and cultures have begun to emerge, based in large part on increased knowledge and sensitivity brought about by *NAGPRA*. Museums, universities, and federal agencies already have learned a great deal about their collections that they would otherwise never have known. Native people have learned that there are people and institutions of good faith in the museum and scientific communities who can be trusted.

The pace of *NAGPRA* implementation is much slower than most expected. Contrary to fears that museum collections would be gutted, fewer than 250 sacred objects or objects of cultural patrimony have been repatriated as of 1996. Several thousand associated funerary objects have been returned. Some 2,700 human remains have been repatriated. It is estimated that 100,000 Native American human remains still reside in agencies that receive federal funds, and so the number of human remains returned to tribes is likely to increase over the next several years.

Lack of sufficient funding from Congress is among the roadblocks to more rapid implementation of *NAGPRA*. To date, tribes and affected agencies have spent in excess of $50 million to implement the Act. Neither tribes nor museums are readily prepared to meet these costs, and Congress has funded less than 10 percent of the expense.

Outlook for the Future

What will be the long-term consequences of *NAGPRA*? A new spirit of cooperation, mutual understanding, and respect will likely emerge in the relationships among many museums, federal agencies, universities, and tribes. To date, *NAGPRA* has not been tested in court, as no disputes have been taken to that level. This fact alone shows that, on the whole, a good faith effort is underway to make *NAGPRA* work, notwithstanding numerous difficulties.

NAGPRA has changed fundamentally and forever the way archaeology and related studies of Native peoples will be practiced in the United States. The youngest members of the scientific community, especially, understand and accept the fact that much of their professional work will be done only with the approval and support of tribes.

At a more general level, museum officials and scientists have been forced to deal with difficult ethical issues regarding their professions' past treatment of Native Americans. Although museums have long been advocates for Native people, they have also been guilty of serious infractions against Native American rights. Acceptance of this realization has been painful for a group of generally liberal individuals who have long considered themselves among the least ethnocentric of Americans. But this realization, along with other forces unrelated to *NAGPRA*, has sparked a genuine commitment by museums to more carefully analyze and question ethical and historical issues. Recent controversies in history and art museums stem from a more thoughtful and honest approach to representing diverse viewpoints. *NAGPRA* did not produce this change, but it certainly is part of the movement away from the role of museums as purveyors of national myth.

The underlying gulf between prevailing Judeo-Christian tenets and Native American ideas and beliefs has not disappeared as a result of *NAGPRA*. Many Americans have great difficulty separating their myths about Native Americans from reality. Over time, new approaches to interpreting Native American lifeways, both historical and contemporary, will result in greater appreciation and understanding, in part as a result of dialogue created by implementation of *NAGPRA*. Eventually, the old myths will drop away and Native Americans will be seen and appreciated in a truer light. Native people will, for their part, be able to function with a distinct identity and as real people in the larger society. On the whole, this will be healthy because the nation must, at some point, come to grips with the history of ethnic cleansing upon which it is based.

NAGPRA represents a major victory for Native American human rights and political advocacy. It has underscored the fact that Native people can make advances, however difficult and painfully slow, through legislation and the political process. The return and reburial of their ancestors provides a source of spiritual renewal to many Native Americans. Among the most hoped-for outcomes will be a greater sense of cultural and spiritual integrity for many Native people as they move into the twenty-first century.

Notes

1. Henry Clay, Annals of Congress, 15th Cong. 2nd sess., 639.

2. "The Indian Tribes of the United States," *De Bow's Review* 17 (July 1854): 76.

3. See Sherburne F. Cook, *The Indian Population of New England in the Seventeenth Century* (Berkeley: University of California Press, 1976); Henry F. Dobyns, *Their Numbers Became Thinned: Native American Population Dynamics in North America* (Knoxville: University of Tennessee Press, 1973); Russell Thornton, *American Indian Holocaust and Survival: A Population History Since 1492* (Norman: University of Oklahoma Press, 1990).

4. Alfred W. Crosby, Jr., *The Columbian Exchange: Biological and Cultural Consequences of 1492* (Westport, CT: Greenwood Press, 1973).

5. American Indians were not made voting citizens of the United States until 1924.

6. Quoted in Robert E. Bieder, *Science Encounters the Indian 1820–1880* (Norman: University of Oklahoma Press, 1986), 66.

7. *Antiquities Act of 1906, U.S. Code*, vol. 16, sec. 431 (1995).

8. Several leading American artists organized the 1931 *Exposition of Indian Tribal Arts* in New York City. Rene d'Harnoncourt, who eventually became director of the Museum of Modern Art, organized the first "blockbuster" Native American art show at MOMA in the 1940s. These exhibitions helped transform Native American "artifacts" into "art."

9. *Native American Graves Protection and Repatriation Act of 1990, U.S. Code*, vol. 25, secs. 3001–2 (1994).

21

Museums and American Indians: Ambivalent Partners

Karen Coody Cooper

American Indians in Non-Indian Museums

There are nearly 200 tribal museums in North America; yet, there is hardly a better example of a European-derived institution than that of a museum. Museums, like textbooks and other records available to the public, serve to spread the dogma of a nation. Museums in America, as a result, have treated American Indians as outsiders, even though they are the original inhabitants of the continent. It is not without ambivalence that tribal people have set up buildings to house collections, launch exhibits, and emulate the very institutions that have so boldly relegated American Indians to the status of flora and fauna of the "New World." Tribal museums, of course, desire to use their institutions to change public perceptions and to promote their own selves. For many, this self-promotion is unseemly. For others, it is deemed necessary as a defense against the erosion of self-esteem in the face of American denouncements, and as the most valid voice for representing themselves to others.

Probably the first museum display of American Indian objects in America was in Philadelphia in Charles Willson Peale's museum, which opened in 1785. The few objects he displayed were insufficient to reveal much logical information about Native life. Museums in this stage of development were based on the European idea of Curiosity Cabinets. American Indians, in such a setting, were treated as curiosities. William Clarke's Indian Museum was opened in 1816 in St. Louis. During his explorations with Meriwether Lewis, a sizeable collection of items were gathered, but they also were displayed without labels along with pelts and minerals obtained during his journeys. From the beginning of American museum history, Native objects were treated as strange materials. Perhaps there is no better example of this treatment than that of the P. T. Barnum Museum which opened in New York City in 1851. American Indians were treated as "curious beings" in a side show manner. As the number of museums grew (to include the Peabody Museum at Harvard and the National Cabinet of Curiosities in

Washington, DC), collections grew and labeling was introduced. Still, the emphasis was on "curiosities" such as grave goods, human remains, and weapons. Just before the turn of the century, various tribes' objects were lumped together under categories such as transportation, recreation, subsistence, and technology (Lester, 1972).

At the turn of the century, anthropologists began to emphasize how environment affected adaptation, causing natural history museums to begin to focus on culture groups and evolution. At least distinguishing Plains tribes from Eastern Woodland Indians served to recognize the distinctiveness of the various American Indian tribes. Still, as museums revamped their installations, they failed to realize that their interpretations were biased and generally served to support existing stereotypes. Museums often referred to some tribes as "war-like," mistakenly identified pole-cutting axes as weapons, and generally belittled Native religions and intellect. No Native American voice was accorded authority. American Indians, generally, only entered museums when hired to provide a live demonstration of an art or technology—and they often left feeling used and ill-treated. Two early twentieth-century examples of interactions between Natives and museums are found in the cases of Ishi and Minik. Ishi, the last survivor of his slaughtered tribe, served as a living exhibit at the natural history museum of the University of California at Berkeley (Kroeber, 1961). Minik, who came from the Arctic under a deceptive offer, thought he saw New York City's American Museum of Natural History give his father a proper burial, only to discover his father's remains in the museum several years later (Harper, 1986). These examples engender sadness and bitterness in the hearts of most American Indians. In addition, the knowledge that museums participated in theft, or knowingly purchased stolen items, and that some museum items were removed by soldiers from massacred bodies and deserted homes creates a stifling atmosphere for most American Indian visitors to museums. The most sensitive visitors can feel when within museum halls the chaos created by past atrocities.

Protests Reshaping Museums

When the American public became engaged in protests involving civil rights and the war in Vietnam in the middle of this century, some American Indians saw an opportunity to illuminate their own long-ignored grievances. Native protests a century before had only gained massacre, removal, impoundment, further loss of rights and property, and other deprivations, such as removal of their children to boarding schools. After a half-century of relative quiet, American Indians saw that protest might finally gain some inroads into obtaining redress. In 1969, a group seized Alcatraz Island in San Francisco Bay. Part of their demands was that the former prison on the island be turned into an American Indian cultural center (Reyhner & Eder, 1989). A proclamation released by Indians of All Tribes, November 1970, observed

> We feel that this request is but little to ask from a government which has systematically stolen our lands, destroyed a once-beautiful and natural landscape, killed-off the creatures of nature, polluted air and water, ripped open the very bowels of our earth in senseless greed; and instituted a program to annihilate the many Indian Tribes of this land by outright murder which even now continues by the methods of theft, suppression, prejudice, termination, and so-called re-location and assimilation. (Council on International Books for Children, 1971, p. 314)

It was not until 1977, followed by more protests, that the group's demands were met in the creation of the Daybreak Star Arts Center on abandoned military property in Seattle (Graves & de los Angeles, 1980). In 1972, the American Indian Movement (AIM) invaded the Bureau of Indian Affairs in Washington, DC. They set up an armed encampment the following year at Wounded Knee, the site of the nineteenth-century massacre of Native people (Burnette & Koster, 1974). These protests galvanized Native groups across America. Localized protests began to achieve long-denied rights, sometimes at the price of lives and always under tremendous hardships.

During this time protests were taken to museums. One of the most distressing museum sights to Native Americans is the display of human remains. It seems non-Indians never questioned whether they had the moral right to excavate, accession, curate, possess, buy and sell and display buried American Indians. For American Indian traditionalists, not only was this disrespectful treatment of ancestors, but also it was dangerous interference in the affairs of the afterlife. Only after countless protests at dozens of museums have laws been enacted to protect burial sites and to cause museums to return American Indian remains to tribal groups. The most publicized battle over human remains occurred at Dickson Mounds Museum in Lewistown, Illinois, which displayed 237 remains in their partially excavated burial site (Illinois State Museum, 1992). Protests escalated in 1990 and included picketing as well as attempts to blanket the Indian remains and to shovel soil over them. In 1992, the site was covered by an entombment of concrete over planks, which finally removed the remains from display (Franke, 1995). In 1990, the Native American Graves Protection and Repatriation Act (NAGPRA) was enacted, requiring all museums receiving federal support (virtually all museums) to inventory their American Indian collections and to engage in returning human remains as well as burial items and collaterally owned ceremonial objects, to appropriate tribal authorities.

In 1988, the most widely publicized protest involving American Indians and museums occurred during the Winter Olympic Games in Calgary, British Columbia, Canada. The Glenbow Museum launched an exhibit,

"The Spirit Sings," showcasing the indigenous cultures of Canada with many objects borrowed from museums in Europe and the United States (Harrison, 1988). Had museum officials utilized an advisory committee of local Cree Indians, they might have avoided the conflict that arose over their selection of sponsor for the exhibit. Shell Oil Canada, largest contributor to the exhibit, was also the benefactor of drilling rights on the contested lands of the Lubicon Band of Cree. The Cree protested the involvement of Shell Oil with the Indian-focused exhibit (Ames, 1991). Reporters and camera crews from throughout the world carried the story. Several museums withdrew their offers to loan objects. The international organizations of the museum world discussed the demands and statements of the protestors. A task force was established in Canada consisting of equal representation from the national museums organization and the national Native organization. The task force brought together museum leaders and Native spokespeople and created a document that explained the deficiencies of former museum policies and suggested future methods of operation (Assembly of First Nations & Canadian Museums Association, 1992). American museum publications and conferences explored the contents of the report and began to implement the recommendations.

A long-term focus of protest has been the display of ceremonial objects. Although some of these items may be returned to Indians through NAGPRA, not all ceremonial objects were group-owned. Ceremonial pipes, for instance, may have belonged to individuals. Such pipes were stored and used with sanctions. Museums do not always display pipes correctly (the bowl should be separated from the stem), and many Native people are questioning whether display is appropriate at all. A protest in 1992 resulted in the Minneapolis Institute of Arts removing pipes from an exhibit and, rather than rearranging the exhibit, the pipes were simply substituted with a display of stones from nearby rivers, effecting an immediate response to Native concerns (Garfield, 1993). However, in the 1970s museums did not usually respond so quickly to requests. Although the Buffalo and Erie County Historical Society removed Iroquois medicine masks from exhibit in 1975, the Iroquois were still fighting other museums long afterward (American Indian Museums Association, 1979). The Zuni also fought a long battle with various museums regarding their war gods and masks (Ferguson, 1990). Zuni war gods traditionally were placed in remote wilderness altars and were expected to return to nature; instead, most were stolen by non-Indians who considered the wooden carvings to be abandoned. The thefts continued even as the public became informed about the purpose of the war gods in their remote altars. Museums continued to display Zuni war gods. Not until the passage of the American Indian Religious Freedom Act of 1978 did museums begin to relinquish their ownership of Zuni war gods. The Pawnee and other groups have struggled with museums about the display and ownership of medicine bundles. Although NAGPRA will put an end to many of the continuing struggles, there still will be gray areas with which to contend.

One of the latest protests involving exhibitions was the one created by the Florida Museum of Natural History in 1990 to mark the quincentenary of the voyage of Columbus. Although "First Encounters" was not billed as a celebration of Columbus, many American Indians saw it as just that. Upon examining the text and viewing the exhibit, protests were launched that followed the exhibit as it traveled across the nation. The exhibit presented detailed information about Columbus and his voyage while providing very little insight into the Native people of the Caribbean. While hardships endured by Columbus and other explorers were presented sympathetically, the deaths and enslavement of Native people at the hands of the Europeans were described without the depth considered necessary by American Indians. The voyages of Columbus set into motion grievous losses endured by Native Americans, and there was no tolerance by American Indians to allow the quincentenary to become a celebration. In St. Paul, Minnesota, American Indian Movement (AIM) leader Vernon Bellecourt threw a container of his own blood on the sails of the replica of the Niña, Columbus' favorite ship, and tossed overboard a mannequin of Columbus (Silva, 1992).

Several museums developed ways to add Native voices to the exhibit. In St. Paul, Native advisors were invited to develop their own exhibit, and in Albuquerque, Rick Hill, an American Indian museum professional, wrote a Native viewpoint guide for viewing "First Encounters" (1990). Again, publicity was wide and created discussion in museum publications and conferences. Museums, as a result, did little in 1992 to "celebrate" Columbus, and many museums added advisory groups and continued, or began, to seek Indian voices regarding programming and to serve as staff.

New and/or continuing battles will involve cultural property rights (use and ownership of designs and ceremonial information), interpretation of history and cultures, and adequate inclusion of American Indian artists in art museum collections and exhibitions.

Museums in a Native Image

All existing tribal museums are products of this century, and most were established in the latter half of the century. Of course, "tribal museum" should not be confused with "American Indian" museum. Although many museums contain vast collections of American Indian materials, they are not the same as museums that are founded and maintained by American Indians. Many directories and listings of American Indian museums include museums that do not have Native staff or any Native voice at all.

Tribal museums and American Indian cultural centers range from well-designed, finely stocked institutions to rarely opened spare rooms in the back of an office complex. The Museum at Warm Springs, Oregon, for instance, opened in 1993 and proudly exhibits a wealth of objects from the Warm Springs reservation. While on the surface the museum may not appear to be radically different from others, it is different in many respects. First, the storyline equitably details the three distinct cultures of Warm Springs told in a manner that emanates from Native speakers. They describe their lives and history, much as any people would, by depicting early houses, furnishings, tools, decorative objects, useful raw materials, and historical documents that explain how the three disparate tribes came to share one reservation. A wedding ceremony is described in a diorama with alternating spotlights illuminating portions of the exhibit as a taped voice describes objects and regalia.

Another fine example, The Makah Cultural and Research Center, Neah Bay, Washington, focuses on the archaeological discoveries of Ozette, a village, like Pompeii, frozen in time by natural catastrophe. Collections there are managed according to Makah linguistic affinities, and managers adhere to tribal sanctions regarding the viewing and handling of collections. By showcasing a part of their rich past, the Makah have enriched their present. The cultural center has helped to strengthen Native language retention. It has attracted many who had left to return and kept others, who might have wandered away, rooted in the community. The experience of retrieving artifacts of such beauty and in such numbers instills pride in the community's members. Although modern life has diminished the bounty of the sea and the wealth of the forests, the Makah are creating another wealth in the form of cultural energy and cultural tourism.

The Cherokee museums in North Carolina and in Oklahoma provide a full panorama of information, ranging from thousands of years ago to recent history, and include living history methods of translating, as well as popular evening dramas. The drama in North Carolina depicts the events that led up to the eviction of the greater part of the tribe from their southern homeland; the drama in Oklahoma picks up the story through the winter evictions known as the Trail of Tears, which brought those Cherokees who survived the travail to the West and to the establishment of a new nation. While the Oklahoma Cherokee have a living history village depicting pre-contact life, the nearby Chickasaw are considering adding a living history portrayal to describe their nineteenth-century lives. The Indian Pueblo Cultural Center in Albuquerque, New Mexico, comprises the collaboration of 19 Pueblo communities and provides exhibits as well as large shopping areas and Native cuisine eateries. The Kiowa of Carnegie, Oklahoma, showcase six large murals by Kiowa artists depicting legends and historical events, but have a difficult time managing artifacts without adequate storage space, budget, personnel, training, or local supportive interest. In many small tribal museums, artifacts are generally loaned by tribal members, but are retrieved during election years in case the new leadership is not favorably received by the loaners. This strategy, of course, creates difficulties for museum staff.

The Native American Centre for the Living Arts, Niagara Falls, affectionately known as the Turtle because of the architectural shape of the large facility, closed in 1995 after nearly two decades of financial struggle. Other tribal museums have announced delays in opening or continue to fight to keep their doors open. Conversely, the now wealthy Pequot of Connecticut, a largely unheard-of tribe a decade ago, plans to open the largest, most financially secure tribal museum of all time. Casinos and bingo parlors have provided the funds for many tribes to use in opening museums for public audiences.

One of the most unusual tribal museums is the Logging Camp Museum of the Menominee in Keshena, Wisconsin. In recognition of the importance of logging to the tribe's survival, a donor provided a remarkable collection of logging paraphernalia for the tribe to manage. Increasingly, Native Americans are hired by the National Park Service to serve as interpreters for Native sites. Additionally, the Arts and Crafts Board of the Bureau of Indian Affairs manages three museum/craft sites staffed by American Indians. The Institute of American Indian Arts, a federally funded arts program, also manages an art museum, again staffed primarily by American Indians. Across the country, family-owned museums, as well as state-owned, church-owned, and city- or county-owned facilities, function as "tribal" museums in that they are staffed and managed primarily by Native Americans.

At Plimoth Plantation, Plymouth, Massachusetts, the Wampanoag Indian Program is directed and staffed by American Indians and has served as a way for important information to reach not only tourists, but also the museum world as well. Additionally, by fostering historical research and craftsmanship, area Indians have benefited through increased knowledge and skills. This development has not occurred without rancor and tension, but it has occurred. Whenever people of one culture work for people of another, misunderstandings will happen. When a minority group is managed by members of the empowered group, there are expectations by each of what the other will do. With misreadings of body language, intolerance of requests derived from cultural need, and suspicion and mistrust, there is soon intolerable friction. For the Wampanoag, there is a special sensitivity regarding America's Thanksgiving Day. This holiday, along with Columbus Day celebrations in much of New England, become trying times for Native people in the Northeast. Their own holidays are ignored. Other situations that create tensions for Indians working for or with non-Indians include teasing that might bring forth comments such as, "Hey chief, did YOU or your squaw make it rain?" At Plimoth, there were additional problems, including the inability of the Wampanoag to speak the language they spoke in 1627, which would be required to be on a par with the Pilgrim enactors. Also, there is the reality that the Pilgrim enactors are enactors while the Wampanoag are actually Wampanoag, and are not role-playing in the way the "pilgrims" are. In addition to these dilemmas, add the problem that fewer dollars were expended to develop the Wampanoag village than applied to the Pilgrim re-creation, and one can understand the tension.

Most tribal museums operate on shoe-string budgets. But the success of gaming will soon demonstrate what wealth can do for tribal interpretations. The Mashantucket Pequot have already broken ground for a 300,000 square-foot museum which will spare no expense to tell the stories they want told. The massacre of a Pequot village by a colonial hero will certainly be one of those stories. So, too, will be told the stories of their long repression and of their recent successes.

Museums, themselves, have discovered that they are a dynamic, ever-changing social institution. With this ability to change, it is possible that American Indians will bring ever greater change to modern museums. As tribal museums grow in numbers and experience, they will have much to share about collections management, audience satisfaction, and museum ethics. Meanwhile, American Indians look forward to the innovative exhibitions of the National Museum of the American Indian, scheduled to open in 2001 on the National Mall in Washington, DC, as part of the Smithsonian Institution (Forgey, 1996). But, even as this historic event approaches, and despite the protests American Indians have held in America's museums, it is hoped that museums across the country will continue to produce exhibits that create dialogue and learning about American Indians for all Americans to experience. The success of the National Holocaust Museum suggests that Americans might be ready to face the harsh facts surrounding American Indian diasporas and the genocidal drive fostered by Manifest Destiny. The future holds many exciting possibilities regarding American Indians and museums.

References

American Indian Religious Freedom Act of 1978. Pub. L. No. 95–341, 92 Stat. 469.

Ames, M. (1988). Boycott the politics of suppression: Museums and politics: The Spirit Sings and the Lubicon boycott. *Muse 11* (3), 15–16.

Assembly of First Nations & Canadian Museums Association. (1992). *Task force report on museums and First Peoples* (3rd ed.). Ottawa: Author.

Burnette, R., & Koster, J. (1974). *The road to Wounded Knee*. New York: Bantam Books.

Council on Interracial Books for Children. (1971). *Chronicles of American Indian protest*. New York: Author.

Ferguson, T. J. (1990). The repatriation of ahayu:da Zuni war gods. *Museum Anthropology, 11* (2), 9–10.

Forgey, B. (1996, May 17). Indian museum gets design go-ahead. *The Washington Post*, pp. B1–B2.

Franke, J. A. (1995). A new view of the past: The renovation of Dickson Mounds. *The Living Museum, 57* (1), 3–4.

Garfield, D. (1993, January/February). Notes. *Museum News*.

Graves, M., & de los Angeles, A. J. (Eds.). (1980). *United Indians of All Tribes Foundation: A ten year history*. Seattle, WA: Author.

Harper, K. (1986). *Give me my father's body: The life of Minik, the New York Eskimo*. Frobisher Bay, NWT, Canada: Blacklead Books.

Harrison, J. (1988). The Spirit Sings and the future of anthropology. *Anthropology Today, 4* (6), 6–9.

Hill, R. (1990). *First Encounters*. Albuquerque, NM: Albuquerque Museum.

Illinois State Museum. (1992). *Biennial report*. Springfield, IL: Author.

Kroeber, T. (1961). *Ishi in two worlds*. Berkeley: University of California Press.

Lester, J. (1972). The American Indian: A museum's eye view. *The Indian Historian, 5* (2), 25–31.

Native American Graves Protection and Repatriation Act of 1990, Pub. L. No. 101–601 (1990).

Reyhner, J., & Eder, J. (1989). *A history of Indian education*. Billings, MT: Council for Indian Education.

Risser, M. (Ed.). (1979). *First national conference papers*. Washington, DC: American Indian Museums Association, Smithsonian Institution, Center for Museum Studies.

Silva, T. (1992, June 2). UF Indian exhibit damaged in Minnesota. *The Gainesville Sun*, p. B1.

Contributors

Ellen L. Arnold is a psychologist and a doctoral candidate in Interdisciplinary Studies at Emory University's Graduate Institute of the Liberal Arts. She is currently working on a study of contemporary Native American novelists and "new science" theories of chaos and complexity. Her research and professional presentations have focused on multicultural counseling, women's studies, Native American literature and religion, and representations of Native Americans in film and popular culture.

William Asikinack is Anishinabe (Ottawa/Potawatomi/Ojibwa) from the Walpole Island First Nations Band in Ontario. He has been teaching in Indian schools for 36 years. His experience ranges from the kindergarten to the university level. Presently, Mr. Asikinack is an Assistant Professor at the Saskatchewan Indian Federated College, Regina, Saskatchewan, and is the President of the Canadian Indian/Native Studies Association. His formal education includes a B.A. from the University of Western Ontario and an M.A. in Education from the University of Regina, Saskatchewan. He is currently enrolled in an Ed.D. program.

Debra K. S. Barker (Rosebud Sioux) is an Assistant Professor of English at the University of Wisconsin-Eau Claire. She teaches courses in American Indian Literatures and American Literature and serves as Chair of the American Indian Studies Committee and Co-Director of the American Indian Studies Program. Her publications include articles on American Indian biographies, American Indian grave desecration, John Steinbeck, and George Meredith.

Laura Browder earned her Ph.D. in English from Brandeis University. She is the recipient of a Networks grant from the Massachusetts Council on the Arts and Humanities and a grant from the Massachusetts Foundation on Humanities and Public Policy. Dr. Browder is an Assistant Professor of English at Virginia Commonwealth University. Her book *Rousing the Nation: Radical Culture in Depression America* is forthcoming from the University of Massachusetts Press.

Karen Coody Cooper began her museum career in 1979 at the American Indian Archaeological Institute (now the Institute of American Indian Studies) in Washington, Connecticut. In 1989, she served as a consultant to the Connecticut Museum of Natural History, preparing the text for the Museum's first permanent exhibit on Southern New England Indian lifeways. Other positions include Curator of Education at the Museum of the Great Plains, Lawton, Oklahoma, and Administrator of Education for Jefferson Patterson Park and Museum, St. Leonard, Maryland. Since 1994, Ms. Cooper has been Curriculum Program Manager of the American Indian Museum Studies Program, Center for Museum Studies, Smithsonian Institution. She is currently completing her master's thesis on the topic, "American Indian Protests Affecting Museum Exhibition Policies and Practices," at the University of Oklahoma. She is an enrolled member of the Cherokee Nation of Oklahoma.

Ross Enochs received his Ph.D. in Religious Studies from the University of Virginia. Currently he teaches at Boston College and Merrimack College. His book, *The Jesuit Mission to the Lakota Sioux: Pastoral Theology and Ministry, 1886–1945*, was published in 1996.

Jane Frazier holds a Ph.D. in English from the University of Mississippi and teaches for East Georgia College. She has written on the poet W. S. Merwin for *South Dakota Review* and has articles forthcoming on Merwin in *Style* and *Weber Studies*. At present she is preparing a book-length manuscript on W. S. Merwin's poetry, entitled "From Origin to Ecology: Nature and the Poetry of W. S. Merwin."

Miriam R. Jorgensen is an economist and a doctoral candidate in Political Economics at Harvard University. Her research explores the ways in which formal political and administrative structures interact with "social capital" to promote economic development in Indian Country. Since 1989, Ms. Jorgensen has worked as a Research Associate for the Harvard Project on American Indian Economic Development. In that capacity, she has served as a consultant on government reform to the Standing Rock Sioux and White Mountain Apache Tribes, written cases for Oglala Lakota College's "Manager as Warrior" program, and taught in the National Executive Education Program for Native American Leadership (NEEPNAL).

Pauleena MacDougall received her Ph.D. in History from the University of Maine in 1995. Her dissertation is entitled "Indian Island, Maine: 1780–1930." She holds a Bachelor of Arts in Anthropology and a Master's in Quaternary Studies. Dr. MacDougall currently teaches history part-time at the University of Maine and administers the Maine Folklife Center. In addition, she has been the Managing Editor of *Northeast Folklore* since 1989.

Tom Matchie is a Professor of English at North Dakota State University in Fargo, North Dakota, where he teaches American Literature. He has published numerous articles on Native American writers, including Louise Erdrich, Michael Dorris, Mary Crow Dog, Ella Deloria, Elizabeth Cook-Lynn, and Thomas King.

Eric Mazur (B.A., M.A., University of Virginia; C. Phil., University of California, Santa Barbara), is a doctoral candidate in the Department of Religious Studies at the University of California, Santa Barbara (UCSB), where he focuses on issues of religion and American law. His work has appeared in the *Journal of Church and State* and *Epoche: The University of California Journal for the Study of Religions*. Before coming to UCSB, Mr. Mazur served as a lobbyist for constitutional issues in Washington, DC.

Sally Midgette received her Ph.D. from the University of New Mexico in 1987, specializing in the Navajo language. She assisted Robert W. Young and William Morgan, Sr., in preparing the *Analytical Lexicon of Navajo*, and her book, *The Navajo Progressive in Discourse*, was published by Peter Lang Publishing in 1995. Dr. Midgette is also a co-editor of *Athabaskan Language Studies*. She is an Adjunct Professor at the University of New Mexico.

Mary Alice Money earned her B.S. and M.A. in English at the University of Tennessee in her hometown of Knoxville, and her Ph.D. in American Literature at the University of Texas at Austin with a dissertation on Popular Westerns. A Professor of English at Gordon College in Barnesville, Georgia, she has presented papers on Westerns and science fiction at sessions of the Popular Culture Association in the South.

Dan L. Monroe is Executive Director of the Peabody Essex Museum in Salem, Massachusetts, and a past Chairman of the American Association of Museums. He played a central role in the creation and passage of the *Native American Graves Protection and Repatriation Act of 1990* and serves as a member of the Federal Repatriation Review Committee. The author of numerous publications and an award-winning filmmaker, Mr. Monroe has extensive experience with Native American art and culture.

Dane Morrison earned his B.A. in History from Boston College, his M.A. from Salem State College, and his Ph.D. from Tufts University; all were in History. An Assistant Professor of History at Salem State College and Visiting Lecturer at Tufts University, both in Massachusetts, he is the author of *A Praying People: Massachusett Acculturation and the Failure of the Puritan Mission, 1600–1690*, published by Peter Lang in 1995.

Irene Moser received her M.A. in Folklore and Mythology from the University of California, Los Angeles, and her Ph.D. in twentieth-century American and British literature from the University of North Carolina, Chapel Hill. While teaching writing and literature at Western Carolina University at Cullowhee and at Cherokee, she also studied the Cherokee language. Dr. Moser is now Associate Professor of English at The College of West Virginia, Beckley, where she teaches writing, literature, and interdisciplinary studies. Literary spaces designed by writers with Native American heritages were the focus of her dissertation and remain one of her interests as a folklorist, literary critic, and reader.

Robert M. Nelson is a Professor of English at the University of Richmond. He has been teaching courses there in Native American literatures since 1989. He is a co-editor of *Studies in American Indian Literatures*. His book, *Place and Vision: The Function of Landscape in Native American Fiction*, was published in 1993 by Peter Lang Publishing. The book is now in its second printing.

Jon Reyhner, Ed.D., is coordinator of the bilingual multicultural education program at Northern Arizona University. He taught Native American Studies and Education classes for nine years at what is now Montana State University-Billings. Previously, he was a teacher and school administrator in reservation schools for thirteen years. Dr. Reyhner is the editor of *Teaching American Indian Students* (University of Oklahoma Press, 1992) and co-author of *A History of Indian Education* (Eastern Montana College, 1989).

Wayne J. Stein, Ed.D., is a member of the Turtle Mountain Chippewa of North Dakota. He is an Associate Professor of Higher Education of the Center for Native American Studies at Montana State University-Bozeman. He has a wide variety of experiences in "Indian business," with a decade spent working with tribally controlled colleges, highlighted by five years as President of Sitting Bull College and one year as President of the American Indian Higher Education Consortium. His book, *Tribally Controlled Colleges: Making Good Medicine*, was published by Peter Lang in 1992.

Gabrielle A. Tayac, a Piscataway Indian Nation citizen, is a doctoral candidate in the Department of Sociology at Harvard University. Her research interests currently focus on the intersections of identity and politics. An activist for indigenous peoples' rights, she co-founded the League of Indigenous Sovereign Nations of the Western Hemisphere and has served in staff and advisory capacities of numerous organizations, including Amnesty International, USA, and Survival International. Ms. Tayac currently resides not far from Moyaone, in Maryland, with her husband and son.

Ron Welburn began teaching Native American writers at Syracuse University in 1974 and continued after receiving his Ph.D. from New York University in 1983. He teaches in the English Department at the University of Massachusetts-Amherst and chairs the Five Colleges American Studies Committee. Dr. Welburn's publications appear in *Choice, MELUS Journal,* and *Notable Native Americans*; he reviews jazz CDs; and he is a widely published poet and member of the Wordcraft Circle. He is an enrolled member of the Southeastern Cherokee Confederacy and shares Conoy Indian and Black ancestry from the Delmarva peninsula.

Index